TREATMENTS OF
PSYCHIATRIC DISORDERS

INDEXES

American Psychiatric Association Task Force on Treatments of Psychiatric Disorders

TREATMENTS OF PSYCHIATRIC DISORDERS

A Task Force Report of the
American Psychiatric Association

INDEXES

Published by the
American Psychiatric Association
1400 K Street, N.W.
Washington, DC 20005
1989

The findings, opinions, and conclusions of this report do not necessarily represent the views of the officers, trustees, or all members of the Association. Each report, however, does represent the thoughtful judgment and findings of the task force of experts who composed it. These reports are considered a substantive contribution to the ongoing analysis and evaluation of problems, programs, issues, and practices in a given area of concern.

The paper used in this publication meets the minimum requirements of the American National Standard for Information Sciences—Permanence of Paper for Printed Library Materials ANSI Z39.48-1984.   ∞

Correspondence regarding copyright permissions should be directed to the Division of Publications and Marketing, American Psychiatric Association, 1400 K Street, N.W., Washington, DC 20005.

The correct citation for this book is:

American Psychiatric Association: Treatments of Psychiatric Disorders: A Task Force Report of the American Psychiatric Association. Washington, DC, American Psychiatric Association, 1989.

Library of Congress Cataloging-in-Publication Data
Treatments of psychiatric disorders.

  "American Psychiatric Association Task Force on Treatments of Psychiatric Disorders" —P. facing t.p.
  Includes bibliographies and indexes.
  1. Psychiatry. 1. American Psychiatric Association. Task Force on Treatments of Psychiatric Disorders. [DNLM: 1. Mental Disorders—therapy. WM 400 T7866]
RC454.T69   1989   616.89′1   89-248
ISBN 0-89042-201-X (set : alk. paper)

ISBN 0-89042-202-8   VOLUME 1
ISBN 0-89042-203-6   VOLUME 2
ISBN 0-89042-204-4   VOLUME 3
ISBN 0-89042-205-2   INDEXES

Contents

List of Consultants xxxi

Foreword xxxvii
  Paul J. Fink, M.D.

Introduction xxxix
  Toksoz Byram Karasu, M.D.

Acknowledgments xliii
  Toksoz Byram Karasu, M.D.

Cautionary Statement xliv

VOLUME 1

SECTION 1
Mental Retardation

C. Thomas Gualtieri, M.D., *Chairperson*

1 **Introduction** 3
  C. Thomas Gualtieri, M.D.

2 **Psychopathology in the Mentally Retarded** 4
  C. Thomas Gualtieri, M.D.
  Johnny L. Matson, Ph.D.
  Jane M. Keppel

  Psychiatric Disorders in Mentally Retarded People

3 **Introduction** 9
  C. Thomas Gualtieri, M.D.
  Stephen R. Schroeder, Ph.D.
  Jane M. Keppel

4 **Affective Disorders** 10
  C. Thomas Gualtieri, M.D.

5 **Anxiety Disorders** 14
  Jeffrey J. Fahs, M.D.

6 **Antisocial Behavior, Aggression, and Delinquency**   20
   James A. Mulick, Ph.D.
   Jason R. Dura, M.A.

7 **Schizophrenia**   27
   Frank J. Menolascino, M.D.

   Neurobehavioral Syndromes Associated with Mental Retardation

8 **Introduction**   29
   C. Thomas Gualtieri, M.D.
   Stephen R. Schroeder, Ph.D.
   Jane M. Keppel

9 **Down's Syndrome**   30
   C. Thomas Gualtieri, M.D.

10 **Self-Injurious Behavior**   32
   Johannes Rojahn, Ph.D.
   Joanne Dixon, M.A.

11 **Lesch-Nyhan Syndrome**   37
   C. Thomas Gualtieri, M.D.

12 **Fragile X Syndrome**   39
   Gail Spiridigliozzi, Ph.D.

13 **Rectal Digging, Feces Smearing, and Coprophagy**   43
   Stephen R. Schroeder, Ph.D.

14 **Abnormal Stereotyped Behaviors**   44
   Stephen R. Schroeder, Ph.D.

15 **Prader-Willi Syndrome**   50
   C. Thomas Gualtieri, M.D.
   Jane M. Keppel

16 **Pica in the Mentally Retarded**   51
   Stephen R. Schroeder, Ph.D.

17 **Rumination**   53
   Stephen R. Schroeder, Ph.D.

18 **Rituals, Preoccupation with Sameness, and
   Tyrannical Behavior**   55
   C. Thomas Gualtieri, M.D.

19 **Behavior-Related Eating Problems**   57
   Thomas W. Jones, Ph.D.

Pharmacotherapy

20 Introduction   67
    C. Thomas Gualtieri, M.D.
    Stephen R. Schroeder, Ph.D.
    Jane M. Keppel

21 Monitoring Psychopharmacology in Programs
    for the Retarded   68
    Jane M. Keppel
    C. Thomas Gualtieri, M.D.

22 Neuroleptics   71
    Michael G. Aman, Ph.D.

23 Antidepressant Drugs and Lithium   77
    C. Thomas Gualtieri, M.D.

24 Antianxiety and Sedative-Hypnotic Agents   85
    Jeffrey J. Fahs, M.D.

25 Psychostimulant Drugs   91
    Michael G. Aman, Ph.D.

26 Anticonvulsant Drugs   94
    Randall W. Evans, M.D.
    Michael G. Aman, Ph.D.
    C. Thomas Gualtieri, M.D.

Psychological, Educational, Vocational, and Residential Services

27 Counseling Families of Children with Mental Retardation 100
    Mark L. Wolraich, M.D.

28 General Counseling Services   104
    Mary E. Van Bourgandien, Ph.D.

29 Psychotherapy   108
    Mark Chandler, M.D.

30 Behavior Therapy   111
    Stephen R. Schroeder, Ph.D.

31 Special Education   123
    J. Gregory Olley, Ph.D.
    Pamela DiLavore, M.A.

32 Transition from School to Work   129
    Gary Mesibov, Ph.D.

33 **Vocational Rehabilitation**   **132**
    John L. Gifford, Ph.D.
    Julia W. Wilson, M.A.
    Frank R. Rusch, Ph.D.

34 **Normalization and Deinstitutionalization: Philosophy, Public
    Policy, and Personal Decision**   **140**
    Susan A. Mouchka-Fossum, Ph.D.

35 **The Association for Retarded Citizens**   **147**
    Frank J. Menaliscino, M.D.

    Section 1 References   **149**

SECTION 2

Pervasive Developmental Disorders

Magda Campbell, M.D., *Co-Chairperson*
Eric Schopler, Ph.D., *Co-Chairperson*

36 **Introduction**   **179**
    Magda Campbell, M.D.
    Eric Schopler, Ph.D.

37 **Diagnosis and Evaluation for Treatment Planning**   **180**
    Lee M. Marcus, Ph.D.
    Magda Campbell, M.D.

38 **Education for Children with Autism**   **192**
    J. Gregory Olley, Ph.D.
    Lee M. Marcus, Ph.D.

39 **Language and Communication Therapy**   **201**
    Linda R. Watson, Ed.D.

40 **Behavior Modification**   **217**
    Lowell T. Anderson, Ph.D.

41 **Pharmacotherapy**   **226**
    Magda Campbell, M.D.

42 **The Family in the Treatment of Autism**   **249**
    Marie M. Bristol, Ph.D.
    Eric Schopler, Ph.D.

43 **Other Treatment Modalities**   **266**
    Gary B. Mesibov, Ph.D.

    Section 2 References   **275**

SECTION 3

Specific Developmental Disorders

Theodore Shapiro, M.D., *Chairperson*

Introduction

44 **Overview of the Specific Developmental Disorders**   **297**
    Theodore Shapiro, M.D.

45 **Early Developmental Environment of the Child with
    Specific Developmental Disorder**   **301**
    Jean Zadig, Ph.D.
    Ludwik Szymanski, M.D.

Clinical Description

46 **Learning Problems**   **308**
    Larry Silver, M.D.

47 **Developmental Language, Phonologic, and
    Fluency Problems**   **313**
    Audrey Eisen, Ph.D.

48 **Specific Mathematics Disorder**   **317**
    Joan Shapiro, Ed.D.

Evaluation and Intervention

49 **Evaluation and Treatment: A Psychiatric Perspective**   **319**
    Larry Silver, M.D.

50 **Evaluation and Treatment of Reading, Learning, and
    Mathematics Disabilities: A Special Education Perspective**   **328**
    Joan Shapiro, Ed.D.

51 **Evaluation and Treatment of Language, Articulation, and
    Fluency Problems: A Speech Pathology Perspective**   **339**
    Audrey Eisen, Ph.D.

52 Treatment and Education: Effect of Public Law 94-142   347
     James Harris, M.D.

     Section 3 References   353

SECTION 4

Attention-Deficit Hyperactivity Disorder and Conduct Disorder

Maureen Donnelly, M.D., *Chairperson*

53 Attention-Deficit Hyperactivity Disorder and
     Conduct Disorder   365
     Maureen Donnelly, M.D.

     Section 4 References   390

SECTION 5

Anxiety Disorders of Childhood or Adolescence

John F. McDermott, Jr., M.D., *Chairperson*

54 Anxiety Disorders of Childhood or Adolescence   401
     John F. McDermott, Jr., M.D.
     John Werry, M.D.
     Theodore Petti, M.D.
     Lee Combrinck-Graham, M.D.
     Walter F. Char, M.D.

     Section 5 References   443

SECTION 6

Eating Disorders

Katherine A. Halmi, M.D., *Chairperson*

55 Introduction   449
     Katherine A. Halmi, M.D.

Treatment of Anorexia Nervosa

56 Medical Evaluation and Management   451
     William Owen, M.D.
     Katherine A. Halmi, M.D.

57 **Hospital Treatment** 455
Arnold Andersen, M.D.

58 **Outpatient Treatment** 462
Pauline Powers, M.D.

59 **Drug Therapy** 471
B. Timothy Walsh, M.D.

60 **Behavior Therapy** 475
Elke Eckert, M.D.

61 **Cognitive Therapy** 482
David Garner, Ph.D.

62 **Family Therapy** 491
Joel Yager, M.D.

63 **Group Therapy** 508
James E. Mitchell, M.D.

64 **Psychodynamic Individual Psychotherapy** 510
Regina C. Casper, M.D.

Treatment of Bulimia Nervosa

65 **Medical Evaluation and Management** 517
William Owen, M.D.
Katherine A. Halmi, M.D.

66 **Hospital Treatment** 520
Katherine A. Halmi, M.D.
William Owen, M.D.

67 **Outpatient Treatment** 523
James E. Mitchell, M.D.

68 **Drug Therapy** 528
B. Timothy Walsh, M.D.

69 **Behavior Therapy** 532
Elke Eckert, M.D.

70 **Cognitive Therapy** 537
David Gardner, Ph.D.

71 **Family Therapy** 543
Joel Yager, M.D.

72 Group Therapy   549
    James E. Mitchell, M.D.

73 Psychodynamic Individual Psychotherapy   555
    Regina Casper, M.D.

            Treatment of Other Eating Disorders

74 Rumination   564
    Barton J. Blinder, M.D.
    Stanley Goodman, M.D.
    Phyllis Henderson, M.D.

75 Pica   579
    Barton J. Blinder, M.D.
    Stanley Goodman, M.D.
    Phyllis Henderson, M.D.

76 Atypical Eating Disorders   589
    Arnold Andersen, M.D.
    Angela Mickalide, Ph.D.

    Section 6 References   595

SECTION 7

Paraphilias and Gender Identity Disorders

James L. Mathis, M.D., *Chairperson*

77 Pedophilia   617
    R. Edward Turner, M.D., F.R.C.P.(C)

78 Fetishism and Transvestism   633
    Thomas N. Wise, M.D.

79 Sexual Sadism and Sexual Masochism   647
    David B. Marcotte, M.D.

80 Transsexualism   656
    Eugene A. Kaplan, M.D.

81 Gender Identity Disorder of Childhood   661
    Kenneth J. Zucker, Ph.D.
    Richard S. Green, M.D.

82 **Exhibitionism and Voyeurism** 670
    John M. Rhoads, M.D.

Section 7 References 674

SECTION 8
Tic Disorders

Donald J. Cohen, M.D., *Co-Chairperson*
James F. Leckman, M.D., *Co-Chairperson*
Kenneth E. Towbin, M.D., *Co-Chairperson*

83 **Tic Disorders** 687
    Kenneth E. Towbin, M.D.
    Donald J. Cohen, M.D.
    James F. Leckman, M.D.

Section 8 References 711

SECTION 9
Elimination Disorders

Mark A. Riddle, M.D., *Chairperson*

84 **Elimination Disorders** 717
    Mark A. Riddle, M.D.
    Soo Churl Cho, M.D.

Section 9 References 727

SECTION 10
Other Disorders of Infancy, Childhood, or Adolescence

Joseph M. Green, M.D., *Chairperson*

85 **Introduction** 733
    Joseph M. Green, M.D.

86 **Reactive Attachment Disorder of Infancy** 734
    Joseph Fischhoff, M.D.

87 **Schizoid Disorder of Childhood or Adolescence** 747
    John B. Griffin, Jr., M.D.

88 Treatment of Elective Mutism   762
    Paul C. Laybourne, Jr., M.D.

89 Oppositional and Other Immature Personality Disorders
    of Childhood   772
    Jack C. Westman, M.D.

90 Identity Disorder   782
    William J. Swift, M.D.

    Section 10 References   792

VOLUME 2

SECTION 11

Organic Mental Syndromes

Lissy F. Jarvik, M.D., Ph.D., *Chairperson*

91 The Importance of Diagnosis   799
    Lissy F. Jarvik, M.D., Ph.D.

92 The Geriatric Patient   800
    Gene D. Cohen, M.D., Ph.D.

93 Delirium   804
    Edward H. Liston, M.D.

94 Dementia and Amnestic Syndromes   815
    Gary W. Small, M.D.

95 Organic Delusional Syndrome and Organic Hallucinosis   831
    Daniel A. Plotkin, M.D.

96 Organic Personality Disorder, Explosive Type   839
    Stuart C. Yudofsky, M.D.
    Jonathan Silver, M.D.
    Beth Yudofsky, M.D.

97 Organic Mood Syndrome   853
    James E. Spar, M.D.

98 Organic Personality Syndrome   857
    James E. Spar, M.D.

99 **The Patient with Parkinson's Disease**   860
    Gerard Addonizio, M.D.

100 **The Patient with Stroke**   867
    Stephen F. Signer, M.D., C.M., F.R.C.P.(C)
    Stephen L. Read, M.D.

101 **The Patient with Epilepsy**   877
    George S. Alexopoulos, M.D.

102 **The Patient with Cardiovascular Disease**   894
    Robert Greenberg, M.D.

103 **The Patient with Renal Disease**   915
    Barnett S. Meyers, M.D.

104 **The Patient with Hepatic Disease**   930
    Hira C. Jain, M.D., M.R.C.Psych.
    Charles A. Shamoian, M.D., Ph.D

105 **The Patient with Lung Disease**   939
    Michael A. Jenike, M.D.

106 **The Patient with Sensory Impairment**   948
    Balu Kalayam, M.D.

107 **Multi-Infarct Dementia**   961
    Robert C. Young, M.D.

108 **Dementia of the Alzheimer Type**   965
    Barnett S. Meyers, M.D.
    Robert C. Young, M.D.

109 **Economic Issues**   979
    Benjamin Liptzin, M.D.

110 **Legal Aspects**   983
    Mark J. Mills, J.D., M.D.
    Spencer Eth, M.D.

111 **Ethical Issues**   994
    Spencer Eth, M.D.
    Mark J. Mills, J.D., M.D.

    Section 11 References   1009

SECTION 12

Psychoactive Substance Use Disorders (Alcohol)

Marc Galanter, M.D., *Chairperson*

Treatment of Alcoholism

112 **Introduction**   1063
     Marc Galanter, M.D.

113 **Typologies**   1065
     Roger Meyer, M.D.

114 **Goals of Treatment**   1072
     Marc A. Schuckit, M.D.

115 **Treatment of Organic Mental Disorders**   1076
     Donald M. Gallant, M.D.

116 **Individual Management and Psychotherapy**   1093
     Sheldon Zimberg, M.D.

117 **Psychodynamic Psychotherapy**   1103
     Richard J. Frances, M.D.
     Edward J. Khantzian, M.D.
     John S. Tamerin, M.D.

118 **Family Therapy**   1111
     Peter Steinglass, M.D.

119 **Group Therapy**   1117
     E. Mansell Pattison, M.D. (deceased)
     Jeffrey M. Brandsma, Ph.D.

120 **Behavior Therapy**   1125
     Gloria Litman, Ph.D.

Special Treatment Contexts

121 **Office Management**   1132
     Marc Galanter, M.D.

122 **Inpatient Programs**   1137
     Jack H. Mendelson, M.D.

123 **Employee Assistance Programs**   1143
     Gloria Litman, Ph.D.

124 **Community-Based Treatment**   1147
     James H. Shore, M.D.
     Lial Kofoed, M.D.

125 **Alcoholics Anonymous**   1151
     Chad D. Emrick, Ph.D.

     Section 12 References   1163

SECTION 13

Psychoactive Substance Use Disorders (Not Alcohol)
Herbert D. Kleber, M.D., *Chairperson*

126 **Clinical Assessment of Drug Abusers**   1183
     Bruce J. Rounsaville, M.D.

127 **Substance Abuse Etiology**   1192
     Dan Lettieri, Ph.D.

128 **The Hallucinogens**   1203
     Sidney Cohen, M.D. (deceased)

129 **Phencyclidine Abuse and Dependence**   1209
     Amin N. Daghestani, M.D.
     Sidney H. Schnoll, M.D.

130 **Stimulants**   1218
     Frank H. Gawin, M.D.
     Everett H. Ellinwood, Jr., M.D.

131 **Cannabis Abuse and Dependence**   1241
     Robert Millman, M.D.

132 **Tobacco Withdrawal and Tobacco Dependence**   1261
     Judith K. Ockene, Ph.D.
     Jean L. Kristeller, Ph.D.
     Gerard J. Donnelly, Ph.D.

133 **Barbiturate, Sedative, Hypnotic Agents**   1294
     David E. Smith, M.D.
     Mim J. Landry
     Donald R. Wesson, M.D.

134 **Opioids: General Issues and Detoxification**   1309
     Jerome H. Jaffe, M.D.
     Herbert D. Kleber, M.D.

135 **Antagonist Treatment: Naltrexone**   1332
     Charles P. O'Brien, M.D., Ph.D.
     George E. Woody, M.D.

136 **Methadone Maintenance** 1341
Edward C. Senay, M.D.

137 **Inpatient Treatment of Addiction** 1359
Charles A. Dackis, M.D.
Mark S. Gold, M.D.
Todd W. Estroff, M.D.

138 **Treatment in Residential Therapeutic Communities** 1379
George De Leon, Ph.D.
Mitchell S. Rosenthal, M.D.

139 **Family Therapy in Substance Abuse Treatment** 1397
Edward F. Kaufman, M.D.

140 **Individual Psychotherapy for Substance Abuse** 1417
George E. Woody, M.D.
Lester Luborsky, Ph.D.
A. Thomas McLellan, Ph.D.
Charles P. O'Brien, M.D., Ph.D.

141 **Behavioral Treatment of Drug Abuse** 1430
Maxine L. Stitzer, Ph.D.
George E. Bigelow, Ph.D.
Janet Gross, Ph.D.

Section 13 References 1448

SECTION 14
Schizophrenia

Robert Cancro, M.D., *Chairperson*

142 **Introduction** 1485
Robert Cancro, M.D.

143 **Selective History of the Concept and Treatment
of Schizophrenia** 1487
Robert Cancro, M.D.
Herbert Weiner, M.D.
Heinz E. Lehmann, M.D.
Shervert H. Frazier, M.D.

144 **The Concept of a Disease: Schizophrenia**   1489
Herbert Weiner, M.D.
Robert Cancro, M.D.
Heinz E. Lehmann, M.D.
Shervert H. Frazier, M.D.

145 **Diagnosis of Schizophrenia**   1493
Jack A. Grebb, M.D.

146 **Psychopharmacologic Treatments**   1501
Heinz E. Lehmann, M.D.
Robert Cancro, M.D.
Herbert Weiner, M.D.
Shervert H. Frazier, M.D.

147 **Psychotherapy of Schizophrenia**   1515
Norman Sussman, M.D.
Robert Cancro, M.D.

148 **Individual Psychodynamic Psychotherapy of Schizophrenia**   1519
Daniel P. Schwartz, M.D.

149 **Group Therapy in Schizophrenia**   1529
Stephen A. Cole, M.D.

150 **Family Treatment of Schizophrenia**   1543
Stephen A. Cole, M.D.
Jane Jacobs, Ed.D.

151 **Rehabilitation in Schizophrenic Disorders**   1567
Robert P. Liberman, M.D.
Shirley M. Glynn, Ph.D.
Catherine C. Phipps, M.S.

Section 14 References   1584

SECTION 15
Delusional (Paranoid) Disorders
Sir Martin Roth, M.D., F.R.C.P., F.R.C.Psych., *Chairperson*

152 **Delusional (Paranoid) Disorders**   1609
Sir Martin Roth, M.D., F.R.C.P., F.R.C.Psych.

Section 15 References   1649

SECTION 16

Psychotic Disorders Not Elsewhere Classified

Allen J. Frances, M.D., *Chairperson*

153 **Introduction**   1655
       Allen J. Frances, M.D.

154 **Treatment of Schizophreniform Disorder**   1656
       Samuel J. Keith, M.D.
       Nina R. Schooler, Ph.D.

155 **Treatment of Schizoaffective Disorders**   1666
       Judith H. V. Crosset, M.D., Ph.D.
       Nancy C. Andreasen, M.D., Ph.D.
       William H. Coryell, M.D.

156 **Treatment of Brief Reactive Psychosis**   1677
       William T. Carpenter, Jr., M.D.
       Diana A. Jauch, M.D.

157 **Treatment of Induced Psychotic Disorder**   1685
       Michael H. Sacks, M.D.

158 **Treatment of Atypical Psychosis**   1697
       Richard B. Rosse, M.D.
       Martha B. Martin, M.D.
       John M. Morihisa, M.D.

     Section 16 References   1713

VOLUME 3

SECTION 17

Mood Disorders

Gerald L. Klerman, M.D., *Chairperson*

159 **Preface**   1725
       Gerald L. Klerman, M.D.

160 **Introduction**   1726
       Gerald L. Klerman, M.D.

161 **Goals of Treatment**   1745
     Jules R. Bemporad, M.D.

162 **Diagnostic Considerations in the Treatment of
     Mood Disorders**   1751
     Hagop S. Akiskal, M.D.

163 **The Choice of Treatment Setting**   1766
     William A. Frosch, M.D.

164 **Antidepressants: Pharmacology and Clinical Use**   1773
     Elliott Richelson, M.D.

165 **Drug Treatment of Resistant Depression**   1787
     Jerrold F. Rosenbaum, M.D.
     Alan J. Gelenberg, M.D.

166 **Electroconvulsive Therapy**   1803
     Charles A. Welch, M.D.

167 **Psychotherapy in the Treatment of Depression:
     New Techologies and Efficacy**   1814
     Myrna M. Weissman, Ph.D.

168 **Intensive Psychotherapy and Psychoanalysis**   1824
     Jules R. Bemporad, M.D.

169 **Cognitive-Behavioral Psychotherapy for Depression**   1834
     Robin B. Jarrett, Ph.D.
     A. John Rush, M.D.

170 **Behavioral Approaches to the Treatment of
     Unipolar Depression**   1846
     Harry Hoberman, Ph.D.
     Peter M. Lewinsohn, Ph.D.

171 **Interpersonal Psychotherapy**   1863
     Myrna M. Weissman, Ph.D.
     Gerald L. Klerman, M.D.

172 **Short-Term Dynamic Therapies for Depression**   1872
     Hans H. Strupp, Ph.D.

173 **Couples and Family Therapy**   1885
     Ira D. Glick, M.D.
     John F. Clarkin, Ph.D.
     Gretchen L. Haas, Ph.D.

174 **Light Therapy**   1890
     Norman E. Rosenthal, M.D.

175 **Psychosurgery**   1896
     William A. Frosch, M.D.

                Treatments of Specific Subdisorders

176 **Secondary Depressions**   1898
     Barbara Mason, Ph.D.
     William A. Frosch, M.D.

177 **Bipolar Disorders**   1925
     Hagop S. Akiskal, M.D.

178 **Dysthymic Disorder**   1940
     James H. Kocsis, M.D.

179 **Adustment Disorder with Depressed Mood**   1946
     Jules R. Bemporad, M.D.

180 **Affective Disorders in Children and Adolescents**   1950
     Jules R. Bemporad, M.D.

     Section 17 References   1959

SECTION 18

Anxiety Disorders

Martin T. Orne, M.D., Ph.D., *Co-Chairperson*
Fred H. Frankel, M.B.Ch.B., D.P.M., *Co-Chairperson*

181 **Introduction**   2007
     Martin T. Orne, M.D., Ph.D.
     Fred H. Frankel, M.B.Ch.B., D.P.M.

182 **Psychoanalytic Psychotherapy**   2010
     George G. Fishman, M.D.

183 **Behavior Therapy**   2025
     G. Terence Wilson, Ph.D.

184 **Treatment with Antianxiety Agents**   2036
     Carl Salzman, M.D.

185 **Strategies of Relaxation, Self-Control, and Fear-Mastery**   2052
     Fred H. Frankel, M.B.Ch.B., D.P.M.
     Martin T. Orne, M.D., Ph.D.

186   **Posttraumatic Stress Disorder**   **2065**
      Mardi J. Horowitz, M.D.

      Section 18 References   **2083**

SECTION 19
Obsessive Compulsive Disorders
Joseph Zohar, M.D., *Chairperson*

187   **Behavior Therapy and Pharmacotherapy**   **2095**
      Joseph Zohar, M.D.
      Edna B. Foa, Ph.D.
      Thomas R. Insel, M.D.

188   **Psychodynamic Psychotherapy**   **2105**
      Leon Salzman, M.D.

      Section 19 References   **2112**

SECTION 20
Somatoform and Factitious Disorders
Robert Kellner, M.D., *Chairperson*

189   **Introduction**   **2119**
      Robert Kellner, M.D.

190   **Somatoform Pain Disorders**   **2120**
      Barry Blackwell, M.D.
      Harold Merskey, D.M.
      Robert Kellner, M.D.

191   **Hypochondriasis and Body Dysmorphic Disorder**   **2138**
      Robert Kellner, M.D.

192   **Undifferentiated Somatoform Disorder and Somatoform
      Disorder Not Otherwise Specified**   **2147**
      Robert Kellner, M.D.

193   **Conversion Disorders**   **2152**
      Harold Merskey, D.M.

194   **Factitious Disorder with Physical Symptoms**   **2159**
      Stuart J. Eisendrath, M.D.

195 **Factitious Disorder with Psychological Symptoms**   2165
     Harold Merskey, D.M.

196 **Somatization Disorder**   2166
     Robert Kellner, M.D.

     Section 20 References   2172

                              Section 21
                      Dissociative Disorders
           (or Hysterical Neuroses, Dissociative Type)
                  Marc H. Hollender, M.D., *Chairperson*

197 **Introduction**   2185
     Marc H. Hollender, M.D.

198 **Psychogenic Amnesia**   2186
     Louis Linn, M.D.

199 **Psychogenic Fugue**   2190
     Charles V. Ford, M.D.

200 **Multiple Personality Disorder**   2197
     Cornelia B. Wilbur, M.D.
     Richard P. Kluft, M.D.

201 **Depersonalization Disorder (or Depersonalization Neurosis)** 2217
     Richard I. Shader, M.D.
     Edward L. Scharfman, M.D.

202 **Dissociative Disorder Not Otherwise Specified**   2222
     Paul C. Horton, M.D.

     Section 21 References   2227

                              Section 22
                         Sexual Disorders
                  Harold I. Lief, M.D., *Chairperson*

203 **Introduction**   2237
     Harold I. Lief, M.D.

204 **Evaluation of Sexual Disorders**   2238
     Connie Moore, M.D.

205   **Atypical Psychosexual Disorder**   2248
        Harold I. Lief, M.D.

206   **Psychiatric Disorders and Sexual Functioning**   2253
        Avodah K. Offit, M.D.

207   **Hypoactive Sexual Desire and Other Problems of
        Sexual Desire**   2264
        Stephen B. Levine, M.D.

208   **Female Sexual Arousal Disorder and Inhibited
        Female Orgasm**   2279
        Connie Moore, M.D.

209   **Dyspareunia and Vaginismus**   2291
        Philip M. Sarrel, M.D.
        Lorna J. Sarrel, M.S.W.

210   **Premature Ejaculation and Inhibited Male Orgasm**   2299
        Domeena C. Renshaw, M.D.
        Dennis J. Krauss, M.D.

211   **Male Erectile Disorder**   2318
        R. Taylor Segraves, M.D.

212   **Surgical Treatment of Impotence**   2330
        Terence Malloy, M.D.
        Alan J. Wein, M.D.

213   **Individual and Couple Therapy**   2334
        R. Taylor Segraves, M.D.

214   **Drug Therapy**   2343
        Theresa L. Crenshaw, M.D.
        James P. Goldberg, Ph.D.

215   **Special Approaches**   2359
        Joshua S. Golden, M.D.

216   **Special Populations and Sexual Dysfunctions**   2366
        Carol C. Nadelson, M.D.

217   **Basic Research Relevant to Treatment of
        Psychosexual Dysfunctions**   2384
        Raul C. Schiavi, M.D.

        Section 22 References   2395

SECTION 23

Sleep Disorders

David J. Kupfer, M.D., *Co-Chairperson*
Charles F. Reynolds III, M.D., *Co-Chairperson*

218 **Introduction**   2419
     Charles F. Reynolds III, M.D.
     David J. Kupfer, M.D.

219 **Parasomnias in Children**   2419
     J. Christian Gillin, M.D.

220 **Primary Insomnia**   2424
     Peter J. Hauri, Ph.D.

221 **Insomnia Related to Medical Conditions: Sleep Apnea
     and Nocturnal Myoclonus**   2433
     Wallace B. Mendelson, M.D.

222 **Narcolepsy**   2439
     David J. Kupfer, M.D.
     Charles F. Reynolds III, M.D.

223 **Sleep-Wake Schedule Disorders**   2440
     Timothy H. Monk, Ph.D.

224 **Sleep Disturbances in Late Life**   2444
     Charles F. Reynolds III, M.D.
     David J. Kupfer, M.D.

     Section 23 References   2450

SECTION 24

Impulse Control Disorders Not Elsewhere Classified

Richard C. Marohn, M.D., *Chairperson*

225 **Introduction**   2457
     Richard C. Marohn, M.D.

226 **Pathologic Gambling**   2463
     Robert Custer, M.D.
     Robert D. Linden, M.D.

227 **Kleptomania**   2466
     John Meeks, M.D.

228 **Pyromania**   2468
     Eugene Bumpass, M.D.

229 **Intermittent Explosive Disorder**   2473
     John R. Lion, M.D.

230 **Atypical Impulse Control Disorder**   2477
     James L. Cavanaugh, Jr., M.D.
     Richard D. Marciniak, M.D.

231 **Trichotillomania**   2481
     Richard A. Ratner, M.D.

232 **Conclusion**   2487
     Richard C. Marohn, M.D.

     Section 24 References   2488

SECTION 25
Adjustment Disorder

Joseph D. Noshpitz, M.D., *Co-Chairperson*
R. Dean Coddington, M.D., *Co-Chairperson*

233 **Introduction**   2497
     R. Dean Coddington, M.D.

234 **Adjustment Disorders in Adulthood and Old Age**   2504
     Jeffery C. Hutzler, M.D.

235 **Adjustment Disorders in Childhood and Adolescence**   2510
     Jerry M. Wiener, M.D.
     Paul Prunier, M.D.

236 **Crisis Intervention: Theory and Technique**   2520
     William C. Swanson, Ph.D.
     Janice B. Carbon, M.S.W.

237 **Stress Management by Behavioral Methods**   2532
     Richard M. Suinn, Ph.D.

238 **Brief Dynamic Psychotherapy**   **2548**
     Mardi J. Horowitz, M.D.

239 **Individual Child Psychotherapy**   **2557**
     Donald J. Carek, M.D.

240 **Family Therapy**   **2566**
     Edward M. Beal, M.D.

241 **Group Therapy**   **2578**
     Myron F. Weiner, M.D.

242 **Pharmacotherapy**   **2585**
     Kevin V. Kelly, M.D.
     William A. Frosch, M.D.

243 **Religion as Ego Support**   **2590**
     Paul L. Whitehead, M.D.
     R. Jan Stout, M.D.

244 **Self-Help and Mutual Aid Groups for Adults**   **2596**
     Leonard D. Borman, M.D. (deceased)

245 **Self-Help, Mutual-Help, and Peer-Helping Services
     for Youth**   **2607**
     Milton F. Shore, Ph.D.
     Fortune V. Mannino, Ph.D.

     Section 25 References   **2617**

SECTION 26

Personality Disorders

John G. Gunderson, M.D., *Chairperson*

246 **Introduction**   **2633**
     John G. Gunderson, M.D.

Treatment Modalities

247 **Psychoanalysis and Dynamic Psychotherapy**   **2639**
     Jerome A. Winer, M.D.
     George H. Pollock, M.D., Ph.D.

248 **Behavior Therapy**   **2649**
     J. Christopher Perry, M.P.H., M.D.
     Raymond B. Flannery, Jr., Ph.D.

249 **Family and Couples Therapy**   2660
     Edward R. Shapiro, M.D.

250 **Group Therapy**   2667
     Molyn Leszcz, M.D., F.R.C.P.(C)

251 **Somatic Therapy**   2678
     Michael R. Liebowitz, M.D.

252 **Residential Treatment**   2689
     Thomas H. McGlashan, M.D.

Treatment of Specific Disorders

253 **Paranoid Personality Disorder**   2705
     William W. Meissner, M.D.

254 **Schizoid Personality Disorder**   2712
     Michael H. Stone, M.D.

255 **Schizotypal Personality Disorder**   2719
     Michael H. Stone, M.D.

256 **Histrionic Personality Disorder**   2727
     Paul Chodoff, M.D.

257 **Narcissistic Personality Disorder**   2736
     Gerald Adler, M.D.

258 **Antisocial Personality Disorder**   2742
     William H. Reid, M.D., M.P.H.
     William J. Burke, M.D.

259 **Borderline Personality Disorder**   2749
     John G. Gunderson, M.D.

260 **Avoidant Personality Disorder**   2759
     Allen J. Frances, M.D.
     Thomas Widiger, Ph.D.

261 **Dependent Personality Disorder**   2762
     J. Christopher Perry, M.P.H., M.D.

INDEXES

List of Consultants

C. Alex Adsett, M.D.
W. Stewart Agras, M.D.
C. Knight Aldrich, M.D.
Arnold Allen, M.D.
Kenneth Z. Altshuler, M.D.
Wayne R. Anable, D.O.
Nancy C. Andreasen, M.D., Ph.D.
Paul A. Andrulonis, M.D.
Laurie Appelbaum, M.D.
Gary K. Arthur, M.D.
Stuart S. Asch, M.D.
Boris M. Astrachan, M.D.

Hrair M. Babikian, M.D.
Thomas H. Babor, Ph.D.
William E. Bakewell, Jr., M.D.
Cornelis B. Bakker, M.D.
Ross J. Baldessarini, M.D.
Gail M. Barton, M.D.
B. Lynn Beattie, M.D., F.R.C.P. (C)
Aaron T. Beck, M.D.
Alan S. Bellack, Ph.D.
Jules Bemporad, M.D.
Elissa P. Benedek, M.D.
R. Scott Benson, M.D.
Norman B. Bernstein, M.D.
Norman R. Bernstein, M.D.
Shashi K. Bhatia, M.D.
Subash C. Bhatia, M.D.
Raman Bhavsar, M.D.
Kay H. Blacker, M.D.
Barry Blackwell, M.D.
Barton J. Blinder, M.D., Ph.D.
Irvin Blose, M.D.
Daniel B. Borenstein, M.D.
Jonathan F. Borus, M.D.
Peter G. Bourne, M.D.
Malcolm B. Bowers, Jr., M.D.
David L. Braff, M.D.
Reed Brockbank, M.D.

Kirk Brower, M.D.
William E. Bunney, Jr., M.D.
Ann W. Burgess, R.N., D.N.Sc.
Ewald W. Busse, M.D.

Dennis P. Cantwell, M.D.
Bernard J. Carroll, M.D., Ph.D.
Stanley Cath, M.D.
Richard D. Chessick, M.D., Ph.D., P.C.
Eve S. Chevron, M.S.
James Claghorn, M.D.
Norman A. Clemens, M.D.
C. Robert Cloninger, M.D.
Raquel E. Cohen, M.D.
Calvin A. Colarusso, M.D.
Bernice E. Coleman, M.D.
Gregory B. Collins, M.D.
Liane Colsky, M.D.
Shirley M. Colthart, M.D.
Arnold M. Cooper, M.D.
Rex W. Cowdry, M.D.
Thomas J. Craig, M.D., M.P.H.
Miles K. Crowder, M.D.
Thomas J. Crowley, M.D.
Homer Curtis, M.D.
Thomas E. Curtis, M.D.

Amin N. Daghestani, M.D.
I. Deborah Dauphinais, M.D.
John M. Davis, M.D.
Jorge G. De La Torre, M.D.
Marian K. DeMyer, Ph.D.
Martha B. Denckla, M.D.
Bharati Desai, M.D.
Daniel A. Deutschman, M.D.
Robert De Vito, M.D.
William G. Dewhurst, M.D.
Leon Diamond, M.D.
Alberto Di Mascio, Ph.D.
David F. Dinges, Ph.D.

C. Wesley Dingman II, M.D.
Susan R. Donaldson, M.D.
John Donnelly, M.D.
Mina K. Dulcan, M.D.
David L. Dunner, M.D.
Jack Durell, M.D.
Maurice Dysken, M.D.

Felton Earls, M.D.
Marshall Edelson, M.D., Ph.D.
Irene Elkin, Ph.D.
Donald E. Engstrom, M.D.
Nathan B. Epstein, M.D.
Jack R. Ewalt, M.D.

Louis F. Fabre, Jr., M.D.
Peter J. Fagan, Ph.D.
Howard Farkas, B.A.
Beverly J. Fauman, M.D.
Ronald R. Fieve, M.D.
Stuart M. Finch, M.D.
Max Fink, M.D.
Paul J. Fink, M.D.
Joseph A. Flaherty, M.D.
Stephen Fleck, M.D.
Don E. Flinn, Jr., M.D.
Marc A. Forman, M.D.
Richard J. Frances, M.D.
Robert O. Friedel, M.D.

Warren J. Gadpaille, M.D.
Pierre N. Gagne, M.D.
Robert S. Garber, M.D.
Max Gardner, M.D.
Russell Gardner, Jr., M.D.
Joseph Gaspari, M.D.
Francine L. Gelfand, M.D.
Robert W. Gibson, M.D.
Stanley Gitlow, M.D.
Rachel Gittelman, Ph.D.
Alexander H. Glassman, M.D.
Ira D. Glick, M.D.
Richard L. Goldberg, M.D.
Charles Goldfarb, M.D.
Stuart J. Goldman, M.D.

Gerald Goldstein, M.D.
Michael J. Goldstein, Ph.D.
Donald Goodwin, M.D.
Tracy Gordy, M.D.
Fred Gottlieb, M.D.
Marvin E. Gottlieb, M.D.
Louis A. Gottschalk, M.D., Ph.D.
Paul Graffagnino, M.D.
Harry Grantham, M.D.
Wayne H. Green, M.D.
Harvey R. Greenberg, M.D.
Lester Grinspoon, M.D.
William N. Grosch, M.D.
Mortimer D. Gross, M.D., S.C.

Seymour Halleck, M.D.
Abraham L. Halpern, M.D.
James A. Hamilton, M.D.
Edward Hanin, M.D.
Richard K. Harding, M.D.
Saul I. Harrison, M.D.
Lawrence Hartmann, M.D.
Irwin N. Hassenfeld, M.D.
Leston Havens, M.D.
David R. Hawkins, M.D.
Robert G. Heath, M.D.
John E. Helzer, M.D.
Hugh C. Hendrie, M.B.Ch.B.
Marvin I. Herz, M.D.
David B. Herzog, M.D.
A. Lewis Hill, M.D.
Douglas P. Hobson, M.D.
James Hodge, M.D.
Charles J. Hodulik, M.D.
Charles C. Hogan, M.D., P.C.
Jimmie C.B. Holland, M.D.
Steven D. Hollon, Ph.D.
Harry C. Holloway, M.D.
Daniel W. Hommer, M.D.
Jeffrey L. Houpt, M.D.

David Israelstam, M.D., Ph.D.

Marc Jacobs, M.D.
Kay R. Jamison, Ph.D.

Michael S. Jellinek, M.D.
Keith H. Johansen, M.D.
Mary Ann Johnson, M.D.
Merlin H. Johnson, M.D.
Charles R. Joy, M.D.
Lewis L. Judd, M.D.
Nalini V. Juthani, M.D.

Nicholas Kanas, M.D.
Sylvia R. Karasu, M.D.
Jack L. Katz, M.D.
Edward Kaufman, M.D.
Jerald Kay, M.D.
David Kaye, M.D.
Alan E. Kazdin, Ph.D.
John F. Kelley, M.D.
Philippe J. Khouri, M.D.
Elizabeth Khuri, M.D.
Chase P. Kimball, M.D.
Donald F. Klein, M.D.
Arthur H. Kleinman, M.D.
Lawrence Y. Kline, M.D.
William Klykylo, M.D.
Peter T. Knoepfler, M.D.
Michael F. Koch, M.D.
Jonathan E. Kolb, M.D.
Lawrence C. Kolb, M.D.
Donald S. Kornfeld, M.D.
Douglas A. Kramer, M.D.
Peter D. Kramer, M.D.
Robert F. Kraus, M.D.
Daniel Kripke, M.D.
Markus Kruesi, M.D.
John W. Kuldau, M.D.

Yves Lamontagne, M.D., F.R.C.P.(C)
Ronald Langevin, Ph.D.
Donald G. Langsley, M.D.
Camille Laurin, M.D.
Ruth L. La Vietes, M.D.
Robert L. Leon, M.D.
Denis Lepage, M.D.
Joseph B. Leroy, M.D.
Stanley Lesse, M.D.
H.J. Leuchter, M.D.

Stephen B. Levine, M.D.
Peritz H. Levinson, M.D.
David J. Lewis, M.D., F.R.C.P.(C)
Robert Paul Liberman, M.D.
Paul Lieberman, M.D.
Rudolf W. Link, M.D.
Margaret W. Linn, Ph.D.
John R. Lion, M.D.
Marvin H. Lipkowitz, M.D.
Zbigniew J. Lipowski, M.D.
Melvin M. Lipsett, M.D.
James W. Lomax, M.D.
Catherine E. Lord, Ph.D.
Maria Lorenz, M.D.
Earl L. Loschen, M.D.
Reginald S. Lourie, M.D.
Eugene L. Lowenkopf, M.D.
Joseph F. Lupo, M.D.

K. Roy MacKenzie, M.D.
John A. MacLeod, M.D.
Leslie F. Major, M.D.
Michael J. Maloney, M.D.
David B. Marcotte, M.D.
John Markowitz, M.D.
Judd Marmor, M.D.
Ronald L. Martin, M.D.
Jules H. Masserman, M.D.
Thomas A. Mathews, M.D.
Kenneth L. Matthews, M.D.
Teresita McCarty, M.D.
Layton McCurdy, M.D.
John J. McGrath, M.D.
F. Patrick McKegney, Jr., M.D.
George N. McNeil, M.D.
Beverly T. Mead, M.D.
Herbert Y. Meltzer, M.D.
James R. Merikangas, M.D.
Harold Merskey, D.M.
Heino F. L. Meyer-Bahlburg, Dr.rer.nat.
Robert Michels, M.D.
Larry Michelson, Ph.D.
Ira Mintz, M.D.
Steven M. Mirin, M.D.
Arnold H. Modell, M.D.

Gordon L. Moore II, M.D.
Robert A. Moore, M.D.
Loren R. Mosher, M.D.
David A. Mrazek, M.D., M.R.C.Psych.
Frances J. Mulvihill, M.D.
Cecil Mushatt, M.D.

Carol C. Nadelson, M.D.
Theodore Nadelson, M.D.
Donald F. Naftulin, M.D.
Carlos Neu, M.D.
Theodore W. Neumann, Jr., M.D.
Robert G. Niven, M.D.
Grayson Norquist, M.D.
John I. Nurenberger, Jr., M.D.

Charles P. O'Brien, M.D., Ph.D.
William C. Offenkrantz, M.D.
Donald Oken, M.D.
Harold S. Orchow, M.D.
Emily Carota Orne, B.A.
Morris G. Oscherwitz, M.D.
Helen J. Ossofsky, M.D.

Lee C. Park, M.D.
Dean X. Parmalee, M.D., F.A.A.C.P.
Robert J. Pary, M.D.
Robert O. Pasnau, M.D.
William Patterson, M.D.
Chester A. Pearlman, Jr., M.D.
William S. Pearson, M.D.
Roger Peele, M.D.
William E. Pelham, Jr., Ph.D.
Irwin N. Perr, M.D.
Helen M. Pettinati, Ph.D.
Betty Pfefferbaum, M.D.
Irving Philips, M.D.
Edward Pinney, M.D.
William Pollin, M.D.
Harrison C. Pope, Jr., M.D.
Robert M. Post, M.D.
Harry Prosen, M.D.
Brigette Prusoff, Ph.D.
Joaquim Puig-Antich, M.D.
H. Paul Putman II, M.D.

Robert Racusin, M.D.
Judith L. Rapoport, M.D.
Allen Raskin, Ph.D.
Robert J. Reichler, M.D.
William H. Reid, M.D., M.P.H.
Karl Rickels, M.D.
Arthur Rifkin, M.D.
Louis Rittelmeyer, M.D.
Lee N. Robins, M.D.
Nicholas L. Rock, M.D.
Paul Rodenhauser, M.D.
Rita R. Rogers, M.D.
John Romano, M.D.
Howard P. Rome, M.D.
Patricia Rosebush, M.D.
Maj-Britt Rosenbaum, M.D.
Milton Rosenbaum, M.D.
Loren H. Roth, M.D.
Bruce Rounsaville, M.D.
Donald K. Routh, Ph.D.
Lester Rudy, M.D.

Benjamin Sadock, M.D.
Virginia Sadock, M.D.
Clifford J. Sager, M.D.
Watt T. Salmon, M.D.
Carl Salzman, M.D.
Alberto Santos, M.D.
Burhan Say, M.D.
Nina R. Schooler, Ph.D.
John Schowalter, M.D.
John J. Schwab, M.D.
Harvey J. Schwartz, M.D.
James H. Scully, M.D.
Peter M. Semkiw, M.D.
Mohammad Shaffii, M.D.
Charles Shagass, M.D.
Brian Shaw, M.D.
Kailie R. Shaw, M.D.
Michael H. Sheard, M.D.
David V. Sheehan, Ph.D.
Edwin Shneidman, Ph.D.
Miles Shore, M.D.
Michael Shostak, M.D.
Lorraine D. Siggins, M.D.

Peter M. Silberfarb, M.D.
Donald J. Silberman, M.D.
Archie A. Silver, M.D.
Joel J. Silverman, M.D.
Everett C. Simmons, M.D.
Bennett Simon, M.D.
George M. Simpson, M.D.
Margaret Singer, M.D.
Phillip R. Slavney, M.D.
William Sledge, M.D.
Gary W. Small, M.D.
Joyce G. Small, M.D.
Erwin R. Smarr, M.D.
Gail Solomon, M.D.
David Spiegel, M.D.
Robert L. Spitzer, M.D.
Daniel J. Sprehe, M.D.
Robert St. John, M.D.
Stephen M. Stahl, M.D., Ph.D.
Monica N. Starkman, M.D.
Dorothy A. Starr, M.D.
Roy Steinhouse, M.D.
Peter E. Stokes, M.D.
John S. Strauss, M.D.
Max Sugar, M.D.
David W. Swanson, M.D.

Zebulin C. Taintor, M.D.
John A. Talbott, M.D.
Allan Tasman, M.D.
Sam D. Taylor, M.D.
Lenore C. Terr, M.D.
Alexander Thomas, M.D.
Gary Tischler, M.D.
Arnold Tobin, M.D.
Garfield Tourney, M.D.
Darold A. Treffert, M.D.
Margaret Owen Tsaltas, M.D.
Gary J. Tucker, M.D.
William M. Tucker, M.D.
Ann R. Turkel, M.D.

Kathleen Bell Unger, M.D.
Yogendra Upadhyay, M.D.

George E. Vaillant, M.D.
Bessel Van der Kolk, M.D.
Christian D. Van der Velde, M.D.
Hugo Van Dooren, M.D.
Herman M. van Praag, M.D., Ph.D.
Ilza Veith, Ph.D., M.D.
Milton Viederman, M.D.

Thomas Wadden, Ph.D.
Raymond Waggoner, M.D.
Richard L. Weddige, M.D.
Walter Weintraub, M.D.
James M.A. Weiss, M.D.
Kenneth J. Weiss, M.D.
Sidney H. Weissman, M.D.
William D. Weitzel, M.D.
Elizabeth B. Weller, M.D.
Charles E. Wells, M.D.
Paul H. Wender, M.D.
Jack C. Westman, M.D.
Kerrin L. White, M.D.
Wayne Whitehouse, Ph.D.
Roy M. Whitman, M.D.
Jan N. Williams, M.D.
C. Philip Wilson, M.D.
G. Terence Wilson, Ph.D.
Ronald Wintrob, M.D.
Michael G. Wise, M.D.
Joseph Wolpe, M.D.
Edward A. Wolpert, M.D., Ph.D.
David R. Wood, M.D.
William M. Wood, M.D.
Sherwin M. Woods, M.D.
Henry H. Work, M.D.
Richard W. Worst, M.D.
Lyman C. Wynne, M.D., Ph.D.

Irvin D. Yalom, M.D.
Alayne Yates, M.D.

Robert G. Zadylak, M.D.
Leonard S. Zegans, M.D.
Norman Zinberg, M.D.
Charlotte M. Zitrin, M.D.
Joel P. Zrull, M.D.

Foreword

T. Byram Karasu and the hundreds of our colleagues who have contributed to this massive effort deserve our highest respect and admiration.

The sheer magnitude of the undertaking would have discouraged most, but the enormous complexity provided the challenge that Dr. Karasu and the APA Task Force on Treatments of Psychiatric Disorders needed to endure this seven-year process. The APA is particularly grateful to Dr. Karasu for his patience, thoughtfulness, and comprehensive intelligence about psychiatric therapies. The result is a work of unprecedented significance. Even though, in its present four volumes, it is by no means a definitive work, this report is a major contribution to the literature and a basis on which much more will be accomplished in the years to come.

Coming to fruition just at the end of my presidency of the American Psychiatric Association, the report advances two of my major interests and concerns. It is the first major attempt to clarify and specify the tools available to psychiatry. As such it will serve as the basis for our continuing effort to describe and define our profession within the world of medicine.

The eradication of stigma has been the theme of my presidency, and it is my hope that *Treatments of Psychiatric Disorders* can help us to demonstrate to the public the positive effective treatments in the psychiatric armamentarium. In its present form it serves to educate the profession, but I hope it will be refined and condensed into material for the general public so that there can be broader understanding of the effectiveness of psychiatric treatment.

Paul J. Fink, M.D.
President, American Psychiatric Association (1988–1989)

Introduction

Science provides only interim knowledge.

Psychiatric treatment, like the rest of medicine, is inherently a flexible and open system which will continuously be influenced by new knowledge. This report represents a description of clinically useful current approaches for the treatment of mental disorders with a balanced perspective. It is important to emphasize that a treatment plan inherently must be an open system. Thus, this report is a working document reflecting a combination of cumulative scientific knowledge and clinical judgment about the treatment of psychiatric patients.

Historical Background

This undertaking began with the establishment of a previous Commission on Psychiatric Therapies in 1977 by Jules Masserman, M.D., then the president of the American Psychiatric Association. The charge was to examine critically the somatic, dyadic, group/family, and social therapies in current use—and to recommend criteria for evaluating therapeutic approaches.

In its attempt to meet this difficult task, the Commission produced two publications, both published by the American Psychiatric Association. The first was a critical review of a large body of evaluation research, entitled *Psychotherapy Research: Methodological and Efficacy Issues* (American Psychiatric Association Commission on Psychiatric Therapies 1982). This work pointed to the complexity of the variables involved in defining both the nature of a psychotherapeutic treatment and its outcome. The second publication, *The Psychiatric Therapies* (American Psychiatric Association Commission on Psychiatric Therapies 1984), was a comprehensive compendium of the many psychosocial and somatic treatment modalities currently in use.

In continuation of the previous Commission, Daniel X. Freedman, M.D., then the president of the APA, established a Task Force on Treatment of Psychiatric Disorders in 1982 to produce a comprehensive document that would describe the state of the art for treatment of psychiatric disorders.

The Process of Development

Because of the multiplicity of psychiatric disorders and their related approaches, the Task Force designated Chairpersons for 26 Panels, each of whom would draw together a working group to review the treatment of a different disorder or group of disorders. Chairpersons and Panel members were chosen from among many well-qualified individuals on the basis of certain criteria: the publication of research or clinical reports concerned with the treatment of a specific category of mental illness; and nomination

by peers based on acknowledged eminence in clinical practice, national reputation, past accomplishments, and broad perspective. In order to assist them in their task, each Panel was empowered to retain the specialized services of a wide variety of consultants and representatives of consultant organizations.

The consultants were selected so as to represent a breadth of disciplines and orientations, in appreciation of the diverse patient and treatment variables important in these fields. They encompass expertise in general psychiatry, child psychiatry, psychoanalysis, psychotherapy, pharmacotherapy, and biological and social psychiatry, as well as exposure to treatments in diverse settings. This method of selecting contributors and consultants, and the desire for integration and synthesis of divergent views, led to multiple responses and challenges. We believe this approach has had a salutary effect on the outcome of the report.

Panels were assigned psychiatric diagnostic groups for which they were to provide treatment considerations. They identified distinct categories within the given diagnostic groupings which deserved full narration and discussed the variation of treatment as applied to other categories. The Panels operated on the basis of the clinical model that assumes that, for an individual with specific characteristics who is suffering from a given disorder or combination of disorders, there are one or more preferred treatments and/or combinations as well as acceptable alternative and possibly adjunct treatments.

Once a draft was prepared by the contributors, that document marked the beginning of an elaborate review process, as follows: 1) it was sent to a number of consultants, chosen by the contributor(s) for comments; 2) Draft II was prepared by the contributor(s) on the basis of the consultants' suggestions; 3) the Task Force sent Draft II to five to ten consultants; 4) the comments and critiques of these individuals were sent to the original contributors(s) for preparation of Draft III; and 5) Draft III was then reviewed and finalized by the Task Force. This complex process of consultation and review produced sections that reflect the input and ideas of many experts. Although in some sections a single author, in others a group of authors, and in still others individual chapters are given credits depending upon the level of contribution, the completed product represents the original work of the primary author(s), views of the Chairperson and Consultants of each Panel, and the Members of the Task Force.

Format

As there was no precedent for us to use as a model, and also recognizing that the consideration of treatment for various disorders may require different approaches to their subjects, the Panels were given a relatively free rein as to the format, style, and length of their presentations.

The sections do not deal with the issues of diagnosis, but assume the reader's prior knowledge. Where there was a need for further elaboration of the *Diagnostic and Statistical Manual of Mental Disorders* in its utilization for treatment planning, these issues were discussed. The work progressed during the transitional stage from DSM-III to DSM-III-R. Whenever we were able, we tried to keep the pace.

Naturally, some topics were repeated to varying degrees in different chapters. This also helped to state some of the finer points between them. At times a clinical example was presented to clarify differential diagnostic issues.

In discussion of treatment of a condition from more than one perspective, an attempt was made to integrate multiple points of view within a single section. Wher-

ever this was not feasible, multiple chapters are included from diverse perspectives. A clinician must be able to consider each clinical problem at several conceptual levels in designing the most appropriate treatment program. Often combined applications are included to describe complementary models that are in use. Wherever empirical data were available, they were cited. In newer fields there are detailed discussions of studies instead of conclusions, to allow a proper perspective on the data. Special references were added in the text for readers who may want to study the subject in greater depth.

Use of This Report

This report is a professional document designed to suggest useful treatments for psychiatric disorders as an aid for treatment planning. It is not intended to impose rigid methods. It aims to demonstrate the complexity of the treatment planning process and its application, the true nature of comprehensive diagnosis, and the depth and breadth of knowledge that is required to assess a patient's need for the provision of treatment.

Proper use of this document requires specialized training that provides both a body of knowledge and clinical skills. Furthermore, many specific factors will influence the treatment needs for a particular individual. The chapters in this report do not dictate an exclusive course of treatment or procedures to be followed and should not be construed as excluding other acceptable methods of practice. Therefore, it would be incorrect to assert that any single treatment in this book automatically fits any single patient. Sound use of this book requires a clinician's judgment based on knowledge of a patient and a valid background of training and practice in psychiatry. Ultimately, it is individual practitioners—based upon their clinical judgment, experience, and assessment of the scientific literature—who will determine the usefulness of various therapeutic approaches. Futhermore, the mental disorders discussed in this report do not encompass all of the conditions that a psychiatrist may legitimately treat.

Future Directions

It is also important to note that this report reflects current assessment from an evolving knowledge base. Psychiatry participates in the continual expansion of knowledge that is taking place in all areas of science and medicine. New psychotropic drugs and other somatic approaches are constantly being tested and evaluated. Similarly, new psychotherapeutic and psychosocial techniques are being developed and assessed. In addition, combinations of treatment which hold promise are being evaluated. The continual accrual of new information will need to be integrated into these formulations in an ongoing way.

An important implication of the attempt to systemize our knowledge is that as the Task Force proceeded with its work, both what is known as well as what needs to be known became more evident. In particular, there is a need for increasing refinement of significant variables toward a greater understanding of individual differences in response to different therapeutic approaches. Such refinement will depend upon ongoing research which must take into account specific interventions, specific disorders or patient subgroups of responders and nonresponders, specific dosages,

specific durations, and specific combinations and sequences of the treatments—in short, the ultimate establishment of carefully delineated criteria for titrating the nature and timing of various therapies and their combinations to be utilized in a biopsychosocial approach to the treatment of psychiatric disorders (Karasu 1982).

Toksoz Byram Karasu, M.D.

References

American Psychiatric Association Commission on Psychiatric Therapies: Psychotherapy Research: Methodological and Efficacy Issues. Washington, DC, American Psychiatric Association, 1982

American Psychiatric Association Commission on Psychiatric Therapies: The Psychiatric Therapies. Volume 1 (Somatic Therapies) and Volume 2 (Psychosocial Therapies). Washington, DC, American Psychiatric Association, 1984

Karasu TB: Psychotherapy and pharmacotherapy: toward an integrative model. Am J Psychiatry 139:7, 1982

Acknowledgments

This work was accomplished with the generous help of many people. Both the size of this project as well as the spirit of cooperation by which it was undertaken are demonstrated by the large number of clinicians involved and cited as contributors and consultants. I am deeply indebted to all.

I would like to thank the Chairpersons of the Panels and all contributors who not only prepared scholarly documents, but also gracefully allowed their original works to be modified through the consultation process. I would also like to express my gratitude to the consultants for their productive criticism.

I am most thankful for the support of Daniel X. Freedman, M.D., founder President of the Task Force, and Paul J. Fink, M.D., who presided during the crucial stage of the project, as well as to Keith H. Brodie, M.D., George Tarjan, M.D., John A. Talbott, M.D., Carol C. Nadelson, M.D., Robert O. Pasnau, M.D., George H. Pollock, M.D., Herbert Pardes, M.D., who served as Presidents, and also Lawrence Hartmann, M.D., William R. Sorum, M.D., Harvey Bluestone, M.D., Fred Gottlieb, M.D., Roger Peele, M.D., Irvin M. Cohen, M.D., and John S. McIntyre, M.D., who served as Speakers of the Assembly during the lifetime of the Task Force.

My special thanks to Melvin Sabshin, M.D., Medical Director of the American Psychiatric Association, for his unfailing leadership and the wisdom which he provided with great generosity, and to Harold Alan Pincus, M.D., Director, Office of Research, who gave administrative direction to the project and who, jointly with Paul J. Fink, M.D., the chairman of the Joint Ad Hoc Review Committee, weathered the most complicated organizational issues and skillfully brought this project to a successful conclusion.

I want to express my gratitude to Sandy Ferris for her organizational ability; to Philomena Lee, who maintained the highly complicated correspondence with a large number of people and corrected final drafts with exemplary patience, good humor, and dedication; to Betty Meltzer for her elegant editorial assistance; and to Louise Notarangelo, Rita Segarra, and Shirley Kreitman, who assisted them with equal competence and generosity.

My sincere appreciation and gratitude to Ronald E. McMillen, General Manager of the American Psychiatric Press, Inc., Timothy R. Clancy, Editorial Director, and Richard E. Farkas, Production Manager, for their leadership, and to their dedicated staff, Christine Kalbacher, Project Coordinator, Karen E. Sardinas-Wyssling and Lindsay E. Edmunds, Principal Manuscript Editors; to Editorial Experts, Inc., specifically Mary Stoughton and the staff editors, Pat Caudill and the staff proofreaders, and June Morse and the staff indexers, and to Robert Elwood and Nancy Borza at Harper Graphics, Typesetter, and Tom Reed at R. R. Donnelley & Sons Company, Printer, whose expert labors have facilitated the transformation of the raw material into four carefully wrought and handsome volumes.

Toksoz Byram Karasu, M.D.

Cautionary Statement

This report does not represent the official policy of the American Psychiatric Association. It is an APA task force report, signifying that members of the APA have contributed to its development, but it has not been passed through those official channels required to make it an APA policy document.

THIS REPORT IS NOT INTENDED TO BE CONSTRUED AS OR TO SERVE AS A STANDARD FOR PSYCHIATRIC CARE.

Subject Index

AA. *See* Alcoholics Anonymous
L-AAM. *See* L-Alpha-acetylmethadiol
Aberrant motivational syndrome. *See*
    Cannabis abuse and
    dependence
Aberration, 648
Abnormal involuntary movements
    autistic children, 243–244
    delirium, 805
Abnormal Involuntary Movements
    Scale (AIMS), 244
Abortion and adolescent's family
    relationships, 2368
Absences. *See* Epilepsy, generalized
    seizures
Abstinence
    and Alcoholics Anonymous, 1158
    as alcoholism treatment goal, 1075–
        1076, 1097–1098, 1103, 1133
    and psychotherapy, 1098, 1108
Abulia and stroke, 868
Abuse. *See* Child abuse or neglect;
    Elder abuse reporting; Spouse
    abuse reporting
Academic skills disorders, 298, 328–
    339
    See also Learning disabilities
Acceptance of autistic child's disability,
    257
Accidents
    alcohol abuse and automobile
        accidents, 846

automobile accident statistics, 846
and depression, 846
drug abuse and automobile
    accidents, 846
proneness to in posttraumatic stress
    disorder, 2074
Acetaminophen
    hepatic disease, 938
Acetazolamide
    atypical psychosis, 1705
    epilepsy, 889
    interaction with other drugs, 960
    menses-associated psychosis, 1708
Acetylcholine
    and antidepressant drugs, 1774
Acetylcholinesterase
    Tourette's syndrome, 691
Acetylsalicylic acid
    dementia, 826
    and electroconvulsive therapy, 1811
    and hypertension, 847
    insomnia, 2430
    interaction with other drugs, 927
    and lithium, 1926
    multi-infarct dementia, 962
    stroke, 869
Acid-base disturbances
    and delirium, 806
    and organic mental syndromes, 897
Acidification treatment for
    phencyclidine abuse and
    dependence, 1213, 1215

Acidosis
  and antianxiety drugs, 945
  and epilepsy, 881
  and lung disease, 940
  and renal disease, 916
Acne from lithium, 1930
ACNP *Review of a Generation of
    Progress*, 1814
Acquired immunodeficiency syndrome
    (AIDS)
  differential diagnosis, 1701
  note on exclusion from sexual
    disorders section, 2238
  precautions for drug addicts,
    hospital treatment, 1363, 1365
  risk, drug abuse side effect, 1185,
    1328
  with secondary depression, 1792,
    1901, 1912
Acromegaly
  pharmacotherapy, 833
  and secondary depression, 1902
Acting out
  adjustment disorders, 2570, 2584
  impulse control disorders not
    elsewhere classified, 2458, 2459,
    2461, 2462
Acupuncture for relief of chronic pain,
    2132
Acute paranoid reaction. *See* Brief
    reactive psychosis
Acute porphyria
  differential diagnosis, 1701
  and secondary depression, 1902
  See also Hepatic disease
Addiction Severity Index, 1187, 1433,
    1444
Addison's disease
  differential diagnosis, 1701
  and secondary mania, 1914
ADHD. *See* Attention-deficit
    hyperactivity disorder
Adjustment disorders
  adulthood and old age
    bereavement, 2507

conversion disorders,
    differentiation, 2507
  course and prognosis, 2507–2508
  depression, differentiation, 2507
  diagnosis, 2504–2506
  dissociative disorders,
    differentiation, 2507
  education, 2509
  hospitalization, 2510
  posttraumatic stress disorder,
    differentiation, 2506
  psychogenic pain disorders,
    differentiation, 2507
  psychotherapy, 2509, 2510
  suicide, 2510
  symptoms, 2505
  treatment, 2508–2510
  vulnerability to stress, 2504, 2508
childhood and adolescence
  concept, 2510–2511
  course and prognosis, 2513–2516
  crisis theory, 2514
  diagnosis, 2512
  DSM-III-R diagnostic criteria, 2513
  environmental manipulations,
    2517–2518
  history, 2511–2512
  hospital versus outpatient
    treatment, 2519
  long-term stressors, 2514, 2515
  posttraumatic play, 2519
  posttraumatic stress disorder,
    differentiation, 2512
  prevention techniques, 2516–
    2517
  psychic trauma, 2515
  recovery rates, 2513–2514
  release therapy, 2518–2519
  stress, response to, 2513
  stress reduction, 2518
  treatment, 2516–2519
  vulnerability of children, 2514,
    2515–2516
combat fatigue, 2514, 2515
DSM-III-R diagnostic criteria, 2497,
    2498

environmental manipulation in
  treatment, 2508, 2509
family therapy
  acting out, 2570
  anxiety, 2570, 2571, 2575, 2576
  biofeedback, 2577
  case vignettes, 2574–2577
  child focus and impairment, 2570–
    2571, 2573
  compensatory mechanisms for
    stress, 2572–2578
  differentiation of self, 2571–2572
  emotional attachment and
    equilibrium, 2571, 2572, 2573
  emotional distance, 2570
  emotional reactivity, 2576
  family as system, 2567–2568
  guilt, 2574
  marital conflict, 2569–2570
  nuclear/extended family emotional
    systems, 2569–2572
  operation of therapy, 2572–2578
  overfunctioning, 2576–2578
  principles, 2566
  relationship patterns, 2568–2569
  response patterns, 2567
  spouse dysfunction, 2570
  stability preservation, 2569
  stress in family relationships,
    2566, 2568, 2569, 2570, 2571,
    2572–2578
  stressors, 2572, 2575
  symptoms, 2573
group therapy
  acting out, 2584
  affect, 2584
  attribution of meaning, 2582–2583
  burnout, 2579
  catharsis, 2581–2582
  classes and clubs, 2583
  countertransference, 2584
  desensitization, 2582
  education, 2580
  emotional issues, 2581
  formats, 2583
  job stress, 2578, 2579, 2580

  nurse-support groups, 2581, 2582,
    2583, 2584, 2585
  optimism as therapeutic element,
    2580
  physical illness groups, 2579,
    2581, 2583, 2584, 2585
  principles, 2579–2580
  problems, 2584
  rationale, 2578–2579
  reframing, 2581
  self-identification, 2582
  structure, 2585
  termination, 2583–2584
  therapeutic elements, 2580–2583
  therapist attitudes, 2584
  therapist qualifications, 2579–2580
in mentally retarded persons, 18
Navy enlisted personnel study, 2513
patient history, 2508
and personality disorders, 2506, 2507
pharmacotherapy
  affect block, 2587
  amobarbital interview, 2587
  antianxiety drugs, 2587–2588
  antidepressant drugs, 2588–2589
  antipsychotic drugs, 2586, 2589
  beta-adrenergic blocking drugs,
    2590
  contraindications and precautions,
    2586, 2587
  controversies, 2585–2586
  depression, indications, 2588
  grief, acute, 2586
  insomnia, 2587
  panic disorders and phobias, 2587
  placebo effect, 2587
  posttraumatic stress symptoms,
    2588–2589
  principles, 2586–2587
  psychotic symptoms, 2589
  sedative-hypnotic drugs, 2587
  stress response, acute, 2587
posttraumatic stress disorders,
  differentiation, 2503
psychotherapy, brief dynamic
  case vignette, 2551–2552

Adjustment disorders (cont)
  defensive maneuvers, 2553, 2554
  early phase, 2550
  histrionic style of personality, 2555
  late phases, 2553
  memory role, 2549, 2550
  middle phases, 2552–2553
  mutual help groups, 2550
  narcissistic style of personality,
    2556
  personality styles, 2553–2556
  rationale, 2549–2550
  role relationship models, 2551–
    2552
  self-concepts, 2551–2552
  self-esteem problems, 2550, 2552
  state formulation procedures,
    2550–2551
  symptomatology, 2550
  termination of therapy, 2553
  therapeutic alliance, 2549, 2550,
    2552
  transference, 2552–2553
psychotherapy, child, individual
  affect, 2559–2560
  case vignettes, 2561–2562, 2562–
    2563, 2563–2564
  contributions, 2565–2566
  crisis intervention, 2557–2558
  developmental capability, 2560–
    2562
  developmental issues, 2564
  focal inquiry, 2560
  interventions, 2560–2562
  play therapy, 2562–2563
  resistance management, 2560
  short-term therapy, 2558–2559
  therapeutic relationship, 2559
  therapist activity, 2563–2564
rape victims, 2535, 2536, 2538, 2541,
    2542–2543
religion as ego support, 2590–2595
signal to noise ratio, 2502
stressors
  psychosocial, 2498–2500
  responses, 2500–2502, 2513
  stress response syndromes, 2548–
    2549
  symptom remission, 2502–2503
  U.S. Army draftee study, 2497
See also Stress management
Adjustment disorder with depressed
    mood
  differential diagnosis, 1900, 1946–
    1949
  incidence, 1727
  pharmacotherapy, 1743, 1949
  psychotherapy, 1743, 1948
Adolescent pedophilia, 619, 620–621
  homosexual vs. heterosexual, 621
Adolescents
  contraceptive use, 2366–2367
  identity formation, 782–785
  mood disorders, 1950–1958
    diagnostic considerations, 1763–
      1764
    family history, 1763
  parenting, 2369–2370
  personality disorders
    behavior therapy, 2655
    dependent personality disorder,
      2765
    family therapy, 2662–2663, 2740
    residential treatment, 2696
    treatment, 2652–2653, 2654
  pregnancy, 2368–2369
  pregnancy prevention and
    intervention programs, 2369
  psychotherapy for schizoid disorder,
    755–757
  psychotherapy issues, 789–790
  sexual activity statistics, 2366
  sexuality and treatment planning,
    2375–2376
  substance abuse, 1192
  tumultuous course through
    adolescence, 784–785
See also Identity disorder
Adolescent support groups. See
    Mutual-help services for youth;
    Peer-helping services for youth;
    names of specific organizations

Adolescent-type behavior in impulse control disorders not elsewhere classified, 2457, 2458, 2460

Adrenal insufficiency and brief reactive psychosis, 1680

Adult attention deficit disorder. *See* Attention deficit disorder, residual type

Adult children of alcoholics (ACOAs), 1110–1111
  Al-Anon groups for, 1160
  See also Children of alcoholics

Adult Diagnostic and Treatment Center, treatment of sexual offenders, 625

Advocacy as a form of coping, 259

Aesthenic personality, 2759, 2763, 2766
  See also Dependent personality disorder

Affect block, 2587

Affect in adjustment disorders, 2559–2560, 2584

Affect intensity problems, 2457

Affective disorders. *See* Mood disorders

Affective Style index, 1551

Affirmation, 2012

Aftercare groups, 2599
  alcoholism, 1122
  schizophrenia, 1569

Age as factor
  amnestic syndromes, 817–818
  antidepressant pharmacotherapy, 827–828
  benzodiazepines dosage, 2042
  bipolar disorders, 1668, 1756, 1758
  cannabis abuse and dependence, 1242, 1243, 1244
  cocaine abuse, 1219
  cognitive-behavioral psychotherapy, 1839
  delirium, 979
  dementia, 817–818, 827–829, 831, 900, 979, 994–995
  digitalis toxicity, 907
  dysthymia, 1757

economic issues, 979–983
efficacy of nortriptyline, 1871
electroconvulsive therapy, 1807
fragile X syndrome, 40
hallucinogen abuse, 1204
heroin addicts, life expectancy, 1327–1328
organic aggressive syndrome, 853
organic mental syndromes, 800–803, 900
Parkinson's disease, 862, 863
phencyclidine abuse and dependence, 1217
psychodynamic psychotherapy, 2647
psychogenic fugue, 2193
psychosocial stressors, response, 2500–2501, 2504
pyromania, 2469
schizoaffective disorder, 1668
spontaneous improvement in antisocial personality disorder, 2743
stroke, 875
trichotillomania, 2481, 2486

Ageusia, 949, 953, 956

Aggression
  anxiolytic agents, contraindications, 86
  and intermittent explosive disorder, 2473, 2474, 2475, 2476

Aging and sexuality, 2280, 2285, 2370–2375

Agitation and neuroleptic drugs, 1514

Agnosia and dementia, 816

Agoraphobia
  behavior therapy, 2029–2034
  distinguished from panic, 2015
  exposure treatment, 2029–2034
    compared with imipramine treatment, 2033–2034
    compared with other treatments, 2033–2034
    couples training, 2030–2031
    limitations, 2032
    long-term efficacy, 2031
    outcome, 2031–2032

Agoraphobia *(cont)*
  pharmacotherapy, 2033–2034
  psychoanalytic psychotherapy, 2015–2019
Agranulocytosis and neuroleptic drugs, 1514, 1906
AIDS. *See* Acquired immunodeficiency syndrome
Akathisia
  and antipsychotic drugs, 849, 1511, 1512
  and Tourette's syndrome, 692, 706, 707
Akinesia
  and neuroleptic drugs, 1514, 1662
  and Parkinson's disease, 860–861
Akinetic mutism and stroke, 871
Akinetic seizures. *See* Epilepsy, generalized seizures
Alanon. *See* Al-Anon
Al-Anon, 1091, 1115–1116, 1160, 1399, 1401, 1411
Alaproclate
  dementia of the Alzheimer's type, 975
Alateen. *See* Al-ateen
Al-ateen, 1160, 1161, 2613
Albuterol, side effects, 944
Alcohol abuse
  and automobile accidents, 846
  and brief reactive psychosis, 1681
  and cannabis abuse and dependence, 1243
  and chronic mania, 1936
  and delirium, 806, 810
  and delusional (paranoid) disorders, 1648
  and dementia, 818, 820, 822
  differential diagnosis, 885
  distinguished from alcohol dependence, 1063, 1067
  DSM-III-R diagnostic criteria, 1063–1064, 1067
  and epilepsy, 885, 887
  and hepatic disease, 932–933, 934, 935, 939
  and methadone maintenance, 1351

and mood disorders
  bipolar disorders, 1759–1760
  depressive disorders, 854, 1765, 1792
and opioid abuse, 1313, 1314, 1329
and organic aggressive syndrome, 842–843, 848, 852
and organic hallucinosis, 833
and other substance abuse, 1149, 1184
and personality disorders, 2684, 2688, 2696, 2698
  avoidant personality disorder, 2762
  borderline personality disorder, 2750
and psychiatric problems, 1185
and psychogenic fugue, 2194
and renal disease, 918
and schizoaffective disorder, 1668
self-reporting, veracity, 1191
and sexual disorders, 2240
and smoking, 1283–1284
symptoms, 1079
and tobacco dependence and withdrawal, 1283–1284
treatment, 846–847
See also Alcohol dependence; Alcoholism
Alcohol amnestic disorder, 826, 1067, 1091
Alcohol and brain function, 1067, 1071, 1091–1093, 1105
Alcohol as antianxiety agent
  anxiety disorders, 2037–2038, 2074
  sexual anxiety, 2309, 2361
Alcohol dependence
  blood alcohol levels and intoxication, 1077
  distinguished from alcohol abuse, 1063, 1067
  DSM-III-R diagnostic criteria, 1064
  severity and treatment outcome, 1068
  severity related to frequency and quantity of consumption, 1068

See also Alcohol abuse; Alcoholism
Alcohol dependence syndrome, 1067–
  1068
Alcohol detoxification
  inpatient
    adjunctive medical care, 1138–1139
    adjunctive psychosocial care, 1139
    admission criteria, 1137
    discharge and follow-up, 1139
    pharmacotherapy, 1087–1090,
      1137–1138
  outpatient, 1150
  social, 1150
  See also Alcohol withdrawal; Hospital
    treatment
Alcohol hallucinosis, 1067, 1089
Alcoholic blackout, 1082–1084
Alcoholic dementia. *See* Dementia
  associated with alcoholism
Alcoholic family, 1112
  See also Adult children of alcoholics;
    Children of alcoholics; Families
    of alcoholics; Family problems;
    Parent role in alcoholism
Alcoholic liver disease, 932–933
  See also Hepatic disease
Alcoholics Anonymous (AA)
  alcoholic's process of involvement,
    1096
  anonymity requirement, 1152
  compared with professional
    treatment, 1158
  disapproval of disulfiram, 1102
  effectiveness, 1156–1158
  evaluation studies, 1157–1158
  history and development, 1152
  meeting formats, 1156
  membership characteristics, 1152–
    1154
  model for group therapy, 1117, 1378
  model for self-help groups, 2596,
    2598, 2599, 2600, 2603, 2604,
    2608, 2611, 2613, 2616, 2695
  policy, 1151–1152
  for prevention and treatment of

organic aggressive syndrome,
    846, 887
  and psychotherapy, 1096, 1107
  referral, 1159
  role in alcoholism treatment, 1076,
    1096, 1101–1102, 1107, 1134
  role in drug abuse treatment, 1299,
    1316, 1378, 1390, 1399, 1420
  sponsors, 1155–1156
  therapeutic procedures, 1154–1156
  Twelve Step structure and
    philosophy, 1152, 1154–1155
  and withdrawal, 1090–1091
Alcohol idiosyncratic intoxication
  defined, 1082–1083
  treatment, 1083–1084
Alcohol intoxication
  amnesic behavior in alcohol
    intoxication, 1083
  differential diagnosis, 884, 1076–1078
  emergency procedures, 1067, 1070–
    1071, 1079–1082
  and organic personality disorder,
    840
  physician's attitude, 1079
  sex differences, 1077
  signs and symptoms, 1077
  treatment, 1079–1082
  See also Alcohol idiosyncratic
    intoxication; Alcohol metabolism
Alcoholism
  and antisocial personality disorder,
    2656
  associated with pedophilia, 621, 632
  behavior therapy, 1076, 1125–1131,
    1862
  cognitive impairment, 1067, 1071,
    1105
  community-based treatment, 1147–
    1151
  cost effectiveness of treatment,
    1142–1143
  and criminality, 1072, 1083
  diagnosis, 1063–1064, 1065–1072,
    1073, 1093–1094

Alcoholism *(cont)*
  differentiation of alcohol abuse and
      alcohol dependence, 1063, 1067
  familial, Types I and II, 1072
  family therapy, 1111–1117, 2664
  genetic predisposition, 1096, 1114
  group therapy, 1102, 1117–1125
  indications of alcohol-related
      problems, 1144–1146
  inpatient treatment, 1102, 1137–1143
  multimodal treatment, 1103, 1129–
      1130, 1140–1141
  new chronic patient, 1151
  office management, 1132–1136
  outpatient treatment, 1102, 1147–
      1149
  and passive-aggressive personality
      disorder, 2784
  pharmacotherapy, 1075, 1076, 1085,
      1087–1089, 1090, 1137–1138,
      2686
  predictors of treatment outcome,
      1071, 1103, 1139, 1151
  prevalence in workforce, 1146
  prevalence of multiple drug abuse,
      1149, 1184
  and psychiatric disorders, 1069,
      1073–1074, 1094
  psychodynamics of, 1094–1097
  and psychopathology, 1067–1072,
      1094
  psychotherapy, 1093–1111
  relapse prevention, 1130–1131, 1135
  and retarded ejaculation, 2313–2314
  risk factors, 1069–1070, 1094–1096,
      1111
  and secondary depression, 1067,
      1068, 1069, 1070–1071, 1094,
      1903, 1915, 1918–1920
  signs and symptoms, 1078–1079
  stages of recovery, 1098–1099
  term not used in DSM-III, 1063
  treatment goals, 1072–1076
  treatment intervention points, 1096–
      1097

  treatment planning considerations,
      1072–1074
  typologies, 1065–1072
  See also Alcohol abuse; Alcohol
      dependence
Alcohol metabolism
  blood alcohol levels, 1077
  and menstrual cycle, 1077
  and oral contraceptives, 1077
  sex differences, 1077
Alcohol-methadone interaction, 1348
Alcohol-related organic mental
      disorders
  categories, 1067
  irreversible, 1091–1093
  treatment goals, 1074
  See also names of specific disorders
Alcohol-related pathologies, 1067–
      1072, 1094
Alcohol withdrawal
  and Alcoholics Anonymous, 1090–
      1091
  convulsions, 1088
  hallucinosis, 1067, 1089
  inappropriate use of intravenous
      fluids, 1082–1088
  mild to moderate (uncomplicated),
      1067, 1084–1086
  multiple drug users, 1088–1089
  pharmacotherapy, 1087–1090, 1137–
      1138
  protracted, 1089–1091
  seizures, 884
  severe (alcohol withdrawal
      delirium), 1086–1087
  signs and symptoms, 1085–1086,
      1372
  treatment, 1084–1091
  See also Detoxification
Alcohol withdrawal delirium
  indications for hospitalization, 1086–
      1087
  pharmacotherapy, 1087–1090
  treatment, 811–812
  See also Alcohol detoxification

Alexithymia
  barrier to treatment of alcoholism,
    1106
  and impulse control disorders, 2457,
    2471
  in schizoid disorder, 760
Allergic diseases and antidepressant
    drugs, 1782, 1874
Alliance for the Mentally Ill, 2604–2605
Allopurinol
  interaction with other drugs, 947
L-Alpha-acetylmethadiol (L-AAM)
  as alternative to methadone
    maintenance, 1325, 1359
Alpha adrenergic blocking drugs
  and retarded ejaculation, 2243
  and sexual disorders, 2240
Alpha adrenergic stimulating drugs
  orgasmic dysfunctions, 2357
Alprazolam
  anxiety disorders, 2039, 2050–2051,
    2052
  anxiety in sexual disorders, 2247
  borderline personality disorder,
    2682, 2755
  dementia, 829
  effects on cardiovascular system, 903
  interaction with other drugs, 915
  mood disorders, 1739
  in treatment nonresponders, 1798
Altruism as therapy in self-help and
    mutual aid groups for adults,
    2603
Aluminum hydroxide gel
  interaction with other drugs, 921
  metabolic acidosis with renal failure,
    921
Alzheimer's disease
  confidentiality of diagnosis, 989
  and depressive disorders, 828
    differential diagnosis, 1910
    nonresponsiveness to
      antidepressant treatment, 1792
  distinguished from alcoholic
    dementia, 1091
  and Down's syndrome, 12, 30–32

ethical issues of treatment, 1004–
    1005
  and organic aggressive syndrome,
    842–843
  pharmacotherapy, 828, 829
  treatment, 803
  See also Dementia of the Alzheimer's
    type
Alzheimer's Disease and Related
    Disorders Association, 2605
  diagnostic criteria, 818
  family therapy, 830
  lobbying efforts, 982
Alzheimer's Disease Research Centers,
    982
Amantadine
  cocaine withdrawal, 1922
  countermeasure for side effects of
    neuroleptic drugs, 1511, 1629
  hypokinetic syndrome, 1512
  and organic psychosis, 833
  Parkinson's disease, 863, 865
  renal disease, 924
Amenorrhea and stroke, 876
American Association for the
    Advancement of Science, 1733
American Association of Retired
    Persons (AARP), 980
American Foundation for the Blind,
    957
American Lung Association program
    on cigarette smoking, 1278, 1279
American Medical Association Patient
    Medication Instruction Sheet
    (PMI) "MAOI Antidepressants,"
    1785
American Medical Systems model 600
    flexible penis prosthesis, 2332,
    2333
American Medical Systems model 700
    penile prosthesis, 2334
American Psychiatric Association
  Commission on Psychiatric
    Therapies, 1729
  Commission on Psychotherapies,
    1516

American Psychiatric Association *(cont)*
  Manual of Psychiatric Peer Review,
    1769–1772
  neuroleptic drug use study, 1569
  tardive dyskinesia study, 1513
  Task Force on Electroconvulsive
    Therapy, 1805, 1806
  Task Force on the Use of Laboratory
    Tests in Psychiatry, 1779
Amikacin
  auditory effects, 958
Amiloride
  renal disease, 925
Aminophylline
  lithium excretion, 906
Amitriptyline
  borderline personality disorder,
    2681, 2682
  classification, 1774
  dementia, 827
  dementia of the Alzheimer's type,
    975
  effectiveness, 1841
  effects on cardiovascular system, 902
  and electroconvulsive therapy, 1813
  histrionic personality disorder, 2735
  interaction with other drugs, 891
  with interpersonal psychotherapy,
    1868, 1869, 1870
  mentally retarded persons, 82
  mood disorders, 1793, 1886
    depressive disorders, 946, 1742,
      1819, 1820, 1821, 1868, 1869,
      1870, 1903, 1904, 1906, 1908,
      1912, 1917, 1919, 1920, 1922,
      1942
  neurotransmitter blockade, 1775,
    1776
  obsessive compulsive disorders, 2103
  premature ejaculation, 2353, 2357
  reaction with disulfiram, 1100
  schizoaffective disorder, 1673
  sex drive reduction, 2356
  side effects, 948
  somatoform pain disorder, 2129

and specific medical diseases, 946,
    1781–1783, 1784
  stroke-related syndromes, 874
  trichotillomania, 2482–2483
  vaginismus, 2358
Ammonium chloride
  delirium, 814
Amnesia. *See* Psychogenic amnesia
Amnesic episodes in alcohol
    intoxication. *See* Alcoholic
    blackout
Amnestic disorder
  alcohol amnestic disorder, 826, 1067,
    1091
  barbiturate-sedative-hypnotic abuse,
    1300
  DSM-III-R diagnostic criteria, 1300
Amnestic episodes in alcohol
    intoxication. *See* Alcohol
    intoxication
Amnestic episodes in multiple
    personality disorder, 2211
Amnestic syndromes
  age factor, 817–818
  alcohol disorder, 826
  anterograde amnesia, 816–817
  benign senescent forgetfulness, 821
  diagnostic criteria, 815–817
  differential diagnosis, 806, 816–817,
    818–822
  from drug effects, 820–821, 948
  epilepsy-related, 878, 880, 883, 884
  immediate memory (digit span), 817
  incidence, 817–818
  long-term (remote) memory, 817,
    821
  and lung carcinoma, 942
  patient evaluation, 822–826
  retrograde amnesia, 817
  and secondary depression, 821
  and sensory impairment, 949, 952
  short-term (recent) memory, 816–
    817, 821
  and stroke, 871–872
  thiamine deficiency, 818, 819, 820

treatment of underlying causes, 826
See also Amnestic disorder;
    Psychogenic amnesia
Amobarbital
    alcohol withdrawal, 1088
    atypical psychosis evaluation, 1700
    depersonalization disorder, 2221
    dissociative disorder, 806
    epilepsy, 890
Amobarbital interview
    adjustment disorders, 2587
    dissociative disorder not otherwise
        specified, 2223
    psychogenic amnesia, 2188
    psychogenic fugue, 2192, 2195–2196
Amodiaquine
    ocular effects, 958
Amok, 1685, 1699, 2165
Amoxapine
    borderline personality disorder, 2684
    classification, 1774
    effects on cardiovascular system, 904
    and ejaculatory pain, 2317
    extrapyramidal symptoms, 1779
    interaction with other drugs, 1779
    pharmacokinetics, 1780
        neurotransmitter blockade, 1776
        neurotransmitter receptor
            blockade, 1779
    and specific medical diseases, 1782,
        1783, 1784
    in treatment nonresponders, 1798
d-Amphetamine
    dementia of the Alzheimer's type,
        975
    neurotransmitter blockade, 1776
Amphetamine abuse
    delusions, 1223
    emergency medical treatment, 1224
    half-life, 1221
    history and epidemiology, 1218–1220
    neurochemical activity, 1220–1222
    urine tests, 1235
    See also Hallucinogen abuse;
        Stimulant abuse

Amphetamine-barbiturate
    combinations
    mood disorders, 1735
Amphetamine or similarly acting
        sympathomimetic delusional
        disorder. *See* Organic delusional
        syndrome
Amphetamines
    accident risk, 846
    attention-deficit hyperactivity
        disorder, 373, 374
    autistic disorder, 241–242
    and dementia of the Alzheimer's
        type, 974
    depersonalization disorder, 2221
    hyperactive children, 73
    interaction with other drugs, 913
    and mania, 854
    mood disorders, 1734, 1735, 1744
    and organic aggressive syndrome,
        852
    and organic delusional syndrome,
        832–833, 834, 837
    and organic personality syndrome,
        858
    and secondary depression, 1913
    sexual effects, 2355
    side effects, 241–242
    Tourette's syndrome, 690
Amputation of sexual organs in
        transsexualism, 656, 658
Amylophagia, 586
Amytal. *See* Amobarbital
Anafranil. *See* Clomipramine
Anal character and personality
        disorders, 2639–2640, 2661
    and obsessive compulsive
        personality disorder, 2771
Analgesia and phencyclidine delirium,
        813
Analgesic drugs
    dementia, 826
    hepatic disease, 938
    and organic psychosis, 833
    secondary depression, 1904

Androcur. See Cyproterone acetate
Androgen levels and sexual
    sadomasochism, 649
Androgynization with age, 2372
Androphilia, conversion from
    pedophilia, 628
Anejaculatory orgasm
  distinguished from retarded
    ejaculation, 2243
Anemia
  and delirium, 806, 808
  and renal disease, 920
  side effect of phenytoin, 910
Anergia and bipolar disorders, 1760
Anger and neuroleptic drugs, 1514
Angioma and hepatic disease, 933, 935
Anhedonia
  differential diagnosis, 919
  and monoamine oxidase inhibitors,
    1743
  and mood disorders, 1754
  and neuroleptic drugs, 1514
  and schizoid personality disorder,
    2712
  and schizotypal personality disorder,
    2720
  in stimulant abuse, 1230–1231
Annuracetam
  dementia of the Alzheimer's type,
    973
Anorectal physiological dysfunction
  and functional encopresis, 724
Anorexia nervosa
  aftercare program, 459–460, 469, 481
  amenorrhea, 453
  atypical form, 590
  and atypical psychosis, 1699, 1706
  behaviorally based treatment
    program, 477–481
  behavior therapy, 456, 461, 467, 469,
    475–481
  binge eating and purging
    management, 467, 479
  bulimia nervosa, differentiation,
    511–512, 524
  bulimic complications, 462

case history, 465
chronic type, 462
cognitive model, 482–484
cognitive therapy, 461, 481, 482–491
computed tomography in
    assessment, 454
control over body as patient goal,
    514–515
criteria for inpatient treatment, 460–
    462
criteria for outpatient treatment,
    464–465
dichotomous reasoning, 486
differential diagnosis, 919
electroencephalogram in assessment,
    454
electrolyte imbalance, 452
endocrine assessment, 453
enmeshment in patients' families,
    495
enzyme levels in, 452
etiology, 510–512
evaluation of outpatient treatment,
    464–465
family role in outpatient behavior
    therapy, 479
family therapy, 459, 461, 463, 469,
    479, 491–508, 2663
group therapy, 508–510
hematology tests for, 452
and hepatic disease, 933, 935
hormone impairment, 453
hospital treatment, 455–462, 479–
    481, 501–502
inpatient behavior therapy, 479–480
laboratory tests for, 451–453, 465
medical assessment, 451–454
medical treatment, 454–455
metabolic problems, 452, 460
mind-body split, 463
motivation for treatment, 484–485
nasogastric feeding, 457–458
nutritional counseling, 470, 479–480,
    485, 509
outpatient treatment, 462–470, 478–
    479

personality problems, 513
pharmacotherapy, 457, 469, 471–474
psychopathology, 458–460, 481, 513–514
psychotherapy, 459, 481, 510–516, 561, 567–568
psychotherapy, concepts, 513–514
reasoning errors in, 486–488
refeeding, 454–455, 456
relapse prevention technique, 467
and secondary depression, 460, 1915, 1916–1917
symptoms, 451–453
treatment goals, 470, 479–480, 500–501
treatment issues, 514–515
treatment team, 470
weight gain and weight restoration, 456–458, 464, 466–467, 479–480
weight restoration-psychotherapy relationship, 459, 468
Anorgasmic women. See Inhibited female orgasm
Anosmia, 949, 952, 953, 955
Anosognosia
and organic delusional syndrome, 834
psychogenic amnesia, 2187
Anoxia
and amnestic syndromes, 819
and delirium, 807–808
and dementia, 816
and epilepsy, 881
and hepatic disease, 936
and stroke, 873
Antabuse. See Disulfiram
Antacids
interaction with other drugs, 921
Anterograde amnesia, 816–817
See also Amnestic syndromes
Antiandrogen drugs
fetishism, 638
pedophilia, 629–630
sexual effects, 2344
transvestic fetishism, 644, 645–646

See also names of specific drugs
Antianxiety drugs
abuse, 1184
adjustment disorders, 2587–2588
alcoholism, 1096
alcohol withdrawal, 1074, 1090
anorexia nervosa, 473
anxiety disorders, 2036–2052
anxiety disorders of childhood or adolescence, 407
avoidant personality disorder, 2762
cannabis abuse effects, 1249, 1252
dementia, 828–829
hepatic disease, 937
hypochondriasis with anxiety, 2145
impotence, 2347, 2357
inhibited female sexual response, 2286, 2290
insomnia, 85, 2587
mentally retarded persons, 85–88
obsessive compulsive disorder, 2103–2104
obsessive compulsive personality disorder, 2780
in patients with lung disease, 945–946, 948
posttraumatic stress disorder, 2073–2075
premature ejaculation, 2353
schizotypal personality disorder, 2725
secondary depression, 948, 1904
sexual effects, 2347
sexual sadomasochism, 651
side effects, 828
See also names of specific drugs
Antiarrhythmic drugs
interaction with other drugs, 913, 915
neuropsychiatric effects, 909–910
sexual effects, 2344
stroke, 867, 869
Antiatherogenic drugs
stroke, 869

Antibiotic drugs
  interaction with other drugs, 947
Anticancer drugs. *See* Antineoplastic
    drugs
Anticholinergic-antihistaminergic
    drugs
  dystonia, 1512
Anticholinergic drugs
  countermeasure for side effects of
    neuroleptic drugs, 1511, 1629
  delirium, 814
  extrapyramidal symptoms, 1675
  and female genital vasocongestion,
    2283–2284, 2349
  interaction with other drugs, 959
  Parkinson's disease, 862, 863, 865
  with a sensory-impaired patient, 958
  sexual effects, 2344
  side effects, 958
  substance-induced psychosis, 1371
Anticholinesterase
  delirium, 813
Anticoagulant drugs
  and dialysis dementia, 918
  interaction with other drugs, 913–915
  multi-infarct dementia, 962
  stroke, 867
Anticonvulsant drugs
  alcohol withdrawal, 1088
  atypical psychosis, 1705
  bipolar disorders, 1932
  and electroconvulsive therapy, 1808–
    1809
  fetishism, 637
  mentally retarded persons
    behavioral studies, 94–97
    clinical studies, 98–99
    cognitive studies, 95–97
    dosage, 98
    psychotropic aspects, 94
    research issues, 97–98
    side effects, 98
  organic aggressive syndrome, 850–
    851
  organic delusional syndrome, 837
  and organic psychosis, 833

personality disorders, 2687
  antisocial personality disorder,
    2746
  borderline personality disorder,
    2682, 2686
  obsessive compulsive personality
    disorder, 2780
and secondary depression, 1912,
    1913
stroke-related syndromes, 874
See also names of specific drugs
Antidepressant drugs
  adjustment disorders, 2588–2589
  alcoholism, 1075, 1096, 1101
  alcohol withdrawal, 1138
  anorexia nervosa, 473
  anxiety disorders, 2033–2034, 2048–
    2049, 2051
  anxiety disorders of childhood or
    adolescence, 408
  atypical psychosis and depression,
    1704
  autistic disorder, 235–239
  avoidant personality disorder, 2762
  borderline personality disorder, 2684
  brief reactive psychosis, 1682
  bulimia nervosa, 521, 525, 529–531
  choosing a drug, 1781–1787
  dementia, 827–828, 829, 831
  depersonalization disorder, 2221
  dosage, 1779–1781, 1784–1786, 1788–
    1789, 1790, 1792
  duration, 1785, 1786, 1788, 1789,
    1790, 1792
  effects on cardiovascular system,
    901–905
  elective mutism, 771
  and epilepsy, 1914
  hepatic disease, 937
  histrionic personality disorder, 2735
  hypochondriasis with depression,
    2145
  induced psychotic disorder, 1695
  insomnia, 2587
  interaction with other drugs, 913,
    928, 944, 959, 1777

lung disease, 945, 946, 948

mentally retarded persons, 77–82
  guidelines, 83–85

monosymptomatic hypochondriasis,
  1705, 2146

mood disorders, 1744, 1773–1787
  children and adolescents, 1957–
    1958
  in drug addicts, 1375
  dysthymia, 1945
  effectiveness, 1839
  secondary depression, 948, 1903,
    1909, 1911–1912, 1915, 1917

morbid jealousy, 1644

multi-infarct dementia, 964

multiple personality disorder, 2210

obsessive compulsive disorder, 708,
  709

obsessive compulsive personality
  disorder, 2780

organic mood syndrome, 856, 1910

passive-aggressive personality
  disorder, 2787

patient compliance, 1788, 1789–1790

pharmacokinetics, 1774–1781

posttraumatic stress disorder, 2074–
  2075

premature ejaculation, 2357

and retarded ejaculation, 2243

schizoid disorder, 760

with self-control therapy, 1859

with a sensory-impaired patient, 958

sex drive reduction, 2356

sexual effects, 2344, 2347, 2353

sexual sadomasochism, 651

and SIADH, 898

side effects, 827–828, 876, 1777,
  1778, 1781

somatoform pain disorder, 2129,
  2130

and specific medical diseases, 1781–
  1783

termination of therapy, 1786

Tourette's syndrome, 708

See also Monoamine oxidase

inhibitors; Tricyclic antidepressant drugs; names of
  specific drugs

Antiepileptic drugs
  epilepsy, 887–893
  interaction with other drugs, 890–
    893

Anti-estrogenic fertility drugs, sexual
  effects, 2355

Antihistaminic drugs
  anxiety disorders, 2047
  anxiety disorders of childhood, 407
  delirium, 809
  and female genital vasocongestion,
    2283–2284
  organic aggressive syndrome, 850
  secondary depression, 1904
  sexual effects, 2344
  See also names of specific drugs

Antihypertensive drugs
  and female sexual arousal disorder,
    2284
  and inhibited female orgasm, 2286
  interaction with other drugs, 912–
    913, 914, 927, 1777
  and mood disorders, 1791
    depressive disorders, 854, 1764
  neuropsychiatric effects, 910–912
  and orthostatic hypotension, 928
  sexual effects, 2240, 2344
  stroke, 869

Anti-inflammatory drugs
  dementia, 826
  and depressive disorders, 854

Antimalarial drugs
  ocular effects, 958

Antineoplastic drugs
  interaction with other drugs, 944
  sexual effects, 2344
  side effects, 944–945

Antiobsessive drugs
  obsessive compulsive personality
    disorder, 2780

Antiparkinsonian drugs
  anticholinergic properties, 1512

Antiparkinsonian drugs *(cont)*
  and delirium, 812
  delusional (paranoid) disorders,
      1629, 1631
  dystonia, 1512
  extrapyramidal symptoms, 866, 1928
  hypokinetic syndrome, 1512
  schizophrenia, 1506, 1511
  secondary depression, 1923
  side effects, 862–864, 1512
  See also names of specific drugs
Antiplatelet drugs
  stroke, 867, 869
Antipsychotic drugs
  adjustment disorders, 2586, 2589
  alcoholism, 1074, 1075
  amnestic syndromes, 826–827
  anorexia nervosa, 471–472
  anxiety disorders, 2046–2047
  APA task force report, 1513, 1569
  attention-deficit hyperactivity
      disorder, 376–377
  atypical psychosis, 1704
  brief reactive psychosis, 2589
  conduct disorder, 387
  contraindicated for alcohol
      withdrawal, 1087
  contraindicated for brief reactive
      psychosis, 2589
  dementia, 826–827, 831
  effects on cardiovascular system,
      906–907
  and hypertension, 847
  and hypokinetic syndrome, 1512
  interaction with other drugs, 851,
      914–915, 959
  menses-associated psychosis, 1708
  monosymptomatic hypochondriacal
      psychosis, 1705
  organic aggressive syndrome, 849–
      850, 852
  in patients with lung disease, 945
  periodic catatonia, 1709
  personality disorders, 2679
    borderline personality disorder,
      2683

    paranoid personality disorder,
      2710
    schizotypal personality disorder,
      2683
  postpartum psychosis, 1707, 1708
  posttraumatic stress disorder, 2075
  premature ejaculation, 2357
  schizoaffective disorder, 1672, 1673,
      1674, 1675, 1676
  schizophrenia, 1502, 1503–1511,
      1513–1515, 1580–1581, 1583
  schizophreniform disorder, 1661
  secondary depression, 1906
  sex drive reduction, 2356
  sexual effects, 2344, 2348
  and SIADH, 898
  side effects, 849–850, 1510–1511,
      1513
  and tardive dyskinesia, 387, 1512–
      1513, 1704
  young males, adverse effects, 1511
  See also Neuroleptic drugs; names of
      specific drugs
Antiserotonic drugs
  autistic disorder, 235, 245–246
  See also names of specific drugs
Antisocial behavior
  drug addicts, hospital treatment,
      1374
  in mentally retarded persons
    assessment, 23–24
    biologic basis, 21
    classification, 23–24
    description, 8, 20–26
    etiology, 21–23
    incidence, 20–21
    neurologic basis, 5, 21
    treatment, 24–26
  neurologic basis, 5, 21
  See also Behavior problems
Antisocial personality disorder
  and alcoholism, 1067, 1068, 1069–
      1070, 1072, 1105, 1918, 2656
  and attention deficit disorder, 2746
  behavior therapy, 2657, 2746
  countertransference, 2745

criminals and convicts, 2636, 2743–
2745
diagnostic criteria, 2636, 2742–2745
limitation of available research
material, 2636
and organic aggressive syndrome,
841
and organic personality syndrome,
840
pharmacotherapy, 2679, 2680, 2682,
2746–2747
psychotherapy, 2642, 2745–2746
family therapy, 2665, 2666, 2746
group therapy, 2668, 2674
psychoanalytic psychotherapy,
2646
residential treatment, 2689, 2747–
2749
incarceration, 2690
special institutions, 2748
therapeutic community programs,
2747–2748, 2749
resistance, 2697
splitting, 2743
spontaneous improvement, 2743
substance abusers, 1330, 1383, 1385
wilderness programs, 2749
Antitrypsin deficiency and liver
transplantation, 933
Antituberculosis drugs
side effects, 944
Antiulcer drugs
sexual effects, 2344
Anton's syndrome and stroke, 870
Anxiety
adjustment disorders, 2570, 2571,
2575, 2576
alcohol abuse, 1076, 1094, 1373
and benzodiazepines, 1506
crisis intervention, 2523
hallucinogen abuse, 1208
and hypochondriasis, 2134, 2145
and impotence, 2320–2321
as motivation for treatment of
fetishism, 638
and neuroleptic drugs, 1514

obsessive compulsive disorder, 2095,
2099, 2111
opioid abuse, 1313, 1314, 1329
and sexual disorders, 2320–2321,
2361–2362
somatoform pain disorder, 2129
stimulant abuse, 1223
substance abuse, general, 1373
tobacco dependence, 1285
See also Anxiety disorders
Anxiety disorders, 2005–2092
adjunctive therapy procedures,
2052–2065
behavior therapy, 2025–2036
disparity and integration of
treatment theory and practice,
2008–2009
in drug addicts, hospital treatment,
1373–1374, 1376
incidence, 2007
mentally retarded persons
definitions, 14–15
description, 7, 14–19
diagnosis, 16–18
incidence, 15–16
symptoms, 17
treatment, 18
and personality disorders, 2685
avoidant personality disorder,
2685, 2759
passive-aggressive personality
disorder, 2656, 2685, 2787
pharmacotherapy, 2036–2052
psychoanalytic theory, 2010–2012
psychotherapy, 2010–2025
Anxiety disorders of childhood or
adolescence
assessment for treatment plan, 402
avoidant disorder, 433–441
background, 401–402
behavior therapy, 403–405, 413–416,
424–426, 433–435
biochemical model, 405–407
case histories, 412–441
conditioning and
counterconditioning, 403, 405

Anxiety disorders of childhood or adolescence *(cont)*
  diagnosis, 402
  DSM-III-R categories, 401
  etiology, 402
  extinction, 403, 404
  family environment, 411, 412
  family therapy, 411–412, 421–423
  loss theory of anxiety, 409
  modeling, 404, 405
  multimodal treatment, 442
  overanxious disorder, 423–433
  pharmacotherapy, 405–408, 416–418, 426–428, 435–436
  play therapy, 410
  psychodynamic development concept, 409
  psychotherapy, 408–411, 418–421
  secondary gain, 404, 405
  self-control, 405
  separation anxiety disorder, 406, 409, 413–423
  tardive dyskinesia as side effect of neuroleptic drugs, 408
  treatment, 403–412
Anxiety management training (AMT)
  impulse disorders, 2537
  phobic disorders, 2537
  stress management, 2536–2537
Anxiety tolerance, 2014–2015
Anxiolytic drugs. *See* Antianxiety drugs
Aphasia
  and alcoholic liver disease, 933
  and dementia, 816
  and digitalis toxicity, 908
  and Parkinson's disease, 864
  with sensory impairment, 956
  and stroke, 868, 872, 874
Apomorphine
  alcoholism, 1127
  fetishism, 639
Apotreptic therapy for obsessive compulsive disorder, 2098–2099
Apraxia
  and dementia, 816
  and organic delusional syndrome, 834

and subacute sclerosing panencephalitis, 952
Arbovirus and sensory impairment, 952
Arecoline
  dementia of the Alzheimer's type, 969, 970–971
Arousal disorder. *See* Female sexual arousal disorder; Male erectile disorder
Artane. *See* Trihexyphenidyl
Arteriosclerotic cardiovascular disease and organic mental syndromes, 801
Articulation disorders
  developmental evaluation, 343–344
  Fisher-Logeman Test of Articulation Competence, 344
  Goldman-Fristoe Test of Articulation, 344
  mild impairment, 345
  phonologic process treatment approach, 344
  stuttering, treatment, 345–346
Arylcyclohexylamines
  and delirium, 813–814
  and organic delusional syndrome, 833, 834
  See also Hallucinogen abuse; Phencyclidine abuse and dependence
Ascorbic acid
  organic delusional syndrome, 838
Asian sexuality, 2312, 2381
Asparaginase
  and secondary depression, 1912, 1913
Asperger's syndrome, 180, 747–748
Aspirin. *See* Acetylsalicylic acid
Assertiveness training
  depressive disorders, 1855, 1858
  personality disorders, 2649, 2652, 2657
    avoidant personality disorder, 2761
    passive-aggressive personality disorder, 2787
  for somatoform pain disorder, 2134

in treatment for exhibitionism, 672, 673

in treatment for pedophilia, 623, 624, 626, 627, 628

in treatment for voyeurism, 672, 673

Assessment of Children's Language Comprehension, 208

Association for Retarded Citizens, 102, 106, 123, 147–148

Asterixis
and cardiovascular disease, 930
and delirium, 805
and hepatic disease, 822, 930, 931, 934, 935, 936
and hyponatremia, 898
and metabolic disorder, 822

Asthma and organic mental syndromes, 939

Atarax. *See* Hydroxyzine

Ataxia
and delirium, 808, 813
and dementia, 818
and digitalis toxicity, 908
and drug intoxication, 891, 892
and hepatic disease, 935, 936, 938
side effect of phenytoin, 910
and subacute cerebellar degeneration, 941

Atenolol
and lithium, 1930
neuropsychiatric effects, 909

Athetosis, 692

Atonic seizures. *See* Epilepsy, generalized seizures

Atropine
dementia of the Alzheimer's type, 969
and electroconvulsive therapy, 1808, 1811
neurotransmitter blockade, 1776
secondary depression, 1906
with a sensory-impaired patient, 958

Attachment disorder. *See* Reactive attachment disorder of infancy

Attention deficit disorder, residual type (ADD-R)
and alcoholism, pharmacotherapy, 2686

and personality disorders, 2685–2686, 2746

Attention deficit disorders
and atypical impulse control disorder, 2478–2479
distinguished from bipolar illness, 1957
and intermittent explosive disorder, 2474

Attention deficit disorder with hyperactivity. *See* Attention-deficit hyperactivity disorder

Attention-deficit hyperactivity disorder
aggression association, 377
and alcoholism, 1094
anorexia nervosa as side effect of stimulants, 375
behavior rating scales, 381
behavior therapy, 377–378
clinical issues, 370–371
clinical management, 380
cognitive therapy, 378
and conduct disorder, 383
definition and diagnosis, 365–370
developmental approach to evaluation, 372
and developmental reading disorder, 365
dietary treatments, 379
differential diagnosis, 372, 373, 857
distinguished from bipolar illness, 1957
DSM-III-R diagnostic criteria, 366
educational treatment, 380
evaluation of patient, 371–373
family environment, 373
imipramine therapy, 239
and language problems, 300
learning problems, 373
motor impairments, 303
multimodal treatment, 370, 378–379, 389
and oppositional defiant disorder, 365–366
and organic aggressive syndrome, 842

Attention-deficit hyperactivity disorder
(cont)
  and organic personality syndrome,
    841
  parent role in treatment, 373
  pharmacotherapy, 373–377
  psychotherapy, 378
  research issues, 370
  sex as factor, 365
  social skills training, 378
  special education, 379–380
  stimulant abuse in adults, 1239, 1240
  stimulants therapy, 241
  therapists' approaches, 442
  tics as side effects of stimulants, 375
  and Tourette's syndrome, 373, 688–
    689, 692, 694, 695, 697, 707–708
  treatment, 371–381
  See also Attention deficit disorder,
    residual type
Attention-focusing procedure, 1571–
  1572
  See also Social skills training
Atypical antidepressants
  mood disorders, 1737–1738
Atypical bipolar disease, 1689
Atypical depression
  diagnostic considerations, 1753
  pharmacotherapy, 1737, 1943
  treatment, 1743
  See also Mood disorders
Atypical eating disorders
  anorexia nervosa and bulimia
    nervosa, atypical, 590
  classification, 591
  definition, 589–590
  and mood disorders, 593
  nutritional rehabilitation, 592
  preoccupation with weight, 591
  preventive approach, 593
  psychodynamic therapy, 593
  treatment, 592–594
  weight restoration, 592–593
Atypical ejaculatory problems, 2250–
  2251

Atypical factitious disorder. See
  Factitious disorder
Atypical impulse control disorder
  and attention deficit disorders, 2478–
    2479
  childhood-adolescence onset, 2478
  clinical experience, 2478
  and criminality, 2477
  diagnosis and differential diagnosis,
    2477
  history of treatment, 2478
  hospitalization, 2480
  instant gratification, 2477
  organic personality disorder,
    differentiation, 2477
  and other conduct disorders, 2478
  pharmacotherapy, 2479–2480
  psychotherapy, 2478, 2480
  research, 2478–2479
  self-destructive behavior, 2477
  social/occupational dysfunction,
    2478, 2480
  tension, 2477
  therapeutic alliance, 2480
  treatment modalities, 2479–2480
  violence, 2477
Atypical mania
  and delusional (paranoid) disorders,
    1631
Atypical psychosexual disorder, 2248–
  2253
Atypical psychosis
  and bipolar disorder, 1706
  and borderline personality disorder,
    1706
  cycloid psychosis, 1671, 1672, 1706,
    1708–1709, 1711
  diagnostic criteria, 1697–1699
  differential diagnosis, 1672, 1679
  distinguished from schizophrenia,
    1497
  future directions for research, 1710–
    1712
  hospitalization, 1703–1704
  menses associated, 1699, 1708

patient evaluation, 1699–1703
periodic catatonia, 1709
postpartum psychosis, 1699, 1707–1708
prognosis, 1710
and stroke, 868
substance-induced chronic psychosis, 1709
treatment, 1703–1710
See also Schizoaffective disorder
Atypical somatoform disorder. *See* Undifferentiated somatoform disorder
Atypical transsexual, 642
Autism. *See* Autistic children; Autistic disorder
Autism Society of America, 259
Autistic children
behavior problems, 196–197
dopaminergic activity in, 242
education for, 192–201
language and communication therapy, 201–217
punishment, 197, 224–226
serotonin levels in, 239, 245–246
teaching methods, 194–197
thyroxine (T₄) levels in, 240
See also Autistic disorder; Pervasive developmental disorders
Autistic disorder
assessment instruments, 185–187
behavior therapy, 217–226, 233
diagnosis and evaluation, 182–192
distinguished from schizophrenia, 1495
DSM-III-R diagnostic criteria, 180–182
early trauma hypothesis, 249
family studies, 249–250
and fragile X syndrome, 40–41
hierarchy of risks, 252–253
language and communication therapy, 201–217
mentally retarded persons, 8
pharmacotherapy, 76, 226–248
predictors for outcome, 184

psychostimulant drugs, contraindications, 92, 93
reformulation in DSM, 179, 180
rituals, 56
treatment methods, 266–274
treatment plan implementation, 190–192
See also Autistic children; Pervasive developmental disorders
Autistic psychopathy. *See* Asperger's syndrome
Autocastration in transvestic fetishism, 645
Autogenic training for anxiety disorders, 2053
Autonomic nervous system stimulation sexual sadomasochism, 649
Aversion conditioning
alcoholism, 1097, 2649
mental retardation, 46, 113
trichotillomania, 2484, 2485
Aversion therapy
alcoholism, 1126–1128
cannabis abuse and dependence, 1260
drug abuse, 1438
exhibitionism, 672, 673
fetishism, 639
obsessive compulsive disorder, 2098
pedophilia, 624, 627, 628–629
personality disorders, 2653
obsessive compulsive personality disorder, 2780
smoking, 1277
substance abuse, 1440
tobacco withdrawal and tobacco dependence, 1277
transvestic fetishism, 646
voyeurism, 672, 673
See also Chemical aversion therapy; Electric aversion therapy
Aversive behavior, 115, 116
Aversive conditioning. *See* Aversion conditioning
Aversive therapy. *See* Aversion therapy

Avoidance conditioning. *See* Aversion conditioning

Avoidance therapy. *See* Aversion therapy

Avoidant disorder of childhood or adolescence
  behavior therapy, 433–435
  distinguished from schizoid disorder of childhood or adolescence, 749
  family therapy, 439–441
  group therapy, 434
  pharmacotherapy, 435–436
  psychotherapy, 437–439
  reinforcement, 434

Avoidant personality disorder
  and anxiety disorders, 2685, 2759
  associated with phobias, 2636
  behavior therapy, 2761
  cognitive therapy, 2761
  and delusional (paranoid) disorders, 1637
  diagnostic criteria, 2759, 2760
  limitation of available research material, 2636
  and panic disorder, 2762
  pharmacotherapy, 2762
  psychotherapy, 2642, 2759–2762
    family therapy, 2762
    group therapy, 2671, 2674, 2761–2762
    individual psychotherapy, 2760–2761
    interpersonal therapy, 2760–2761
    psychoanalytic psychotherapy, 2645, 2646
    psychodynamic psychotherapy, 2760
  resistance, 2697

Azotemia
  and chronic hepatic failure, 932
  and renal disease, 925, 926

B aclofen
  and secondary depression, 1912, 1913

Ballism, 692

Barbiturate abuse. *See* Sedative and hypnotic drug abuse

Barbiturates
  adjustment disorders, 2588
  anxiety and lung disease, 945
  anxiety disorders, 2038
  delirium, 809, 812
  and depression, 854
  and electroconvulsive therapy, 1808–1809, 1810
  hepatic disease, 937, 938
  interaction with other drugs, 915, 944, 947
  and organic aggressive syndrome, 842, 850
  organic delusional syndrome, 838
  and secondary depression, 1912, 1913
  side effects, 809, 876
  withdrawal seizures, 884

Beck Depression Inventory (BDI), 1186, 1187, 1849, 1854, 2125, 2129
  cognitive-behavioral therapy effectiveness, 1839, 1842
  depression and cancer, 1905
  personality disorders, 2681
  secondary depression, 1919, 1920, 1922

Bedwetting. *See* Functional enuresis

Behavioral baseline in mentally retarded persons, 8

Behavioral couples group therapy
  alcoholism, 1120

Behavioral group therapy
  alcoholism, 1122, 1125
  See also Group therapy

Behavioral Performance Situations, test, 1444

Behavioral rating scales for autistic disorder, 185, 229

Behavioral techniques. *See* Behavior therapy

Behavioral theory of rumination, 569–570

Behavioral toxicity
and neuroleptic drugs, 1510, 1514
as sign of excess dose in children, 232

Behavioral treatment. *See* Behavior therapy

Behavior analysis. *See* Behavior therapy

Behavior assessment in drug abuse, 1432–1433

Behavior modification. *See* Behavior therapy

Behavior problems
antianxiety drugs, contraindications, 86
autistic children, 196–197
cannabis abuse and dependence, 1241–1242, 1245
learning disabled children, 311
mentally retarded persons
aggression, 20–26
antisocial behavior, 20–26
causes, 5, 6
counseling, 105
delinquency, 20–26
eating disorders, 59
fragile X syndrome, 40
taxonomy, 7

Behavior therapy
agoraphobia, 2029–2034
alcoholism, 1076, 1125–1131
anorexia nervosa, 456, 457, 461, 467, 475–481
anxiety disorders, 2025–2036
anxiety disorders of childhood or adolescence, 403–405, 413–416, 424–426, 433–435
attention-deficit hyperactivity disorder, 377–378
atypical psychosis, 1705–1706
autistic disorder, 217–226
avoidant disorder of childhood, 433–435
bulimia nervosa, 521, 527, 532–537
cannabis abuse and dependence, 1260
childhood gender identity disorder, 664–665
cognitive techniques, 118
conduct disorder, 384–385, 388
consequence, definition, 113
conversion disorders, 2158
coping skills training in drug abuse, 1436–1437
cost effectiveness of anorexia nervosa outpatient treatment, 478
covariation, 121–122
dialectical behavior therapy, 2653
drug abuse, general, 1430–1447
elective mutism, 767–768, 770–771
epilepsy, 893–894
exhibitionism, 672, 673
factitious disorder with physical symptoms, 2164
family therapy, 2663
fetishism, 639
functional enuresis, 721–722
hallucinogen-induced anxiety, 1208
identity disorder, 791
immature personality disorders, 775, 778, 779, 781, 782
impotence, 2319, 2322–2323, 2326–2327, 2328, 2329
incentive systems, 115, 116
insomnia, primary, 2430–2433
language disorders in children, 341, 346
mentally retarded persons, 18, 111–123
behavior analysis, 118
effectiveness, 117
evaluation, 121
guidelines, 118
intervention procedures, 120–122
learning and personality development, 112–115
misconceptions, 116–117
observational learning, 114–115
practical therapy, 117–120

Behavior therapy *(cont)*
  stereotyped behaviors, abnormal,
    46, 49, 119
  mood disorders, 1729, 1731, 1801
  communication training, 1858
  Coping with Depression Course,
    1857–1858, 1862
  couples and family therapy, 1886–
    1887, 1889
  current and future directions,
    1861–1862
  depressive disorders, 1846–1862
  diagnostic and functional
    assessment, 1849–1850
  effectiveness, 1839, 1840, 1847
  major depression, 1817–1822
  operant reinforcement, 1860
  Pleasant Events Schedule, 1850,
    1851, 1852, 1854, 1855
  practical concerns, 1854–1855
  self-control therapy, 1858, 1859,
    1861
  social interaction therapy, 1858
  social skills training, 1859, 1861,
    1862
  treatment strategy, 1849–1861
  Unpleasant Events Schedule, 1850,
    1851, 1854, 1855
  multiple personality disorder, 2201
  nonphobic anxiety, 2034
  obsessive compulsive disorder,
    2098–2100
  operant conditioning, 55, 113–115,
    305, 403, 456, 476, 628
  organic aggressive syndrome, 848–
    849
  overanxious disorder of childhood,
    424–426
  paraphiliac men, 2277
  pedophilia, 624, 625, 628–629
  personality disorders, 2637, 2649–
    2659, 2668, 2689
    antisocial personality disorder,
      2657, 2746
    avoidant personality disorder,
      2761
    borderline personality disorder,
      2653, 2754
    controversies, 2657–2659
    dependent personality disorder,
      2769
    duration of treatment, 2651–2652
    effectiveness, 2655–2656
    histrionic personality disorder,
      2657, 2735
    obsessive compulsive personality
      disorder, 2717, 2771, 2772–2773,
      2774, 2779–2780, 2781, 2782
    paranoid personality disorder,
      2710
    passive-aggressive personality
      disorder, 2651, 2787–2788
    recommendations, 2656–2657
    residential treatment, 2696
    resistance, 2657–2659
    schizoid personality disorder, 2717
    schizotypal personality disorder,
      2724–2725, 2726
    self-destructive behavior, 2653
    treatment techniques, 2652
  pervasive developmental disorders,
    217–226
    extinction, 221–222
    generalization and maintenance,
      223–224
    pharmacotherapy combined with,
      226
    procedures, 218–226
    prompting and fading, 223
    punishment, 224–226
    rewards, 218–221
    shaping, 223
    time-out, 222
    treatment strategy, 217–218
  phobias, 2779
  pica, 120, 586, 587
  pyromania, 2471
  reinforcement, 113, 116
  respondent conditioning, 112, 114–
    115, 405, 475
  restraint guidelines, 117
  rumination, 577–578

schizoid disorder of childhood or adolescence, 759–760
schizophrenia, 1569–1570, 1576–1580
self-injurious behavior, 34–36, 119
separation anxiety disorder of childhood, 413–416
sexual sadomasochism, 653, 654
smoking, 1276–1278
social validity, 121
somatic-behavioral therapy, 2538–2541
stimulant abuse, 1233–1234
stress management, 2532–2548
suppression, 120–121
Tourette's syndrome, 701–702
transvestic fetishism, 643, 644–645
treatment manuals, 1816
trichotillomania, 2482, 2484, 2486
vaginismus, 2297
verbal mediation, 118
voyeurism, 672, 673
See also Contracts in behavior therapy; Sex therapy; Social skills training
Belief systems of self-help and mutual aid groups for adults, 2602, 2603
Belladonna alkaloids and delirium, 812
Benadryl. *See* Diphenhydramine
Bender Visual Motor Gestalt Test, 330
Benhaven, 270–271
Benperidol
sex drive reduction, 2356
Benzenepropanamine
neurotransmitter blockade, 1776
pharmacokinetics, 1780
Benzodiazepines
adjustment disorders, 2587
advantages as antianxiety agents, 2039–2041
affect block, 2587
age and dosage, 2042
akathisia, 1512
alcoholism, 1075, 1091, 1101
alcohol withdrawal, 1075, 1085, 1087–1088, 1090, 1091, 1101, 1138

anxiety and lung disease, 945
anxiety disorders, 2039–2046
anxiety disorders in mentally retarded persons, 87
anxiety disorders of childhood or adolescence, 407
atypical impulse control disorder, 2479
atypical psychosis, 1704
brief reactive psychosis, 1681, 1682
and cocaine combination, intoxication, 1295
delirium, 809, 811–812
dementia, 828–829
dependence on, 2042–2044
depersonalization disorder, 2221
duration of action, 1303
elective mutism, 771
and electroconvulsive therapy, 1808, 1810
epilepsy, 890
epilepsy in mentally retarded, 87–88
hepatic disease, 937
hypochondriasis, 2145
insomnia, 831, 2430, 2587
interaction with other drugs, 890, 891, 892
intermittent explosive disorder, 2476
intoxication, 1294–1295
mood disorders, 1729, 1730, 1739
adjustment disorder with depressive mood, 1743
bipolar disorders, 1932
secondary depression, 1369
uncomplicated bereavement, 1743
nocturnal myoclonus, 2438
organic aggressive syndrome, 850
panic disorders and phobias, 2587
panic due to hallucinogen abuse, 1207
Parkinson's disease, 865
in patients with lung disease, 946
personality disorders, 2687
borderline personality disorder, 2682
pharmacology, 2041–2042

Benzodiazepines *(cont)*
  phencyclidine-induced delirium,
    1215
  posttraumatic stress disorder, 2075
  prevalence of use, 85–86, 88
  principles of use, 2045
  related withdrawal syndromes, 1299
  renal disease, 921, 922, 923–924
  repeated single dose regimen, 2045–
    2046
  schizophrenia, 1506
  schizophreniform disorder, 1661
  seizure disorders, 87–88
  side effects, 1739
  side effects and tolerance, 87
  sleep disturbances in late life, 2447–
    2448
  somatic symptoms in patients with
    anxiety disorders, 2151–2152
  tardive dyskinesia, 1513
  as transitional objects, 2014
  treatment nonresponders, 1798
  withdrawal, 1296–1297, 1298, 1304,
    1305, 1306, 1307, 2039, 2042–
    2044, 2052
  withdrawal seizures, 884
  See also names of specific drugs
Benztropine
  and hypokinetic syndrome, 1512
  in patients with lung disease, 946
Benztropine mesylate
  secondary depression, 1923
Bereavement, 2507
  distinguished from posttraumatic
    stress disorder, 2069–2070
Beri-beri
  and secondary depression, 1902
Beta-adrenergic blocking drugs
  anxiety disorders of childhood or
    adolescence, 408
  hepatic disease, 938
  interaction with other drugs, 914,
    915
  and lithium, 1930
  neuropsychiatric effects, 908–909,
    911

  and nonresponsiveness to
    antidepressant treatment, 1792
  organic aggressive syndrome, 851
  personality disorders, 2687
  renal disease, 928
  sexual effects, 2240
  stress-related conditions, 2590
Betahistine
  multi-infarct dementia, 963
Bethanechol
  dementia of the Alzheimer's type, 971
  and neuroleptic drug side effects,
    1514
Biliary cirrhosis
  and chronic hepatic failure, 932
Binge eating and purging
  anorexia nervosa, 467, 479
  bulimia nervosa, 519, 520, 521, 522,
    524, 528–529, 532, 534, 536–537,
    538, 557
Binswanger's disease, 868
Biofeedback training
  adjustment disorders, 2577
  alcoholism, 1076
  anxiety disorders, 2052–2055, 2063–
    2065
  case histories, 2056–2058
  cultural perspective and
    effectiveness of treatment, 2055
  epilepsy, 894
  generalized anxiety disorder, 2034,
    2054–2055
  headaches, 2150
  panic disorder, 2035
  patient-therapist relationship, 2055
  pedophilia, 628
  somatoform pain disorder, 2131
  See also Relaxation therapy and
    training
Biological Therapies in Psychiatry, 1661
Biologic therapy
  fetishism, 637–638
  transvestic fetishism, 643, 644
Bipolar disorders
  age factor, 1668, 1756
  and atypical psychosis, 1698, 1706

bipolar disorder not otherwise
     specified
  additional diagnoses, 1758
  classification, 1925
  clinical presentation, 1759
  diagnostic considerations, 1753,
     1758
  pharmacotherapy, 1934
classification, 1757–1760
cyclothymia, 1742, 1752, 1753, 1754,
     1759, 1925, 1933–1934
diagnosis of phases, 1760–1762
diagnostic considerations, 1700,
     1752, 1753, 1754
differential diagnosis, 1674, 1709
electroconvulsive therapy, 1742
and epilepsy, 882
family history, 1669–1671, 1935, 1937
hypomanic episode, 853, 854, 1752,
     1758, 2687
incidence, 1752
and induced psychotic disorder,
     1694
maniacal grief reaction, 1761
opioid abuse, 1329
and organic delusional syndrome,
     838
and Parkinson's disease, 866
and personality disorders, 2684
pharmacotherapy, 909, 1741–1742,
     1754, 1927–1936
  patient compliance, 1938–1939,
     1940
postpartum mania, 1928
procainamide exacerbation, 910
psychoanalytic psychotherapy, 1826
psychotherapy, 1936–1937
rapid cycling, 1758, 1934–1936
  risk factors, 1935
and renal disease, 924
and sexual disorders, 2254–2255
soft bipolar spectrum, 1935, 1939
Bisexual pedophilia, 618, 627
Bittersweet Farms, 271, 273
Blackouts and organic personality
     disorder, 840

Black patch psychosis. *See* Sensory
     impairment, bilateral eye
     patching
Black sexuality, 2380–2381
Bleomycin
  auditory effects, 958
  side effects, 944
Bleuler diagnostic system for
     schizophrenia, 1487–1488, 1490,
     1498–1499
Blindness
  visual hallucinations, 835
Blocking procedures in behavior
     therapy, 2098
Blood alcohol concentration and
     intoxication, 1077, 1084
Body Awareness Resource Network
     (BARNY), 2611
Body-conceptualization disturbance in
     bulimic females, 521, 538
Body dysmorphic disorder, 2146
Body image as sexual concern, 2249–
     2250
Body rocking. *See* Stereotyped
     behaviors, abnormal
Bondage
  sexual sadomasochism, 652
  transvestic fetishism, 641
Bonding, 734–736, 2011–2012
  See also Reactive attachment disorder
     of infancy
Borderline personality disorder
  and alcoholism, 1094, 1104–1105
  and anorexia nervosa, 468, 545
  and atypical psychosis, 1706
  behavior therapy, 2653, 2657, 2754
  and bipolar disorder not otherwise
     specified, 1758
  and borderline personality
     organization, 2636, 2737
  countertransference, 2757, 2759
  and dependent personality disorder,
     2763
  diagnostic criteria, 2636, 2749–2750
  differential diagnosis, 843, 1679,
     2706

Borderline personality disorder (cont)
  distinguished from schizophrenia,
    1497
  drug addicts, hospital treatment,
    1374
  ego diffusion, 2721–2722
  family history, 2637, 2686
  fetishism, 637, 638, 639
  limitation of available research
    material, 2636
  and organic aggressive syndrome,
    841
  in parents of children with gender
    identity disorder, 666
  pharmacotherapy, 2679, 2680, 2683,
    2684, 2741, 2754–2755, 2759
    cautions, 2688
    noncompliance, 2755
  psychotherapy, 2642
    family therapy, 2665, 2666, 2753,
      2759
    group therapy, 2668, 2673–2674,
      2741, 2753–2754, 2759
    individual psychotherapy, 2738,
      2750–2752, 2759
    psychoanalytic psychotherapy,
      2645, 2646, 2647, 2751–2752
    short-term psychotherapy, 2752
    supportive psychotherapy, 2752
  regression, 2697
  residential treatment, 2689, 2690,
    2697, 2741, 2759
    day care, 2756
    halfway houses, 2756
    indications, 2755–2756
    long- versus short-term, 2757–2758
    principles of treatment, 2756–2757
  resistance, 2697
  with secondary depression, 2656,
    2681, 2750
  splitting, 2743
  transference, 2755
  transvestic fetishism, 642
Borderline personality organization
  and borderline personality disorder,
    2636, 2737

and narcissistic personality disorder,
    2737, 2739
Boston Collaborative Drug Surveillance
    Program, 909, 943
Boston University Medical Center
  sexual problems study, 2335
  study on schizophreniform disorder,
    1659
Bouffée delirante (BD), 1613, 1620–1621
Bowen Family Systems, 2566
Bradyarrhythmias, differential
    diagnosis, 884
Bradykinesia and Parkinson's disease,
    862
Brain Age Quotient, 1071
Brain damage
  alcohol-related, 1067, 1071, 1091–
    1093, 1105
  and epilepsy, 881
  hallucinogen abuse, 1209
  and intermittent explosive disorder,
    854
  and organic aggressive syndrome,
    848
  and organic personality syndrome,
    857–858
  and schizophrenia, 1491
  seat belts and prevention of, 846
  and secondary depression, 854
  and tic disorders, 691
  See also Head injury
Brain dimorphism and sexual
    sadomasochism, 649
Brain metastases and lung disease, 939
Brain opioid activity and autistic
    disorder, 247–248
Brain syndromes and intermittent
    explosive disorder, 2474
Brain tumors
  amnestic syndromes, 819
  dementia, 822
  differential diagnosis, 861, 935, 1910
  and electroconvulsive therapy, 1806
  epilepsy, 885–886, 893
  and exhibitionism/voyeurism, 671

and fetishism, 637
organic aggressive syndrome, 842
organic personality disorder, 840
and secondary mania, 854, 1761
sensory impairment, 949, 952–953
Brainwashing as cause of dissociative
disorder not otherwise
specified, 2222, 2223, 2225–2226
Brentwood VA Job Finding Club,
1574–1575
Brentwood VA Medical Center, 1581
Brief Alcoholism Screening Test, 1078–
1079
Brief dynamic psychotherapy
depressive disorders, 1872–1884
effectiveness, 1839, 1883
psychodynamic formulation of
depression, 1873–1874
short-term anxiety-provoking
psychotherapy, 1877
supportive-expressive
psychotherapy, 1732, 1822,
1882–1883, 1921
time-limited dynamic psychotherapy, 1877–1878, 1881–
1882
time-limited psychotherapy, 1877–
1878
treatment strategies, 1874–1883
The Montreal Group, 1879–1881
The Tavistock Group, 1878–1879
The Vanderbilt Group, 1881–1882,
1884
Brief Psychiatric Rating Scale
secondary depression, 1920
Brief reactive psychosis
and delusional (paranoid) disorders,
1612
diagnosis, 1679–1680, 1699–1700
differential diagnosis, 1655, 1660,
1677–1679, 1682, 1699, 1702
distinguished from posttraumatic
stress disorder, 2069
distinguished from schizophrenia,
1497

DSM-III-R diagnostic criteria, 1678
duration, 1677–1678, 1679
patient evaluation, 1679–1680
treatment
integration of approaches, 1683–
1684
interpersonal strategies, 1681–
1682, 1683, 1685
pharmacotherapy, 1681–1682,
1684, 2589
phenomenological basis, 1682–
1683
pitfalls, 1684–1685
underlying causes, 1680–1681
Brigance Diagnostic Inventory of Early
Development, 187
Briquet's syndrome
electroconvulsive therapy, 2170
group therapy, 2168
somatization disorder,
differentiation, 2167
British Journal of Psychiatry on
psychosurgery, 1897
Broca's syndrome and stroke, 870
Bromazepam
obsessive compulsive personality
disorder, 2780
Bromides
anxiety disorders, 2038
epilepsy, 889
and secondary mania, 1914
Bromocriptine
dementia of the Alzheimer's type,
975, 976
hepatic disease, 936
neuroleptic malignant syndrome,
1805
and organic psychosis, 833
Parkinson's disease, 863
sexual effects, 2350
Bruxism (tooth grinding), 2424
Bulbar palsy and lung carcinoma, 941
Bulimia nervosa
alcoholism in patient's family,
prevalence, 545

Bulimia nervosa (cont)
  anorexia nervosa, differentiation,
    511–512, 524
  as anxiety-based disorder, 532
  atypical form, 590
  behaviorally based treatment
    program, 534–537
  behavior theory of etiology, 532–534
  behavior therapy, 521, 527, 532–537
  binge eating and purging, 519, 520,
    521, 522, 524, 528–529, 532, 534,
    536–537, 538
  case history, 559–563
  cognitive-behavioral treatment, 533,
    534
  cognitive model, 539–540
  cognitive therapy, 525, 537–543
  contracts and goal setting in
    outpatient treatment, 526
  control over body as patient goal,
    522, 540
  dieting consequence, 533
  electrolyte imbalances, 518
  endocrine abnormalities, 518–519
  enzyme abnormalities, 518
  etiology, 539–540
  family problems, 545–546
  family role in treatment, 528, 548
  family therapy, 521, 543–548
  gastric dilatation, 517
  group therapy, 525–526, 549–555
  hospital treatment, 520–523
  and impulse-ridden character
    disturbance, 544–545
  interpersonal problems, 521
  medical assessment in
    hospitalization, 521
  medical screening in outpatient
    treatment, 525
  medical treatment, 517–519
  misconceptions, patient, 539–540
  and mood disorder, 544, 545
  morbid obesity alternative, 544
  motivation for treatment, 540–541
  normalization of eating and weight,
    541–542
  nutritional rehabilitation in
    outpatient treatment, 524
  outpatient treatment, 523–528
  patient education in outpatient
    treatment, 526, 535
  peer pressure as cause, 544
  pharmacotherapy, 521, 525, 528–531
    with secondary depression, 2684–
    2685
  post-hospital follow-up, 522–523
  psychoeducational material, 541
  psychotherapy, 525–526, 555–563
  reasoning errors, 542
  reinforcement, 532–533, 539
  relapse prevention, 528, 536–537
  and rumination, 566, 567
  and secondary depression, 520, 525,
    544, 1916, 1917–1918
  self-control strategies, 536, 538
  self-esteem problems, 520–521, 536,
    538
  self-monitoring techniques, 526, 535,
    538
  social skills training, 522, 536
  stimulus control, 541–542
  symptoms, 517
  treatment goals, 500–501, 557–558
  treatment prognosis, 534, 542–543
  two-track treatment, 540
  vicious cycle aspect, 538–540
  vocational problems, 521
Bunney-Hamburg Rating Scale, 1923
Buprenorphine for opioid
    detoxification maintenance, 1325
Bupropion
  classification, 1774
  effects on cardiovascular system, 903
  pharmacokinetics, 1776, 1779, 1780
  sexual effects, 2353
  and specific medical diseases, 1782,
    1783
  in treatment nonresponders, 1798
Burnout, adjustment disorder, 2579

Buspirone
anxiety disorders, 2047
Butorphenol, pharmacology, 1309
Butyrophenones
delirium, 809–810, 814
effects on cardiovascular system,
906–907
mentally retarded persons
autistic disorder, 76
self-injurious behavior, 36
organic aggressive syndrome, 849
organic delusional syndrome, 838
and retarded ejaculation, 2243
side effects, 849
stereotypic behavior, 76
See also Neuroleptic drugs
Butyrylcholinesterase
and Tourette's syndrome, 691

Calcium channel blockers
bipolar disorders, 1932
interaction with other drugs, 915
neuropsychiatric effects, 909
Camarillo State Hospital
personal grooming training, 1572
study on schizophreniform disorder,
1659
token economy, 1577–1578
Camberwell Family Interview, 1550
Canadian National Population Survey,
statistics on pedophilia, 621–622
Cancer
differential diagnosis, 1701
and secondary depression, 1901,
1904–1907
self-help and mutual aid groups for
adults, 2605, 2606
sexual effects, 2379
Cancer of the liver, 933
See also Hepatic disease
Cannabis
and sexual anxiety, 2361
sexual effects, 2344

Cannabis abuse and dependence
abstinence syndrome, 1254
and alcohol use, 1243
anxiety, 1373
assessment and evaluation
age as factor, 1242, 1243, 1244
diagnosis, 1245–1247
DSM-III-R diagnostic criteria, 1246
laboratory tests, 1246–1247
need for treatment, 1260
patient attitudes, 1245
procedures, 1245–1246
symptoms, 1246
urine tests, 1246–1247, 1253–1254
and cigarette smoking, 1284–1285
epidemiology, 1242–1243
history of use, 1243–1244
in hospitalized patients, detection,
1370
and organic delusional syndrome,
833, 834
and organic personality syndrome,
858
and other drug abuse, 1244–1245
physiological effects
adverse reactions, 1248
chronic cannabis syndrome, 1252–
1253
intoxication, 1247–1248
prevalence of use, 1242
psychological effects
anxiety and panic attacks, 1248
behavior problems, 1241–1242,
1245
delirium, 1249
delusional disorder, 1248–1249
flashback syndrome, 1249
other problem behaviors, 1250
psychiatric disorders, chronic,
1250–1253
psychiatric reactions, acute, 1247–
1249
psychosocial correlates, 1250
psychotic disorders and
symptoms, 1251–1252, 1371,
1372

Cannabis abuse and dependence
(cont)
    and schizophrenia, 1250–1252
    secondary mania, 1914
  recovery, early, 1254–1255
  self-medication with cannabis, 1250
  treatment
    behavior therapy, 1260
    education program, 1253, 1258
    facilities, 1255–1260
    family therapy, 1258
    general, 1253–1255
    group therapy, 1258–1259
    hospitalization, 1256
    long-term treatment, 1255
    outpatient programs, 1257
    pharmacotherapy, 1249, 1252, 1254
    psychotherapy, 1249, 1257–1258
    rehabilitation program, 1256
    relapse prevention, 1254–1255
    self-help groups, 1259
    therapeutic communities, 1256
    Twelve Step program for
      substance abuse, 1255, 1256,
      1259–1260
  use cessation, 1253–1254
Cannabis delusional disorder. See
    Organic delusional syndrome
Capgras' syndrome
  etiology, 834, 836
  side effect of nifedipine, 909
  and stroke, 874
Captopril
  and secondary depression, 1914
Carbamazepine
  atypical impulse control disorder,
    2479
  atypical psychosis, 1705, 1711
  behavioral-cognitive effects in
    mentally retarded persons, 96
  bulimia nervosa, 531
  epilepsy, 882, 887, 888–889, 1739,
    1931
  fetishes, 637
  interaction with other drugs, 891,
    892–893, 947

intermittent explosive disorder, 2476
  mood disorders, 1729, 1738, 1739
    bipolar disorders, 876, 1763, 1929,
      1931, 1934, 1936
    in mentally retarded persons, 95
    secondary depression, 1912
    secondary mania, 893
  and nonresponsive patients, 1799–
    1800
  organic aggressive syndrome, 850
  organic mood syndrome, 856
  personality disorders, 2687
    borderline personality disorder,
      2682, 2754, 2755
  rage, 2686
  schizoaffective disorder, 1674, 1675
  schizophrenia, 1503
  schizophreniform disorder, 1931
  and SIADH, 898
  side effects, 889, 892–893, 1739, 1932
  stroke, 876
Carbonic anhydrase inhibitors
  interaction with other drugs, 914
Carbon monoxide in cigarette smoke,
  1262–1263, 1271
Carbon monoxide poisoning
  and delirium, 808
  differential diagnosis, 861
Carcinoid malignancy and secondary
    depression, 1902
Cardiac arrhythmias and delirium, 806,
    808
Cardiac dysrhythmias and dementia,
    821
Cardiac tumors and organic mental
    syndrome, 894, 896
Cardiopulmonary disorders and
    delirium, 806
Cardiovascular disease
  acid-base disturbances, 894, 897–898
  cardiac tumors, 894, 896
  choosing antidepressant drugs,
    1781–1783
  and dementia, 821
  and electroconvulsive therapy, 1805–
    1806

hyperkalemia, 899
hypernatremia, 898–899
hypertensive encephalopathy, 897
hypokalemia, 899
hyponatremia, 898
infective endocarditis, 896–897
and multi-infarct dementia, 962
pharmacotherapy, 900, 901–915
psychotherapy, 900–901
and secondary depression, 1900,
1901, 1902, 1907–1908
sexual effects, 2379
Cardiovascular drugs
hepatic disease, 938
Carotid endarterectomy
stroke, 869, 870
Castration anxiety
childhood gender identity disorder,
666
fetishism, 635, 637
sexual sadomasochism, 649
transvestic fetishism, 643
Castration as treatment for pedophilia,
623, 628, 629
Catapres. *See* Clonidine
Catatonia
and atypical psychosis evaluation,
1700
and brief reactive psychosis, 1678
electroconvulsive therapy, 1804
and schizoaffective disorder, 1671
Catatonic excitement and atypical
psychosis, 1699
Catatonic schizophrenia, 1498
and hepatic disease, 935
Catchment Area Program. *See*
Epidemiologic Catchment Area
Survey
Catecholamines
and dementia of the Alzheimer's
type (DAT), 978
multi-infarct dementia, 962
stress response, 2070–2071
Catharsis in adjustment disorders,
2581–2582
CD. *See* Conduct disorder

Center for Epidemiologic Studies-
Depression Scale (CES-D), 1849
Center for the Study of Neuroses,
University of California, San
Francisco, 2078
Center for the Study of Sex Education
in Medicine, 2360
Central nervous system depressant
drugs
sexual effects, 2344
Central sleep apnea, 2436
Centrophenoxine
dementia of the Alzheimer's type,
973
Cerebral arteriosclerosis
differential diagnosis, 935
and exhibitionism/voyeurism, 671
and Parkinson's disease, 861
and secondary depression, 1902
Cerebral atrophy
and organic delusional syndrome,
834
and Parkinson's disease, 864
Cerebral infarction
and lung disease, 941
and organic delusional syndrome,
834
and organic mood syndrome, 856
and secondary depression, 854
side effect of guanethidine, 912
Cerebral vascular disease and organic
aggressive syndrome, 846–847
Cerebral vasculature, 868
Change points, 1531
Character neuroses, 2634
Character structures, 772–774
Checking as obsessive compulsive
disorder, 2096, 2100, 2109
Chemical aversion therapy
alcoholism, 1126–1127
See also Disulfiram
The Chemistry of Love, 2354
Chemotherapeutic agents
and organic psychosis, 833
Chestnut Lodge follow-up study, 1675

Chewing-speech relationship in eating disorders of mentally retarded persons, 61–62
Chickenpox encephalitis and organic delusional syndrome, 836
Child abuse or neglect
  and attachment disorder, 735, 736, 744–745
  ethical issues, 1000
  legal intervention, 744–745, 993
  and multiple personality disorder, 2199, 2208, 2212, 2213
  and vaginismus, 2295
Child Behavior Checklist, 351, 373, 382, 389, 402, 435
Child development, normal
  interactions with developmental disorders, 302–303
  language and speech disorders, effects, 302–303
  motor impairments, effects, 301–302
  neurologic deficits, effects, 301
  parental expectations, 303–304
  sensory impairments, effects, 301
Childhood Autism Rating Scale (CARS), 185, 229
Childhood gender identity disorder, 661–670
  cross-dressing, 662, 663, 664
  cross-gender identification, 662, 663, 664, 667, 668, 669, 670
  disavowal of sexual anatomy, 663
  etiology, 662, 666
  and homosexuality, 662, 669
  importance of same-sex or opposite-sex therapist, 668
  oedipal factors, 666
  parent role, 664, 666, 667–669
  preoedipal factors, 666, 667
  and transsexualism, 661–662, 669
  treatment, 664–670
Childhood sleep disorders. See Parasomnias in children
Childhood trauma
  and autistic disorder, 249

and transvestic fetishism, 635, 642, 643
Child molesting. See Pedophilia
Child-onset insomnia, 2425–2426, 2427, 2428
Children
  immigrant children concerns, 763, 769, 771
  mood disorders, 1950–1958
    diagnostic considerations, 1763–1764
    family history, 1763
  nightmares, 2420–2422, 2562
  observations of transvestic fetishism, 642
  personality disorders
    diagnosis, 733–734, 749, 750, 772, 781
    pharmacotherapy, 2682
    treatment, 2652
  pharmacotherapy issues, 232, 234
  pyromania, 2457, 2460, 2461, 2469
  rating conditions, 231–232
  sexuality and treatment planning, 2375–2376
  tardive and withdrawal dyskinesias in, 244–245
  See also Child abuse or neglect; Immature personality disorders; Infants
Children, autistic. See Autistic children
Children as sexual objects. See Pedophilia
Children of alcoholics (COAs)
  sons, 1072
  teenage support groups, 1120
  Types I and II, 1072
  See also Adult children of alcoholics
Children's Psychiatric Rating Scale (CPRS), 229
Chloral hydrate
  delirium, 809, 810
  interaction with other drugs, 915
  organic aggressive syndrome, 850
  organic delusional syndrome, 838

Chloramphenicol
  ocular effects, 958
Chlorazepate
  alcohol withdrawal, 1087
  epilepsy, 889
Chlordiazepoxide
  alcohol withdrawal, 1087, 1088, 1101
  anxiety and lung disease, 945
  anxiety disorders, 2039
  borderline personality disorder, 2755
  delirium, 811, 812
  hepatic disease, 937
  renal disease, 922
  secondary depression, 1920
  somatic symptom, 2151
  withdrawal, 1296, 1304
Chlorimipramine
  obsessive compulsive personality
      disorder, 2780
  secondary depression, 1917
Chloroquine
  ocular effects, 958
Chlorpromazine
  and agranulocytosis, 1514
  anorexia nervosa, 471
  autistic disorder, 242
  borderline personality disorder,
      2680–2681, 2684
  compared with lithium, 239–240
  conduct disorder, 387
  dementia and amnestic syndromes,
      827
  dependent personality disorder,
      2770
  effects on cardiovascular system,
      906, 907
  interaction with other drugs, 852,
      891, 914, 915, 928
  mentally retarded persons, 71–73
  mood disorders, 1736
    acute manic episode, 1741
    bipolar disorders, 1925, 1931
    secondary mania, 1914
  organic delusional syndrome, 838
  passive-aggressive personality
      disorder, 2770, 2789

  schizoaffective disorder, 1673, 1674
  schizophrenia, 1507, 1508
  schizophreniform disorder, 1658,
      1661
  seizure-associated psychoses, 839
  seizures as side effect, 227, 884
  side effects, 884, 1514
Cholecystokinin-like immunoreactivity
      in dementia of the Alzheimer's
      type, 977
Cholestatic jaundice and neuroleptic
      drugs, 1514
Cholesterol and stroke, 869
Choline
  dementia of the Alzheimer's type,
      969, 970, 971
Choline acetyltransferase
  and dementia of the Alzheimer's
      type, 829, 967–968, 969
  and Parkinson's disease, 861
Cholinesterase inhibitors
  dementia of the Alzheimer's type,
      970
Chordee, 2242, 2243
Chorea, 692
Choreoathetosis and Wilson's disease,
      934
Chromatopsia and digitalis toxicity,
      908
Chromosomal abnormalities
  Down's syndrome, 30
  fragile X syndrome, 39–42
  Lesch-Nyhan syndrome, 37–38
  Prader-Willi syndrome, 50–51
Chromosomal damage from
      hallucinogen abuse, 1209
Chromosomal typing in
      transsexualism, 658
Chronic hepatic failure, 932
  See also Hepatic disease
Chronic obstructive pulmonary disease
      (COPD)
  and organic mental syndromes, 939–
      948
  See also Lung disease

Chronic respiratory disease
and organic mental syndromes, 939–940
See also Lung disease
Cigarette smoke
carbon monoxide in, 1262–1263, 1271
nicotine in, 1263
physiologic effects, 1262–1264
tar in, 1263
Cigarette smoking. *See* Smoking
Cimetidine
interaction with other drugs, 947
and secondary depression, 1912
Cinchonism
side effect of quinidine, 909
Cingulumotomy
mood disorders, 1741, 1897
Cinnarizine
multi-infarct dementia, 962, 963
Circadian realignment in sleep-wake schedule disorders, 2442, 2443
Cirrhosis
and chronic hepatic failure, 932
and liver transplantation, 933
Cis-Platinum
auditory effects, 958
and cancer, 1906
Civil commitment, 985–986, 988, 991–992, 993
Clinical Evaluation of Language Functions—Revised, 330
Clinical Global Impressions Scale (CGI), 229, 1942
Clinical management
mood disorders, 1731
Clomid. *See* Clomiphene
Clomiphene
sexual effects, 2355
Clomiphene citrate
menses-associated psychosis, 1708
Clomipramine
obsessive compulsive disorder, 709, 2100–2102, 2103, 2685
obsessive compulsive personality disorder, 2685

premature ejaculation, 2353
sexual anxiety, 2356
Clonazepam
atypical psychosis, 1705
bipolar disorders, 1932, 1934
epilepsy, 888, 889
Tourette's syndrome, 691
Clonazepam for nocturnal myoclonus, 2437–2438
Clonidine
attention-deficit hyperactivity disorder, 374, 376
dementia of the Alzheimer's type, 975
and depression, 854
interaction with other drugs, 913, 928, 1782, 1914
mania, 911
neuropsychiatric effects, 911
nicotine craving and withdrawal symptoms, 1276
obsessive compulsive disorder, 911
opioid detoxification, 1316, 1319, 1320–1322, 1355
posttraumatic stress disorder, 2071
side effects, 707, 876
Tourette's syndrome, 691, 697, 705, 706–707, 708, 709, 911
Clonus and hepatic disease, 936
Clophenoxate
multi-infarct dementia, 963
Clorgyline
bipolar disorders, 1934
Clumsiness in Tourette's syndrome, 692
Cocaine
and organic aggressive syndrome, 842
and organic delusional syndrome, 832, 833, 834
and organic personality syndrome, 858
and secondary mania, 854
and sex drive, 2356
and sexual anxiety, 2361
sexual effects, 2354–2355

Cocaine abuse
  age as factor, 1219
  anxiety, 1373
  and benzodiazepine combination,
      intoxication, 1295
  bingeing, 1227
  and cannabis use, 1244
  contingency contracting, 1233
  "crack," 1218, 1219, 1920
  delusions, 1223
  emergency medical treatment, 1224
  history and epidemiology, 1218–1220
  nasal irritation, 1185
  neurochemical activity, 1220–1222
  and opioid abuse, 1315
  and psychiatric problems, 1185
  with secondary depression, 1369–
      1370, 1920–1922
  urine tests, 1235
  withdrawal, 1229–1231
  See also Stimulant abuse
Cocaine Anonymous, 1316, 1378, 1399
Cocaine delusional disorder
  differential diagnosis, 1709
Cocanon, 1401, 1411
Codeine dependence
  methadone treatment, 1355
Cogentin. *See* Benztropine
Cognitive-behavioral psychotherapy
  automatic thoughts, 1837–1838
  cognitive triad, 1834–1835
  course of therapy, 1836–1838
  logical errors, 1835–1836
  mood disorders, 1729, 1731, 1732,
      1801, 1834–1846, 1862
    cognitive theory of depression,
        1834–1836
    dysthymia, 1943, 1945
    effectiveness, 1838–1846
    intermittent depressive disorder,
        1943–1944
    major depression, 1822, 1943–1944
    marital therapy, 1887
    and pharmacotherapy, 1838, 1839,
        1840–1841, 1842, 1843, 1845–
        1846

  prophylactic effects, 1834, 1842,
      1846
  secondary depression, 1921
  specific effects, 1842–1843
  personality disorders, 2652
    passive-aggressive personality
        disorder, 2788
  self-monitoring, 1837
  silent assumptions, 1834, 1835,
      1837–1838
Cognitive decrement and organic
    mental syndromes, 800
Cognitive factors in antisocial behavior
    of mentally retarded persons, 23
Cognitive impairment
  and alcoholism, 1067, 1071, 1105
  and schizophrenia, 1530–1531, 1570,
      1571
Cognitive-linguistic treatment of
    language disorders in children,
    341–342, 346
Cognitive model
  anorexia nervosa, 482–484
  bulimia nervosa, 539–540
  distortions, 464, 468, 481
  reasoning errors, 481, 486–488
Cognitive restructuring, 2542–2543
Cognitive self-reinforcement in bulimia
    nervosa, 539
Cognitive therapy
  alcoholism, 1130
  anorexia nervosa, 461, 482–491
  anxiety disorders, 2036
  attention-deficit hyperactivity
      disorder, 378
  basic techniques, 488–490
  beliefs, articulating and
      operationalizing, 489
  bulimia nervosa, 525, 537–543
  challenge concept, 489
  course and duration, 491
  decatastrophizing and decentering,
      489
  family therapy, 2663
  generalized anxiety disorders, 2035
  headaches, 2150

Cognitive therapy (cont)
 hypothesis testing, 490
 insomnia, primary, 2431–2433
 as integration of behavioral and
  psychodynamic theories, 2009
 mood disorders, 1733, 1801
  combined with pharmacotherapy,
   1821
  depressive disorders, 900–901,
   1817–1822, 1871
  efficacy, 1816–1817
  long-term effectiveness, 1822
 motivation for anorexia nervosa
  treatment, 484–485
 motivation for bulimia nervosa
  treatment, 540–541
 pain, chronic, somatoform, 2130–
  2131
 panic disorder, 2035
 pedophilia, 626, 627
 personality disorders
  avoidant personality disorder, 2761
  obsessive compulsive personality
   disorder, 2774
 psychoeducational material, 485–486
 schizoaffective disorder, 1675
 smoking, 1276
 stress inoculation training, 2541–
  2543
 treatment manuals, 1816
 trichotillomania, 2484
Coital headache, 2251
Coitus interruptus, 2311
Coitus reservatus, 2311–2312
Collateral behaviors to drug abuse,
  assessment and treatment,
  1444–1446
Collective psychosis
 differential diagnosis, 1688
 epidemic hysteria, 1693
 shared paranoia, 1692, 1693
Columbia Presbyterian Medical Center,
  842
Coma
 anticholinergic overdose, 812
 and stroke, 871

Combative patients, 991–992
Commitment. See Civil commitment
Communication deviance and
  schizophrenia, 1549–1550, 1552,
  1557
Communication patterns of families of
  anorectic patients, 497
Communication skills assessment in
  pervasive developmental
  disorders, 204–210
Communication therapy
 depressive disorders, 1858
 distinguished from language
  therapy, 201–202
 educational approaches for autistic
  children, 197–198
 pervasive developmental disorders,
  201–217
  alternative systems of
   communication, 212–214
  goals, 202–204, 210–211
  horizontal and vertical
   programming, 203
  motivation, 216
  skills assessment, 204–210
  therapeutic settings and agents,
   211–212, 215
  treatment methods, 210–217
Communicative comprehension in
  autistic children, 207–210
Communicative functions, 206
Community assessment for pervasive
  developmental disorders, 190
Community-based treatment
 alcoholism
  drunk driver diversion programs,
   1149–1150
  medical versus psychiatric
   treatment models, 1147
  multiple drug use, 1149
  outpatient treatment, 1147–1149
 for mentally retarded persons, 141,
  143–145, 146
 pyromania, 2472
 schizophrenia, 1569, 1578–1580
 See also Residential treatment

programs; Therapeutic communities for substance abuse

Community resources for crisis intervention, 2530

Community role in treatment
disaster response and posttraumatic stress disorder, 2072–2073, 2081–2082
mentally retarded persons, 107
pervasive developmental disorders, 183–184, 190
See also Education

Community Services for Autistic Citizens (CSAC), 269, 270, 274

Compassionate Friends, 2598, 2599–2600, 2602

Compensation and disability payments, role in pain disorders, 2136

Competency standards
ethical issues, 998–999
research participation, 1006–1008
See also Ethical issues; Legal issues; Professional issues

Complex partial seizures. *See* Epilepsy, partial seizures

Compulsion neurosis. *See* Obsessive compulsive disorder

Compulsive personality disorder
distinguished from obsessive compulsive disorder, 2097
and obsessive compulsive personality disorder, 2685
and secondary depression, 1901

Computed tomography (CT)
alcohol and brain function, 1071
atypical psychosis diagnosis, 1702
delirium diagnosis, 807
dementia diagnosis, 823–825, 961
epilepsy diagnosis, 885–886, 887
hepatic disease diagnosis, 934
organic aggressive syndrome diagnosis, 842, 845–846
organic mental syndromes diagnosis, 837

organic mood syndrome diagnosis, 855
organic personality syndrome diagnosis, 859
Parkinson's disease diagnosis, 864
prior to electroconvulsive therapy, 1807

Conditioned cues for stimulant abuse, 1231–1232

Conduct disorder
aggressive type
haloperidol effects, 234
alcohol dependence in parent, 367, 383
antisocial personality disorder in parent, 367, 368, 383
and attention-deficit hyperactivity disorder, 383
behavior therapy, 384–385, 388, 2649
in children, 20
clinical issues, 370–371
clinical management, 388
definition and diagnosis, 365–370
developmental perspective, 382
and developmental reading disorder, 365
drug addicts, hospital treatment, 1374
DSM-III-R diagnostic criteria, 368
evaluation of patient, 382–384, 388
family therapy, 385–386
institutional, residential, and day-treatment programs, 385–386
learning problems, 383
and mental retardation, 383
and mood disorder, 383
multimodal treatment, 370, 387, 389
and oppositional defiant disorder, 365–366
and organic aggressive syndrome, 841
and organic mental disorder, 383
and organic personality disorder, 840
parent management training, 384
pharmacotherapy, 386–387

Conduct disorder *(cont)*
  and posttraumatic stress disorder, 383
  prepubertal onset, 367
  psychopathology in family members, 383
  psychotherapy, 386
  and reading disorder, 298
  research issues, 370
  social skills training, 384–385
  suggested reformulation of classification for children, 772
  treatment, 381–389
Confabulation and stroke, 873
Confidentiality
  in alcoholism treatment, 1134
  ethical issues, 999–1001
  legal issues, 989–991, 992, 993
  of self-reported drug abuse, 1191
Conflict avoidance in families of anorectic patients, 495
Conflict in alcoholics, 1094–1096, 1106, 1107–1108
Conflict resolution, 2012
Confusional states
  age factor, 900
  and brief reactive psychosis, 1682, 1683
  and epilepsy, 881
  and Parkinson's disease, 861, 863, 865
  side effect of clonidine, 911
Congestive heart failure
  and delirium, 806
  and electroconvulsive therapy, 1805–1806
  and organic mental syndromes, 897–898
  and secondary depression, 1902, 1908
Conjugal paranoia, 1642
Conjugal psychosis. *See* Induced psychotic disorder
Conners' Parent and Teacher Rating Scales, 229, 373, 413, 424, 428, 433, 693, 694, 695

Constitutional psychosis. *See* Brief reactive psychosis
Contingency contracting. *See* Contracts in behavior therapy
Contingency management
  Tourette's syndrome, 701
Contingent punishment
  abnormal stereotyped behavior in mentally retarded persons, 46
  rumination, 54
Continuous positive air pressure (CPAP) as sleep apnea therapy, 2435, 2436
Contraceptive drugs
  alcohol metabolism effect, 1077
  interaction with other drugs, 893
  menses-associated psychosis, 1708
  and secondary depression, 1913
Contraceptives use by adolescents, 2366–2367
Contracts in behavior therapy
  alcoholism, 1097–1098, 1101, 1120, 1128–1129
  anorexia nervosa, 478
  bulimia nervosa, 526
  cannabis abuse and dependence, 1260
  cocaine abuse, 1233
  drug abuse, general, 1440, 1441–1444
  family therapy for substance abuse, 1407
  personality disorders, 2650, 2651, 2652, 2653, 2656, 2657
  stimulant abuse therapy, 1233–1234
  tobacco withdrawal and tobacco dependence, 1276–1277, 1293
Contracts in crisis intervention, 2530
Controlled breathing for panic disorder, 2035
Controlled drinking as alcoholism treatment goal, 1075, 1097, 1102–1103
Control Your Depression, 1857
Conversion disorders
  adjustment disorders of adulthood

and old age, differentiation, 2507

adverse reactions
  pharmacotherapy, 2155
  symptom removal, 2154

behavior therapy, 2158

differential diagnosis, 883

electroconvulsive shock therapy, 2158

epidemic outbreaks in school children, 2159

hypnosis, 2156–2157

hysterical reaction, 2153

lithium therapy, 2158

neuroanalysis, 2157

organic disease correction, 2155–2156

and other disorders
  depression, 2153, 2154, 2156
  personality problems, 2153
  schizophrenia, 2153, 2156
  somatoform pain disorder, 2121–2122

pharmacotherapy, 2158

prognosis, 2153–2154

psychological support, 2155, 2156

psychotherapy, insight, 2157

religious-ritual procedures for alleviation, 2159

seizures, 2155

social therapy, 2159

stress, 2153

suggestion, direct, 2156

symptoms, 2152, 2153

treatment aims, 2155

treatment principles, 2153–2155

Convulsions
  and acute porphyria, 932
  and hallucinogen abuse, 1209
  and hepatic disease, 931

Convulsive therapy. *See* Electroconvulsive therapy

Coping in stress management
  development, 2538–2540, 2543
  styles, 2532, 2540, 2547

Coping with Depression, 1836

Coping with Depression Course, 1857–1858

Copper blood level. *See* Wilson's disease

Coprolalia in Tourette's syndrome, 687

Coprophagy in mental retardation, 43–44

Copropraxia in Tourette's syndrome, 688

Cornelia de Lange syndrome in self-injurious behavior, 32

Coronary disease. *See* Cardiovascular disease

Cor pulmonale and digitalis toxicity, 907

Corticosteroid drugs
  epilepsy, 889
  ocular effects, 958
  and secondary depression, 1912, 1913
  and secondary mania, 854
  side effects, 947

Corticotropin
  epilepsy, 889

Cortisone
  and secondary depression, 1912, 1913
  side effects, 943

Cost effectiveness
  alcoholism treatment, 1142–1143
  anorexia nervosa outpatient treatment, 478
  deinstitutionalization of mentally retarded persons, 141, 143–145
  family therapy in schizophrenia treatment, 1555

Counseling
  alcoholism, 1075, 1076
  autistic disorder, 266–268
  conduct disorder in children, 386
  developmental disorders, 322–324
  distinguished from psychotherapy, 254
  mentally retarded persons
    families of, 100–104

Counseling *(cont)*
  guilt feelings of parents, 101
  initial interview, 100–102
  parents as resource, 103
  patients, 104–107
  physician-parent relationship,
    100–101
  sibling conflicts, 102–103
  spouse relationship, 102
  teachers as resource, 107
  methadone treatment programs,
    1420
  mood disorders, 1731
  opioid abuse and dependence, 1327
  pervasive developmental disorders,
    266–268
  therapeutic communities for
    substance abuse, 1392
  See also Family counseling; Parent
    counseling; Psychotherapy
Counterconditioning in drug abuse,
  1438
Countertransference
  personality disorders, 2643, 2644,
    2698, 2700
  antisocial personality disorder,
    2745
  borderline personality disorder,
    2688, 2757, 2759
  dependent personality disorder,
    2767
  histrionic personality disorder,
    2731
  narcissistic personality disorder,
    2739
  paranoid personality disorder,
    2708–2709, 2714
Couples group therapy
  alcoholism, 1119–1120, 1124
Couples sex therapy. *See* Sex therapy
Couples therapy
  mood disorders, 1732, 1885–1890
  personality disorders, 2660–2666
    duration of treatment, 2665
    histrionic personality disorder,
      2735

indications and contraindications,
    2665–2666
  narcissistic personality disorder,
    2740–2741
Covert modeling and childhood
  gender identity disorder, 665
Covert sensitization
  alcoholism, 1127–1128
  antisocial personality disorder, 2653
  exhibitionism, 672, 673
  pedophilia, 624, 626, 627
  transvestic fetishism, 644
  voyeurism, 672, 673
"Crack." *See* Cocaine abuse
Crashing in stimulant abuse, 1223–
    1224, 1228–1229
Crime
  and alcoholism, 1072, 1083
  and atypical impulse control
    disorder, 2477
  and impulse control disorders not
    elsewhere classified, 2459
  and opioid abuse, 1330, 1345–1346
  sexually criminal acts and
    prescription of sexually
    potentiating drugs, 2359
Crisis intervention
  anxiety and tension, 2523
  assessment, 2528–2529
  case review, 2531
  case vignette, 2524, 2526
  child psychotherapy, 2557–2558
  community resources, 2530
  contracts, 2530
  crisis development, 2522
  definition, 2521
  formulation, 2529
  generic versus individual treatment,
    2527
  goals, 2525, 2526, 2529–2530
  hospitalization, 2529
  implementation, 2530
  magical thinking, 2526, 2529
  model, 2521, 2525–2526
  patient losses, 2528, 2531
  patient selection, 2527–2528

patient's responsibility, 2529
precipitant and reintegration, 2523
sequence, 2521–2524
suicide risk assessment, 2529
support network, 2526, 2528, 2530
termination, 2530–2531
theory, 2520
therapeutic framework, 2524–2525
therapeutic intervention, 2528–2531
therapist-patient relationship, 2526,
    2529, 2531
vulnerability, 2521
Cross-dressing, 638, 640
    childhood gender identity disorder,
        662, 663, 664
    See also Transvestic fetishism
Cross-gender identification and
        childhood gender identity
        disorder, 662, 663, 664, 667, 668,
        669, 670
Crown-Crisp Experiential Inventory in
        somatoform pain disorder
        diagnosis, 2125
Cruelty to animals and pyromania
        association, 2469
Cue exposure in alcoholism relapse
        prevention, 1130–1131
Cults. *See* Induced psychotic disorder
Culture and sexuality, 2285, 2311–
        2312, 2380–2383
Cushing's syndrome
    and dementia, 822
    differential diagnosis, 1701
    and lung disease, 943, 945
    and organic personality syndrome,
        858
    secondary depression, 1909
    secondary mania, 1914
Cyclandelate
    dementia of the Alzheimer's type,
        972
    multi-infarct dementia, 962, 963
Cycloid psychosis, 1671, 1672, 1706,
        1708–1709, 1711
    See also Atypical psychosis
Cyclopentolate
    with a sensory-impaired patient, 958

Cyclophosphamide
    side effects, 944
Cycloserine
    and secondary depression, 1912,
        1913
    side effects, 944
Cyclothymia
    classification, 1925
    clinical presentation, 1759
    diagnostic considerations, 1752
    differential diagnosis, 855
    and hypomanic episode, 1758
    and personality disorders, 2684
    pharmacotherapy, 1742, 1933–1934
    rapid cycling, 1754
    reclassification as mood disorder,
        2679
Cyproheptadine
    anorexia nervosa, 469, 472–473
Cyproterone acetate
    sex drive reduction, 2356
    in treatment of pedophilia, 629

Daily Record of Dysfunctional
        Thoughts, 1837
Daily Smoking Record, 1269, 1288–
        1289
Dalmane. *See* Flurazepam
Dantrolene
    neuroleptic malignant syndrome,
        1805
DAT. *See* Dementia of the Alzheimer's
        type
Daughters and Sons United, 2613
Day care residential treatment
    borderline personality disorder, 2756
Deafness
    auditory hallucinations, 835
    and induced psychotic disorder,
        1694
Decongestant drugs
    and secondary mania, 1914

Defenses and personality disorders,
       2634
Degenerative disease and delirium, 806
Dehumanization in fetishism, 635
Dehydration and delirium, 811
Deinstitutionalization
   of mentally retarded persons
      cost effectiveness as issue, 141,
         143–145
      definition of terms, 140–142
      institutionalization as personal
         decision, 145–146
      philosophy, 142–143
      policy issues, 143–145
   of schizophrenics, 1547, 1568, 1576
Deja vu
   from brain damage, 835
   in depersonalization disorder, 2219
   in dissociative disorder not
      elsewhere specified, 2225
   epilepsy-related, 878, 880, 883
Delayed ejaculation. See Retarded
      ejaculation
Delayed postanoxic encephalopathy,
      896
Delayed sleep phase syndrome
   phototherapy, 1895–1896
Delinquency. See Conduct disorder
Delinquent behavior and impulse
      control disorders not elsewhere
      classified, 2458, 2459, 2460
Delirium
   and acute porphyria, 932
   age factor, 900, 979
   and alcohol hallucinosis, 835
   from anticholinergic drugs, 958, 967
   anticholinergic side effect, 1906
   from antineoplastic drugs, 944
   from antituberculosis drugs, 944
   associated features, 805
   from asthma drugs, 943
   barbiturate-sedative-hypnotic
      withdrawal, 1300
   and brief reactive psychosis, 1680,
      1681

   cannabis abuse and dependence,
      1249
   clinical subtypes, 805
   confidentiality of diagnosis, 989
   diagnostic criteria, 804–805
   differential diagnosis, 806, 807–808,
      819–820, 836, 855, 857, 918
   and digitalis toxicity, 908
   electroconvulsive therapy
      emergence, 814
   etiology, 805–806
   and hepatic disease, 934
   and hypernatremia, 899
   incidence, 805
   and insomnia, 810, 812
   and lung disease, 940, 943, 947
   and organic delusional syndrome,
      832
   and organic mood syndrome, 853
   and organic personality syndrome,
      841
   patient evaluation, 807, 837
   phencyclidine-induced, 1215
   and renal disease, 929
   and sensory impairment, 949, 956,
      957
   side effect of propranolol, 908
   stimulant abuse, 1223
   and stroke, 871
   treatment, 807–814
      alcohol withdrawal, 811–812
      anticholinergic delirium, 812–813
      electroconvulsive therapy, 810
      pharmacotherapy, 809–810, 811–
         814
      phencyclidine delirium, 813–814
      sedative, hypnotic or anxiolytic
         withdrawal, 812
   See also Confusional states
Delirium in alcohol withdrawal. See
      Alcohol withdrawal delirium
Delirium tremens
   and alcoholic liver disease, 933
   and hepatic disease, 934
   See also Alcohol withdrawal; Alcohol
      withdrawal delirium

Delusional (paranoid) disorders, 1607–
 1652
  acute stage treatment, 1625–1626
  alcohol abuse and, 1648
  assessment, 1624–1625
  and atypical psychosis, 1698
  classification, 1611–1612
  DSM-III-R classifications, 1611–1612
  electroconvulsive therapy, 1632–1633
  etiology, 1612–1622
  history of concept, 1609–1611
  incidence, 1609
  late paraphrenia, 836
  long-term treatment, 1626–1627
  monosymptomatic hypochondriacal
   psychosis, 1695
  neurobiological research, 1633–1634
  as nonreactive psychosis, 1620–1622
  and other psychiatric syndromes,
   1612–1622
  pharmacotherapy, 1627–1632
  prognosis, 1647–1648
  psychoanalytic theories, 1622–1624
  psychogenic, 1613, 1618–1620
  as psychogenic or reactive disorders,
   1616–1618
  and schizophrenia, 1497, 1609, 1612,
   1614–1616, 1647–1648
  somatic, 2146
  specific paranoid conditions, 1634–
   1648
  treatment principles, 1626
  See also Organic delusional
   syndrome; Paranoia
Delusions
  and acute porphyria, 932
  amphetamine abuse, 1223
  and atypical psychosis, 1699, 1702,
   1704
  and brief reactive psychosis, 1678
  cannabis abuse and dependence,
   1248–1249
  and cycloid psychosis, 1708
  and dementia, 821
  and digitalis toxicity, 908
  and hepatic disease, 935

  and induced psychotic disorder,
   1686, 1690, 1691, 1695
  and infective endocarditis, 896
  and lung disease, 941, 947
  and mood disorders, 1740, 1767
  and multi-infarct dementia, 964
  and Parkinson's disease, 863
  and postpartum psychosis, 1707
  and schizoaffective disorder, 1667
  and sensory impairment, 950, 953
  stimulant abuse, 1223
  and Wilson's disease, 934
Delusions, hypochondriacal, 2146
Dementia
  age factor, 817–818, 827–829, 831,
   900, 979, 994–995
  alcoholic liver disease, 933
  confidentiality of diagnosis, 989
  diagnostic criteria, 815–817
  differential diagnosis, 806, 818–822,
   819–820, 836, 855, 858, 864, 918,
   1751, 1764
  from drug effects, 820–821, 944
  and hepatic disease, 935
  incidence, 817–818
  and induced psychotic disorder,
   1689, 1694
  and insomnia, 827, 828
  Korsakoff's syndrome, 818, 820
  and lung disease, 941, 942
  and organic personality syndrome,
   841
  and Parkinson's disease, 861–862,
   865, 866
  patient evaluation, 822–826
  Pick's disease, 818–819
  psychotherapy, 829
  and renal disease, 919
  and secondary depression, 821, 827–
   829
  and stroke, 868, 871, 872
  and subacute cerebellar
   degeneration, 941
  treatment
   pharmacotherapy, 826–829, 831
   underlying symptoms, 826, 831

Dementia (cont)
  Wernicke's encephalopathy, 818, 822
  and Wilson's disease, 934
  See also Dementia associated with
    alcoholism; Dementia of the
    Alzheimer's type; Multi-infarct
    dementia
Dementia associated with alcoholism,
    820, 822, 1067, 1091–1093
Dementia of the Alzheimer's type
    (DAT)
  biogenic amines, 973–974
  cholinergic hypothesis, 967–971
  confidentiality of diagnosis, 990
  diagnostic criteria, 965–967
  differential diagnosis, 818–819, 820,
    821, 825, 826, 961
  distinguished from alcoholic
    dementia, 1091
  economic issues, 981
  ethical issues of treatment, 1005
  gamma-aminobutyric acid (GABA),
    973
  incidence, 817
  metabolic enhancers, 973
  multi-infarct dementia, 972
  and Parkinson's disease, 862
  treatment, 828, 829, 974–979
    cholinergic hypothesis, 969
    pharmacotherapy, 963, 967–979
    senile, 961, 964
  vasodilators, 971–973
  See also Dementia
Dementia praecox, 1487, 1488, 1567–
    1568
  differential diagnosis, 1666–1667
  See also Schizophrenia
Demyelination and epilepsy, 886
Dengue fever and depression, 854
Denial and personality disorders, 2669
Dependence disorder. See Substance
    abuse
Dependent personality disorder
  age factor, 2765
  and agoraphobia, 2764
  and anxiety disorders, 2685
  behavior therapy, 2769

and borderline personality disorder,
    2763
  in children, 772, 775, 780–781
  countertransference, 2767
  diagnostic criteria, 2762–2766
  group therapy, 2769
  and histrionic personality disorder,
    2763
  identification, 2768
  and induced psychotic disorder,
    1696
  and passive-aggressive personality
    disorder, 2763, 2764, 2770
  pharmacotherapy, 2675, 2770
  psychotherapy, 2642
    group therapy, 2675, 2769
    individual psychodynamic
      psychotherapy, 2767–2769
    problems, 2766
    psychoanalytic psychotherapy,
      2646
    short- versus long-term treatment,
      2768–2769, 2770
  residential treatment, 2764, 2770
  resistance, 2697
  with secondary depression, 2764
  transference, 2767
Depersonalization disorder
  case vignettes, 2217–2218
  defensive maneuver, 2220
  definition, 2218–2219
  deja vu, 2219
  dissociative disorder classification,
    2219
  DSM-III-R diagnostic criteria, 2219
  estrangement feelings, 2218
  etiology, 2219–2220
  frequency and linkages, 2219
  future directions, 2221–2222
  and other psychiatric disorders, 2219
  pharmacotherapy, 2221, 2222
  phenomenology, 2217–2218
  physiologic basis, 2220
  stress, 2219
  treatment, 2220–2221
Depersonalization neurosis. See
      Depersonalization disorder

Depo-Provera. *See* Medroxyprogesterone acetate
Deprenyl
effects on cardiovascular system, 905
interaction with other drugs, 867
sexual effects, 2354
Depression
adjustment disorders of adulthood
and old age, differentiation,
2507
behavioral formulation, 1847–1848
cognitive formulation, 1834–1836
and conversion disorders, 2153,
2154, 2156
definitions, 1727
and dissociative disorder not
otherwise specified, 2224
and hypochondriasis, 2138, 2145
interpersonal psychotherapy
formulation, 1863–1866
and kleptomania, 2468
and multiple personality disorder,
2209–2210
and pathologic gambling, 2464, 2465
pharmacotherapy, 2588
and primary insomnia, 2428
psychoanalytic formulation, 1827–
1829
psychodynamic formulation, 1873–
1874
and psychogenic fugue, 2191, 2192,
2193, 2194
and somatoform pain disorder, 2121,
2123, 2129
and stress management, 2539, 2542
See also Depressive disorders;
Secondary depression
Depressive Adjective Checklist
(DACL), 1851
Depressive adjustment disorders. *See*
Adjustment disorder with
depressed mood
Depressive disorders
accident risk, 846

adjustment disorder with depressed
mood
diagnostic criteria, 1900, 1946–1949
incidence, 1727
treatment, 1743, 1948, 1949
atypical depression, 2685
brief dynamic psychotherapy, 1872–
1884
children and adolescents
diagnostic criteria, 1950–1952
impact on development, 1952–
1956
cognitive-behavioral psychotherapy,
1834–1846
conversion from paranoid
personality disorder, 2708
couples therapy, 1885–1890
depressive disorder not otherwise
specified
diagnostic considerations, 1753
differential diagnosis, 918, 2706
double depression, 1757, 1789, 1942,
1943–1944
drug addicts, hospital treatment,
1368–1370
dysthymia, 1940–1945
classification, 1727, 1728
diagnostic considerations, 1753–
1754, 1756–1757, 1949–1942
incidence, 1727
treatment, 1743–1745, 1756, 1789,
1942
family therapy, 1885–1890
intermittent depressive disorder,
1943–1944
interpersonal psychotherapy, 1863–
1872
learning disabled children, 311
major depression, 1752, 1753, 1756,
1803, 1817–1822, 1942–1944
classification, 1727, 1728
diagnostic considerations, 1754–
1755
treatment, 1742–1744, 1943–1944
vulnerability factors, 1748

Depressive disorders (cont)
  melancholia, 1752, 1790, 1832
  and mental retardation, 10–13
  neurotic depression, 1743
  in parents of children with gender identity disorder, 666
  and personality disorders, 2684
  pharmacotherapy
    risk of orthostatic hypotension, 902–903
  psychosurgery, 1729, 1741, 1896–1897
  reactive depression, 1743
  and rumination, 570
  seasonal affective disorder (SAD), 1801, 1891–1896
  secondary depression. See Secondary depression
  situational depression, 1743
  vulnerability factors, 1748
  See also Depression
Depressive stupor, 1740
Desamino-D-arginine vasopressin (DDAVP)
  functional enuresis, 723
Desensitization. See Systematic desensitization
Desipramine
  cannabis withdrawal, 1254
  classification, 1774
  dementia, 827
  dosage, 1789
  effects on cardiovascular system, 902, 903
  functional enuresis, 723
  interaction with other drugs, 928
  mood disorders, 1799
    melancholia, 1790
    secondary depression, 946, 1903, 1912, 1917, 1922
  obsessive compulsive disorder, 2103
  Parkinson's disease, 865
  personality disorders, 2687
  pharmacokinetics, 1779, 1780, 1786
    neurotransmitter blockade, 1775, 1776, 1777

phencyclidine-induced depression, 1217
  and specific medical diseases, 1782, 1783, 1784
  and specific medical disorders, 946
  stimulant abuse, 1236
Desmethyldiazepam
  epilepsy, 888
  renal disease, 922
Desmethylimipramine
  and ejaculatory pain, 2316
Desyrel. See Trazodone
Detoxification. See specific substance
Development, normal, of child. See Child development, normal
Developmental articulation disorders. See Articulation disorders, developmental
Developmental disorders, pervasive. See Pervasive developmental disorders
Developmental disorders, specific. See Specific developmental disorders
Developmental fluency disorders. See Fluency disorders, developmental
Developmental language and speech disorders. See Language and speech disorders, developmental
Developmental pattern of pedophiles, 621
Developmental phonologic disorders. See Phonologic disorders, developmental
Developmental reading disorders. See Reading disorders, developmental
Developmental Test of Visual-Motor Integration, 330
Deviant behaviors. See Stereotyped behaviors, abnormal
Deviant sexual behaviors. See Paraphilias

Dexamethasone
stroke, 875
Dexamethasone suppression test (DST)
alcohol effects on, 1071, 1138
depressive disorders diagnosis, 1903,
1905, 1917, 1921
depressive disorders in children and
adolescents, 1951
organic mood syndrome diagnosis,
1910
Dexedrine
secondary depression, 1912
Dextroamphetamine
mood disorders, 1799
secondary depression, 1906
Dextroamphetamine for temper
outbursts in children, 2476
Diabetes
and impotence, 2319, 2331
and multi-infarct dementia, 962
and renal disease, 918, 920
with secondary depression, 1909
and stroke, 869
treatment, 846
Diabetic ketoacidosis and brief reactive
psychosis, 1680
*Diagnostic and Statistical Manual of
Mental Disorders* (DSM)
controversial issues in sexual
disorders classification, 2237,
2248
evaluating for schizophrenia
diagnosis, 1499, 1500, 1501
homosexuality dropped from
DSM-III-R, 2237, 2252
identity disorder recognized in
DSM-III, 750, 762, 783
new classification of personality
disorders, 2678–2679
partial deletion of neurotic
depression, 1755–1756
reclassification of affective and mood
disorders, 1726, 2679
reformulation of other disorders of
infancy, childhood, or
adolescence, 733–734

reformulation of pervasive
developmental disorders, 179,
180
schizoid disorder classification
dropped, 733, 750, 762
shifts in personality disorder
diagnosis, 2636
suggested reformulation of
immature personality disorders,
733–734, 772
Diagnostic interpretative conference
for pervasive developmental
disorders, 191
Diagnostic overshadowing, 11
Diagnostic Questions for Early or
Advanced Alcoholism, 1078
Diagnostic systems other than DSM
evaluation criteria, 1499–1501
schizophrenia, 1498–1501
Dialectical behavior therapy for
personality disorders, 2653
Diaphoresis
and delirium, 813
and lung disease, 941
side effect of clonidine, 911
Diaphragm pacing therapy for central
sleep apnea, 2436
Diathesis-stress theory of
schizophrenia, 1548
Diazepam
alcohol withdrawal, 1087, 1088, 1101
anxiety and lung disease, 945
anxiety disorders, 2039, 2040
anxiety disorders of childhood, 407
anxiety due to cannabis abuse, 1249,
1252
avoidant disorder of childhood, 435–
436
delirium, 811, 812, 814
dementia, 828
drug switching, 1307
and electroconvulsive therapy, 1811
epilepsy, 888, 889, 890
hepatic disease, 937
interaction with other drugs, 915,
921

Diazepam (cont)
  mood disorders, 1798
    major depression, 1819
    secondary depression, 1912, 1913, 1920
  organic delusional syndrome, 838
  overanxious disorder of childhood, 427, 428
  Parkinson's disease, 866
  renal disease, 922
  schizoid disorder, 760
  sedative-hypnotic drug withdrawal, 1296, 1304
  side effects, 876
  somatic symptoms, 2151
  Tourette's syndrome, 691
  vaginismus, 2358
Diazoxide
  interaction with other drugs, 891
Dibenzoxazepines
  neurotransmitter blockade, 1776
  pharmacokinetics, 1780
Diclofenac
  interaction with other drugs, 927
Dicoumarol
  interaction with other drugs, 890
Diethylstilbestrol
  sex drive reduction, 2356
Differential reinforcement of other behavior (DRO), 113
  See also Reinforcement
Digitalis
  neuropsychatric effects, 907
  ocular effects, 958
Digitalis toxicity
  and electroconvulsive therapy, 1806
  and hyperkalemia, 899
  and phenytoin, 910
Digitoxin
  hepatic disease, 938
  interaction with other drugs, 891
Digoxin
  hepatic disease, 938
  interaction with other drugs, 890, 909, 913, 914, 915

Dihydroergotoxine
  dementia of the Alzheimer's type, 972, 978
  multi-infarct dementia, 962, 963
Dihydrostreptomycin
  auditory effects, 958
Dilantin. See Diphenylhydantoin
Diltiazem
  neuropsychiatric effects, 909
Diphenhydramine
  insomnia in opioid detoxification, treatment, 1318
  mentally retarded persons, 88
  neurotransmitter blockade, 1776
Diphenylhydantoin
  hepatic disease, 938
  organic aggressive syndrome, 850
  reaction with disulfiram, 1100
  secondary depression, 1904
Diplopia
  from drug intoxication, 892
  and hepatic disease, 936
Dipyridamole
  stroke, 869
Disabilities, sexual effects, 2375–2378
Discriminative stimulus, 113
Disease concept and schizophrenia, 1489–1493
Disease phobia in hypochondriasis, 2143
Diseases of mood. See Mood disorders
Disinhibition syndrome, 840
  See also Organic personality disorder
Disopyramide
  effects on cardiovascular system, 901
  interaction with other drugs, 913
  neuropsychiatric effects, 910
  and secondary depression, 1912, 1913
Disorders of affect. See Mood disorders
Disorganized subtype of schizophrenia, 1498
Displacement and obsessive compulsive personality disorder, 2772

Disruptive behavior disorder. *See*
Conduct disorder; Oppositional
defiant disorder
Dissociative disorder not otherwise
specified
amytal interview, 2223
brainwashing, 2222, 2223, 2225–2226
communicative incompetence, 2226
definition, 2222–2223
deja vu, 2225
and depression, 2224
derealization, 2225
indoctrination, 2222, 2223, 2225–2226
meditation experience, 2223, 2224
reassurance in therapy, 2226
religious/mystical aspects, 2223–2224
schizophrenia, differentiation, 2225
stress, 2226
thought control and thought reform
cultism, 2222, 2223, 2225–2226
trance-like states, 2223–2225
Dissociative disorders
adjustment disorders of adulthood
and old age, differentiation,
2507
classification, 2185
depersonalization disorders, 2217–
2222
differential diagnosis, 883, 884
dissociative disorder not otherwise
specified, 2222–2226
multiple personality disorder, 2197–
2216
psychogenic amnesia, 2186–2190
psychogenic fugue, 2190–2196
Distar instructional system for
remediation of mathematics
disorders, 338
Distractibility and learning disabilities,
310, 311
Disulfiram
contracts for use, 1097–1098, 1101,
1120, 1129
disapproval of by AA members,
1102
interaction with other drugs, 890

mechanism of action, 1100
periodic catatonia, 1709
role in alcoholism treatment, 1075,
1100–1103, 1113, 1126–1127,
1134–1135, 1149–1150
and secondary depression, 1912,
1913
side effects, 1100
toxic reactions with other drugs,
1100
Diuretics
auditory effects, 958
hepatic disease, 932, 935, 936, 937–
938
and hyperkalemia, 899
interaction with other drugs, 913,
914, 927, 960
and lithium, 906, 1926
neuropsychiatric effects, 912
renal disease, 925, 928–929
sexual effects, 2344
Division TEACCH, 199, 205, 253, 269–
270, 273–274
DMT (dimethyltryptamine). *See*
Hallucinogen abuse
L-Dopa. *See* Levodopa
Dopamine
and antidepressant drugs, 1775–1777
and dementia of the Alzheimer's
type, 973–974
effects on cardiovascular system, 903
and electroconvulsive therapy, 1813
interaction with other drugs, 913
link with psychosis, 833
and Parkinson's disease, 861
release with amphetamines, 832
and reserpine, 1734, 1795
stimulant abuse role, 1220–1221
stress response, 2071
stroke, 871
and Tourette's syndrome, 690–691,
705, 706
Dopamine receptor sensitivity and
schizophrenia, 1491
Dopaminergic activity in autistic
children, 242

Dopaminergic drugs
  impotence, 2357
  orgasmic dysfunctions, 2357
  sex drive, 2356
Doppler assessment of penile vascular
    function, 2242, 2329, 2331
Double bind theory of schizophrenia,
    753, 1544, 1545
Double depression. *See* Mood
    disorders
Doubting, pathologic, as obsessive
    compulsive disorder, 2096, 2100,
    2109
Down's syndrome
  and Alzheimer's disease, 12, 30–32
  premature aging, 31
  Trisomy 21 as cause, 30
Doxepin
  classification, 1774
  dementia, 827, 828
  effects on cardiovascular system, 902
  interaction with other drugs, 891, 928
  mood disorders
    dysthymia, 1942
    secondary depression, 1903, 1906,
      1920, 1921–1922
  pharmacokinetics, 1780
    neurotransmitter blockade, 1776
  and specific medical diseases, 1782,
    1783, 1784
Doxorubicin
  side effects, 944
DRO. *See* Differential reinforcement of
    other behavior
Droperidol
  delirium, 809–810, 814
  and electroconvulsive therapy, 1811
  side effects, 810
Dropouts Anonymous, 2612
Drug abuse
  acute effects, 1189
  AIDS risk, 1185
  antianxiety drugs, 1184
  assessment interviews, 1186–1187,
    1190
  and automobile accidents, 846

as behavior problem, 1380–1381
and brief reactive psychosis, 1680,
    1681
chronic effects, 1189–1190
clinical assessment, 1183–1193
and delirium, 806, 810, 812
differential diagnosis, 885
drug-induced mental states, effects
    on assessment, 1187–1191
and epilepsy, 885, 887
guidelines for evaluating symptoms,
    1190
half-life of drugs, 1188
and hepatic disease, 935, 939
and induced psychotic disorder,
    1694
legal aspects, 1185
medical problems, 1185
and mental disorders, 1189
and mood disorders, 1759–1760,
    1765, 1792
  bipolar disorders, 1762
  secondary depression, 1901, 1920–
    1922
occupational problems, 1185–1186
and organic aggressive syndrome,
    842–843
and organic delusional syndrome,
    832, 837, 838
and organic hallucinosis, 832, 837
and organic personality syndrome,
    860
paraprofessional assistance, 1186–
    1187
and personality disorders, 2684,
    2688, 2696, 2698
  avoidant personality disorder,
    2762
  borderline personality disorder,
    2750
prognosis, 1185–1186
psychopathology, 1185, 1189–1190
and schizoaffective disorder, 1668
self-reporting, 1186, 1191
and sexual disorders, 2240, 2344
social problems, 1185–1186

type and severity, 1184
urine and blood tests, 1191, 1235,
    1246–1247, 1253–1254
withdrawal effects, overview, 1190
See also Alcohol abuse; Hospital
    treatment for drug addiction;
    Substance abuse; Substance-
    induced chronic psychosis;
    Therapeutic communities for
    substance abuse; names of
    specific drugs
Drug Abuse Reporting Project, 1343–
    1344
Drug Abuse Warning Network
    (DAWN), 1224
Drug counselors in methadone
    treatment programs, 1420
Drug dependence in somatoform pain
    disorder, 2128
Drug-induced mental states, effects on
    assessment of drug abuse, 1187–
    1191
Drug interactions in naltrexone
    antagonist treatment for opioid
    dependence, 1341
Drugs as reinforcers, 1431–1432
Drug switching, adverse effects, 1307
Drug therapy. *See* Pharmacotherapy
Drunk driver diversion programs,
    1149–1150
DSM. *See Diagnostic and Statistical
    Manual of Mental Disorders*
DST. *See* Dexamethasone suppression
    test
Dupuytren's contractures and hepatic
    disease, 935
Dynamic psychotherapy. *See*
    Psychodynamic psychotherapy
Dysarthria
    and delirium, 813
    and hepatic disease, 936
    renal disease, 917
    side effect of lidocaine, 909
    side effect of phenytoin, 910
    and subacute cerebellar
        degeneration, 941

and Wilson's disease, 934
Dyscalculia, mathematics disorder, 317
Dyskinesias
    levodopa-induced, 866
    See also Tardive dyskinesia;
        Withdrawal dyskinesia
Dysmorphophobia, 2146
Dyspareunia
    causes, 2243–2244, 2291–2293
    and depression, 2254
    DSM-III-R diagnostic criteria, 2291
    and inhibited female sexual
        response, 2284
    psychological reactions, 2293
    tests for physical causes, 2243–2244
Dysphagia and subacute cerebellar
    degeneration, 941
Dysphasia
    and delirium, 805
    renal disease, 917
    transient ischemic attacks, 885
Dysphoria
    and brief reactive psychosis, 1681
    hallucinogens, 1206
    methadone maintenance,
        prevention, 1349
    naltrexone antagonist treatment for
        opioid dependence, 1333
    and neuroleptic drugs, 1510, 1514
    and stimulants, 1223–1224, 1228–
        1229, 1230–1231
    and Tourette's syndrome, 697
Dysthymia
    character spectrum disorders, 1941
    diagnostic considerations, 1753–
        1754, 1756–1757, 1940–1942
    differential diagnosis, 855
    incidence, 1727
    and passive-aggressive personality
        disorder, 2787
    with personality disorders, 1940
    reclassification as mood disorder,
        2679
    secondary dysphoria, 1941
    and somatoform pain disorder, 2121
    thymoleptic responsive, 1941

Dysthymia *(cont)*
  treatment
    pharmacotherapy, 1756, 1789, 1942
    psychotherapy, 1943–1945
Dystonia
  and antipsychotic drugs, 1511
  distinguished from tic disorders, 692
  incidence in young male patients,
    1511, 1512
  and neuroleptic drugs, 1512, 1682

Early childhood education
  autistic children, 198
  learning disabled, 304–305
  mentally retarded, 126–127
Early trauma hypothesis of autistic
    disorder, 249
Eating disorders
  anorexia nervosa, 451–516
  atypical eating disorders, 589–594
  bulimia nervosa, 517–563
  diagnostic criteria, 450, 1752
  and kleptomania, 2468
  mentally retarded persons
    behavior therapy, 64–65
    chewing-speech relationship, 61–
      62
    classification, 57–58
    etiology, 57, 58–59
    food texture and consistency as
      factors, 63, 65
    hyperphagia, 50–51
    incidence, 59–60
    motivation, 62–63
    neurodevelopmental therapy, 63–
      64
    neuromotor disabilities, 58
    normalization goals, 61
    nutritional aspects, 60–61
    psychotherapy, 62
  overview, 449–450
  and personality disorders, 2750
  pica, 51–53, 579–589
  rumination, 53–55, 564–579

and secondary depression, 1915–
    1918
Eaton-Lambert syndrome and lung
    disease, 942
Ebstein's anomaly, 1931
Echolalia in Tourette's syndrome, 687,
    688
Economic factors in treatment of
    depression, 1751
Economic issues
  institutionalization of antisocial
    personality disorder patients,
    2748
  Medicare patients, 979–980, 981,
    982, 983
  public policy issues, 982
  residential treatment, 2703–2704
  treatment of organic mental
    syndromes, 799, 802–803
  See also Cost effectiveness
ECT. *See* Electroconvulsive therapy
Education
  attention-deficit hyperactivity
    disorder, 379–380
  autistic children, 192–201
  bulimic patients, 526, 535
  children with immature personality
    disorders, 774, 782
  children with specific developmental
    disorders
    learning disabilities, evaluation,
      321
    planning and programs, 304–305,
      347–352
  coping skills training in drug abuse,
    1436–1437
  employment skills training
    programs, 1445
  legal requirements, 123–124. 132,
    193–194
  mentally retarded persons
    classroom placement, 125, 126
    curriculum and teaching methods,
      125–126, 127
    early intervention in moderate and
      severe retardation, 127

labeling as issue, 124–126
legal requirements, 123–124
profound retardation, issues, 128
programs, 127, 128
parent involvement, 124, 194, 198,
200
psychiatrist involvement, 200–201
shift toward social skills training,
197, 198, 267, 268
work as education in therapeutic
community, 1386
See also Early childhood education;
Education for All Handicapped
Children Act; Sex education;
Social skills training
Education for All Handicapped
Children Act (PL 94-142)
amendments of 1983 (PL 98-199),
123, 200
categories, 349–350
handicap, legal definition, 347
interaction with mental health
professionals, 300, 349
learning disabled children, 300, 304
overview, 193–194, 348–349
parent involvement, 200
provisions, 104, 123, 193–194
screening teams, 348
services, legal provision, 347
special education, 349–352
Educative interventions in family
therapy, 2663, 2664
Ego
and personality disorders, 2640,
2644, 2674
antisocial personality disorder,
2743
Ego-dystonic behavior, 2096–2097,
2457
Ego-dystonic homosexuality dropped
from DSM-III-R, 2237, 2252
Ejaculation disorders. *See* Ejaculatory
pain; Premature ejaculation;
Retarded ejaculation
Ejaculation process, 2299–2301
Ejaculatory incompetence. *See*
Retarded ejaculation

Ejaculatory pain, 2316–2317
Elavil. *See* Amitriptyline
Elder abuse reporting, 984, 993, 1000
Elective mutism
behavior therapy, 767–768, 770–771
definition, 762–763
etiology, 763–764
family therapy, 769–771
paraverbal therapy, 768–769
pharmacotherapy, 771
psychotherapy, 764–767
relaxation technique, 768
stimulus fading, 768, 771
treatment, 764–771
Electric aversion therapy
alcoholism, 1097, 1126
exhibitionism, 672
legality and ethical issues, 225
pervasive developmental disorders,
224–226
voyeurism, 672, 673
See also Aversion therapy
Electric skin shock. *See* Electric
aversion therapy
Electrocardiography (EKG)
atypical psychosis diagnosis, 1701
bradyarrhythmia diagnosis, 884
with carbamazepine, 1932
cardiac conduction impairment, 2687
during electroconvulsive therapy,
1809
preparation for lithium therapy, 1926
Electrocochleogram, 955
Electroconvulsive therapy (ECT)
adverse effects, 1809, 1810, 1811–
1812
atypical psychosis, 1704
and benzodiazepines, 1808, 1810
Briquet's syndrome, 2170
and cardiovascular disease, 1917
compared with pharmacotherapy for
schizophrenia, 1502
consent, 1806–1807
continuation therapy, 1813
conversion disorders, 2158
delirium treatment, 810, 814

Electroconvulsive therapy (ECT) *(cont)*
  delusional (paranoid) disorders,
    1632–1633
  dementia, 828
  dementia of the Alzheimer's type,
    977
  drug-induced psychosis, 943
  effects on cardiovascular system,
    903–904
  elderly patients, 1807
  electrocardiography during, 1809
  and electroencephalography, 1807,
    1810, 1812
  emergence delirium, 814
  fetishism, 639
  hallucinogen abuse, 1207
  hypochondriasis, 2145
  indications, 1803–1805
  induced psychotic disorder, 1695
  and lithium, 1808
  mechanism of action, 1812
  menses-associated psychosis, 1708
  and monoamine oxidase inhibitors,
    1808
  mood disorders, 1729, 1734, 1736,
    1737, 1740, 1764, 1768, 1785,
    1787, 1803–1813
    bipolar disorders, 1742, 1760,
      1927–1928, 1936
    depressive stupor, 1740
    major depression, 1742
    secondary depression, 1908, 1909,
      1915, 1917
    secondary mania, 1914
  multi-infarct dementia, 964
  nonresponsive patients, 1801
  obsessive compulsive disorder, 2104
  organic mood syndrome, 856, 1910
  organic personality syndrome, 859
  pain, chronic, somatoform, 2133
  Parkinson's disease, 865, 866
  periodic catatonia, 1709
  phencyclidine abuse and
    dependence, 1215
  postpartum psychosis, 1708
  risk factors, 1805–1806, 1807

  schizoaffective disorder, 1672, 1673–
    1674
  schizophreniform disorder, 1659
  seizures, 884
  side effects, 947
  somatization disorder, 2170
  somatoform pain disorder, 2133
  stroke, 875
  tardive dyskinesia, 1513
  transvestic fetishism, 643
  treatment technique, 1807–1811
  and tricyclic antidepressant drugs,
    1808
Electroencephalography (EEG)
  anorexia nervosa assessment, 454
  antisocial behavior in mentally
    retarded persons, diagnosis, 23
  atypical psychosis diagnosis, 1701
  delirium diagnosis, 806
  dementia diagnosis, 825
  and electroconvulsive therapy, 1807,
    1810, 1812
  epilepsy diagnosis, 877, 880, 883,
    884, 893, 2687
  hepatic disease diagnosis, 930–931,
    934
  organic aggressive syndrome
    diagnosis, 842, 845
  organic mood syndrome diagnosis,
    855
  organic personality syndrome
    diagnosis, 859
  personality disorder diagnosis, 2681,
    2683
    borderline personality disorder,
      2686
  preparation for lithium therapy, 1926
  secondary depression with AIDS
    diagnosis, 1912
Electrolysis in transsexualism, 659
Electrolyte imbalance
  and anorexia nervosa, 454
  and brief reactive psychosis, 1680
  and bulimia nervosa, 518
  and delirium, 806, 808, 811
  and hepatic disease, 935

and renal disease, 929
Electromyographic (EMG) biofeedback.
    See Biofeedback training
Electroretinography, 955
Elementary partial seizures. *See*
    Epilepsy, partial seizures
Elimination disorders, 715–730
Emetine
  alcoholism, 1097, 1127
EMIT (enzyme multiplied immuno-
    assay test). *See* Urine tests in
    drug abuse
Employee assistance programs
  alcoholism, 1143–1146
  constructive confrontation versus
    self-referral, 1146
  referral indications, 1144
  referral procedures, 1145–1146
  weaknesses of, 1145–1146
Employment
  autistic adults, 272–274
  drug abusers
    Job Seekers' Workshop, 1445, 1447
    occupational problems, 1185–1186
    skills training, 1445
  mentally retarded persons, 132–138
  schizophrenics, 1573–1575
  See also Vocational training
Encephalitis
  and amnestic syndromes, 819
  and brief reactive psychosis, 1680
  and organic aggressive syndrome,
    842
  and Parkinson's disease, 861
  and psychogenic fugue, 2194
  and secondary depression, 854, 1902
  and sensory impairment, 952
  and SIADH, 898
Encopresis. *See* Functional encopresis
Encounter groups for alcoholism
    treatment, 1121
Endocrine abnormalities
  anorexia nervosa, 453
  bulimia nervosa, 518–519
  and delirium, 806
  in drug addicts, 1366

with secondary depression, 1901,
    1902, 1908–1909
Endocrine changes in naltrexone
    antagonist treatment for opioid
    dependence, 1340
Endogenomorphic syndrome
  and stroke, 875
β-Endorphin
  dementia of the Alzheimer's type,
    977
Endorphins
  schizophrenia, 1503
Enkephalin
  dementia of the Alzheimer's type,
    977
Enuresis. *See* Functional enuresis
Environment as factor
  antisocial behavior in mentally
    retarded persons, 24
  atypical psychosis, 1700
  behavior problems in mentally
    retarded persons, 5, 6
  delirium, 808
  dementia, 829–830
  employment of mentally retarded
    persons, 136–137
  induced psychotic disorder, 1690–
    1691
  mood disorders, 1749
    treatment, 1885–1890
  mood disorders in mentally retarded
    persons, 13–14
  schizophrenia, 1509, 1548
  schizophreniform disorder, 1663
  stereotyped behavior, abnormal, in
    mentally retarded persons, 45–
    46
  substance abuse, 1197, 1199–1200,
    1201
  Tourette's syndrome, 690
  See also Family environment as factor
Environment modification
  brief reactive psychosis, 1681
Enzyme abnormalities
  anorexia nervosa, 452
  bulimia nervosa, 518

Enzyme deficiency as cause of Lesch-
    Nyhan syndrome, 37
Ephedrine
    interaction with other drugs, 913
    side effects, 944
Epidemic hysteria
    differential diagnosis, 1688, 1693
    See also Induced psychotic disorder
Epidemiologic Catchment Area (ECA)
        Survey
    alcoholism, 1063
    antisocial personality disorder, 2743
    dementia study, 817–818
    obsessive compulsive disorders, 2097
Epilepsy
    and amnestic syndrome, 880
    associated with fetishism, 637
    and atypical psychosis, 1698
    behavioral disorders, 879–883
    contraindication for antidepressants,
        1914
    coping skills training, 2540
    diagnostic criteria, 877–879
    differential diagnosis, 873, 883–885,
        935
    generalized seizures, 878–879, 881,
        883, 885
        pharmacotherapy guidelines, 889
    and mania, 854
    and organic aggressive syndrome,
        842, 846, 850
    and organic personality syndrome,
        840, 858, 859
    partial seizures, 878, 880, 881, 883,
        884, 885, 888
        pharmacotherapy guidelines, 889
    patient evaluation, 885–886
    and psychogenic fugue, 2194
    with secondary depression, 854,
        1910
    self-help and mutual help groups,
        2598, 2605, 2606
    and stroke, 874
    suicide risk, 882, 883
    treatment, 886–894
        behavior methods, 893–894

    pharmacotherapy, 882, 887–893,
        894
    surgery, 893
    vocational rehabilitation, 886–887
    twilight states, 880, 881
    unclassified seizures, 879
    unilateral seizures, 879
Epinephrine
    interaction with other drugs, 913,
        914
    stress response, 2070–2071
Episodic dyscontrol syndrome, 840
    See also Organic personality disorder
Epstein-Barr virus and depression, 854
Erectile dysfunction. See Male erectile
        disorder
Erotomania and atypical psychosis,
        1698
Erotomanic delusional states, 1646–
        1647
Erythromycin
    interaction with other drugs, 947
Esophageal motor dysfunction in
        rumination, 572
Esophageal sphincter pressure in
        rumination, 573
Essentials of English, test, 330
Estrogen
    interaction with other drugs, 1779
    sex drive reduction, 2356
    with tricyclic antidepressant drugs,
        1795–1796
Estrogen deficiency
    and aging, 2292, 2373–2374
    and dyspareunia, 2292, 2373
    and female sexual arousal disorder,
        2242, 2283
    and impaired sexual desire, 2241
Ethacrynic acid
    auditory effects, 958
    interaction with other drugs, 927
    renal disease, 925
Ethanol intoxication. See Alcohol
        intoxication
Ethanol metabolism. See Alcohol
        metabolism

Ethclorvynol
  adjustment disorders, 2588
  anxiety and lung disease, 945
Ethical issues
  biopsychosocial aspects of old age,
      994–995
  child abuse reporting, 993, 1000
  confidentiality, 989, 999–1001, 1134,
      1191
  countertransference, 1004–1005
  diagnostic concerns, 996–998
  economic reimbursement, 982, 996–
      997
  elder abuse reporting, 1000
  euthanasia, 1002–1004
  institutional care constraints, 1001–
      1002
  involuntary commitment, 2702
  patient consent, 998–999, 1513
  for physicians participating in
      gender reassignment, 660, 661
  prescribing sexually potentiating
      drugs, 2358–2359
  punishment, 225, 2659
  research concerns, 1005–1008
  role of ethics, 995–996
  sexological examination, 2365
  sexual provocation from patients,
      991–992
  sexual surrogates, 2363–2364
  terminal care, 1002–1004
  termination of treatment, 2004
  in treatment of organic mental
      syndromes, 799
  truth-telling, 997–998
  See also Legal issues; Professional
      issues
Ethionamide
  and secondary depression, 1912,
      1913
  side effects, 944
Ethosuximide
  behavioral-cognitive effects in
      mentally retarded persons, 96–
      97
  borderline personality disorder, 2686

epilepsy, 888, 889
  interaction with other drugs, 890
  and secondary depression, 1912,
      1913
Euphoria
  and antituberculosis drugs, 944
  barbiturates, sedatives, and hypnotic
      agents, 1294–1295
  and depressive disorders, 805
  and digitalis toxicity, 908
  side effect of lidocaine, 909
  stimulant abuse, 1220, 1221, 1226
  tobacco as euphoriant, 1261
Euthanasia, 1002–1004
Exertional hypotension
  side effect of guanethidine, 912
Exhibitionism, 670–673
  and antisocial personality disorder,
      2653
  definition, 671–672
  deriving from somatic disorders, 671
  incidence, 670–671
  in pedophilia, 618–619, 622
  physical causes, 673
  recidivism, 619, 672
  and sadomasochism, 670
  stroke-related, 877
  treatment, 672–673
Exploratory insight-oriented (EIO)
      psychotherapy for
      schizophrenia, 1517–1518
Explosive aggressive behavior in
      mentally retarded persons, 119
Explosive personality disorder. *See*
      Intermittent explosive disorder;
      Organic personality disorder;
      Organic personality syndrome
Exposure treatment, 2099–2100
  agoraphobia, 2029–2034
    compared with imipramine
      treatment, 2033–2034
    compared with other treatments,
      2033–2034
    couples training, 2030–2031
    limitations, 2032
    long-term efficacy, 2031

Exposure treatment *(cont)*
  outcome, 2031–2032
  posttraumatic stress disorder, 2080–2081
  simple phobias, 2027–2028
  See also Behavior therapy
Expressed emotion and schizophrenia
  causal factor, 1551–1552
  family intervention strategies, 1552–1557
  relapse factor, 1493, 1550–1552
Extinction
  in behavior therapy, 113, 221–222, 403, 404
  personality disorders, 2650
  in substance abuse, 1231–1232, 1238, 1437–1438
Eysenck Personality Inventory in somatoform pain disorder diagnosis, 2125

Face-Hand Test for delirium diagnosis, 807
Factitious disorder
  differential diagnosis, 806, 883, 884, 1679
  with physical symptoms
    behavior therapy, 2164
    child abuse and deprivation as causes, 2161
    definition, 2159
    dependency need as cause, 2162
    diagnosis, 2162–2163
    differential diagnosis, 2160–2161
    DSM-III-R diagnostic criteria, 2160
    etiology and pathogenesis, 2161–2162
    family involvement, 2163
    health-related background of patients, 2161–2162
    history, 2160
    malingering, 2161
    motivation, 2160

Munchausen-type patients, 2160, 2161
    pharmacotherapy, 2163
    prevalence, 2161
    prognosis, 2161
    psychiatric consultant, 2162
    psychotherapy, 2163–2164
    recognition, 2162
    simulation and self-infliction, 2161
    staff attitude as factor in therapy, 2163
    treatment options, 2163–2164
  with psychological symptoms
    DSM-III-R diagnostic criteria, 2160, 2165, 2166
    historical background, 2165
    hysterical psychoses, 2165
    as schizophrenia precursor, 2165–2166
    treatment, 2166
Fagerstrom Nicotine Addiction scale, 1265, 1267, 1286–1287
Failure to thrive in infants and attachment disorder, 735, 736–737, 742
Fainting. *See* Vasovagal attacks
Familial bipolar disorder, 1761
  See also Mood disorders
Families of alcoholics, 1072, 1112–1114
  See also Adult children of alcoholics; Children of alcoholics; Family problems; Parent role in alcoholism
Family assessment
  alcoholism, 1112–1113
  anorexia nervosa, 492–494, 495
  bulimia nervosa, 521
  pervasive developmental disorders, 187–190
  reactive attachment disorder of infancy, 738–740
Family counseling
  bulimia nervosa, 521
  conduct disorder in children, 386
  learning disabilities, 322–325
  mental retardation, 100–104

specific developmental disorders, 322–324
See also Family therapy; Parent counseling
Family environment as factor
alcoholism, 1111, 1112, 1113–1114
anorexia nervosa, 494–495
attention-deficit hyperactivity disorder, 373
atypical psychosis, 1707
autistic disorder, 249
childhood gender identity disorder, 666, 667–669
dependent personality disorder, 780
elective mutism, 764, 769
identity disorder, 784
impulse control disorders not elsewhere classified, 2458
induced psychotic disorder, 1690–1692
mood disorders, 1885–1890
opioid abuse and dependence, 1314–1315
pedophilia, 621, 632
personality disorders, 2660–2666
dependent personality disorder, 2765
histrionic personality disorder, 2728–2729
obsessive compulsive personality disorder, 2773
reactive attachment disorder of infancy, 735, 736
schizoid disorder of childhood or adolescence, 752, 753
schizophrenia
early theories, 1544–1545
expressed emotion and communication deviance, 1549–1552
relapse, 1493, 1509, 1545
tension and stress, 1583
teen pregnancy, 2368
See also Environment as factor
Family history of mood disorders in mentally retarded, 12

Family problems
alcohol-associated, 1067, 1112–1114
autistic disorder, 257–262
bulimia nervosa, 545–546
confidentiality of diagnosis, 989–991
learning disabled children, 311–312
mentally retarded persons, 145–146
pervasive developmental disorders, 257–262
schizophrenia, 1547–1548, 1559, 1575, 1583
See also Family environment as factor; Family therapy
Family relationships
pedophilia, 621
Family role in treatment
alcoholism, 1115, 1133–1134, 1139
anorexia nervosa, 479, 502
atypical psychosis assessment, 1702–1703
authorization, 987
autistic disorder, 249–266
brief reactive psychosis, 1681
bulimia nervosa, 528, 548
cardiac disease with organic mental syndromes, 900
dementia, 830
drug abuse behavior therapy, 1442
factitious disorder with physical symptoms, 2163
hepatic disease assessment, 935
induced psychotic disorder, 1694–1697
mood disorders, 1885–1890
pervasive developmental disorders, 183, 194, 200, 249–266
reactive attachment disorder of infancy, 740, 741, 743–744
schizoid disorder, 756–757
schizophrenia, 1548
schizophreniform disorder, 1660–1661, 1663–1665
sensory impairment assessment, 954
sexual sadomasochism, 651
stroke, 876
Tourette's syndrome, 698–699

Family role in treatment (cont)
  transvestic fetishism, 646
  See also Family therapy; Parent role
    in treatment; Sibling role in
    treatment
Family support groups
  for families of alcoholics, 1091, 1115–
    1116, 1120, 1160, 1161, 1399,
    1401, 1411
  for families of substance abusers,
    1316, 1378, 1399
  for families of the mentally ill, 1543,
    1548, 1560, 1563
  See also Mutual-help services for
    youth; Self-help and mutual aid
    groups for adults; names of
    specific organizations
Family systems theory
  alcoholism, 1112–1113
  schizophrenia, 1545
Family therapy
  adjustment disorders, 2566–2578
  alcoholism
    family-oriented diagnosis, 1112
    family systems therapy, 1114–1115
    indications for, 1111–1113
    literature review, 1116–1117
    methods, 1113–1116
    social network therapy, 1115
  anorexia nervosa
    assessment of family, 494–498
    background, 491–492
    communication techniques, 503–
      504
    environment and attitudes as
      factors, 493–496
    evaluation, 508
    family commitment and
      expectations, 498
    family structures and processes,
      497–498
    family transmission of eating
      disorders, 492
    guidelines, 500–507
    indications for, 498–499
    paradoxical techniques, 506–507
    prescriptive techniques, 504–506
    problems, 507
    prudent approach, 502–503
    psychoeducation, 503
    rationale, 461, 463, 492–494
    stress reactions, 493–494
    therapeutic interventions, 503–507
    treatment goals and strategies,
      500–501
  anxiety disorders of childhood or
    adolescence, 411–412, 421–423
  avoidant disorder of childhood, 439–
    441
  bulimia nervosa
    background, 543–545
    evaluation, 548
    family assessment, 546
    indications for, 546–547
    rationale, 545–546
    strategies for family intervention,
      547–548
    treatment goals, 547
  conduct disorder, 385–386
  dementia, 830
  elective mutism, 769–771
  fetishism, 639
  identity disorder, 791
  immature personality disorders, 774,
    775, 776, 778, 779, 781, 782
  induced psychotic disorder, 1696
  mood disorders, 1885–1890
    in children and adolescents, 1953
    inpatient family intervention (IFI),
      1887, 1889
    major depression, 1817
  organic aggressive syndrome, 847–
    848
  organic personality syndrome, 860
  overanxious disorder of childhood,
    431–433
  personality disorders, 2637, 2648,
    2652, 2660–2666, 2695
    antisocial personality disorder,
      2665, 2666, 2746
    avoidant personality disorder,
      2762

borderline personality disorder,
2665, 2666, 2753, 2759
duration of treatment, 2665
histrionic personality disorder,
2734–2735
indications and contraindications,
2665–2666
narcissistic personality disorder,
2740–2741, 2742
obsessive compulsive personality
disorder, 2778–2779
paranoid personality disorder,
2710
schizoid personality disorder,
2665, 2666, 2716–2717
and psychoanalysis, 2664
pyromania, 2471
reactive attachment disorder of
infancy, 740, 743–744
and residential treatment, 2690, 2699
schizoaffective disorder, 1656
schizoid disorder of childhood or
adolescence, 757–759
schizophrenia
cost effectiveness, 1555
crisis intervention, 1546–1547,
1553, 1559
expressed emotion and communication deviance, 1552–1557
family consultation, 1561, 1563,
1567
family systems therapy, 1545, 1564
home-based, 1554–1555, 1562
multiple relatives' group
intervention, 1553–1554, 1562–
1563, 1575, 1576
phase-oriented, 1557–1567
principles of, 1565–1567
procedures, 1564–1565
psychoeducational strategies,
1552, 1561, 1575
relapse prevention, 1503, 1557,
1560–1563, 1575–1576
and social skills training, 1555–
1557, 1575–1576

supportive, 1561–1562, 1563–1564
survival skills workshop, 1556,
1561–1562
treatment assignment, 1557–1559,
1567
schizophreniform disorder, 1656,
1663–1665
separation anxiety disorder of
childhood, 421–423
sexual sadomasochism, 651
somatoform pain disorder, 2135
Tourette's syndrome, 699
trichotillomania, 2485–2486
See also Family role in treatment;
Family therapy in substance
abuse; Marital therapy
Family therapy in substance abuse
aftercare, 1416
cannabis abuse and dependence,
1258
drug-free state, establishing and
maintaining
abstinence achievement, 1399–
1400
family participation, 1401
hospitalization, 1400
intervention technique, 1400–1401
patient history, 1398–1399
efficacy, 1397–1398
ethnicity as factor, 1412–1413
family readjustment, 1416
integrated approach
behavior therapy, 1406
Bowen's system, 1406
countertransference, 1404–1405
family dysfunctions, diagnosis,
1403
family of origin technique, 1405
genogram, 1403
psychodynamic therapy, 1404–
1405
resistance, 1405
structural-strategic therapy, 1403–
1404
techniques, overview, 1403–1406
life-cycle phase of family, 1411, 1415

Family therapy in substance abuse
(cont)
　schizophrenic drug abusers, 1420
　sex as factor, 1416
　structural techniques
　　actualization, 1408
　　balancing and unbalancing, 1410
　　boundaries, 1409
　　contingency contracting, 1407
　　cotherapy, 1410–1411
　　intensity creation, 1410
　　joining, 1407, 1408
　　maintenance, 1407–1408
　　mimesis, 1408
　　paradox, 1410
　　reframing, 1409
　　self-esteem enhancement, 1408
　　task assignment, 1409
　　tracking, 1408
　variations for different needs
　　absent families, 1414–1415
　　depression in family members,
　　　1415
　　disintegrated, enmeshed, and
　　　functional families, 1414
　　family reactivity, 1413–1415
　　female substance abusers, 1416
　　modification by drug type, 1411–
　　　1412
　　peer group approaches, 1415
Family with an alcoholic member, 1112
　See also Adult children of alcoholics;
　　Children of alcoholics; Families
　　of alcoholics; Family problems;
　　Parent role in alcoholism
Fantasy absence problems, 2457, 2461
Fear of castration. See Castration
　anxiety
Feces smearing in mental retardation,
　43–44
Feedback for trichotillomania, 2484
Feedback with behavior therapy for
　personality disorders, 2650, 2657
Female dyspareunia
　causes, 2243–2244, 2292
　and depression, 2254

DSM-III-R diagnostic criteria, 2291
　and inhibited female sexual
　　response, 2284
　psychological reactions, 2293
　tests for physical causes, 2243–2244
Female sexual arousal disorder
　added in DSM-III-R to replace
　　inhibited sexual excitement,
　　2237, 2283
　aging and responsivity, 2280
　case history, 2286–2290
　defined, 2282–2283
　DSM-III-R inclusion of psychic
　　component, 2283
　excitement and orgasm phases in
　　women, 2279–2280
　menstrual cycle and responsivity,
　　2282
　physical causes, 2242, 2283–2284
　prevalence, 2283–2284
　psychological causes, 2284
　tests for physical problems, 2242
Fenfluramine
　autistic disorder, 232, 245, 246–247
Fenoterol
　side effects, 944
Fertility drugs
　potential effects on offspring, 2359
　sexual effects, 2355
Fetishism, 633–646
　characteristics, 636–637
　definition, 636
　etiology, 634–636, 638
　in pedophilia, 619
　treatment, 636, 637–640
　　aversion therapy, 639
　　behavior therapy, 639, 2653
　　biological therapy, 637–638
　　doubts about self-report, 637, 639
　　pharmacotherapy, 637–638
　　psychotherapy, 638–639
Fetor hepaticus as sign of hepatic
　disease, 935
Finney flexi-rod penile prosthesis,
　2332, 2333

Fire-setting in impulse control disorders not elsewhere classified, 2457, 2460, 2461, 2468–2473

Fisher-Logeman Test of Articulation Competence, 344

Flagyl. *See* Metronidazole

Flapping tremor. *See* Asterixis

Flashbacks
cannabis abuse and dependence, 1249
hallucinogen abuse, 1208
in stress-related disorders, 2536, 2540

Flexible System for diagnosis of schizophrenia, 1500

Flooding
agoraphobia, 2029–2032
avoidant personality disorder, 2761
obsessive compulsive personality disorder, 2780
simple phobias, 2026–2027
social phobias, 2028
See also Behavior therapy; Exposure treatment

Fludrocortisone
orthostatic hypotension, 903

Fluency disorders, developmental
description, 315–316
evaluation, 339–341
parent-child interaction, 339–340
phonetic errors, 345
stuttering, 316–317, 345–346
tensions as factor, 346

Fluid imbalance and delirium, 806

Fluoxetine
classification, 1774
effects on cardiovascular system, 903, 904–905
and monoamine oxidase inhibitors, 1785, 1787
obsessive compulsive disorder, 708, 709, 2102
pharmacokinetics, 1775, 1776, 1777, 1779–1781
premature ejaculation, 2357
and specific medical diseases, 1782, 1783, 1784
in treatment nonresponders, 1798

Fluphenazine
autistic disorder, 242
bipolar disorders, 1929
and dystonia, 1512
organic mood syndrome, 856
in patients with lung disease, 946
schizoaffective disorder, 1675
schizophrenia, 1509
secondary depression, 1924
sex drive reduction, 2356
Tourette's syndrome, 690, 705, 706

Fluphenazine decanoate
delusional (paranoid) disorders, 1629
late paraphrenia, 1641
schizophrenia, 1506

Fluphenazine enanthate
schizophrenia, 1506

Fluphenazine esters
and depressive mood changes, 1514

Flurazepam
insomnia in opioid detoxification, treatment, 1318
as sedative-hypnotic agent, 90

Fluvoxamine and fluoxetine for obsessive compulsive disorder, 2102

Focal cerebral epilepsy. *See* Epilepsy

Folic acid deficiency
and organic delusional syndrome, 836, 837

Folic acid treatment of fragile X syndrome, 42

Folie à deux
clinical subtypes, 1687–1688
cults, 1692
definition, 1686
heredity, 1689
between mother and child, 1691

Folie à douze, 1688
See also Induced psychotic disorder

Folie à famille, 1688, 1693
treatment, 1696

Folie à famille *(cont)*
See also Induced psychotic disorder
Folie à pleusirs, 1688
See also Induced psychotic disorder
Folie à quatre, 1688
See also Induced psychotic disorder
Folie à trois, 1688
See also Induced psychotic disorder
Folie collective, 1693
See also Induced psychotic disorder
Follicle-stimulating hormone
transvestic fetishism, 635
Food and Drug Administration (FDA)
non-approval of medroxyprogesterone acetate for sex
offenders, 630
oxazepam administration, 945
Forensic psychiatry
kleptomania, 2466
multiple personality disorder, 2215–
2216
Fort Steilacom, Washington, treatment
of sexual offenders, 625
Fountain House-Sears program, 1573
Four-Factor Theory of Etiology, 2202
Fragile X syndrome in mental
retardation
age as factor, 40
autistic disorder, 40–41
behavioral characteristics, 40
description, 39–42
diagnosis, 42
folic acid treatment, 42
physical abnormalities, 39, 41–42
sex as factor, 41
speech and language dysfunctions,
40
Frontalis muscle feedback. See
Biofeedback training
Frontal lobe syndrome, 845
Fugues, epilepsy-related, 880
Fulminating hepatic failure, 932
See also Hepatic disease
Functional encopresis
assessment, 725
DSM-III-R diagnostic criteria, 723

epidemiology, 724
etiology, 724–725
factors associated with treatment
failure, 726
history and definition, 723–724
toilet training effects, 724
treatment, 725–726
Functional enuresis
definition, 717
diagnosis and assessment, 721
DSM-III-R diagnostic criteria, 717
epidemiology, 718
etiology, 718–721
genetic factors, 718–719, 2423
history, 717
and parasomnias in children, 2423–
2424
physical factors, 719–720
and pyromania, 2469
sex differences, 718
social factors, 720
stressful life events effect, 720
subclassification, 718
toilet training effects, 720
treatment, 721–723
Furosemide
auditory effects, 958
interaction with other drugs, 914,
927
renal disease, 925

Galactosemia and liver
transplantation, 933
Galvanic skin response (GSR)
pedophilia, 629
Gamblers Anonymous, 2464, 2465,
2466
Gambling. See Pathologic gambling
Gamma-aminobutyric acid (GABA)
benzodiazepine complex, 2041–2042
dementia of the Alzheimer's type,
973, 978

Gang behavior
impulse control disorders not
elsewhere classified, 2460
mutual-help services for youth, 2613
Ganglionic blockers and retarded
ejaculation, 2243
Ganser's syndrome, 2165
See also Factitious disorder, with
psychological symptoms
Gastrointestinal disease and
antidepressant drugs, 1782, 1874
Gate control theory of pain relief, 2132
Gates-MacGinitie Reading Tests, 330
Gates-McKillop-Horowitz Reading
Diagnostic Tests, 330
Geigy Laboratories
imipramine development, 1734, 1737
Gelastic epilepsy. *See* Epilepsy, partial
seizures
Gender ambiguity psychosis, 641
Gender as factor. *See* Sex as factor
Gender dysphoria
childhood gender identity disorder,
669
transvestic fetishism, 638, 640, 641–
642, 644, 645–646
See also Transsexualism
Gender identity
potential effects of sex-affecting
drugs on offspring, 2359
and sexual motivation, 2267
Gender identity boards, 656
Gender identity disorders, 615–683
of childhood, 661–670
and low sexual motivation, 2274–
2275
Gender identity formation, 656–657
Gender orientation, 2252–2253
potential effects of sex-affecting
drugs on offspring, 2359
Gender reassignment, transsexualism,
658, 659
General anesthesia
epilepsy, 890
Generalized anxiety disorder
behavior therapy, 2034–2035
biofeedback training, 2034, 2053

psychoanalytic theory, 2012–2015
relaxation training, 2034–2035
Generalized seizures. *See* Epilepsy,
generalized seizures
Genetic counseling
autistic disorder, 256–257, 264–265
Genetic history of families of anorectic
patients, 496
Genetic predisposition
alcoholism, 1096, 1114
enuresis, 2423
mood disorders
bipolar disorders, 1935, 1937
familial bipolar disorder, 1761
sleepwalking, 2422
stimulant abuse, 1227
Genetic syndromes
Down's syndrome, 30–32
fragile X syndrome, 39–42
Lesch-Nyhan syndrome, 37–38
Prader-Willi syndrome, 50–51
Genital character type of personality
disorders, 2640
Gentamycin
auditory effects, 958
Geophagia, 586, 588
Geriatric patients
organic mental syndromes, 800–803,
994–1008
Gestalt group therapy for alcoholism,
1121
Global Assessment Scale, 693, 695,
1617
Glomerulonephritis
and renal disease, 920
Glutamic acid decarboxylase (GAD)
dementia of the Alzheimer's type,
978
Glycogen storage disease and liver
transplantation, 933
Glycopyrrolate and electroconvulsive
therapy, 1808, 1811
Goldman-Fristoe Test of Articulation,
344
Gonorrheal infections and ejaculatory
pain, 2293

Good prognosis schizophrenia, 1672
  See also Schizoaffective disorder
Graded exposure
  avoidant personality disorder, 2761
Grafenberg spot, 2286
Grandiose delusions and stroke, 874
Grandiosity in obsessive compulsive
      disorder, 2110
Gray-Oral Reading Test, 330
Grief
  distinguished from posttraumatic
      stress disorder, 2069–2070
  pharmacotherapy, 2586
Group psychoses
  differential diagnosis, 1688
  in hallucinogen abuse, 1208
Group therapy
  adjustment disorders, 2578–2585
  alcoholism
      benefits, 1102, 1117–1119
      outcome issues, 1123–1125
      types, 1119–1122
  anorexia nervosa, 508–510
  anorgasmic women, 2290
  avoidant disorder of childhood, 434
  Briquet's syndrome, 2168
  bulimia nervosa, 525–526, 549–555
      alternative behaviors, 554
      cognitive restructuring, 554
      controlled treatment trials, 550–
          552
      establishing eating patterns, 553
      logistics of therapy, 552
      psychoeducation, 553
      self-help groups, 549–550
      treatment components, 553–555
  cannabis abuse and dependence,
      1258–1259
  exhibitionism, 673
  fetishism, 639
  hypochondriasis, limitations, 2144
  identity disorder, 791
  impulse control disorders not
      elsewhere classified, 2462
  mentally retarded persons, 110–111
  mood disorders, 1729

  depressive disorders, 1732, 1817,
      1857
  multiple personality disorder, 2201–
      2202
  nurse support groups, 2581, 2582,
      2583, 2584, 2585
  pedophilia, 621, 623, 625, 628, 631–
      632
  personality disorders, 2648, 2652,
      2667–2678, 2695
    available evidence, 2668
    avoidant personality disorder,
        2761–2762
    borderline personality disorder,
        2668, 2673–2674, 2741, 2753–
        2754, 2759
    combined with individual
        psychotherapy, 2667, 2676, 2677
    controversies, 2677
    dependent personality disorder,
        2675, 2769
    duration of treatment, 2669
    effectiveness, 2668–
    goals of treatment, 2669–2670
    histrionic personality disorder,
        2671–2672, 2717, 2734
    indications and contraindications,
        2676
    narcissistic personality disorder,
        2741
    obsessive compulsive personality
        disorder, 2675, 2717, 2779
    paranoid personality disorder,
        2670–2671, 2710
    passive-aggressive personality
        disorder, 2675, 2788
    in residential treatment, 2690
    schizoid personality disorder,
        2671, 2717–2718
    schizotypal personality disorder,
        2671, 2725
  physical illness groups, 2579, 2581,
      2583, 2584, 2585
  posttraumatic stress disorder, 2081
  premature ejaculation, 2307
  principles, 1532

reactive attachment disorder of
infancy, 741–742
schizoid disorder of childhood or
adolescence, 759
schizophrenia, 1529–1543
assignment strategies, 1537–1538
benefits, 1531
comparison of social learning and
interaction-oriented, 1540–1541,
1542
evaluation studies, 1533–1535
functions of, 1532–1533
guidelines, 1535–1537
insight-oriented, 1533, 1537
interaction-oriented, 1534–1535,
1536, 1538, 1539–1542, 1543
overstimulation, 1530–1531, 1536,
1539
procedures, 1538–1542
social learning, 1530, 1534, 1535,
1536, 1537, 1538, 1542, 1543
sources of change, 1533
treatment planning considerations,
1530–1531
schizophreniform disorder, 1658,
1662, 1665
self-help and mutual aid groups,
2596–2607, 2607–2616
sexual sadomasochism, 651, 652
smoking, 1279
somatization disorder, 2168
special training and qualifications of
therapists, 2676
stress management, 2578–2585
voyeurism, 673
See also Psychotherapy
GROW, self-helf group, 2598, 2604
GSR. *See* Galvanic skin response
Guanabenz
interaction with other drugs, 1782
Guanadrel
interaction with other drugs, 1777,
1782
Guanethidine
interaction with other drugs, 912–
913, 914, 928, 1777, 1782, 1783

neuropsychiatric effects, 911–912
side effects, 876
Guilt feelings of parents
anorexia nervosa patients, 459, 493,
499
learning-disabled children, 311–312
maternal guilt in rumination, 575
maternal guilt in separation anxiety,
413
mentally retarded persons, 101
paternal guilt in separation anxiety,
419–420
schizophrenics, 1547–1548
Guilt feelings of patient
adjustment disorders, 2574
drug abusers in therapeutic
communities, 1382
fetishism, 638
impulse control disorders not
elsewhere classified, 2459, 2461
overanxious disorder of childhood,
429–430
rumination, 577
unhealthy religious groups, 2594,
2595
Gynecomastia
and alcoholic liver disease, 933
and hepatic disease, 935

Habit reversal and Tourette's
syndrome, 701, 702
Hair pulling. *See* Trichotillomania
Haldol. *See* Haloperidol
Half-way houses. *See* Residential
treatment programs;
Therapeutic communities for
substance abuse
Hallucinations
and acute porphyria, 932
from anticholinergic drugs, 958
from antineoplastic drugs, 944
from antituberculosis agents, 944
from asthma drugs, 943, 944

Hallucinations *(cont)*
  and atypical psychosis, 1699, 1702, 1704
  and brief reactive psychosis, 1678
  and cycloid psychosis, 1708
  and delirium, 804, 805, 811
  and digitalis toxicity, 908
  and epilepsy, 878, 880, 881, 883, 884
  and hepatic disease, 934, 935
  and induced psychotic disorder, 1690, 1691
  and infective endocarditis, 896
  and lung disease, 847, 941, 942
  and multi-infarct dementia, 964
  and Parkinson's disease, 863
  and postpartum psychosis, 1707
  and schizoaffective disorder, 1667, 1671, 1672
  with sensory impairment, 949, 950, 951, 953
  side effect of clonidine, 911
  side effect of phenytoin, 910
  side effect of procainamide, 910
  side effect of propranolol, 908
  side effect of reserpine, 910
  and systemic lupus erythematosus, 952
  See also Organic hallucinosis
Hallucinogen abuse
  age as factor, 1204
  anxiety, 1208, 1373
  brain damage, 1209
  and cannabis use, 1244
  chromosomal damage, 1209
  cognitive effects, 1205
  complications, 1206–1209
  convulsions, 1209
  detoxification, 1209
  diagnosis, 1206
  dysphoria, 1206
  electroconvulsive shock therapy, 1207
  emotional responses, 1205
  flashbacks, 1208
  laboratory tests, 1206
  neurologic reactions, 1209

  and organic delusional syndrome, 833
  and organic hallucinosis, 833
  paranoid disorder, shared, 1208–1209
  paranoid state, acute, 1207
  pharmacotherapy, 1208
  physiologic effects, 1204
  and psychiatric problems, 1204
  psychological effects, 1205
  psychosis induction, 1206, 1371, 1372
  psychosocial aspects, 1204
  psychotomimetic reactions
    acute, 1206–1207
    chronic, 1207–1209
  schizophrenic reactions, 1207
  and secondary depression, 1207
  symptoms, 1204–1205
  See also Therapeutic communities for substance abuse
Hallucinogen delusional disorder. *See* Organic delusional syndrome
Hallucinogen hallucinosis. *See* Organic hallucinosis
Hallucinogenic drugs
  autistic disorder, 235
  classification, 1203–1204
  and organic aggressive syndrome, 852
  and organic delusional syndrome, 832, 833, 834
  and organic hallucinosis, 833
  See also Hallucinogen abuse; names of specific drugs
Hallucinosis. *See* Organic hallucinosis
Haloperidol
  autistic disorder, 184, 226, 233–234, 242–243, 248
  borderline personality disorder, 2681, 2682
  cannabis abuse effects, 1249, 1252
  conduct disorder, 387
  conduct disorders, aggressive type, 234

delirium, 809, 810, 814
dementia and amnestic syndromes,
    826–827
drug-induced psychosis, 943
and dystonia, 1512
effect on IQ, 184
effect on seizures, 839
and ejaculatory pain, 2317
and electroconvulsive therapy, 1811
extrapyramidal symptoms, 810
interaction with other drugs, 914,
    915, 928
mentally retarded persons, 75–76
mood disorders, 1736
    acute manic episode, 1741
    bipolar disorders, 1928
neurotransmitter blockade, 1776
organic delusional syndrome, 838
organic mood syndrome, 856
Parkinson's disease, 865
in patients with lung disease, 946
phencyclidine-induced delirium,
    1215
premature ejaculation, 2309, 2357
rumination, 574
schizoaffective disorder, 1673, 1674,
    1675
schizoid disorder, 760
schizophrenia, 1509
schizotypal personality disorder,
    2682–2683
side effects, 706, 810, 947
stroke, 874, 875
tardive or withdrawal dyskinesias,
    234, 243
Tourette's syndrome, 690, 697, 705–
    706, 707, 709
weight gain as side effect, 245
Haloperidol decanoate
schizophrenia, 1506
Halothane
epilepsy, 890
and secondary depression, 1912,
    1913
Halstead-Reitan category subtest,
    1092

Halstead-Reitan neuropsychological
    test battery, 1071
Hamilton Rating Scale for Depression
    alcoholism, 1919
    chronic pain, 2125
    dysthymia, 1942
    mood disorders, 1733, 1788, 1789,
        1871, 1922
    seasonal affective disorder, 1891
Handicaps, legal definition, 347
Hand waving. *See* Stereotyped
    behaviors, abnormal
Headaches, biofeedback, 2150
Head banging, 2424
    in mentally retarded persons, 32, 33
    See also Stereotyped behaviors,
        abnormal
Head injury
    and amnestic syndromes, 819
    and brief reactive psychosis, 1680
    and delirium, 806
    differential diagnosis, 1701
    and epilepsy, 885, 890
    and organic aggressive syndrome,
        842
    and organic personality syndrome,
        840, 859
    and psychogenic fugue, 2194
    and sensory impairment, 952, 953
    See also Brain damage
Head weaving in mentally retarded
    persons, 32, 33
Health maintenance organizations, 982
Health professionals, opioid
        dependence, naltrexone
        treatment, 1335–1336
Heart disease. *See* Cardiovascular
    disease
Hebephilia and exhibitionism, 671
Hebephrenic subtype of schizophrenia,
    1498
Helper therapy principle in mutual
        help groups, 2599, 2603
"Helping" relationship in substance
        abuse, development by
        therapist, 1424–1425

Hemangiomas and epilepsy, 886
Hemianopia and stroke, 868
Hemiparesis and stroke, 868
Hemisensory loss and stroke, 868
Hemochromatosis and liver
        transplantation, 933
Hemodialysis
    lithium excretion, 906
    lithium intoxication, 1931
    schizophrenia treatment, 1502
Hepatic disease
    and alcoholism, 932–933, 934
    clinical stages, 931
    and delirium, 806, 811
    and dementia, 820
    differential diagnosis, 934–935
    and epilepsy, 885
    etiology, 931–934
    impending hepatic coma (precoma),
        930–931, 934
    and organic mental syndromes, 930–
        939
    patient evaluation, 935–936
    prodromal symptoms, 930, 931
    and sexual disorders, 2241
    stupor and coma, 931
    treatment, 936–938, 939
        pharmacological precautions, 937–
        938
    Wilson's disease, 933–935
Hepatic necrosis and neuroleptic
        drugs, 1514
Hepatitis
    and chronic hepatic failure, 932
    and nonresponsiveness to
        antidepressant treatment, 1792
    precautions for drug addicts,
        hospital treatment, 1362, 1365
    with secondary depression, 854,
        1902
Heredofamilial psychoses, 2712
Heroin addiction
    life expectancy, 1328
    naltrexone treatment, 1337–1338
    prevalence, 1309
    reinforcement, 1312–1313

treatment programs, 1325–1326
    withdrawal, 1311–1312
    See also Opioid abuse and
        dependence
Herpes
    and dyspareunia, 2292, 2293
    and fulminating hepatic failure, 932
    and sensory impairment, 952
    and viral hepatitis, 932
Herstedvester, antisocial personality
        disorder treatment, 2748
Heterocyclic antidepressant drugs
    efficacy, 1738
    interaction with other drugs, 912–
        913
    mood disorders, 1729
        bipolar disorders, 1758, 1927,
        1934, 1935, 1936
    in pregnant patients, 1931
    See also Antidepressant drugs; names
        of specific drugs
Heterosexual pedophilia, 617, 618, 627
    in adolescents, 621
    pharmacotherapy, 630
    place of offense, 620
    psychotherapy, 631
    recidivism, 619, 627, 632
Hexobendine
    multi-infarct dementia, 963
High-intensity transition in stimulant
        abuse, 1226–1227
High School Senior Survey, marijuana
        use, 1242
Hispanic sexuality, 2381–2383
Histamine blockade
    antidepressant drugs, 1777
The History of the Psychoanalytic
        Movement, 1825
Histrionic personality disorder
    behavior therapy, 2657, 2735
    and bipolar disorder not otherwise
        specified, 1758
    countertransference, 2731
    and dependent personality disorder,
        2763
    diagnostic criteria, 2727–2729

and hypochondriasis, 2736
limitation of available research
    material, 2636
and mood disorders, 2685
pharmacotherapy, 2735–2736
psychotherapy, 2642, 2729–2735
    brief therapies, 2733
    family therapy, 2734–2735
    group therapy, 2671–2672, 2717,
    2734
    marital therapy, 2735
    psychoanalytic psychotherapy,
    2646, 2729–2733
    short-term anxiety provoking
    psychotherapy, 2733–2734
    residential treatment, 2736
    resistance, 2697
and secondary depression, 2735,
    2736
sex as factor, 2728
transference, 2729, 2731
Holding, 2012
Holistic treatment of language
    problems in children, 342–343,
    346
Holter monitoring during lithium
    therapy, 906
Homatropine
    with a sensory-impaired patient, 958
Home-based family management
    infants of adolescent mothers, 2370
    schizophrenia, 1554–1555, 1562
Homework with behavior therapy for
    personality disorders, 2657
Homosexuality
    and aging, 2374
    and childhood gender identity
    disorder, 662, 669
    dropped from DSM, 2237, 2252
    and sexual disorders, 2383–2384
    transvestic fetishism, 640, 641, 642
Homosexual pedophilia, 617, 618, 627
    in adolescents, 621
    pharmacotherapy, 630
    place of offense, 620
    psychotherapy, 631

recidivism, 619, 627, 632
Homovanillic acid
    and dementia of the Alzheimer's
    type, 974
    and multi-infarct dementia, 962
Hong Kong addict study for
    methadone maintenance
    treatment, 1343
Hopkins Symptom Checklist for
    somatic symptoms, 2151
Hormonal aspects of sexual function
    and dysfunction, 2388–2390,
    2392–2393
Hormonal therapy
    pedophilia, 623, 628
    transsexualism, 656, 658, 659
Horrific temptations in obsessive
    compulsive disorder, 2096
Hospital Anxiety and Depression
    Scale, 2125
Hospital treatment
    adjustment disorders of adulthood
    and old age, 2510
    alcoholism, 1102, 1137–1143
    anorexia nervosa, 455–462, 479–481,
    501–502
    atypical impulse control disorder,
    2480
    bulimia nervosa, 520–523
    crisis intervention, 2529
    detoxification, 1137–1139
    mood disorders
    efficacy, 1887
    multiple personality disorder, 2209
    pathologic gambling, 2465
    psychogenic amnesia, 2187
    rumination, 574–576
    schizophrenia, 1569, 1576–1578
    See also Hospital treatment for drug
    addiction
Hospital treatment for drug addiction
    admission procedures, 1361–1363
    antisocial behavior, 1374
    anxiety disorders, 1373–1374, 1376
    borderline personality disorders,
    1374

Hospital treatment for drug addiction *(cont)*

cannabis abuse and dependence, 1256

conduct disorders, 1374

depressive disorders, 1368–1370

diagnosis, 1363–1367

endocrine abnormalities, 1366

family patterns, 1377

in family therapy, 1400

laboratory tests, 1364

mania, 1371–1372

manic symptoms produced by drug abuse, 1371

medical complications, 1360, 1364, 1365, 1366

motivation for treatment, 1378

panic disorders, 1373–1374, 1376

patients

    activity, 1378

    assessment and evaluation, 1360

    resistance to medication, 1375

personality disorders, 1374, 1376

precautions

    AIDS, 1363, 1365

    hepatitis, 1362, 1365

    overdosing potential, 1363

    withdrawal, 1362

pregnancy complications, 1366–1367

psychiatric evaluation, 1367–1368

psychotic disorders, 1371, 1372, 1375–1376

schizophrenia in addicts, 1372

stimulant abuse, 1236

treatment

    addiction, 1377–1378

    peer group formation, 1377

    pharmacotherapy, 1374–1375

    psychiatric illness in addicts, 1374–1377

    psychotherapy, 1377

urine tests, 1361

Human immunodeficiency virus (HIV)

differential diagnosis, 1701

See also Acquired immunodeficiency syndrome

Human Sexual Inadequacy, 2264, 2338

Huntington's disease

and depression, 854

and nonresponsiveness to antidepressant treatment, 1792

and organic delusional syndrome, 836

and organic personality syndrome, 858

Huxley Institute for research on nutrition and mental health, 2605

Hydergine

dementia, 829

Hydralazine

interaction with other drugs, 913

neuropsychiatric effects, 912

and orthostatic hypotension, 928

Hydrazines

hepatic disease, 937

Hydrocephalus

and dementia, 825

Hydrochlorothiazide

and secondary depression, 908

Hydroxychloroquine

ocular effects, 958

L-5-Hydroxytryptophan

mood disorders, 1800

Hydroxyzine

alcohol withdrawal, 1087

anxiety disorders, 2047

mentally retarded persons, 88

secondary depression, 1904

Hyperactive sexual desire or arousal

case studies, 2276–2278

causes, 2270

not included in DSM, 2237, 2248, 2276

pharmacotherapy consideration for sexual disorders, 2359

Hyperactivity

anxiolytic drugs, contraindications, 86

from asthma drugs, 943

and delirium, 811

imipramine effect, 239

and learning disabilities, 310–311

and mental retardation, 7, 20, 120

neuroleptic drugs effect, 245
stimulants effect, 241
See also Attention-deficit
hyperactivity disorder
Hyperadrenalism with secondary
depression, 1902, 1909
Hyperadrenocorticalism
and organic mood syndrome, 853,
854, 855
and secondary depression, 854
and secondary mania, 854
Hyperaesthetic personality, 2759
Hypercalcemia
diagnosis, 799
and digitalis toxicity, 907
and lung disease, 943
and organic mood syndrome, 855
and secondary depression, 854
Hypercapnia and lung disease, 939,
940, 945
Hypercortisolemia with secondary
depression, 1909
Hyperekplexias, 692
Hyperglycemia from renal disease, 916
Hyperhidrosis and Parkinson's
disease, 861
Hyperinsulinism and secondary
depression, 1902
Hyperlipidemia and multi-infarct
dementia, 962
Hypernatremia and organic mental
syndrome, 898–899
Hyperparathyroidism
differential diagnosis, 1701
and organic mood syndrome, 855
from renal disease, 916
with secondary depression, 854,
1902, 1909
Hyperphagia. *See* Prader-Willi
syndrome
Hyperprolactinemia, pharmacotherapy, 833
Hyperreflexia and delirium, 812
Hypersexuality, pharmacotherapy,
637–640
Hypersomnia disorders. *See*
Narcolepsy; Sleep apnea

Hypertension
and brief reactive psychosis, 1680
and dementia, 826
and electroconvulsive therapy, 1806
and impotence, 2319
and multi-infarct dementia, 962
and organic aggressive syndrome,
852
and organic mental syndromes, 895,
896, 897
and renal disease, 916, 918, 920
and secondary depression, 1729
side effect of clonidine, 911
and stroke, 867, 868, 869, 876
treatment, 846
Hypertension Detection and Follow-
Up Program Cooperative
Group, 847
Hyperthermia
and brief reactive psychosis, 1680
and delirium, 807–808, 811
Hyperthyroidism
and dementia, 821
differential diagnosis, 1701
and mania, 854
and organic mood syndrome, 853,
854, 855
and personality disorders, 2656
with secondary depression, 854,
1902, 1909
Hyperuricemia from renal disease, 916
Hypervitaminosis with secondary
depression, 1902
Hypnosis
anxiety disorders, 2052–2053, 2055–
2056, 2063–2065
case histories, 2057–2063
patient-therapist relationship, 2055
conversion disorders, 2156–2157
cultural perspective and effectiveness of treatment, 2055
jet lag, 2443
multiple personality disorder, 2202,
2203, 2204, 2205–2209, 2212

Hypnosis *(cont)*
  obsessive compulsive personality
     disorder, 2774
  outcome studies, 2063–2064
  pain, chronic, somatoform, 2131–
     2132
  psychogenic amnesia, 2187–2188
  psychogenic fugue, 2195
  rape trauma syndrome, 2061–2063
  relationship of hypnotizability to
     efficacy, 2063–2064
  sexual disorders, 2362
  smoking, 1277–1278, 1279
  transvestic fetishism, 644
  trichotillomania, 2483, 2485, 2486
  vaginismus, 2297
Hypnotic drugs
  alcohol withdrawal delirium, 1087
  delirium, 809
  dementia, 828–829
  hepatic disease, 937
  insomnia, 2430
  interaction with other drugs, 915
  organic aggressive syndrome, 850,
     852
  organic delusional syndrome, 838
  sexual effects, 2344
  side effects, 850
  uncomplicated bereavement, 1743
  See also names of specific drugs
Hypnotic-sedative drugs
  delirium, 812
Hypoactive sexual desire
  case studies, 2271–2276
  causes, 2269–2270
  cultural impact, 2275
  diagnosis, 2269–2270
  lifelong low sexual desire, 2275–2276
  organic conditions, 2271–2272
  psychological levels, 2245
  relationship problems, 2272–2274
  sexual identity, 2274–2275
  situational, 2270
  treatment, 2271–2276
  treatment effectiveness, 2278–2279

Hypoadrenalism
  and nonresponsiveness to
     antidepressant treatment, 1792
  with secondary depression, 1902
Hypoadrenocorticalism
  and depression, 854
  and organic mood syndrome, 853,
     854, 855
Hypoalbuminemia and renal disease,
     922, 923
Hypocalcemia
  and epilepsy, 885
  and secondary mania, 1914
  visual changes, 949
Hypochondriasis
  and anxiety, 2139, 2145
  definition, 2138
  and depression, 2138, 2145
  differential diagnosis, 859, 1751
  disease phobia, 2143
  electroconvulsive shock therapy,
     2145
  etiology, 2139
  exercise, physical, in therapy, 2143
  and grief reaction, 2143
  and histrionic personality disorder,
     2736
  hypochondriacal reaction, 2138
  and narcissistic personality disorder,
     2738
  and organic personality syndrome,
     858
  pain and residual somatic
     symptoms, 2144
  and panic disorder, 2138, 2145
  pharmacotherapy, 2140–2142, 2143,
     2144–2145
  physical examination, 2140
  psychological exploration, 2140–2141
  psychosurgery cautions, 2146
  psychotherapy
    empathy of therapist, 2142–2143
    explanations and information,
      2141–2142
    insight, 2143
    persuasion, 2141

repetition and suggestion, 2142
   session frequency, 2141
   and schizotypal personality disorder,
      2723–2724
   therapeutic alliance, 2142–2143
   therapeutic strategies, 2140, 2144
Hypoglycemia
   and alcohol intoxication, 1082
   and brief reactive psychosis, 1680
   and delirium, 806, 807, 811
   differential diagnosis, 884, 885
   and epilepsy, 885, 889
   and exhibitionism/voyeurism, 671
   and hepatic disease, 936
   and lung disease, 942, 943
   and mood disorders in children and
      adolescents, 1951
   and personality disorders, 2656
   visual changes, 949
Hypokalemia
   and chronic hepatic failure, 932
   and delirium, 811
   and digitalis toxicity, 907
   and hepatic disease, 936
   and organic mental syndrome, 899
   resemblance to lithium side effects,
      905
Hypokinesia and stroke, 871
Hypokinetic syndrome
   and antiparkinsonian drugs, 1512
   and antipsychotic drugs, 1511, 1512
Hypomagnesemia
   and delirium, 811
   and secondary depression, 1902
Hypomania
   and organic mood syndrome, 853,
      854
   in transvestic fetishism, 644
   See also Bipolar disorders
Hypometamorphosis and organic
      personality syndrome, 858
Hyponatremia
   and hepatic disease, 935
   and lung disease, 943
   and organic mental syndrome, 898

Hypoparathyroidism
   differential diagnosis, 861, 1701
   with secondary depression, 1902,
      1909
Hypoperfusion states and brief
      reactive psychosis, 1680
Hypopituitarism and secondary
      depression, 1902
Hypotension
   and delirium, 808
   and Parkinson's disease, 861, 866
   and secondary depression, 1902
   side effect of neuroleptic drugs, 827
   and stroke, 873
Hypotensive drugs and impotence,
      2329
Hypothalamic-pituitary axis
      dysfunction and sexual
      disorders, 2241
Hypothalamus disturbance as factor in
      antisocial behavior, 50
Hypothemic disorder, 1758
   See also Mood disorders, bipolar
      disorders
Hypothermia and hepatic disease, 935
Hypothyroidism
   and dementia, 821
   differential diagnosis, 1701
   and digitalis toxicity, 907
   from lithium, 1930, 1938
   and nonresponsiveness to
      antidepressant treatment, 1792
   and organic delusional syndrome, 837
   and organic mood syndrome, 853,
      854, 855
   with secondary depression, 854,
      1902, 1909
Hypovolemia and renal disease, 920
Hypoxemia
   from antianxiety drugs, 945
   and lung disease, 940, 945
Hypoxia
   and amnestic syndromes, 895
   and brief reactive psychosis, 1680
   and chronic hepatic failure, 932
   and delirium, 807–808, 895

Hypoxia (cont)
    and dementia, 821, 895
    and digitalis toxicity, 907
    extrapyramidal symptoms, 895
    and hyperkinesis, 895
    and lung disease, 939, 940
Hysterectomy, sexual effects, 2374
Hysteria. See Conversion disorders;
        Somatization disorder
Hysteria, chronic. See Somatization
        disorder
Hysterical neuroses, dissociative type.
        See Dissociative disorders
Hysterical personality disorder. See
        Histrionic personality disorder
Hysterical reaction in conversion
        disorders, 2153
Hysterical states and brief reactive
        psychosis, 1683
Hysteroid dysphoria, 1743, 2683, 2685,
        2736
    pharmacotherapy, 2741

Ibuprofen
    interaction with other drugs, 927
Id
    and personality disorders, 2640, 2644
        antisocial personality disorder,
        2743
Idealization
    psychoanalysis of narcissistic
        personality disorder, 2738
Identity disorder
    case studies, 786–787
    diagnosis, 787–788
    distinguished from schizoid disorder
        of childhood or adolescence, 749
    DSM-III-R diagnostic criteria, 785
    etiology, 785–786
    history and definition, 782–783
    prevalence, 783
    recognition in DSM-III, 734, 783
    treatment, 788–791
    See also Gender identity disorders

Identity disturbance in multiple
        personality disorder, 2198
Identity formation, 782–785
    See also Identity disorder
Ideologies of self-help and mutual aid
        groups for adults, 2603
Idiosyncratic intoxication. See Alcohol
        idiosyncratic intoxication
Illinois Test of Psycholinguistic
        Abilities, 330
Illusions in delirium, 804, 805
Imaginal desensitization. See
        Systematic desensitization
Imaginal exposure treatment. See
        Exposure treatment
Imaginal flooding. See Flooding
Imaging techniques
    personality disorders, 2652, 2653,
        2656
Imipramine
    agoraphobia, 2033–2034
    anxiety and panic-related disorders
        in mentally retarded persons, 88
    anxiety disorders, 2047, 2048–2049,
        2050–2051
    autistic disorder, 239
    classification, 1774
    with cognitive-behavioral psycho-
        therapy for mood disorders,
        1839, 1840–1841, 1842, 1843
    dementia, 827, 828
    depression-hypochondriasis
        combination, 2145
    dosage, 1788
    effects on cardiovascular system,
        902, 903, 905
    and ejaculatory pain, 2316
    and electroconvulsive therapy, 1813
    functional enuresis, 722–723
    hyperactivity, 239
    interaction with other drugs, 891,
        928
    and monoamine oxidase inhibitors,
        1785, 1787
    mood disorders, 1733, 1734, 1735,
        1737, 1744, 1793, 1798

in children and adolescents, 1957

dysthymia, 1743, 1942

effectiveness, 1803, 1871

major depression, 1818, 1820, 1821

secondary depression, 946, 1903, 1906, 1907, 1912, 1917, 1919–1920, 1922, 1923–1924

night terrors, 2589

obsessive compulsive disorder, 708, 709, 2103

panic attacks, 2489

personality disorders, 2687

    borderline personality disorder, 2682, 2684

    dependent personality disorder, 2770

    obsessive compulsive personality disorder, 2685

    passive-aggressive personality disorder, 2789

    with secondary depression, 2684

pharmacokinetics, 1779, 1780, 1786

    neurotransmitter blockade, 1776

posttraumatic stress disorder, 2355

rape trauma syndrome, 2355

renal disease, 923, 929

schizoaffective disorder, 1674

schizoid disorder, 760

separation anxiety disorder of childhood, 416–417

sex drive reduction, 2356

sexual anxiety, 2356

sexual effects, 2355–2356

side effects, 239, 723, 948

somatic symptoms, 2151

and specific medical diseases, 946, 1781–1783, 1783, 1784

Immature personality disorders

character structures and, 773

classification, 775

diagnosis in children, 733–734, 749, 750, 772, 781–782

suggested reformulation of personality disorders classification, 733–734, 772

treatment, 774–775, 782

treatment principles, 774

See also names of specific disorders

Immigrant children, proneness to elective mutism, 763, 769, 771

Impaired sexual desire. *See* Hypoactive sexual desire; Sexual desire problems

Implosive therapy

    obsessive compulsive disorder, 2099

    stress management, 2535, 2536

    See also Exposure treatment; Flooding

Impotence. *See* Male erectile disorder

Impulse control disorders

    anxiety management training, 2537

    associated with fetishism, 537, 638

    behavior therapy, 2649

    See also Impulse control disorders not elsewhere classified; names of specific disorders

Impulse control disorders not elsewhere classified

    acting out, 2458, 2459, 2461, 2462

    adolescent-type behavior, 2457, 2458, 2460

    alexithymia, 2457

    atypical impulse control disorder, 2477–2480

    behavior patterns, 2460

    childhood conduct problems, 2457

    and criminality, 2459

    definition, 2457

    delinquent behavior, 2458, 2459, 2460

    ego problems, 2457, 2460

    fantasy absence, 2457, 2461

    group therapy, 2462

    guilt and shame feelings, 2459, 2461

    intermittent explosive disorder, 2473–2476

    kleptomania, 2466–2468

    and narcissistic personality, 2457, 2459

    pathologic gambling, 2463–2466

Impulse control disorders not
elsewhere classified (cont)
  perversion and sadomasochism,
    2461, 2462
  pharmacotherapy, 2487
  psychoanalytic concepts, 2458–2460
  psychotherapy difficulties, 2461
  pyromania, 2457, 2460, 2461, 2468–
    2473
  relapse, 2463
  risks and violence tendency, 2461
  self-psychology, 2462
  tension regulation problems, 2457,
    2463
  therapist attitudes, 2461, 2462
  therapist responsibility, 2462
  transference, 2459
  trichotillomania, 2481–2486
Imsak, 2312
Imu, 1685
Incarceration for sexual offenses,
    pedophilia, 623, 624–627
Incidental teaching
  autistic children, 195–196, 198
  schizophrenics, 1570
Incontinence
  epilepsy-related, 883
  and stroke, 868
  See also Functional encopresis;
    Functional enuresis
Incoordination. See Tic disorders
Individualized education program
    (IEP), 124, 194, 197, 199–200
Individual psychotherapy
  alcoholism, 1093–1103
  exhibitionism, 673
  pedophilia, 623, 630–631
  personality disorders, 2635, 2636,
    2637, 2652, 2667
  avoidant personality disorder,
    2760–2761
  borderline personality disorder,
    2738, 2750–2752, 2759
  dependent personality disorder,
    2767–2769
  effectiveness, 2668

histrionic personality disorder,
  2729–2733
narcissistic personality disorder,
  2737–2740, 2742
obsessive compulsive personality
  disorder, 2773–2778
in residential treatment, 2690
schizoid personality disorder,
  2713–2716
schizotypal personality disorder,
  2719–2725
schizophrenia, 1486, 1515–1529
schizophreniform disorder, 1658,
  1662, 1665
sexual disorders, 2247, 2290, 2316,
  2337, 2339, 2341, 2342–2343
sexual sadomasochism, 651, 652
substance abuse, 1417–1430, 1422–
  1429
voyeurism, 673
See also Psychoanalytic
  psychotherapy; Psychodynamic
  psychotherapy; Psychotherapy
Indoctrination as cause of dissociative
  disorder not otherwise
  specified, 2222, 2223, 2225–2226
Indolealkylamine derivatives. See
  Hallucinogen abuse
Indoleamine
  and dementia of the Alzheimer's
  type, 978
  multi-infarct dementia, 962
  stroke-related syndromes, 874
Indomethacin
  interaction with other drugs, 927
  vaginismus, 2358
Induced psychotic disorder
  association between subjects, 1688–
    1692
  communicated psychosis, 1687,
    1688, 1689, 1690, 1694, 1696
  cults, 1688, 1692–1694
  definitions, 1685–1687
  diagnosis of partners, 1688–1689
  differential diagnosis, 1660, 1688
  DSM-III-R diagnostic criteria, 1687

environmental factors, 1690–1691
heredity, 1686, 1689–1690
imposed psychosis, 1687, 1688, 1689, 1690, 1694, 1695–1696
incidence, 1688
induced psychosis, 1687, 1688
simultaneous psychosis, 1687, 1688
treatment, 1686, 1694–1697
See also Delusional (paranoid) disorders
Infantile autism. *See* Autistic children; Autistic disorder
Infantile spasms. *See* Epilepsy, generalized seizures
Infants
car seat use, 846
failure to thrive, 735, 736–737, 742
maturation, internalization, and conflict resolution, 2012
overstimulation and rumination, 568–569
parent-infant bonding, 734–736, 2011–2012
See also Reactive attachment disorder of infancy
Infarction and SIADH, 898
Infective endocarditis and organic mental syndromes, 896–897
Inflatable penile prostheses, 2333–2334
Influenza
and secondary depression, 854, 1902
and secondary mania, 1761
Inhibited female orgasm
behavior therapy, 2247
case history, 2286–2290
and depression, 2254
DSM-III-R diagnostic criteria, 2284
physical causes, 2286
practice effects, 2284–2285
prevalence, 2284, 2335–2336
psychological level, 2245
sociocultural and religious effects, 2285–2286
speculative pharmacotherapy, 2357
treatment approaches, 2286–2290
vaginal versus clitoral preference, 2280–2282

Inhibited male orgasm. *See* Retarded ejaculation
Inhibited sexual desire. *See* Hypoactive sexual desire; Sexual desire problems
Inhibited sexual excitement
DSM-III-R changes to male erectile disorder and female sexual arousal disorder, 2237
Inpatient family intervention (IFI). *See* Family therapy, mood disorders
Inpatient Multidimensional Psychiatric Rating Scale (IMPS), 2681
Inpatient treatment. *See* Hospital treatment
Input and integrative disabilities of learning disabled children, 319–320
Insight-oriented psychotherapy
conversion disorders, 2157
sexual disorders, 2247, 2256
See also Psychotherapy
Insomnia
accident risk, 846
from antituberculosis drugs, 947
child-onset, 2425–2426, 2427, 2428
and delirium, 810, 812
and dementia, 827, 828
and digitalis toxicity, 908
geriatric type, 2446
and liver transplantation, 933
in opioid detoxification, 1318
pharmacotherapy, 2430, 2587
and sensory impairment, 950
side effect of disopyramide, 910
side effect of methyldopa, 911
See also Primary insomnia
Institute of Medicine, 982
Institutionally based self help for alcoholism, 1122
Insulinoma and secondary depression, 1902
Insurance Institute for Highway Safety, 846
Intake-orientation groups, alcoholism treatment, 1119

Integration of theory and practice in
psychiatry, 2008–2009
Integrity groups, 2598, 2599, 2600,
2604
Interactional psychotherapy groups
alcoholism, 1120
schizophrenia, 1534–1535, 1536,
1538, 1539–1542, 1543
Intermediate Care Facility—Mentally
Retarded (ICF-MR), 269–270
Intermetamorphosis, 836
Intermittent explosive disorder
and aggression, 2473, 2474, 2475,
2476
and attention-deficit disorders, 2474
and borderline personality disorder,
2686
and brain injury, 854
and brain syndromes, 2474
clinical experience, 2475
description, 2473–2474
DSM-III-R diagnostic criteria, 840,
2474
history, 2475
incidence, 2475–2476
in mentally retarded persons, 7
pharmacotherapy, 2476
psychotherapy, 2476
research, 2475–2476
temper outbursts, 2473, 2474, 2475,
2476
and violence, 2475
See also Organic personality disorder
Internalization, 2012
International Association for the Study
of Pain, 2122
International Classification of Disease,
9th edition (ICD-9)
delusional (paranoid) disorders,
1611, 1612, 1618
hyperkinetic syndrome, 366
schizoaffective disorder, 1667, 1668,
1671
schizophrenia, 1499
International Clinical and Electro-

encephalographic Classi-
fication of Epileptic Seizures,
877
International Pilot Study of Schizophrenia,
1612–1613
Interpersonal psychotherapy
avoidant personality disorder, 2761
combined with pharmacotherapy,
1821
mood disorders, 1729, 1731, 1732,
1733, 1863, 1863–1872, 1944
attachment bonds, 1864–1865
dysthymia, 1945
effectiveness, 1816–1817, 1822,
1868–1871
interpersonal formulation of
depression, 1863–1866
major depression, 1817–1822
secondary depression, 1921
treatment strategy, 1866–1868
Interpersonal relationship deficits
bulimia nervosa, 521
in mentally retarded persons, 8, 108
Intoxication. See Alcohol intoxication
Introverted personality, 2759
In vivo exposure. See Exposure
treatment
"Invulnerable" parents of autistic
children, 260–261
Iproniazid
effects on cardiovascular system, 905
mood disorders, 1734, 1736, 1737
side effects, 944, 1736
IQ measures, pervasive developmental
disorders, 187
Iron deficiency in pica, 581–583, 585–
586, 587
Irritability/Depression and Anxiety
Scale, 2125
Irritable bowel syndrome,
psychotherapy, 2149
Ischemia
and dementia of the Alzheimer's
type, 972
and stroke, 873
Ischemic score and dementia, 820, 961

Ismak, 2312
Isocarboxazid
  classification, 1774
  pharmacokinetics, 1780
  premature ejaculation, 2353, 2357
  trichotillomania, 2482
Isoetharine
  side effects, 944
Isoniazid
  interaction with other drugs, 890
  mood disorders, 1736
    secondary depression, 1912, 1913
    secondary mania, 1914
  reaction with disulfiram, 1100
  side effects, 944
Isoproterenol
  dementia of the Alzheimer's type,
    975
Isoxsuprine
  dementia of the Alzheimer's type,
    972
  multi-infarct dementia, 962, 963

Jacksonian march, 880
Jactatio capitis nocturna, 2424
Jamais vu
  from brain damage, 835
  epilepsy-related, 878, 880
Jay Nolan Center, 269, 270
Jealousy. *See* Morbid jealousy
Jet lag, 2442–2443
  phototherapy, 1891, 1896
Jewish Chronic Disease Hospital
    Study, 1005
Job Club program, 1573, 1574–1575
Job Seekers' Workshop, 1445, 1447
Job stress, 2578, 2579, 2580
Jonas flexible penile prosthesis, 2332
Juvenile impostor, 2459

Kanamycin
  auditory effects, 958

Kappa statistic, 1500
Karezza, 2312
Kayser-Fleischer corneal ring, Wilson's
    disease, 934
Kemadrin. *See* Procyclidine
Ketamine and delirium, 813–814
Key Math Diagnostic Arithmetic Test
    Revised, 331
Kinsey Institute for Sex Research, 2360
Kleptomania
  associated with fetishism, 637, 640
  childhood onset, 2467
  definition, 2466
  and depression, 2468
  and eating disorders, 2468
  forensic psychiatry, 2466
  motivation, 2467
  sexual perversion, 2467
  shoplifting, 2467–2468
Koro syndrome, 2381
Korsakoff's syndrome and alcoholic
    dementia, 818, 820
Kraepelin diagnostic system for
    schizophrenia, 1487, 1490, 1498,
    1499, 1613, 1614

Labeling of persons
  as handicapped, 304
  as mentally retarded, 124–126
Labetalol
  hypertension from ECT, 1810
Labile affective illness
  and digitalis toxicity, 908
  and renal disease, 929
Laboratory tests
  cannabis abuse and dependence,
    1246–1247
  hallucinogen abuse, 1206
  hospital treatment of drug addicts,
    1364
  phencyclidine abuse and
    dependence, 1212, 1213
Lactulose
  hepatic disease, 936

Language and speech disorders,
    developmental
  behavior problems, 303
  definition, 298, 313–314
  effect on development, 302
  evaluation, 339–341
  fluency disorders, 315–316, 339–346
  phonologic disorders, 314–315
  prevalence, 299–300
  stuttering, 316–317, 345–346
Language problems in children
  behavior therapy, 341, 346
  coding language, 341
  cognitive-linguistic treatment
      approach, 341–342
  diagnosis, 340
  evaluation, 339–341
  holistic approach to treatment, 342
  parent-child interaction, 339–340
  treatment strategies, 342–346
Language therapy
  distinguished from communication
      therapy, 201–202
  See also Communication therapy
Latah, 1685, 1699, 2165
Late-onset schizophrenia and atypical
    psychosis, 1698
Late paraphrenia, 1615, 1640–1642
  differential diagnosis, 836
  See also Paraphrenia
Lead ingestion and lead poisoning in
    pica, 52, 583
League for Emotionally Disturbed
    Children, 2601
Learned helplessness, 2540–2541
  and dyspareunia, 2293
Learning Accomplishment Profile, 187
Learning disabilities
  categories, 308–309
  definition, 308
  and emotional problems, 309
  special education programs, 351–352
  theories, early, 297
  See also Academic skills disorders;
      Learning disabilities, specific
Learning disabilities, specific
  ability training as remediation, 332

  academic skills training, 333
  auditory-perceptual disability, 309,
      320
  behavior therapy, 325
  center-based versus home-based
      programs for children, 305
  controversial therapies, 326–327
  differential diagnosis, 320–321
  and distractibility, 310
  educational evaluation, 328–329
  Education for All Handicapped
      Children Act, 300, 304
  emotional problems, 311–312
  family problems, 311–312
  and hyperactivity, 310
  input, integrative, and memory
      disabilities, 320
  modality matching, 333
  motor output disability, 310
  neurological evaluation, 321
  output disabilities, 320
  pharmacotherapy, 326
  process training, 332–333
  psychological interventions in
      treatment, 325–326
  psychotherapy, 325
  reading disorders, 332–337
  school environment in treatment,
      322
  sequencing difficulties, 323
  social problems, 311–312
  special education programs, 351–352
  treatment, 321–328
  visual-perceptual disability, 309, 319
  See also Specific developmental
      disorders
Learning problems and attention-
    deficit hyperactivity disorder,
    373
Learning strategies of children, 331–
    332
Lecithin
  dementia of the Alzheimer's type,
      969, 970
Legal aspects of multiple personality
    disorder, 2215

Legal issues
  child abuse reporting, 993, 1000
  civil commitment, 985–986, 988,
    991–992, 993, 2702
  combative patients, 991–992
  competency standards, 983–984,
    998–999
  confidentiality of diagnosis, 989–991,
    992, 993
  consent for electroconvulsive
    therapy, 1807
  elder abuse reporting, 984, 993, 1000
  emergency treatment, 985–986
  litigiousness of paranoid personality
    disordered patients, 2709
  power of attorney, 988
  questionable consent, 986–989
  research concerns, 1007
  right to refuse treatment, 993
  seclusion and restraint, 991–992, 993
  sexual provocation from patients,
    991–992
  spouse-abuse reporting, 993
  termination of treatment, 993
  testamentary capacity, 993–994
  in the treatment of organic mental
    syndromes, 799
  See also Ethical issues
Legal problems
  and drug abuse treatment, 1185
  and methadone maintenance
    treatment of opioid abuse, 1346
Legal requirements for education for
    handicapped persons, 123–124,
    132, 193–194
  See also Education for All
    Handicapped Children Act
Lesbianism. *See* Homosexuality
Lesch-Nyhan syndrome
  enzyme deficiency as cause, 37
  failure of skin shock to eliminate
    self-injury, 225
  mentally retarded persons
    chromosomal abnormalities, 37–38
    diagnosis, 38
    symptoms, 37
  pharmacotherapy, 977

Lesions on the brain
  and electroconvulsive therapy, 1806
  and epilepsy, 886
  and organic aggressive syndrome,
    844, 848, 851
  and organic delusional syndrome,
    833–835
  and organic hallucinosis, 835
  and organic mood syndrome, 853,
    854, 855
  and organic personality syndrome,
    840, 841, 843, 858, 860
  See also Stroke
Levine-Pilowsky Depression
    Questionnaire, 2125
Levoamphetamine. *See* Amphetamines
Levodopa
  autistic disorder, 246
  dementia of the Alzheimer's type,
    974–975
  hepatic disease, 936
  interaction with other drugs, 866,
    867
  and mania, 854
  multi-infarct dementia, 962
  and organic psychosis, 833
  Parkinson's disease, 862, 863–864,
    865, 866, 966, 974
  and secondary depression, 1912,
    1913
  and secondary mania, 1914
  sexual effects, 2349–2350, 2358
  side effects, 2358
  stimulant abuse role, 1237
  tardive dyskinesia, 1513
  Tourette's syndrome, 690
Leyton Obsessional Inventory, 402,
    693, 694
LHRH. *See* Luteinizing hormone-
    releasing hormone
Libidinal object constancy, 2012–2013
Librium. *See* Chlordiazepoxide
Lidocaine
  and electroconvulsive therapy, 1810–
    1811
  hepatic disease, 938
  neuropsychiatric effects, 909

Light therapy. *See* Phototherapy
Like Other People, 2378
Limbic encephalopathy
   and depression, 854
   and lung disease, 942
Liothyronine
   adjunct with tricyclic antidepressant
      drugs, 1794–1795
Listening and understanding in
      psychotherapy for substance
      abuse, 1425
Lisuride and organic psychosis, 833
Lithium
   adjunct treatment with other drugs,
      1792, 1793–1794, 1797, 1799
   alcoholism, 1075, 1096, 1919, 1920,
      1927
   anorexia nervosa, 473–474, 478–479
   atypical impulse control disorder,
      2479
   atypical psychosis, 1705, 1706
   autistic disorder, 239–245
   bipolar disorder, 1672
   brief reactive psychosis, 1682
   bulimia nervosa, 531
   cancer, 1906
   conversion disorders, 2158
   cycloid psychosis, 1709
   delirium, 814
   dementia, 828
   drug-induced psychosis, 943, 947
   effects on cardiovascular system,
      905–906
   and electroconvulsive therapy, 1805,
      1808, 1813
   extrapyramidal symptoms, 867
   family history of effectiveness, 2682
   hepatic disease, 937–938
   and hypothyroidism, 1938
   induced psychotic disorder, 1695
   interaction with other drugs, 891,
      893, 914, 927, 960, 1926
   levodopa-induced dyskinesias, 866
   mania, 893
   menses-associated psychosis, 1708

mentally retarded persons
   aggression, 79–80, 83
   animal studies, 79
   bipolar disorder, 78–79, 81, 83
   cyclical temper outburst, 80
   depression, 78, 81, 83
   guidelines, 83
   monitoring of, 83
   self-injurious behavior, 36, 80
   side effects, 83
mood disorders, 1729, 1738, 1752,
      1754, 1764, 1765, 1785, 1787
   acute depressive episode in
      bipolar disorder, 1742
   acute manic episode, 1741–1742
   bipolar disorders, 1752, 1758,
      1759, 1760, 1763, 1849, 1925,
      1926–1933, 1934, 1935–1936,
      1938–1939
   children and adolescents, 1957
   cyclothymia, 1742
   secondary depression, 1903, 1912,
      1917, 1923
   secondary mania, 1915
multiple personality disorder, 2210
nonresponsive patients, 1797, 1799,
      1801
organic aggressive syndrome, 850
organic delusional syndrome, 838
organic mood syndrome, 856, 1910
Parkinson's disease, 866
pathologic gambling, 2465
personality disorders, 2687, 2688
   antisocial personality disorder,
      2682, 2746, 2747
   borderline personality disorder,
      2754
   with secondary depression, 2683,
      2684
postpartum psychosis, 1707–1708
posttraumatic stress disorder, 2075
in pregnant patients, 1806, 1931
premature ejaculation, 2357
prophylactic effects, 1929
rage, 2686
renal disease, 924–927, 929

schizoaffective disorder, 1656, 1672–
1674, 1675, 1676
schizophrenia, 1503
side effects, 905–906, 925–926, 1930–
1931
stimulant abuse, 1240
stroke, 875–876
tardive dyskinesia, 1513
toxicity, 925–927, 1930–1931
unipolar disorder, 1672
Lithium carbonate
alcoholism, 1101
delusional (paranoid) disorders,
1632–1633
Lithium-clomipramine combination
obsessive compulsive disorder, 2103
Litigious delusional states, 1644–1645
Liver disease. *See* Hepatic disease
Liver flap. *See* Asterixis
Liver transplantation, 933
See also Hepatic disease
Lock Wallace Short Marital
Adjustment Scale, 493
Loneliness as a contributing factor to
pedophilia, 621
Lorazepam
alcohol withdrawal, 1087–1088
anxiety and lung disease, 945
anxiety disorders, 2039
bipolar disorders, 1932
delirium, 809, 810, 811
dementia, 828
epilepsy, 890
hepatic disease, 937
narcissistic personality disorder,
2741
renal disease, 921, 922
secondary depression and lung
disease, 948
Loxapine
borderline personality disorder,
2680–2681
dementia and amnestic syndromes,
826
neurotransmitter receptor blockade,
1779
Loyola Sensate Focus, 2307–2308

Loyola Sexual Dysfunction Clinic,
2301, 2309, 2312–2313, 2316
LSD. *See* Lysergic acid diethylamide
Lumbar puncture as diagnostic aid,
799
Lung disease
and delirium, 808
and dementia, 821
and depression, 854
endocrine abnormalities, 943
metastatic disease, 941, 943
and organic mental syndromes, 939–
948
and secondary depression, 948
treatment
pharmacotherapy of associated
psychiatric symptoms, 945–946,
948
side effects of lung medications,
943–945, 947
Lupus erythematosus. *See* Systemic
lupus erythematosus
Luteinizing hormone
transvestic fetishism, 635
Luteinizing hormone-releasing
hormone (LHRH)
sexual disorders, 2351–2352, 2355
D-Lysergic acid diethylamide. *See*
Hallucinogen abuse; Lysergic
acid diethylamide
Lysergic acid diethylamide (LSD)
anxiety and flashbacks, 1208
autistic disorder, 235
classification as hallucinogen, 1203–
1204
Manson "family" episodes, 1208
neurologic reactions, 1209
and organic delusional syndrome,
833
and organic hallucinosis, 833
phencyclidine abuse, differential
diagnosis, 1206
psychosocial aspects, 1204
radioimmunoassay, 1206
and substance-induced chronic
psychosis, 1709
See also Hallucinogen abuse

Machismo, 2382
Macropsia, epilepsy-related, 878, 883
Madonna-prostitute complex, 2252, 2382
Magical thinking, dispelling in crisis intervention, 2526, 2529
Magnesium depletion and digitalis toxicity, 907
Magnesium pemoline
  attention-deficit hyperactivity disorder, 374–375
Magnetic resonance imaging (MRI)
  atypical psychosis diagnosis, 1702
  delirium diagnosis, 807
  dementia diagnosis, 961
  epilepsy diagnosis, 886
  organic aggressive syndrome diagnosis, 845–846
  organic mood syndrome diagnosis, 855
  organic personality syndrome diagnosis, 859
Mainstreaming
  learning disabled children, 305
  mildly mentally retarded persons, 125
Major depression
  chronicity, 1753
  classification, 1727, 1728
  diagnostic considerations, 1754–1755, 1946
  duration, 1756
  and dysthymia, 1942–1943
  incidence, 1727, 1752
  and melancholia, 1753, 1756
  and organic mood syndrome, 853
  and personality disorders, 2684
  seasonality, 1753
  treatment
    electroconvulsive therapy, 1742, 1803
    pharmacotherapy, 1742–1743, 1942–1943
    psychotherapy, 1743–1744, 1817–1822, 1943–1944
  vulnerability factors, 1748

See also Depressive disorders
Major role therapy for schizophrenia, 1517
Maladaptive responses to stress. *See* Adjustment disorders
Malaria and secondary depression, 1902
Male alcoholism subtype, 1072
Male dyspareunia
  added to DSM-III-R, 2248
  causes, 2243, 2293
  and depression, 2254
  DSM-III-R diagnostic criteria, 2291
  tests for physical causes, 2243
Male erectile disorder
  added in DSM-III-R to replace inhibited sexual excitement, 2237
  and aging, 2372–2373
  and anxiety, 2320–2321
  behavior therapy, 2326–2327
  clinical subgroups, 2321
  etiology, 2319–2320
  interpersonal reinforcing pattern, 2325
  and marital discord, 2325, 2328
  mixed etiologies, 2328–2329
  pharmacotherapy, 2357
  physical causes, 2241, 2344
  prevalence, 2318–2319
  primary impotence, 2321, 2327–2328
  secondary impotence, 2321–2322
    acute onset, brief duration, 2323–2324
    insidious onset, and/or long duration, 2324–2325
  in sexual sadomasochism, 654–655
  side effect of antidepressant drugs, 1777
  side effect of disopyramide, 910
  and stroke, 876
  surgical treatment
    diagnosis, 2330–2331
    indications for, 2331–2332
    inflatable prostheses, 2333–2334
    types of prostheses, 2332–2333

tests for physical causes, 2241–2242
treatment, 2322–2323, 2326–2327, 2329–2330
treatment considerations, 2328
Malignant neuroleptic syndrome. *See* Neuroleptic malignant syndrome
Malnutrition and delirium, 811
Manganese poisoning, differential diagnosis, 861
Mania
  from asthma drugs, 943
  and delirium, 804
  and digitalis toxicity, 908
  in drug addicts, hospital treatment, 1371–1372
  and hyponatremia, 898
  and lung disease, 941
  and organic mood syndrome, 853
  pharmacotherapy, 911
  and postpartum psychosis, 1707
  procarbazine-induced, 945
  and renal disease, 924
  and schizoaffective disorder, 1667, 1674
  side effect of depression, 912
  stimulant abuse-induced, 1223
  and stroke, 875
  and systemic lupus erythematosus, 952
Maniacal grief reaction. *See* Mood disorders, bipolar disorders
Manic depressive disorder. *See* Mood disorders
Manic disorder
  and organic aggressive syndrome, 841
  in transvestic fetishism, 644
Mannitol
  lithium excretion, 906
MAOI. *See* Monoamine oxidase inhibitors
Maprotiline
  classification, 1774
  dementia, 827
  effects on cardiovascular system, 904

interaction with other drugs, 913
mood disorders
  secondary depression, 1903, 1906
  pharmacokinetics, 1775, 1776, 1777, 1779–1781
  seizures, 884
  and specific medical diseases, 1781–1783, 1784
  in treatment nonresponders, 1798
Marginal transvestite, 641, 642
Marianismo, 2382
Marijuana. *See* Cannabis; Cannabis abuse and dependence
Marital couples group therapy for alcoholism, 1119–1120, 1124
Marital discord
  and impotence, 2325, 2328
  in parents of anorectic patients, 493
  and sexual disorders, 2246, 2328, 2336–2337, 2358
Marital relationships of pedophiles, 621
Marital therapy
  alcoholism, 1119–1120
  exhibitionism, 672
  impotence, 2319–2320, 2322, 2328, 2329
  mood disorders, 1732, 1885–1890
    major depression, 1817
  pedophilia, 625
  personality disorders, 2648, 2660–2666
    duration of treatment, 2665
    histrionic personality disorder, 2735
    indications and contraindications, 2665–2666
    schizotypal personality disorder, 2725
  reactive attachment disorder of infancy, 743–744
  voyeurism, 672
  See also Family therapy; Sex therapy
Marplan. *See* Isocarboxazid
Maryland State Penitentiary, 630

Masochism
　associated with fetishism, 637, 639
　associated with transvestic fetishism,
　　645
　in women marrying transvestic
　　fetishists, 644
Massachusetts Appeals Court
　euthanasia ruling, 1003
Massachusetts Supreme Court
　euthanasia ruling, 1003
Massachusetts Treatment Center
　pedophilia, 627
Massed negative practice
　Tourette's syndrome, 701
Mass hysteria
　differential diagnosis, 1688
　See also Induced psychotic disorder
Massive seizures. See Epilepsy,
　generalized seizures
Mastectomy, sexual effects, 2374
Masters and Johnson approach for
　　sexual disorders treatment,
　　2238, 2319, 2326, 2327, 2337–
　　2339, 2341, 2363
　pedophilia, 628
Masters-Johnson Foundation, 2301
Masturbation
　fetishism, 638, 639
　pedophilia, 620, 624, 627
　sexual sadomasochism, 650–651,
　　652–653
　transvestic fetishism, 644, 645, 646
Maternal attachment in pedophilia, 632
Maternal communication deviance and
　　schizophrenia, 1549–1550
Maternal depression
　and infant rumination, 576
　and reactive attachment disorder of
　　infancy, 736, 737, 738
Maternal deprivation
　mood disorders in children and
　　adolescents, 1749–1750, 1952
　studies, 735–737.
　See also Reactive attachment disorder
　　of infancy

Maternal role in paraphilias
　childhood gender identity disorder,
　　664, 666, 667–669
　pedophilia, 632
　sexual sadomasochism, 650, 651,
　　653, 654, 655
　transvestic fetishism, 635, 643
Mathematics disorders, specific
　Cuisenaire rods as teaching aids, 338
　description, 317–318
　diagnosis, 328–329
　Distar instructional system for
　　remediation, 338
　dyscalculia, 317
　remediation, 338–339
Maturation, 2012
McLean Hospital study on
　　schizophreniform disorder, 1659
Medicaid, 980, 981
Medicare, 979–983
　age of entitlement, 995
　and organic mental syndromes, 802
Meditation
　alcoholism, 1076
　anxiety disorders, 2052–2053, 2054–
　　2055, 2064–2065
　cultural perspective and effective-
　　ness of treatment, 2055
　generalized anxiety disorder, 2054–
　　2055
　patient-therapist relationship, 2055
　vaginismus, 2298
Medroxyprogesterone acetate
　fetishism, 638
　menses-associated psychosis, 1708
　pedophilia, 629–630
　sex drive reduction, 2356
　transvestic fetishism, 645–646
　treatment for high sexual desire in
　　men, 2277
Megace
　sex drive reduction, 2356
Megavitamins
　autistic disorder treatment, 241
　schizophrenia treatment, 1502

Melancholia
  diagnostic considerations, 1752
  and major depression, 1753, 1756
  nonresponsiveness, 1790
  psychoanalytic psychotherapy, 1832
Melatonin and phototherapy, 1891
Mellaril. *See* Thioridazine
Memory and traumatic events, 2071–2072, 2082
Memory impairment
  from antianxiety drugs, 945–946
  delirium, 804
  and dementia of the Alzheimer's type, 967
  and digitalis toxicity, 908
  from electroconvulsive therapy, 1809, 1811–1812
  in multiple personality disorder, 2198
  and Parkinson's disease, 864
  and renal disease, 916
  and substance abuse, 2186
  and Wilson's disease, 934
  See also Amnestic disorder; Amnestic syndromes; Psychogenic amnesia
Memory training
  cognitive impairment, 901
  dementia and amnestic syndromes, 830
Mended Hearts, 2601, 2602, 2603
Meningeal carcinomatosis and organic mental syndromes, 941
Meningitis
  and brief reactive psychosis, 1680
  and dementia, 821
  diagnosis, 799
  differential diagnosis, 1910
  and SIADH, 898
Menninger Foundation, 1732
Menninger Outcome Study, 2752
Menninger Psychotherapy Project, 2642
Menstrual cycle
  and atypical psychosis, 1699, 1708
  and metabolism of alcohol, 1077
  and sexual responsivity, 2282

Mental retardation
  aggression, 20–26, 850
  antisocial behavior, 8, 20–26
  anxiety disorders, 7, 14–19
  Association for Retarded Citizens, 147–148
  behavior problems, 5–7, 20–26, 40, 59, 105
  behavior therapy, 111–123, 2649, 2656
  classification of psychological disorders, 115–116
  coprophagia, 43–44
  counseling, 100–107
  deinstitutionalization, 140–146
  delinquency, 20–26
  Down's syndrome, 30–32
  eating problems, behavior-related, 57–66
  educational services, 123–129
  education of mildly mentally retarded persons, 124–126
  emotional problems of mentally retarded persons, 104
  employment issues, 132–138
  feces smearing, 43–44
  fragile X syndrome, 39–42
  and induced psychotic disorder, 1689, 1694
  labeling issues, 124–125
  Lesch-Nyhan syndrome, 37–38
  mental health policies, 140–148
  and mood disorders, 7–8, 10–14, 1740
  neuropsychiatric treatment needs, 3–4
  and organic aggressive syndrome, 842
  pharmacotherapy, 67–99, 850
  pica, 51–53, 120
  placebo substitution in research, 97
  Prader-Willi syndrome, 50–51
  preoccupation with sameness, 55–57
  psychopathology in, 4–8
  psychotherapy, 5, 12–14, 62, 108–111

Mental retardation *(cont)*
  quality of life, 138–139
  rectal digging, 43–44
  ritualistic behavior, 55–57
  rumination, 8, 53–55, 568
  schizophrenia, 27–28
  school-work transition, 129–132
  self-injurious behavior, 8, 32–37, 119
  services to patient, 100–139
  stereotyped behaviors, abnormal,
    44–49, 119
  tyrannical behavior, 55–57
  vocational programs, 129–139
Mental Status Questionnaire (MSQ)
  delirium diagnosis, 807
  dementia diagnosis, 823
Mentor Company penile prosthesis,
  2334
Meperidine
  interaction with other drugs, 914
  and monoamine oxidase inhibitors,
    1785
Mephenytoin
  epilepsy, 889
Meprobamate
  adjustment disorders, 2588
  anxiety and lung disease, 945
  anxiety disorders, 2038–2039
Merck manual, 799, 1725
Mescaline
  and organic delusional syndrome, 833
  and organic hallucinosis, 833
Mesoridazine
  interaction with other drugs, 915
  personality disorders, 2679
  secondary depression, 1920
  with a sensory-impaired patient, 958
Mesterolone
  with tricyclic antidepressant drugs,
    1795–1796
Metabolic disorders
  and delirium, 806
  and hypernatremia, 899
  with secondary depression, 1901,
    1902, 1909
Metabolism of alcohol. *See* Alcohol
  metabolism

Metaproterenol
  side effects, 944
Metastatic disease
  and organic mental syndromes, 941,
    942
  and secondary depression, 854
Methadone
  hepatic disease, 938
  naltrexone, differentiation, 1335
  overdosing, 1348
  pharmacology, 1309, 1347–1348
  withdrawal, 1311, 1312, 1317, 1319
  See also Methadone maintenance
Methadone maintenance
  adverse attitudes, 1345
  alcohol interaction, 1348, 1351
  L-alpha-acetylmethadiol (L-AAM) as
    alternative, 1325, 1359
  community relations, 1351
  crime-opioid relationship, 1345–1346
  depressive disorders, 1357–1358
  detoxification, 1353–1355
  dosage, 1350
  drug counselors, 1420
  dysphoria prevention, 1349
  evaluation studies, 1343–1347
  funding, 1346–1347
  future directions, 1358–1359
  health problems of addicts, 1349,
    1357
  history, 1342–1343
  legal aspects of treatment, 1346
  licensing and accreditation of
    programs, 1358
  opioid abuse treatment program,
    1323–1324, 1348–1351
  patient categories, 1352, 1354
  psychological aspects of methadone
    therapy, 1357–1358
  psychological assistance, 1349
  psychopathology, 1358
  psychotherapy, individual, 1423
  reproduction and pregnancy, effects
    on, 1347, 1356
  side effects, 1348
  success rates, 1353
  "take-home" policy, 1350

and therapeutic communities, 1344
training for workers, 1346
withdrawal, 1351–1352
Methamphetamine, "truth serum"
  effect, 2157
Methamphetamine abuse
  history and epidemiology, 1218–1220
  "speed," 1219
  See also Stimulant abuse
Methaqualone
  sexual anxiety, 2361
Methohexital
  and electroconvulsive therapy, 1808–
  1809
Methotrexate
  side effects, 944, 947
Methsuximide
  epilepsy, 888, 889
1-Methyl-*d*-lysergic acid butanolamide
  bimaleate
  autistic disorder, 235
Methyldopa
  dementia, 826
  interaction with other drugs, 913,
  914, 928
  neuropsychiatric effects, 910–911
  and secondary depression, 854,
  1912, 1913, 1914
  side effects, 876
α-Methyldopa
  interaction with other drugs, 1782
  periodic catatonia, 1709
Methylphenidate
  antisocial personality disorder, 2682
  attention deficit disorder, 2685–2686
  attention-deficit hyperactivity
  disorder, 373–374
  autistic disorder, 91, 92
  dementia, 829
  dementia of the Alzheimer's type,
  975
  interaction with other drugs, 890
  mental retardation, 93
  mood disorders, 1735, 1799
  secondary depression, 1912
  secondary mania, 854

organic personality syndrome, 859
stereotypy of mentally retarded
  persons, 73–74
stimulant abuse treatment, 1237,
  1240
temper outbursts in children, 2476
Tourette's syndrome, 690
Methysergide
  autistic disorder, 235
  neurotransmitter blockade, 1776
Metoclopramide and secondary mania,
  1914
Metoclopramide for rumination, 574
Metoprolol
  atypical impulse control disorder,
  2480
  intermittent explosive disorder, 2476
  tremor in alcoholics, 1085
Metrizamide
  and secondary depression, 1912
Metronidazole
  reaction with disulfiram, 1100
Metyrapone
  lung disease, 945
Mianserin
  interaction with other drugs, 913
Michigan Alcoholism Screening Test
  (MAST), 1078, 1079, 1148, 1186
Micropsia
  and epilepsy, 878, 883
Middle-age pedophilia, 619, 621
Midtown Manhattan Study, 2763
Midwinter insomnia. *See* Seasonal
  affective disorder (SAD)
Migraine
  and antidepressant drugs, 1783
  differential diagnosis, 884, 885
  See also Headaches
Milieu
  schizophreniform disorder, 1659
Millon Behavioral Health Inventory in
  somatoform pain disorder
  diagnosis, 2125
Mineral deficiency as cause of pica, 52
Minimal brain dysfunction (MBD),
  2685–2686

Minimal brain dysfunction (cont)
  and personality disorders, 2687
  See also Attention deficit disorders
Mini-Mental State Examination
    (MMSE)
  dementia diagnosis, 817–818, 823,
    824–825
  dementia of the Alzheimer's type,
    975
Minneapolis Veterans Administration
    Medical Center, 2319
Minnesota Multiphasic Personality
    Inventory (MMPI), 737, 1065–
    1067, 1383, 2125, 2223, 2331,
    2420, 2422
  lung disease, 939–940
  organic personality syndrome
    diagnosis, 859
  paranoia in the hard of hearing, 951
  personality disorders, 2650
Mirroring, 2012
Mixed dominance in Tourette's
    syndrome, 692
Modeling
  anxiety disorders of childhood, 404,
    405
  personality disorders, 2650, 2652,
    2654, 2656, 2657
  simple phobias, 2027
  See also Behavior therapy
Molindone
  autistic disorder, 242
  effect on seizures, 839
  interaction with other drugs, 914
  and neuroleptic drug side effects,
    1513
Monoamine oxidase inhibitors (MAOI)
  anxiety disorders, 2048, 2049–2050,
    2051, 2052
  anxiety disorders of childhood, 407
  bulimia nervosa, 530–531
    with secondary depression, 2685
  classification, 1773–1774
  dementia, 828
  dementia of the Alzheimer's type,
    975–976

dosage, 1797
duration, 1797
effectiveness, 1803
effects on cardiovascular system,
    903, 905
and electroconvulsive therapy, 1808
hepatic disease, 937
and hypertension, 847
and inhibited female orgasm, 2286
interaction with other drugs, 851,
    866, 891, 892–893, 913–914, 928,
    959, 1785, 1787
mentally retarded persons, 82
mood disorders, 1729, 1734, 1736–
    1737, 1744, 1791
  acute depressive episode in
    bipolar disorders, 1742
  atypical depressions, 1797
  bipolar disorders, 1760, 1927,
    1929, 1934, 1936
  dysthymia, 1943
  major depression, 1796
  melancholia, 1796
  secondary depression, 1903, 1906,
    1917, 1918, 2683
  uncomplicated bereavement,
    1743–1744
nonresponsive patients, 1792, 1796
obsessive compulsive disorder, 2103
organic mood syndrome, 856
and orthostatic hypotension, 928
panic attacks, 2685
panic disorder in drug addicts, 1376
personality disorders, 2687, 2688
  avoidant personality disorder,
    2762
  borderline personality disorder,
    2682, 2735, 2754, 2755
  histrionic personality disorder,
    2735
  narcissistic personality disorder,
    2741
  paranoid personality disorder,
    2710
  with secondary depression, 2683,
    2684

pharmacokinetics, 1778, 1780
posttraumatic stress disorder, 2074
premature ejaculation, 2309, 2353,
    2357
and secondary mania, 854
sexual anxiety, 2247, 2356
sexual effects, 2344, 2347–2348, 2353,
    2354
special considerations, 1785
and specific medical diseases, 1782,
    1783
stimulant abuse, contraindications,
    1237
trichotillomania, 2482
See also Antidepressant drugs
Monoamine oxidase (type B) levels
        and paranoid form of
        schizophrenia, 1491
Mononucleosis
    nonresponsive patients, 1792
    and secondary depression, 1902
Monosymptomatic hypochondriasis
    and atypical psychosis, 1698
    and dysmorphophobia, 2146
    and organic disease, 836
    pharmacotherapy, 839, 874, 1705
Montreal General Hospital, 1879
The Montreal Group. *See* Brief
        dynamic psychotherapy
Mood disorders
    atypical anxiety disorder, 1728
    and atypical eating disorders, 593
    bipolar disorders, 1727, 1728, 1925–
        1940, 2684
        bipolar disorder, 1760–1762
        bipolar disorder not otherwise
            specified, 1758, 1925
        classification, 1757–1760
        cyclothymia, 1728, 1742, 1758–
            1759, 1925
        familial bipolar disorder, 1761
        hyperthymic disorder, 1758
        hypomanic episode, 1752, 1758,
            2687
        maniacal grief reaction, 1761
        postpartum mania, 1761, 1928

rapid cycling forms, 1934–1936
reactive mania, 1761
secondary mania, 1914–1915
soft bipolar spectrum, 1935, 1939
and brief reactive psychosis, 1678
and bulimia nervosa, 531
categories, 1753–1754
children and adolescents, 1763–1764,
    1950–1958
    diagnostic criteria, 1950–1952
    impact on development, 1952–
        1956
    juvenile bipolar affective illness,
        1956–1957
and depression in Parkinson's
        disease, 863
depressive disorders
    adjustment disorder with
        depressed mood, 1727, 1728,
        1747, 1900, 1946–1949
    atypical depression, 1743, 1753,
        1797, 1943, 2684, 2685
    categories, 1727–1728
    depressive disorders not otherwise
        specified, 1753
    double depression, 1757, 1789,
        1942, 1943–1944
    dysthymia, 1727, 1728, 1753–1754,
        1756–1757, 1789, 1940–1945
    intermittent depressive disorder,
        1943–1944
    major depression, 1727, 1728,
        1742–1744, 1748, 1752, 1753,
        1754–1755, 1756, 1803, 1817–
        1822, 1942–1944, 1946
    melancholia, 1790, 1796
    mood-reactive depression, 1743
    neurotic depression, 1743
    reactive depression, 1743
    seasonal affective disorder (SAD),
        1801, 1891–1896
    secondary depression. *See*
        Secondary depression
    situational depression, 1743
    uncomplicated bereavement, 1728,
        1743–1744, 1748, 1755, 1946

Mood disorders (cont)
vulnerability factors, 1748
diagnostic considerations, 1726–
1727, 1751–1766
family history, 1757
differential diagnosis, 1655, 1656,
1660, 1666, 1671, 1674, 1676,
1679, 1689
distinguished from schizophrenia,
1495
and epilepsy, 881, 882
family history, 1669–1671, 1751,
1755, 1761
and induced psychotic disorder,
1690
mentally retarded persons
description, 7–8, 10–14
diagnosis, 11–12
prevalence, 10–11
treatment, 12–14
and opioid abuse, 1313, 1314, 1329–
1330
organic affective syndrome, 1728
organic mood disorder, 1728
overlap with personality disorders,
2682, 2683–2685
and Parkinson's disease, 864
psychotherapy, 2714
and renal disease, 916
and rumination, 570
versus schizoaffective disorders,
1762–1763
and somatoform pain disorder, 2121
and stimulant abuse, 1227
and stroke, 875
treatment
brief dynamic psychotherapy,
1872–1884
choice of setting, 1766–1773
cognitive-behavioral psychotherapy, 1834–1846
combining drugs and
psychotherapy, 1733–1734,
1786–1787, 1791, 1817, 1819–
1820, 1821, 1823, 1826, 1838,
1839, 1840–1841, 1842, 1843,
1845–1846, 1863, 1885, 1886,
1888, 1890
couples therapy, 1885–1890
effectiveness, 1728–1729
electroconvulsive therapy, 1801,
1803–1813
family therapy, 1885–1890
goals of treatment, 1745–1751
interpersonal psychotherapy,
1863–1872
pharmacotherapy. See Pharmacotherapy
pharmacotherapy in drug addicts,
1375
phototherapy, 1890–1896
psychosocial treatment, 1730–1734
psychosurgery, 1741, 1896–1897
psychotherapy. See Psychotherapy
resistant patients, 1787–1802
Moos Family Environment Scale, 493
Moral issues. See Ethical issues
Moratorium, 1531
Morbid jealousy, 1642–1644
Morphine
hepatic disease, 938
pharmacology, 1309
withdrawal, 1311–1312
Mortality of opioid addicts, 1327–1328
Mother-child relationship in
rumination, 574
Mothers Against Drunk Driving
(MADD), 2613
Motivation for treatment
anorexia nervosa, 484–485
bulimia nervosa, 540–541
fetishism, 638, 639
"Mourning and Melancholia," 1827
Mourning distinguished from
posttraumatic stress disorder,
2069–2070
MRI. See Magnetic Resonance Imaging
MSQ. See Mental Status Questionnaire
Multifocal demyelination and stroke,
868

Multi-infarct dementia (MID)
dementia of the Alzheimer's type, 972
and depressive disorders, 826
differential diagnosis, 818, 820, 826
incidence, 817
and lung disease, 941
research problems, 961–964
risk factors, 962
treatment, 826
pharmacotherapy, 962–964
surgery, 964
See also Dementia
Multiple personality disorder
affect, 2213, 2214
alter egos, communication, 2204, 2212, 2213
amnestic episodes, 2211
child abuse as factor, 2199, 2208, 2212, 2213
childhood onset, 2198
conflict resolution, 2212–2214
and depression, 2209–2210
diagnosis, 2197–2199
dissociative defenses, 2202
DSM-III-R diagnostic criteria, 2198
etiology, 2202
family interventions, 2201
follow-up studies, 2198, 2216
forensic psychiatry considerations, 2215–2216
fusion of alters, 2207–2208, 2214
glossary of terms, 2216
hypnosis, 2202, 2203, 2204, 2205–2209, 2212
identity disturbance, 2198
integration as goal, 2200, 2203
patient communication, 2204
phenomenology, 2197–2199
postfusion therapy, 2214–2215
posttraumatic stress disorder, 2198
prevalence, 2198–2199
psychopathology, 2198, 2204
relapse, 2214
therapeutic alliance, 2203, 2211, 2215
therapy problems, 2210–2211

traumatic symptoms, 2207
treatment
behavior therapy, 2201
course and characteristics, 2210–2214
dyadic psychodynamic therapy, 2204
facilitation, 2204–2209
goals, 2199–2200
group therapy, 2201–2202
hospitalization, 2209
modalities, 2200–2202
pharmacotherapy, 2205, 2209–2210
principles and caveats, 2202–2203
psychoanalysis, 2201, 2211, 2212
staff attitudes as factor, 2209
stages, 2203–2204
videotape techniques, 2202, 2205
Multiple sclerosis
differential diagnosis, 935, 1701, 1910
and impotence, 2319
and organic aggressive syndrome, 842
and organic personality syndrome, 858
with secondary depression, 854, 1902, 1910, 1911
with secondary mania, 854, 1761
and sensory impairment, 949
Munchausen's syndrome. *See* Factitious disorder
Muscular Dystrophy Association, 2601
N-Mustard
auditory effects, 958
Muteness. *See* Mutism
Mutism
from asthma drugs, 943
and atypical psychosis evaluation, 1700
and lung disease, 941
and renal disease, 917
and stroke, 868, 871
Mutism, elective. *See* Elective mutism
Mutual aid groups. *See* Mutual-help services for youth; Self-help and

mutual aid groups for adults;
Support groups for families
Mutual-help services for youth
    Ala-teen, 1160, 1161, 2613
    categories, 2610
    characteristics, 2609–2610
    children of alcoholics, 1120
    criteria, 2612
    definitions and roles, 2608
    drunk driving prevention, 2613
    dysocial groups, 2613
    gangs, 2613
    hospital settings, 2613
    origins, 2607–2608
    political issues, 2609
    services, 2611–2613
    sociopathic peer leaders, 2613
    substance abuse, 2613
    types, 2611–2612
    See also Peer-helping services for
        youth; Self-help and mutual aid
        groups for adults; Self-help
        services for youth
Myasthenia gravis
    differential diagnosis, 1910
    and lung disease, 940, 942
Myocardial infarction
    and delirium, 806, 808
    and dementia, 822, 827
    and electroconvulsive therapy, 1805–
        1806
    and secondary depression, 903,
        1902, 1907
    and sexual aversion, 2252
    sexual effects, 2379
    side effect of guanethidine, 912
    and stroke, 867
Myocardial ischemia and digitalis
    toxicity, 907
Myoclonic seizures. See Epilepsy,
    generalized seizures
Myoclonus, 692
    and delirium, 814
    and renal disease, 917, 918, 919
Myxedema and organic delusional
    syndrome, 836

Nadolol
    neuropsychiatric effects, 909
Nafronyl
    dementia of the Alzheimer's type,
        973
    multi-infarct dementia, 962, 963
NAIM, self-help and mutual aid group
    for widows, 2602
Nalbuphine, pharmacology, 1309
Nalidixic acid
    and secondary depression, 1912,
        1913
Naloxone
    antagonist effect, 1333–1334
    delirium, 813
    dementia of the Alzheimer's type,
        977, 978
    mental retardation, 248
    self-injurious behavior, 36
    See also Naltrexone
Naltrexone
    autistic disorder, 247–248
Naltrexone antagonist treatment for
    opioid dependence
    alternative treatments, comparison,
        1334–1335
    antagonist concept, 1322–1323, 1333
    antagonist effects, 1333–1334
    clonidine combination, 1321–1322
    dependence and withdrawal, lack
        of, 1335
    detoxification, 1338
    disulfiram, differentiation, 1335
    dosage, 1339
    drop-out rate, 1355
    drug interactions, 1341
    dysphoria, 1333
    endocrine changes, 1340
    liver disorders, contraindication,
        1340
    maintenance, 1339–1340
    methadone, differentiation, 1335
    mode of use, 1338–1341
    monitoring, 1339
    naloxone, differentiation, 1333–1334

naloxone testing for residual dependence, 1338–1339
opioid detoxification, 1316
opioid receptor blockage, 1332
patient selection
  health care professionals, 1335–1336
  middle-class/suburban addicts, 1336–1337
  parolees and probationers, 1337
  socioeconomic status as factor, 1336–1338
  street heroin addicts, 1337–1338
rationale, 1332–1333
relapse prevention, 1334
reproductive effect potential, 1341
thioridazine interaction, 1341
Naproxen
  and secondary depression, 1912, 1913
Narcanon, 1399, 1401, 1411
Narcissism in alcoholics, 1096, 1104–1105
Narcissistic partner, 2661
Narcissistic personality and impulse control disorders not elsewhere classified, 2457, 2459
Narcissistic personality disorder, 772, 775, 778–780
  and borderline personality organization, 2737, 2739
  countertransference, 2739
  differential diagnosis, 2706
  DSM-III-R diagnostic criteria, 2737
  and mood disorders, 2685
  and organic aggressive syndrome, 841
  in parents of children with gender identity disorder, 666
  pharmacotherapy, 2741
  projective identification, 2739
  psychotherapy, 2642, 2737–2741, 2742
    couples therapy, 2740–2741
    effectiveness, 2742

family therapy, 2665, 2666, 2740–2741
    goals of treatment, 2639
    group therapy, 2672–2673, 2741
    individual psychotherapy, 2737–2740
    psychoanalytic psychotherapy, 2645, 2738–2739
    short-term psychotherapy, 2740
    supportive psychotherapy, 2740
  regression, 2699
  residential treatment, 2741–2742
  resistance, 2697
  with secondary depression, 1901
  splitting, 2739, 2743
  transference, 2738, 2741
Narcolepsy
  differential diagnosis, 935
  myoclonic movements, 2437
  symptoms, 2439
  treatment, 2440
Narcotic drugs
  interaction with other drugs, 914, 944
  secondary depression, 1906–1907
  and sexual disorders, 2240
Narcotics Anonymous, 887, 1217, 1299, 1316, 1327, 1378, 1390, 1399, 1420
Nardil. *See* Phenelzine
Nasogastric feeding in anorexia nervosa, 457, 458
National Alliance for the Mentally Ill, 1543, 1548, 1560, 2604–2605
National Association of Retarded Citizens. *See* Association for Retarded Citizens
National Commission on the Protection of Human Subjects of Biomedical and Behavioral Research, 996, 1741, 1896, 1897
National Gay Alliance, 2604
National Health Insurance program. *See* Medicare
National Household Survey on Drug Abuse, 1309

National Institute of Health-National
Institute of Mental Health
Consensus Development
Conference, 1740, 1742
National Institute of Mental Health
(NIMH)
choosing marital partners, 2660
Collaborative Study of
Psychotherapy, 1816–1817, 1819
Collaborative Study on Depressive
Disorders, 1732–1733, 1756,
1788, 1816, 1821–1822, 1845
Consensus Development Confer-
ence, 1742
Division TEACCH funding, 269
phototherapy study, 1740
Psychopharmacology Research
Branch, 240, 244
research funding, 982
research on depression, 1746
study on aging versus illness, 800–
801
National Institute of Neurological and
Communicative Disorders and
Stroke, 818, 982
National Institute on Aging, 982, 996
dementia diagnosis, 823
National Safety Council
automobile accident statistics, 846
National Society for Autistic Citizens,
270
Negative transference
personality disorders, 2658
narcissistic personality disorder,
2739, 2740
See also Transference
Negi Negi, factitious disorder, 2165
Neomycin
auditory effects, 958
hepatic disease, 936
Neoplasms
and delirium, 806
and dementia, 821
and epilepsy, 878, 885

and nonresponsiveness to
antidepressant treatment, 1792
and organic mental syndromes, 939
and organic mood syndrome, 856
and organic personality syndrome,
857, 858, 859
and secondary depression, 854, 1904
and sensory impairment, 952–953
Nephrogenic diabetes insipidus, 926
from lithium, 1930
Nerve block therapy for somatoform
pain disorder, 2132–2133
Networks as factor in self-help and
mutual aid groups for adults,
2602, 2603, 2605
Neuroanalysis in conversion disorders,
2157
Neurobehavioral syndromes associated
with mental retardation
coprophagy, 43–44
Down's syndrome, 30–32
feces smearing, 43–44
fragile X syndrome, 39–42
Lesch-Nyhan syndrome, 37–38
pica, 51–53
Prader-Willi syndrome, 50–51
rectal digging, 43–44
self-injurious behavior, 32–37
Neuroleptic drugs
agranulocytosis, 1906
and akinesia, 1662, 1922
anxiety disorders, 2046–2047
anxiety disorders of childhood or
adolescence, 408
atypical impulse control disorder,
2479
autistic disorder, 71–76, 234, 242–
245
brief reactive psychosis, 1680, 1682,
1684
cannabis abuse effects, 1249, 1252
combined with other drugs, 1794,
1795, 1804
contraindicated for alcohol withdrawal, 1087, 1089

delirium, 809, 812
delusional (paranoid) disorders, 1627–1632
dementia and amnestic syndromes, 827
effects on cardiovascular system, 906
extrapyramidal symptoms, 827, 838, 865, 1661, 1682, 1736, 1922
fetishism, 637
hypoactivity, 227
induced psychotic disorder, 1695, 1696, 1697
interaction with other drugs, 866, 891, 892, 914, 928, 944
late paraphrenia, 1615, 1640
and lithium, 1930
mentally retarded persons
  autistic disorder, 71–76
  self-injurious behavior, 36
  stereotypic behavior, 76
mood disorders, 1729, 1734, 1736
  acute manic episode, 1741–1742
  bipolar disorders, 1927, 1928
  secondary depression, 1912, 1923
  secondary mania, 1915
morbid jealousy, 1644
multi-infarct dementia, 964
neuroleptic malignant syndrome, 1804–1805
obsessive compulsive disorder, 2104
organic aggressive syndrome, 849
organic delusional syndrome, 837–838, 839
organic hallucinosis, 837–838
organic mood syndrome, 856
organic personality syndrome, 859
and parkinsonism, 861
and Parkinson's disease, 865
in patients with lung disease, 938, 945, 946
persecutory delusional disorder, 1640
personality disorders, 2679, 2687
  antisocial personality disorder, 2746
  borderline personality disorder, 2680–2681, 2684, 2754

schizotypal personality disorder, 2682
schizoid disorder, 760
schizophrenia
  acute schizophrenic, 1507–1508
  administration, 1505–1506
  American Psychiatric Association task force report, 1513, 1569
  chronic schizophrenic, 1508
  combined with other drugs, 1506
  combined with other treatment, 1519, 1569, 1575, 1580–1581, 1583
  common errors, 1507–1508
  dose requirements, 1507–1508
  dosing strategy, 1505
  informed consent and documentation, 1513
  limitations of, 1569
  long-acting, 1506
  maintenance treatment, 1508–1510, 1550
  noncompliance of patient, 1505–1506, 1509, 1514
  reassessment, 1508
  symptom response time, 1507–1508
  treatment considerations, 1501–1502, 1503, 1515
  treatment goals, 1505
schizophrenia in children, 234
schizophrenic reactions from hallucinogen abuse, 1207
schizophreniform disorder, 1658, 1659, 1661, 1663, 1665
seizures, 884
sensory-impaired patient, 958
side effects, 242, 408, 827, 838, 849, 876, 1510–1511, 1513–1514, 1629–1630
somatic complications, 1514
and specific medical diseases, 1783
stroke-related syndromes, 874, 875, 877
and subjective dysphoria, 1514

Neuroleptic drugs (cont)
  and tardive dyskinesia, 827, 875,
      1510, 1512–1513, 1631, 1662,
      1763, 1775
  Tourette's syndrome, 697, 709
  types of phenothiazines, 1503
  weight gain as side effect, 245, 1511,
      1513
  See also Antipsychotic drugs; names
      of specific drugs
Neuroleptic malignant syndrome,
      1498, 1514, 1630
  electroconvulsive therapy, 1804
Neurological syndromes associated
      with mental retardation
  behavior-related eating problems,
      57–66
  preoccupation with sameness, 55–57
  ritualistic behavior, 55–57
  rumination, 53–55
  stereotyped behaviors, abnormal,
      44–49
  tyrannical behavior, 55–57
Neurologic disorders
  and antidepressant drugs, 1782,
      1783–1784
  and personality disorders, 2685–2686
  with secondary depression, 1902,
      1909–1912
Neuromuscular and joint diseases,
      sexual effects, 2379–2380
Neuropeptides
  dementia of the Alzheimer's type,
      976–977
  role in rumination, 573
  schizophrenia, 1503
  Tourette's syndrome, 691
Neuroses, differential diagnosis, 1751
Neurosyphilis and epilepsy, 885
Neurotic depression, 1743
  See also Mood disorders
Neurotransmitters, stress response,
      2070–2071
New Haven-Boston Collaborative
      Depression Project, 1819, 1863
New Haven Schizophrenia Index,
      1499, 1501

New Jersey Supreme Court euthanasia
      ruling, 1004
New York Association for Help to
      Retarded Children, 2601
New York County Health Services
      Review Organization
  Criteria for Psychiatry, 1772–1773
New York State Psychiatric Institute
  study on aging and organic mental
      syndromes, 801
Niacin
  multi-infarct dementia, 963
Nicotinamide
  delirium, 944
Nicotine dependence
  chewing gum, nicotine-containing,
      1271, 1275, 1279
  DSM-III-R criteria, 1261–1262
  Fagerstrom Nicotine Addiction scale,
      1265, 1267, 1286–1287
  nicotine fading, 1273
  nicotine substitutes, 1271, 1275, 1279
  physiologic assessment, 1267, 1268–
      1269
  physiologic effects, 1263
  and psychiatric disorders, 1285–1286
  smokeless tobacco, 1283
  Tar and Nicotine Content of 28
      Selected Cigarettes, tabulation,
      1292–1293
  withdrawal syndrome, 1262, 1280
  See also Smoking; Tobacco
      withdrawal and tobacco
      dependence
Nicotine in cigarette smoke, 1263
Nifedipine
  effects on cardiovascular system, 909
  interaction with other drugs, 909,
      915
  neuropsychiatric effects, 909
Nightmares and night terrors
  in children, 2420–2422, 2562
  stress management, behavior
      therapy, 2540
Nitroglycerine
  hypertension from electroconvulsive
      therapy, 1810

Nitroprusside sodium
  hypertension from electroconvulsive
    therapy, 1810
Nitrosureas
  side effects, 944
Nocturnal myoclonus
  diagnosis, 2437
  pharmacotherapy, 2437–2438
Nocturnal Oxygen Therapy Trial
    Group, 940
Nocturnal penile tumescence (NPT)
    monitoring, 2239, 2241–2242,
    2303, 2321, 2331, 2385–2386
Nolvadex. *See* Tamoxifen
Nomifensine
  low sex drive, 2356
  in treatment nonresponders, 1798
Nonketonic hyperosmolar states
  and brief reactive psychosis, 1680
Nonmetastatic disease
  and organic mental syndromes, 941–
    942
Nonphobic anxiety
  behavior therapy, 2034
  See also Generalized anxiety disorder;
    Panic disorder
Nonpsychotropic drugs
  schizoaffective disorder, 1674
Nonsteroidal anti-inflammatory drugs
  interaction with other drugs, 927
  and lithium, 1926
  ocular effects, 958
Nootropic drugs
  dementia of the Alzheimer's type,
    973, 978
Noradrenaline
  dementia of the Alzheimer's type,
    973, 974
Noradrenergic activity elevation in
    posttraumatic stress disorder,
    2071
Norepinephrine
  and antidepressant drugs, 1775–1777
  and imipramine, 1735
  interaction with other drugs, 913,
    914, 928

and mood disorders, 1800
  secondary depression, 1916
and reserpine, 1734, 1795
stress response, 2071
Tourette's syndrome, 691, 706
Normalization of eating disorders
  bulimia nervosa, 541–542
  mentally retarded persons, 61
Northwestern Syntax Screening Test,
    208
Nortriptyline
  autistic disorder, 239
  classification, 1774
  and cognitive-behavioral
    psychotherapy, 1839, 1841,
    1842, 1843, 1845
  dementia, 828
  dosage, 1789
  effects on cardiovascular system,
    901–902, 903
  interaction with other drugs, 867
  mentally retarded persons, 82
  mood disorders, 1793
    dysthymia, 1944
    effectiveness, 1871
    major depression, 1820, 1845
    secondary depression, 946, 1906,
      1907, 1911, 1917, 1923
  obsessive compulsive disorder, 2103
  Parkinson's disease, 865
  pharmacokinetics, 1779, 1780, 1786
    neurotransmitter blockade, 1776
  schizoaffective disorder, 1673, 1674
  sleep disturbances in late life, 2448
  and specific medical diseases, 946,
    1781–1783
  stroke, 875
Nuclear transsexual, 641
Nuclear transvestite, 641
Nurse's Global Impressions Scale
    (NGI), 229
Nurse's role in anorexia nervosa
    inpatient treatment, 456
Nurse support groups in adjustment
    disorder therapy, 2581, 2582,
    2583, 2584, 2585

Nursing home care
  ethical issues, 1001–1002
  making the decision, 830
  Medicare, 983
  organic mental syndromes, 803
  schizophreniform disorder, 1664
  and sexuality, 2374–2375
Nutritional counseling
  anorexia nervosa, 470, 479–480, 485,
    509
  bulimia nervosa, 524, 551
Nutritional rehabilitation
  atypical eating disorders, 592
  bulimia nervosa, 524
Nutritional therapy for pica, 588
Nux vomica
  impotence, 2354
Nylidrin
  multi-infarct dementia, 963
Nystagmus
  and delirium, 808, 813
  from drug intoxication, 891, 892
  and hepatic disease, 936, 938
  side effect of phenytoin, 910

O besity
  and multi-infarct dementia, 962
  and stroke, 869
  treatment, 846
Object constancy, 2012–2013
Obscene language in Tourette's
    syndrome, 688
Obscene phone calls associated with
    sexual sadomasochism, 653
Observational learning
  performance, 114
  socialization, 114
Obsessional disorder. See Obsessive
    compulsive disorder
Obsessional neurosis. See Obsessive
    compulsive disorder
Obsessions, pure, 2096

Obsessive compulsive disorder
  and alcoholism, 1068
  anxiety, 2095, 2099, 2111
  apotreptic therapy, 2098–2099
  aversion therapy, 2098
  behavioral treatments, 2098–2100
  behavior therapy, shortcomings,
    2100
  blocking procedures, 2098
  clinical features, 2095–2098
  communication problems, 2106
  compulsive personality disorder,
    differentiation, 2097
  control, patient's need for, 2106,
    2107, 2109, 2110
  diagnosis, 2096–2097
  diagnostic considerations, 1764
  digressions during therapy, 2106,
    2108
  DSM-III-R diagnostic criteria, 2097
  ego dystonic symptoms, 2096–2097
  electroconvulsive shock therapy,
    2104
  exposure and response prevention
    in therapy, 2098–2100
  grandiosity, 2110
  horrific temptations, 2096
  implosive therapy, 2099
  mentally retarded persons,
    diagnosis, 18
  and obsessive compulsive personal-
    ity disorder, 2636, 2685, 2771
  perfectionism, 2108–2109
  pharmacotherapy, 708–709, 911,
    2100–2104
  prevalence, 2097
  psychosurgery, 1896–1897, 2104–
    2105
  psychotherapy, psychodynamic,
    2105–2111
  psychotic-like decompensations,
    2097
  resistance, 2096
  ritualistic behavior, 2095–2096, 2099,
    2106, 2108, 2110
  self-esteem problems, 2106, 2107

systematic desensitization, 2098
therapeutic alliance, 2107–2108, 2110
and Tourette's syndrome, 688, 689–
    690, 692, 693, 694, 700, 708–709
treatment goals, 2111
and trichotillomania, 2483
types
    checking and doubting, 2096,
        2100, 2109
    pure obsessions, 2096
    slowness, primary obsessional,
        2096
    washing, 2095
Obsessive compulsive personality
    disorder
    and anxiety disorders, 2685
    behavior modification, 2771, 2781,
        2782
    behavior therapy, 2717, 2772–2773,
        2774, 2779–2780
    displacement, 2772
    doubting and rituals, 2776–2777
    DSM-III-R diagnostic criteria, 2771–
        2773
    family history, 2773
    limitation of available research
        material, 2636
    and obsessive compulsive disorder,
        2636, 2685, 2771
    pharmacotherapy, 2679, 2685, 2771,
        2780, 2781
    psychosurgery, 2780–2781
    psychotherapy, 2642, 2771, 2781
        family therapy, 2778–2779
        group therapy, 2675, 2717, 2779
        individual psychotherapy, 2773–
            2778
        psychoanalytic psychotherapy,
            2643, 2646, 2777
        psychodynamic psychotherapy,
            2773–2777
        risks, 2776–2777
        short-term therapy, 2778
    residential treatment, 2781
    resistance, 2697
    and secondary depression, 2780

Obstructive sleep apnea
    continuous positive air pressure
        (CPAP) therapy, 2435
    pharmacotherapy, 2435
    surgery, 2436
    weight loss as therapy, 2434–2435
Occupational problems of drug
    abusers, 1185–1186
Occupational therapy
    organic aggressive syndrome, 848
    with residential treatment, 2695
OCD. *See* Obsessive compulsive
    disorder
ODD. *See* Oppositional defiant
    disorder
Oedipal complex
    brief dynamic psychotherapy, 1879
    childhood gender identity disorder,
        666
    impotence, 2319
    sexual sadomasochism, 649
    teen pregnancy, 2368
    transvestic fetishism, 642, 643
Office management of alcoholism
    and Alcoholics Anonymous, 1134
    considerations, 1132–1133
    and disulfiram, 1134–1135
    patient characteristics, 1132
    support network, 1133–1134, 1135–
        1136
    treatment and relapse prevention,
        1135–1136
Oliguria and renal disease, 920, 925
Olivopontocerebellar degeneration,
    differential diagnosis, 861
Oneida community, 2312
Ononism, 2311
"On the Psychical Mechanisms of
    Hysterical Phenomena," 1824
Operant conditioning in behavior
    therapy
    anorexia nervosa, 456, 476
    anxiety disorders of childhood or
        adolescence, 305, 403
    definitions and techniques, 113–115
    pedophilia, 628

Operant conditioning in behavior
    therapy (cont)
  personality disorders, 2650, 2655,
      2656
  satiation as rumination therapy, 55
  self-injurious behavior, 35
  See also Behavior therapy
Ophthalmologic disease and
      antidepressant drugs, 1782, 1874
Ophthalmoplegia and stroke, 871
Opiate antagonists, 1333
Opiate drug addiction
  interpersonal psychotherapy, 1868
  with secondary depression, 1915,
      1918, 1920
Opiates
  dementia of the Alzheimer's type,
      977
Opioid abuse and dependence
  and AIDS, 1328
  and alcohol abuse, 1313, 1314, 1329
  and anxiety, 1373
  biologic factors, 1313–1314
  and cannabis abuse, 1244
  central nervous system effects, 1328
  and cocaine abuse, 1315
  and crime, 1330, 1345–1346
  detoxification, 1316–1317
  diagnosis, 1313
  etiology, 1312–1315, 1330
  evaluation, 1189
  family factors, 1314–1315
  fetal withdrawal syndrome, 1328
  follow-up studies, 1331–1332
  insomnia during detoxification, 1318,
      1321
  learning mechanisms, 1315
  medical complications, 1327–1328,
      1357
  neuroadaptation, 1310–1311
  opioid receptors, 1309, 1310
  pharmacology, 1309–1312
  pregnancy problems, 1328, 1356
  prevalence, 1309
  prognosis, 1330–1331
  psychiatric disorders
    anxiety disorders, 1313, 1314

  mood disorders, 1185, 1313, 1314,
      1329–1330
  personality disorders, 1313, 1314,
      1330
  schizophrenic disorders, 1304
  psychopathology, 1313, 1314, 1316
  reinforcement factors, 1312–1313,
      1315
  relapse, 1331
  sex as factor, 1328
  social factors in dependence, 1312
  symptom evaluation guidelines, 1190
  tolerance and physical dependence,
      1310–1311
  treatment
    counseling and psychotherapy,
        1327
    detoxification, 1316–1317
    general considerations, 1315
    maintenance programs other than
        methadone, 1325
    methadone maintenance, 1323–
        1324, 1342–1359
    opioid antagonists, 1322–1323
    outpatient drug-free programs,
        1327
    pharmacotherapy for
        detoxification, 1316, 1317, 1318,
        1319, 1320–1323
    therapeutic communities, 1326–
        1327, 1330
  withdrawal, 1311–1312, 1315, 1316–
      1319
  See also Heroin addiction; Morphine
Opioid and benzodiazepine
      combination, intoxication, 1295
Opioid receptors
  action, 1309, 1310
  naltrexone blockage, 1332
Opioid treatment for rumination, 573–
      574, 577
Oppositional defiant disorder
  attention-deficit hyperactivity
      disorder and conduct disorder
      association, 365–366
  DSM-III-R diagnostic criteria, 369

Oppositional personality disorder
  case study, 776–777
  definition, 775–776
  suggested reformulation of
      personality disorders
      classification, 733–734, 772
  treatment, 775, 776
  See also Immature personality
      disorders; names of specific
      disorders
Oral character, 2661, 2762
  personality disorders, 2640
Oral contraceptives
  and metabolism of alcohol, 1077
  ocular effects, 958
  and secondary depression, 1912,
      1913
  and stroke, 869
Organic affective syndrome
  differential diagnosis, 841
  See also Organic personality
      syndrome
Organic aggressive syndrome
  age factor, 853
  differential diagnosis, 841–842
  DSM-III-R diagnostic criteria, 841,
      843–845
  incidence, 842–843
  patient evaluation, 845–846
  treatment
    behavior therapy, 848–849
    family therapy, 847–848
    pharmacotherapy, 842, 847, 848,
        849–851, 852
    psychotherapy, 847–848
  See also Organic personality
      syndrome
Organic anxiety syndrome
  differential diagnosis, 806, 841
  See also Organic personality
      syndrome
Organic delusional syndrome
  and delirium, 832
  and delusional (paranoid) disorders,
      1612

differential diagnosis, 832–833, 836–
    837, 841, 855, 859, 1709
DSM-III-R diagnostic criteria, 831–
    832, 834
patient evaluation, 837
and schizophrenia, 832
and secondary depression, 837
seizures, 836
sensory changes, 835
and stroke, 874
treatment, 837–839
    amphetamine-related psychosis,
      838
    cocaine-related psychosis, 838
    seizure-related psychosis, 839
See also Organic personality
    syndrome
Organic depressive syndrome
  differential diagnosis, 854–855
  patient evaluation, 855
  treatment, 855–856
  See also Organic mood syndrome
Organic dyscontrol. *See* Organic
    personality disorder
Organic hallucinosis
  and delirium, 832
  and dementia, 832
  differential diagnosis, 806, 832–833,
      836–837, 855, 859
  DSM-III-R diagnostic criteria, 831–
      832, 834, 835
  patient evaluation, 837
  and schizophrenia, 832
  sensory changes, 835
  and stroke, 873
  treatment, 837–839
Organic manic syndrome
  differential diagnosis, 855
  patient evaluation, 855
  treatment, 855–856
  See also Organic mood syndrome
Organic mental disorder not otherwise
    specified
  phencyclidine abuse as cause, 1215–
      1216

Organic mental disorders
  diagnostic criteria, 1699–1700
  differential diagnosis, 1700
  distinguished from schizophrenia,
    1493–1498
  See also names of specific disorders
Organic mental disorders, alcohol-
    related. *See* Alcohol-related
    organic mental disorders
Organic mental syndromes, 797–1060
  and aging, 800–803, 899
  delirium, 804–815
  diagnosis, 799–800
  differential diagnosis, 1905
  economic considerations, 799, 802
  from electroconvulsive therapy, 1812
  ethical considerations, 799, 994–1008
  geriatric patients, 800–803
  legal considerations, 799, 983–994
  pharmacotherapy, 801
  and secondary depression, 1918
  social factors, 803
  treatment, 799
  See also names of specific syndromes
Organic mood syndrome
  and delirium, 853
  and depressive disorders, 853–854,
    855, 1754
  differential diagnosis, 806, 837, 854–
    855, 858, 1910
  DSM-III-R diagnostic criteria, 853,
    1900
  and epilepsy, 882
  etiology, 853
  incidence, 853
  patient evaluation, 855
  and stroke, 875–876
  treatment, 855–856, 1741
Organic personality disorder, explosive
    type, 839–852
Organic personality syndrome
  atypical impulse control disorder,
    differentiation, 2477
  diagnostic criteria, 841, 843–845, 857,
    883, 884
  differential diagnosis, 837, 858–859

  and epilepsy, 881
  etiology, 858
  incidence, 842–843, 857–858
  patient evaluation, 845–846, 859
  treatment, 859–860
    behavior therapy, 848–849
    family therapy, 847–848
    pharmacotherapy, 847, 848, 849–
      851, 852
    psychotherapy, 847–848
Orgasm
  female, 2279–2282, 2387
  male, 2386
Orgasmic cephalgia, 2317–2318
Orgasmic dysfunctions. *See* Inhibited
    female orgasm; Retarded
    ejaculation
Orgasmic reconditioning
  pedophilia, 627
  sex offenders, 2653
  transvestic fetishism, 644
Orgasm with flaccid penis, 2310
Oriental sexuality, 2312, 2381
Orphenadrine
  countermeasure for side effects of
    neuroleptic drugs, 1629
  secondary depression, 1922, 1923
Orthomolecular therapies
  autistic disorder, 241
  schizophrenia, 1502
Orthostatic hypotension
  from antidepressant drugs, 946
  imipramine side effect, 1908
  increased risk of diuretics, 913
  levodopa-related, 867
  from phenothiazine treated delirium,
    944
  and renal disease, 928–929
  side effect of antidepressants, 827–
    828, 902–903, 904
  side effect of antihypertensives, 912
  side effect of antipsychotic drugs,
    907
  side effect of methyldopa, 911
  side effect of monoamine oxidase
    inhibitors, 905

side effect of neuroleptic drugs, 838
side effect of propranolol, 913, 915
Osteomalacia from renal disease, 916
Othello syndrome. *See* Morbid jealousy
Other disorders of infancy, childhood,
    or adolescence, 731–796
    See also names of specific disorders
Output disabilities of learning disabled
    children, 320
Outward Bound program for
    adolescents, 2501, 2749
Overanxious disorder of childhood
    behavior therapy, 424–426
    cycling effect, 425
    family therapy, 431–433
    pharmacotherapy, 426–428
    psychotherapy, 428–431
Overcorrection
    behavior problems in autistic
      children, 224
    behavior therapy, definition, 113
    pica, 586
    self-injurious behavior, 35
    stereotyped behavior, abnormal, of
      mentally retarded persons, 48
Overdosing
    barbiturate-sedative-hypnotic drugs,
      1301, 1302
    drug addicts, hospital treatment,
      1363
    methadone, 1348
    opioids, naloxone treatment, 1334
    phencyclidine abuse and
      dependence, 1213
    stimulant abuse, management, 1224,
      1225
Overprotectiveness in families of
    anorectic patients, 495, 497
Overstimulation in infants as cause of
    rumination, 568–569
Overt sensitization
    transvestic fetishism, 644
Oxazepam
    alcohol withdrawal, 1087
    anxiety and lung disease, 945
    anxiety disorders, 2039

    delirium, 809, 810, 811
    hepatic disease, 937
    renal disease, 922
Oxiracetam
    dementia of the Alzheimer's type,
      973
Oxybutynin
    functional enuresis, 723

Pacific Crest Outward Bound School
    for antisocial personality
    disorder treatment, 2749
Pagophagia, 585
Pain, chronic, somatoform
    acupuncture, 2132
    and anxiety, 2129
    characteristics, 2122–2123
    cognitive therapy, 2130
    compensation and disability
      payments as factor, 2136
    and depression, 2129
    distinction from physical disorder,
      2123
    electroconvulsive therapy, 2133
    etiology, 2123
    exercise, 2130
    follow-up studies, 2136–2138
    gate control, 2132, 2136
    hypnosis, 2131–2132
    hypochondriasis, 2144
    innovative strategies, 2133
    management program, 2124–2130
    nature, 2122
    nerve blocks, 2132–2133
    outcome studies, 2136–2138
    pain clinics, 2121, 2122, 2123
    peer support, 2136
    pharmacotherapy, 2129
    physical rehabilitation, 2130
    primary physician, role, 2136
    re-entry planning, 2135
    sensory stimulation, 2132
    surgical procedures, 2133

Pain, chronic, somatoform *(cont)*
  transcutaneous nerve stimulation (TNS), 2132
Pain behavior, alteration, 2134, 2135
Pain management, 2124–2130
Pain prone disorder with secondary depression, 1903
Palilalia in Tourette's syndrome, 688
Palmar erythema
  and alcoholic liver disease, 933
  and hepatic disease, 935
Pancreatic carcinoma
  and organic mood syndrome, 855
  and secondary depression, 854, 1902, 1904, 1906
Pancreatitis and delirium, 811
Panel on Depression and Mood Disorders, 1725
Panic attacks
  and personality disorders, 2688
  pharmacotherapy, 2685
Panic disorder
  adjunctive therapy procedures, 2035, 2052–2065
  behavior therapy, 2035
  differential diagnosis, 859, 883, 884, 1764
  distinguished from agoraphobia, 2015
  in drug addicts, hospital treatment, 1373–1374, 1376
  and hypochondriasis, 2138, 2145
  in mentally retarded persons, diagnosis, 17
  and mood disorders, 1755
  pharmacotherapy, 2047–2051, 2587
  psychoanalytic psychotherapy, 2015–2019
  respiratory control method, 2035
  See also Agoraphobia
Papaverine
  dementia of the Alzheimer's type, 972
  multi-infarct dementia, 962, 963
Paper pica, 584
Paradoxical orgasm, 2251

Paradoxical responses to sedative-hypnotic agents by mentally retarded persons, 90
Paradoxical techniques in behavior therapy for anorexia nervosa, 476, 506–507
Paraldehyde
  organic aggressive syndrome, 850
  organic delusional syndrome, 838
Paranoia
  from antituberculosis drugs, 944, 947
  from asthma drugs, 943, 944
  and borderline personality disorder, 2681
  and brief reactive psychosis, 1682, 1683
  from clonidine, 911
  and delirium, 805, 808–809, 813
  and dementia, 826
  effects of hallucinogens, 1207, 1208–1209
  and hepatic disease, 930, 931
  and induced psychotic disorder, 1686–1687, 1691, 1695–1696
  and infective endocarditis, 896
  and organic aggressive syndrome, 841
  and organic personality syndrome, 841, 857, 858
  and Parkinson's disease, 863
  as a psychodynamic factor of pedophilia, 631
  and renal disease, 916
  and schizoaffective disorder, 1671
  and sensory impairment, 950, 951
  and stroke, 874
  term retained in ICD-9, 1612
  See also Delusional (paranoid) disorders; Paranoid personality disorder
Paranoid disorders. *See* Delusional (paranoid) disorders; Paranoid personality disorder
Paranoid personality disorder
  behavior therapy, 2710

countertransference, 2708, 2714
and depressive disorders, 2708,
    2709, 2710
distinguished from schizophrenia,
    1497
DSM-III-R diagnostic criteria, 1612,
    2705–2707
limitation of available research
    material, 2636
pharmacotherapy, 2679, 2680, 2682,
    2710–2711
psychotherapy, 2642, 2707–2708
  with adjunctive therapy, 2709
  autonomy, 2708
  brief therapy, 2710
  family therapy, 2710
  group therapy, 2670–2671, 2710
  psychoanalytic psychotherapy,
    2645, 2646, 2647
  therapeutic alliance, 2707
residential treatment, 2711
resistance, 2697
and schizophrenia, 2705
transference, 2709
See also Delusional (paranoid)
    disorders; Paranoia
Paranoid psychoses, 1621–1622, 1687
Paranoid schizophrenia, 1491, 1498
  amphetamine-related, 832–833
  differential diagnosis, 1687, 1735,
    1760, 1761
  and induced psychotic disorder,
    1696
Paranoid-schizotypal personality
    disorder, differential diagnosis,
    1689
Paraphilias, 615–683
  stroke-related, 877
Paraphrenia
  classification in diagnostic systems
    other than DSM, 1612, 1614,
    1615
  definition, 1689
  and sensory impairment, 951
  See also Late paraphrenia

Paraphrenia, late. *See* Late paraphrenia
Parasomnias in children
  bruxism (tooth grinding), 2424
  definition and categories, 2419
  enuresis (bedwetting), 2423–2424
  etiology, 2420
  nightmares and night terrors, 2420–
    2422, 2562
  psychopathology, 2420
  sex as factor, 2523, 2524
  sleepwalking, 2422–2423
  stress, 2421, 2422, 2424
Parasympathomimetic drugs
  impotence, 2357
Paraverbal therapy for elective
    mutism, 768–769
Paregoric in rumination treatment, 573
Parental factors in substance abuse,
    1200–1201
Parental role in personality disorders,
    2634, 2641–2642, 2644
  narcissistic personality disorder,
    2738
Parental stress
  parents of autistic children, 257–262
  parents of mentally retarded, 106–
    107
  See also Family problems
Parent burnout, parents of autistic
    children, 261–262
Parent-child relationship
  language disabilities, 339–340
  learning disabilities, 347–348
Parent counseling
  autistic disorder, 254–262
  mental retardation, 106–107
  mood disorders in children and
    adolescents, 1954
  pervasive developmental disorders,
    254–262
Parent Daily Report, 382, 389
Parent-infant bonding, 734–736, 2011–
    2012
  See also Reactive attachment disorder
    of infancy

Parent-Infant Growth Program, 746
Parent involvement in education, 124, 194, 198, 200
    learning disabled children, 305–307, 322–325
Parent-physician relationship in treatment of mentally retarded persons, 100–101
Parent role in alcoholism, 1111, 1114
    See also Adult children of alcoholics; Children of alcoholics
Parent role in early identification of developmental disorders, 303–304
Parent role in organic aggressive syndrome, 844
Parent role in paraphilias
    childhood gender identity disorder, 664, 666, 667–669
    pedophilia, 620, 632
    transvestic fetishism, 635, 643
    See also Maternal role in paraphilias; Paternal role in paraphilias
Parent role in pica, 580–581
Parent role in treatment
    autistic disorder, 250–254
    childhood gender identity disorder, 664, 669
    immature personality disorders, 782
    mentally retarded persons, 25, 137
    See also Family role in treatment; Parent involvement in education
Parents Anonymous, 2598, 2599, 2600, 2601, 2611
Parents Without Partners, 2611
Paresis and delirium, 808
Paresthesias
    and acute porphyria, 932
    and digitalis toxicity, 908
    epilepsy-related, 880
    and hyperkalemia, 899
Parkinsonism
    and antidepressant drugs, 849, 1511, 1784
    and organic mood syndrome, 1741

Parkinson's disease
    age factor, 862, 863
    and confusional states, 861, 863, 865
    and dementia, 861–862, 865
    and depressive disorders, 854, 861, 862–863, 864, 865
    differential diagnosis, 935
    DSM-III-R diagnostic criteria, 860–861
    extrapyramidal side effects, 827
    nonresponsiveness to antidepressant treatment, 1792
    patient evaluation, 864
    pharmacotherapy, 863–866, 966, 974, 978
        drug-disease interactions, 866
        drug-drug interactions, 866–867
    psychotic reactions, 863–864
    with secondary depression, 1910
    treatment of accompanying organic mental syndrome, 864–865
Paroxysmal dyskinesias, 692
Partial seizures. See Epilepsy, partial seizures
Passive-aggressive personality disorder
    and anxiety disorders, 2656, 2685, 2787
    behavior therapy, 2651, 2787–2788
    in children, 772, 775, 777–778
    cognitions, 2785
    and dependent personality disorder, 2763, 2764, 2770
    diagnostic criteria, 2783–2784
    and dysthymia, 2787
    pharmacotherapy, 2679, 2784, 2788–2789
        noncompliance, 2789
    psychodynamics, 2785–2786
    psychotherapy, 2642
        group therapy, 2675, 2788
        problems, 2786
        psychoanalytic psychotherapy, 2646
        psychodynamic psychotherapy, 2786–2787

resistance, 2697, 2786, 2787
and secondary depression, 2784,
　　2785, 2787
transference, 2786, 2787
Paternal role in paraphilias
　childhood gender identity disorder,
　　666, 667–669
　pedophilia, 632
　sexual sadomasochism, 650, 651–
　　652, 653, 654, 655
　transvestic fetishism, 635, 643
Pathological intoxication, 1082–1084
Pathologic gambling
　consequences, 2464
　and depression, 2464, 2465
　diagnosis problems, 2463–2464
　etiology, 2465
　history of treatment, 2464
　hospitalization, 2465
　and other psychiatric disorders,
　　2464–2465, 2466
　self-help programs, 2464, 2465, 2466
　suicide attempts, 2465
　treatment modalities, 2465–2466
Patuxent Institution
　antisocial personality disorder
　　treatment, 2748
Pavlovian conditioning. *See*
　　Respondent conditioning
PCP. *See* Phencyclidine abuse and
　　dependence
PDD. *See* Primary degenerative
　　dementia
PDDAT. *See* Primary degenerative
　　dementia of the Alzheimer's
　　type
PEA. *See* Phenylethylamine
Peabody Picture Vocabulary Test
　　Revised (PPVTR), 209, 330
Pedohebephilia, 617–618
Pedophilia
　adolescent pedophiles, 619, 620–621
　age differences, 617
　bisexuals, 618
　etiology, 625, 632
　and exhibitionism, 671

family relationships, 621
features, 617
heterosexuals, 617, 618, 619, 620
homosexuals, 617, 618, 619, 620
incidence, 621–623
middle-age pedophiles, 619, 621
parent effect, 620, 632
pharmacotherapy, 628, 629–630
phenomenology, 618–621
place of offense, 620
recidivism, 619, 622–623, 626, 627,
　　629
relationship between victim and
　　offender, 618, 620, 622
senescent pedophiles, 619, 621
spouse role, 621
treatment, 623–632, 2653
treatment effectiveness, 628
Types I, II, and III, 619
Peer-helping services for youth, 2607–
　　2616
　alternative services, 2615
　behavior changes, 2615
　categories, 2610
　characteristics, 2609–2610
　counseling, 2614–2615
　definitions and roles, 2608–2609
　hazards, 2616
　origins, 2607–2608
　peer influence, 2609–2610
　peer support, 2610
　political issues, 2609
　services, 2614–2616
　tutoring, 2614
　types, 2614
　See also Mutual-help services for
　　youth
Peer pressure and substance abuse,
　　1200
Pellagra
　from antituberculosis drugs, 944
　with secondary depression, 1902
Pemoline
　minimal brain dysfunction, 2686
　Tourette's syndrome, 690

Penfluridol
    Tourette's syndrome, 690
Penicillamine
    Wilson's disease, 934
Penile cavernosal tissue abnormality,
        2242
Penile plethysmography
    fetishism, 639
    pedophilia, 624
Penile pressure, 2242
Penile prosthesis implantation
    diagnosis, 2330–2331
    indications, 2310, 2331–2332
    inflatable prostheses, 2332–2333
    role of the psychiatrist, 2334
    SST deformity, 2332
    types of prostheses, 2332–2333
Penile structural defects, 2242, 2243,
        2293
Pentazocine
    hepatic disease, 938
    and organic psychosis, 833
    pharmacology, 1309
    and secondary depression, 1912
Pentobarbital
    alcohol withdrawal, 1088–1089
    delirium, 812
Pentothal
    epilepsy, 890
Pentoxifylline
    dementia of the Alzheimer's type,
        973
    multi-infarct dementia, 962, 963
Peptic ulcers, psychotherapy, 2149
Perceptual abnormalities and stroke,
        873–874
Perfectionism in obsessive compulsive
        disorder, 2108–2109
Performance anxiety, 2320–2321, 2338
Periodic catatonia, 1709
    See also Atypical psychosis
Periodic psychosis of puberty. See
        Atypical psychosis, menses
        associated
Pernicious anemia
    and secondary depression, 1902

Perphenazine
    depressive disorders
        dysthymia, 1942
        secondary depression, 1922
    interaction with other drugs, 928
    late paraphrenia, 1641
    stroke-related syndromes, 874
Persecutory delusional disorder, 1634–
        1640
Persecutory delusions
    and delirium, 811
Personality disorders
    and adjustment disorders, 2506,
        2507
    affective spectrum of disorders,
        2683–2685
    Alcoholics Anonymous, 2695
    and alcoholism, 1094
    and anorexia nervosa, 513
    antisocial personality disorder, 2742–
        2749
    anxiety spectrum of disorders, 2685
    avoidant personality disorder, 2759–
        2762
    behavioral formulation, 2649
    behavior therapy. See Behavior
        therapy
    biological formulation, 2678–2679
    borderline personality disorder,
        2749–2759
    character structures and, 773
    choosing a treatment, 2659
    conceptual base, 2633–2635
    couples therapy, 2663–2665
    dependent personality disorder,
        2762–2770
    diagnosis in children, 733–734, 749,
        750, 772, 781–782
    differential diagnosis, 884, 1751
    distinction between dystonic and
        syntonic traits, 2640
    distinguished from schizophrenia,
        1497
    in drug addicts, hospital treatment,
        1374, 1376
    duration of treatment, 1637–1638

and dysthymia, 1940, 1942–1943
family theorist formulation, 2660
family therapy, 2637, 2663–2665,
2746, 2762
group therapy, 2761–2762, 2788
histrionic personality disorder, 2727–
2736
limitation of available research, 2636,
2637
marital therapy, 2663–2665
versus mood disorders, 1764
narcissistic personality disorder,
2736–2742
and neurologic disorders, 2685–2686
obsessive compulsive personality
disorder, 2771–2782
opioid abuse and dependence, 1313,
1314, 1330
organic spectrum of disorders, 2685–
2686
overlap with mood disorders, 2682,
2683–2685
paranoid personality disorder, 2705–
2711
passive-aggressive personality
disorder, 2783–2789
pharmacotherapy. *See*
Pharmacotherapy
psychodynamic formulation, 2639–
2640
and psychogenic amnesia, 2186,
2190
psychotherapy. *See* Psychotherapy
resistance, 2640, 2647, 2651, 2656,
2697, 2786, 2787
schizoid personality disorder, 2712–
2718
schizotypal personality disorder,
2719–2726
with secondary depression, 1765
self-destructive behavior, 2653
and sexual disorders, 2256–2264,
2336
splitting, 2669, 2690, 2712, 2714,
2739, 2743

suggested reformulation of
classification, 733–734, 772
with underlying medical conditions,
2656
See also Immature personality
disorders; names of specific
disorders
Personality syndrome. *See* Organic
personality syndrome
Personality traits, 772–774
Pervasive developmental disorders,
177–294
assessment instruments, 185–187
behavior therapy, 217–226
definition, 180
diagnosis and evaluation, 182–192
DSM-III-R diagnostic criteria, 180–
182
evaluation methods, 184–190
individualization of treatment plan,
183, 191, 192
language and communication
therapy, 201–217
pharmacotherapy, 226–248
predictors for outcome, 184
reformulation in DSM, 179, 180
treatment goals, 191
treatment methods, 266–274
treatment plan implementation, 190–
192
See also Autistic children; Autistic
disorder
Perversion, 648
PET. *See* Positron emission tomography
Peyronie's disease, 2242, 2243, 2293
Phallic partner, 2661
Phallometry, 627
Pharmacologic treatment. *See*
Pharmacotherapy
Pharmacotherapy
acromegaly, 833
adjustment disorders, 2585–2590
agoraphobia, 2033–2034
alcoholism, 1075, 1076, 1100–1101,
1126–1127, 1134–1135

Pharmacotherapy *(cont)*
  alcohol withdrawal, 1085, 1087–1089, 1090, 1137–1138
  Alzheimer's disease, 828, 829
  anorexia nervosa, 471
  anxiety disorders, 2036–2052
  anxiety disorders in mentally retarded, 18
  anxiety disorders of childhood or adolescence, 405–408, 416–418, 426–428, 435–436
  attention-deficit hyperactivity disorder, 373–377
  atypical impulse control disorder, 2479–2480
  atypical psychosis, 1704–1705
  autistic disorder, 226–248
  avoidant disorder of childhood, 435–436
  biochemical model of anxiety, 405–407
  bipolar disorder, 909
  brief reactive psychosis, 1680, 1681–1682, 1684
  bulimia nervosa, 521, 525, 528–531
  cannabis abuse and dependence, 1249, 1252, 1254
  cardiovascular disease, 900, 901–905
  child treatment issues, 232, 234
  conduct disorder, 386–387
  conversion disorders, 2158
  delirium, 809–810, 811–814
  delusional (paranoid) disorders, 1627–1632
  dementia, 826–829, 831
  dementia of the Alzheimer's type, 963, 967–979
  depersonalization disorder, 2221, 2222
  elective mutism, 771
  epilepsy, 882, 889, 894
  exhibitionism, 630
  factitious disorder with physical symptoms, 2163
  fetishism, 637–638
  functional enuresis, 722–723

  hallucinogen abuse, 1208
  hepatic disease, 937–938
  hospital treatment for drug addicts, 1374–1375
  hyperprolactinemia, 833
  hypochondriasis, 2140–2142, 2143, 2144–2145
  impotence, 2357
  impulse control disorders, 2487
  induced psychotic disorder, 1695, 1697
  intermittent explosive disorder, 2476
  mania, 911
  measures for untoward effects of drugs, 229
  mentally retarded persons, 67–99
    monitoring, 68–71
    Prader-Willi syndrome, 51
    reduction of use as treatment, 67, 68, 69, 70
  monosymptomatic hypochondriasis, 839, 874, 1705
  mood disorders, 1729, 1730, 1733, 1734–1739, 1744–1745
    bipolar disorders, 1758, 1760, 1938–1939, 1940
    depressive disorders, 1756, 1787–1802, 1817, 1818–1820, 1821, 1839, 1845–1846, 1848, 1863, 1948, 1949
    effectiveness, 1822, 1839
  multi-infarct dementia, 962–964
  multiple personality disorder, 2205, 2209–2210
  nocturnal myoclonus, 2437–2438
  obsessive compulsive disorder, 708–709, 911, 2100–2104
  obstructive sleep apnea, 2435
  opioid detoxification, 1316, 1317, 1318, 1319, 1320–1322, 1322–1323
  organic aggressive syndrome, 842, 847, 848, 849–851, 852
  organic delusional syndrome, 837–839
  organic mental syndromes, 801

organic mental syndromes with sensory impairment, 957–959, 960

organic personality syndrome, 847, 848, 849–851, 852, 859

overanxious disorder of childhood, 426–428

panic anxiety, 2047–2051

panic disorder, 2587

Parkinson's disease, 863–866, 966, 974, 978

pedophilia, 623, 628, 629–630

periodic catatonia, 1709

personality disorders, 2635, 2637, 2659, 2678–2689

   antisocial personality disorder, 2679, 2680, 2682, 2746–2747

   avoidant personality disorder, 2762

   borderline personality disorder, 2679, 2680, 2683, 2684, 2688, 2741, 2754–2755, 2759

   combined with psychotherapy, 2683, 2688–2689

   dependent personality disorder, 2675, 2770

   duration of treatment, 2687

   histrionic personality disorder, 2735–2736

   indications and contraindications, 2688

   narcissistic personality disorder, 2741

   obsessive compulsive personality disorder, 2679, 2685, 2771, 2780, 2781

   paranoid personality disorder, 2679, 2680, 2682, 2710–2711

   passive-aggressive personality disorder, 2679, 2784, 2788–2789

   practicalities of treatment, 2687–2689

   in residential treatment, 2690

   schizoid personality disorder, 2679, 2680, 2682, 2718

schizotypal personality disorder, 2680, 2681, 2682–2683, 2725

pervasive developmental disorders, 226–248

   cognitive measures, 229

   contraindications for, 227

   efficacy assessment, 228–232

   goals, 226–228

   indications for, 227

   literature review, 234–248

   methodology and experimental design, 229–231

   rating conditions, 231–232

phencyclidine abuse and dependence, 1213, 1215

phobias, 2047–2051, 2587

pica, 588–589

polypharmacy avoidance, 98–99, 1506

postpartum psychosis, 1707–1708

posttraumatic stress disorder, 2073–2075

premature ejaculation, 2309

primary insomnia, 2426, 2430

psychiatric symptoms of lung disease, 945–946

and psychotherapy, 1733–1734, 1786–1787, 1791, 1817, 1819–1820, 1821, 1826, 1839, 1863, 1885, 1886, 1888, 1890, 1943, 1945

   cognitive-behavioral, 1838, 1839, 1840–1841, 1842, 1843

   future directions for research, 1823

   interpersonal psychotherapy, 1866

versus psychotherapy, 1818–1819

renal disease, 920–929

rumination, 576–577

schizoaffective disorder, 1656, 1672–1674, 1675, 1676

schizoid disorder of childhood or adolescence, 760

schizophrenia, 1486, 1501–1515

   acute schizophrenics, 1507–1508

   administration, 1505–1506

   benefits, 1502

Pharmacotherapy *(cont)*
    chronic schizophrenics, 1508
    combined with other treatments, 1503, 1519, 1569, 1575, 1580–1581, 1583
    common errors, 1507–1508
    compared with electroconvulsive therapy, 1502
    dosing strategy, 1505, 1507–1508
    full disclosure and informed consent, 1505, 1511
    limitations of, 1569
    maintenance treatment, 1508–1510
    medication management module, 1581
    negative effects, 1510–1511
    noncompliance of patient, 1505–1506, 1509, 1514, 1581
    polypharmacy avoidance, 1506
    reassessment, 1508
    treatment considerations, 1501–1502, 1503, 1507–1508
    treatment goals, 1505
  schizophreniform disorder, 1656, 1657, 1658, 1659–1660, 1661–1662
  secondary depression with cancer, 1905–1907
  secondary depression with cardio-vascular disease, 1907–1908
  secondary depression with chronic pain, 1903–1904
  sensory-impaired patients, 957–959
  separation anxiety disorder of childhood, 416–418
  sexual anxiety, 2247
  sexual disorders, 2247, 2343–2359
    drugs to avoid, 2349
    drugs with positive sexual effects, 2349–2356
    effects of psychotropic drugs, 2346–2348
    ethical issues, 2358–2359
    limitations of available data, 2345–2346
    mechanisms of action for sexually depressive drugs, 2349
    premature ejaculation, 2309
    reduction of sex drive, 2356
    speculations, 2356–2358
    transient and sustained effects, 2358
    treatment considerations, 2358–2359
  sexual effects of commonly prescribed drugs, 2344–2345
  sexual sadomasochism, 651, 652
  side effects, 16, 70
  sleep-wake schedule disorders, 2442
  somatoform pain disorder, 2129–2130
  stereotyped behavior, abnormal, 49
  stimulant abuse, relapse prevention, 1236–1237, 1240
  stroke, 867, 871, 874, 875
  Tourette's syndrome, 692, 695, 696, 697, 701, 703–709, 911
  transvestic fetishism, 643, 644, 645–646
  tremor in alcoholics, 1085
  trichotillomania, 2482–2483, 2486
  violent behavior in alcoholics, 1084
  See also names of specific drugs and classes of drugs
pH disturbances. *See* Acid-base disturbances
Phencyclidine abuse and dependence
  acidification treatment, 1213, 1215
  age as factor, 1217
  anxiety, 1373
  central nervous system effects, 1210
  complications, 1213–1214
  as contaminant in other drugs, 1210
  and delirium, 810, 813–814
  differential diagnosis, 1212
  DSM-III-R diagnostic criteria, 1211
  electroconvulsive shock therapy, 1215
  intoxication, 1211–1214
  laboratory tests, 1212, 1213
  LSD, differential diagnosis, 1206
  management, 1216–1218

and organic aggressive syndrome, 842

and organic delusional syndrome, 833, 834

and organic hallucinosis, 833

overdosing, 1213

overview, 1209–1211

pharmacotherapy, 1213, 1215

psychosis, drug-induced, 1214, 1371, 1372

psychotic reactions, 1210

and secondary depression, 1217

and secondary mania, 854, 1914

seizure and status epilepticus, 1213

symptoms, 1212, 1214

tolerance and withdrawal, 1210

toxicity stages, 1211

treatment techniques, 1212–1213, 1214–1215, 1216–1218

Phencyclidine delusional disorder. *See* Organic delusional syndrome

Phenelzine

anxiety disorders, 2049–2051

anxiety-hypochondriasis combination, 2145

cause of parasitosis delusions, 2146

classification, 1774

depersonalization disorder, 2221

depressive disorders

dysthymia, 1942

secondary depression, 1917

dosage, 1797

effectiveness, 1803

effects on cardiovascular system, 905

and electroconvulsive therapy, 1813

personality disorders, 2687

histrionic personality disorder, 2735

obsessive compulsive personality disorder, 2685

with secondary depression, 2683, 2684

pharmacokinetics, 1780, 1785–1786

posttraumatic stress symptoms in combat veterans, 2588–2589

premature ejaculation, 2353, 2357

side effects, 2049

somatic symptoms, 2151

Phenmetrazine

mood disorders, 1735

Phenobarbital

adverse effects in epileptic children, 96–97

alcohol withdrawal, 1088–1089

epilepsy, 888, 889, 890

interaction with other drugs, 890, 891, 893

side effects, 891

substitution technique, 1296

withdrawal, 1296, 1297

Phenothiazines

anxiety due to hallucinogen abuse, 1207

borderline personality disorder, 2682, 2754

delirium, 809, 813

delusional (paranoid) disorders, 1631

effects on cardiovascular system, 906, 907

interaction with other drugs, 890, 914, 915, 921, 928

late paraphrenia, 1640

mentally retarded persons, 71–75

mood disorders, 1734, 1736

bipolar disorders, 1929

major depression, 1742

ocular effects, 958

organic aggressive syndrome, 849

organic delusional syndrome, 838

and orthostatic hypotension, 928

in pregnancy, 1806

premature ejaculation, 2309

procarbazine-induced delirium, 944

renal disease, 921, 922, 923

schizophrenia, 1503, 1506, 1507, 1516

seizures, 884

with a sensory-impaired patient, 958

side effects, 849, 1922

See also Neuroleptic drugs

Phenoxybenzamine

premature ejaculation, 2357

Phentolamine
  neurotransmitter blockade, 1776
Phenylalanine
  sexual effects, 2354
Phenylalkylamine derivatives. *See*
    Hallucinogen abuse
Phenylbutazone
  hepatic disease, 938
  interaction with other drugs, 891,
    927
Phenylephrine
  interaction with other drugs, 959
  and secondary depression, 1912,
    1913
Phenylethanolamine
  interaction with other drugs, 891
Phenylethylamine
  sexual effects, 2354
Phenylpropanolamine
  interaction with other drugs, 913
Phenytoin
  alcohol withdrawal, 1088
  behavioral effects in mentally
    retarded persons, 94–96
  bulimia nervosa, 529
  epilepsy, 888, 889, 890
  interaction with calcium, 890
  interaction with other drugs, 890–
    891, 892, 893, 915, 947
  menses-associated psychosis, 1708
  neuropsychiatric effects, 910
  and organic psychosis, 833
  and secondary depression, 1912,
    1913
  side effects, 890
Pheochromocytoma
  and secondary depression, 1902
Pheromones, sexual, 2355
Phii Pob, factitious disorder, 2165
Phimosis, 2293
Phobias
  adjunctive therapy procedures,
    2052–2065
  anxiety management training, 2537
  behavior therapy, 2026–2034, 2649,
    2779
  case histories, 2058–2061

diagnostic considerations, 1764
differential diagnosis, 859
disease and germ phobia, 2143
mentally retarded persons,
    diagnosis, 17
modeling, 2540
and personality disorders, 2685, 2688
  dependent personality disorder,
    2764
  paranoid personality disorder,
    2710
pharmacotherapy, 1737, 2047–2051,
    2587, 2685, 2710
psychoanalytic psychotherapy, 2019–
    2022
psychosurgery, 1897
pubic hair phobia in pedophilia, 631
school phobia and Tourette's
    syndrome, 697
See also Anxiety disorders; Simple
    phobias; Social phobias
Phobic character, 2759
Phobic disorders. *See* Phobias
Phonetic errors in mild speech
    disorders, 345
Phonologic disorders, developmental,
    314–315
Phonologic process approach to
    articulation disorders, 344
Phospenes induced by sound, 835
Phosphatidylcholine
  dementia of the Alzheimer's type,
    973
Phosphatidylethanolamine
  dementia of the Alzheimer's type,
    973
Phototherapy
  effectiveness, 1892–1893
  mechanism of action, 1894–1895
  mood disorders, 1729, 1740, 1890–
    1896
    bipolar disorders, 1932–1933
    seasonal affective disorder (SAD),
      1801, 1891–1896
  phase-shifting effects of light, 1895–
    1896
  practical considerations, 1893–1894

side effects, 1894
Physical abnormalities
  eating disorders, 58–59
  fragile X syndrome, 39, 41–42
Physical illness groups
  adjustment disorders, 2579, 2581,
    2583, 2584, 2585
Physical restraint
  behavior therapy guidelines, 117
  legal issues, 991–992, 993
  pica, 588
  self-injurious behavior, 36, 37
Physician-parent relationship in
    treatment of mentally retarded
    persons, 100–101
Physician's attitude toward alcoholics,
    1079
Physicians Desk Reference (PDR), 232,
    234, 1672, 1705
Physostigmine
  anticholinergic crisis, 1681
  brief reactive psychosis, 1681
  delirium, 813, 814
  dementia of the Alzheimer's type,
    967, 968, 969, 970, 971
  side effects, 813
Piblokto, factitious disorder, 2165
Pica
  amylophagia, 586
  animal models of, 581–583
  in Australian aborigines, 584
  behavior therapy, 586, 587
  Bezoars, 585
  clinical description, 584–585
  definition, 579–580
  etiology, 580–581
  food selection studies, 582
  geophagia, 586, 588
  incidence, 583–584
  iron deficiency, 581–583, 585–586,
    587
  iron treatment, 588
  and lead poisoning, 52, 583
  medical complications, 584–586
  mentally retarded persons, 8, 51–53,
    120, 584

nutrient treatment, 588
and other disorders, 584
overcorrection in behavior therapy,
    586
pagophagia, 585
paper pica, 584
parental role, 580–581
pharmacotherapy, 588–589
physical restraint in prevention, 588
prevalence, 583–584
psychosocial treatment, 589
in schizophrenic patients, 570, 585
treatment, 586–589
zinc deficiency, 588
See also Mental retardation
Pick's disease, 818–819
See also Dementia
Pills Anonymous, 1299
Pimozide
  anorexia nervosa, 471, 472
  autistic disorder, 242
  monosymptomatic hypochondriasis,
    839, 874, 2146
  personality disorders, 2679
  side effects, 707
  stroke-related syndromes, 874
  Tourette's syndrome, 690, 695, 697,
    705, 707, 709
Pipamperone for mentally retarded
    persons, 76
Pipradrol
  mood disorders, 1735
Piracetam
  dementia of the Alzheimer's type,
    969–970, 971, 973, 978
Pitowsky Illness Behavior
    Questionnaire in somatoform
    pain disorder diagnosis, 2125
PL 94-142. *See* Education for All
    Handicapped Children Act
PL 98-199. *See* Education for All
    Handicapped Children Act,
    amendments of 1983
Placebo effect in adjustment disorders,
    2587

Planned learning environments
   autistic children, 196
Play therapy
   adjustment disorders, 2562–2563
   autistic disorder, 266
   childhood gender identity disorder,
      662, 664–665
   schizoid disorder of childhood or
      adolescence, 754–755
Pleasant Events Schedule (PES). *See*
      Behavior therapy, mood
      disorders
PLISSIT Model for treatment of sexual
      dysfunctions, 2380
Pneumonia
   and delirium, 811
   and secondary depression, 1902
Polyarteritis nodosa and secondary
      depression, 1902
Polypharmacy avoidance, 98–99, 1506
Positron emission tomography (PET)
   brain uptake of 18-F-
      fluorodeoxyglucose and
      schizophrenia, 1491
   epilepsy diagnosis, 893
Possession by outside forces and
      obsessive compulsive
      personality disorder, 2771
Post-coital pain, 2251
Postencephalitic parkinsonism, 861
   See also Parkinson's disease
Posthallucinogen perception disorder,
      differential diagnosis, 1709
Postictal states and delirium, 806
Postoperative states and delirium, 806
Postpartum mania. *See* Mood
      disorders, bipolar disorders
Postpartum psychosis
   DSM-III-R diagnostic criteria, 1699
   treatment, 1707–1708
   See also Atypical psychosis
Posttraumatic stress disorder (PTSD),
      2065–2082
   and accident-proneness, 2074
   adjustment disorders of adulthood
      and old age, differentiation, 2506

adjustment disorders of childhood
      and adolescence, differentiation,
      2512
   biologic response, 2070–2071
   diagnosis, 2066–2068
   differential diagnosis, 2069–2070,
      2506, 2512
   DSM-III-R diagnostic criteria, 2066
   etiology, 2070–2073
   mentally retarded persons, 18
   multiple personality disorder, 2198
   pharmacotherapy, 2073–2075, 2588–
      2589
   precipitating events, 2066
   prevention, 2081–2082
   psychological response, 2071–2072
   psychotherapy, 2075–2081
   signs and symptoms, 2066–2068
   social response systems, 2072–2073
   traumatic stress response, 2065–
      2066, 2069–2073
   treatment, 2073–2075
Postural hypotension from
      antidepressant drugs, 1790
Potassium
   and alkalosis, 897
   and disopyramide interaction, 910
   and hyperkalemia, 899
   and hypokalemia, 899
Powers of attorney, 988
Prader-Willi syndrome
   mentally retarded persons
      behavior therapy, 51
      diagnosis, 50–51
      genetic syndrome, 50
      symptoms, 8, 50–51
Prazepam
   delirium, 812
Prazosin
   interaction with other drugs, 1782
   neuropsychiatric effects, 912
   and orthostatic hypotension, 928
Precocious aging in Down's syndrome,
      30–31
Prednisolone
   hepatic disease, 938

Prednisone
  hepatic disease, 938
  and secondary depression, 1912,
    1913
  side effects, 943
Prefrontal lobotomy
  mood disorders, 1741
  obsessive compulsive personality
    disorder, 2781
  schizophrenia, 1741
Pregenital factors of transvestic
    fetishism, 643
Pregnancy
  adolescents, 2368–2369
  heterocyclic antidepressant drugs,
    1931
  lithium, 1931
  and opioid abuse, 1328
  treatment restrictions, 1806
Premack technique, 219, 220
Premature ejaculation
  and coitus interruptus, 2311
  described, 2301–2303
  DSM-III-R diagnostic criteria, 2301
  ejaculation process, 2299–2301
  medical work-up, 2303–2305
  pharmacotherapy, 2309, 2357
  physical causes, 2241
  prevalence, 2301
  psychological level, 2245
  and serotonin enhancing
    antidepressants, 2353
  systematic desensitization, 2361
  tests for physical causes, 2242
  transient versus chronic, 2302
  treatment, 2305–2310
    behavior therapy, 2247
    couples sex therapy, 2307
    follow-up, 2309–2310
    group therapy, 2307
    homosexuals, 2309
    Loyola sensate focus, 2307–2308
    pharmacotherapy, 2309, 2357
    phases, 2305–2306
    practice exercises, 2306

Preoccupation with sameness in
    mentally retarded persons, 55–
    57
Pre-oedipal factors
  and childhood gender identity
    disorder, 666, 667
  and obsessive compulsive
    personality disorder, 2771
  and personality disorders, 2648
Present State Examination (PSE/
    CATEGO), 1499, 1500, 1612
President's Commission for Study of
    Ethical Problems in Medicine
    and Biomedical and Behavioral
    Research, 1003
Priapism
  side effect of trazodone, 2354
Primary degenerative dementia of the
    Alzheimer's type (PDDAT), 819
Primary degenerative dementia (PDD),
    818, 826
  See also Dementia; Dementia of the
    Alzheimer's type
Primary impotence, 2321, 2327–2328
  See also Male erectile disorder
Primary insomnia
  arousing thoughts, 2431
  ascending reticular activating system
    (ARAS), 2426, 2427, 2431
  behavior therapy, 2430–2433
  case vignettes, 2425, 2426–2427
  child-onset insomnia, 2425–2426,
    2427, 2428
  cognitive therapy, 2431–2433
  definition, 2425
  and depression, 2428
  diagnosis, 2425–2428
  insomnia complaint without
    objective findings, 2428
  neurologic imbalance, 2426
  persistent psychophysiologic
    insomnia (PPI), 2426–2428
  pharmacotherapy, 2426, 2430
  relaxation therapy, 2430–2431
  as secondary disorder, 2424–2425
  sleep hygiene, 2429–2430

Primary insomnia *(cont)*
  sleep-restriction therapy, 2432–2433
  sleep/wake cycle, 2426
  stimulus control therapy, 2432
  stress, 2427, 2428
  treatment, 2429–2433
Primary Maternal Preoccupation, 738
Primer pheromones, 2355
Primidone
  epilepsy, 888, 889
  interaction with other drugs, 891–892, 893
  and secondary depression, 1912, 1913
Prison Children Anonymous, 2613
Probenecid
  multi-infarct dementia, 962
Procainamide
  effects on cardiovascular system, 901
  hepatic disease, 938
  interaction with other drugs, 913
  neuropsychiatric effects, 909–910
Procarbazine
  secondary depression, 1906
  and secondary mania, 1914
  side effects, 944, 948
Prochlorperazine
  alcohol withdrawal, 1088
Procyclidine
  and hypokinetic syndrome, 1512
  and secondary mania, 1914
Prodromal symptoms and schizophreniform disorder, 1657
Professional issues
  confidentiality in alcoholism treatment, 1134
  economic reimbursement, 982, 996
  full disclosure or informed consent for pharmacotherapy, 1513
  patient consent, 998–999, 1513
  physician's attitude toward alcoholics, 1079
  for physicians participating in gender reassignment, 660, 661
  research concerns, 1005–1008
  sexological examination, 2365

  sexual provocation from patient, 991–992
  sexual surrogates, 2363–2364
  See also Ethical issues; Legal issues
Progestagens
  sex drive reduction, 2356
Progesterone
  stroke-related paraphilias, 877
Progesterone therapy for obstructive sleep apnea, 2435
Progressive relaxation. *See* Relaxation therapy and training
Progressive supranuclear palsy, differential diagnosis, 861
Projective identification
  definition, 2661
  in family therapy, 2666
  and personality disorders, 2669, 2690
    narcissistic personality disorder, 2739
    psychoanalysis, 2714
Prolactin levels in epilepsy, 883
Prolixin decanoate
  schizophreniform disorder, 1662
Promiscuity
  fetishism, 638
  stroke-related, 877
  See also Hyperactive sexual desire or arousal
Prompting and fading, 223, 768
  See also Behavior therapy
Propanediols
  anxiety disorders, 2038–2039
Prophenazine
  major depression, 1742
Propiophenone
  pharmacokinetics, 1780
    neurotransmitter blockade, 1776
Propoxyphene
  interaction with other drugs, 893
Propoxyphene dependence, methadone treatment, 1355
Propranolol
  akathisia, 1512
  alcohol withdrawal, 1089
  anxiety disorders, 2046

anxiety due to substance abuse, 1373
atypical impulse control disorder,
	2480
clinical use, 952
dementia of the Alzheimer's type,
	975
effects on cardiovascular system, 903
hepatic disease, 938
interaction with other drugs, 851,
	852, 913, 914, 915, 947
intermittent explosive disorder, 2476
mentally retarded persons, 88
neuropsychiatric effects, 908–909
organic aggressive syndrome, 842,
	849, 851
organic delusional syndrome, 838
posttraumatic stress disorder, 2075
schizophrenia, 1502
and secondary depression, 854,
	1912, 1913, 1914
side effects, 876, 908–909
somatic symptoms, 2152
tremor in alcoholics, 1085
Prostatis
	sexual effects, 2241, 2373
Protracted withdrawal syndrome,
	1089–1091
See also Alcohol withdrawal
Protriptyline
	classification, 1774
	and ejaculatory pain, 2316
	pharmacokinetics, 1776, 1779–1781
	and specific medical diseases, 946,
		1782, 1783, 1784
Protriptyline for obstructive sleep
	apnea, 2435
Provera. *See* Medroxyprogesterone;
	Medroxyprogesterone acetate;
	Progestagens
Pseudohypoparathyroidism
	and organic delusional syndrome,
		836
Pseudoneurotic schizophrenia, 2679,
	2684
Psilocybin. *See* Hallucinogen abuse,

and organic delusional
	syndrome
Psoriasis from lithium, 1930
Psychedelic drugs. *See* Hallucinogen
	abuse
Psychiatric disorders
	in mentally retarded persons
		aggression and delinquency, 20–
			26
		antisocial behavior, 20–26
		anxiety disorders, 14–19
		assessment, 6
		diagnosis, 7, 9
		frequency, 4, 5, 6
		mood disorders, 10–14
		prognosis, 5
		schizophrenia, 27–28
	and sexual disorders, 2253–2264,
		2336
Psychiatric University Clinic, Berne,
	Switzerland, 2255
Psychiatrist role
	in alcoholism treatment, 1063, 1148–
		1149
	in the classroom, 200–201
	in penile prosthesis implantation,
		2334
Psychiatrist role in treatment of
	alcoholism
	See also Psychotherapy
Psychiatry, integration of theory and
	practice, 2008–2009
Psychoactive drugs
	sex drive reduction, 2356
	sexual effects, 2240
Psychoactive substance abuse
	DSM-III-R diagnostic criteria, 1064
	See also Alcohol abuse; Drug abuse;
		Substance abuse; names of
		specific substances and classes
		of substances
Psychoactive substance dependence
	DSM-III-R diagnostic criteria, 1064
	See also names of specific substances
		and classes of substances

Psychoactive substance use disorders
(alcohol). *See* Alcohol abuse;
Alcohol dependence;
Alcoholism
Psychoactive substance use disorders
(not alcohol). *See* Drug abuse;
Substance abuse; names of
specific substances and classes
of substances
Psychoanalysis. *See* Psychoanalytic
psychotherapy; Psychotherapy
Psychoanalytic psychotherapy
mood disorders, 1824–1833
bipolar disorders, 1826
effectiveness, 1833
and pharmacotherapy, 1826
process of therapy, 1829–1833
psychoanalytic formulations of
depression, 1827–1829
multiple personality disorder, 2201,
2211, 2212
personality disorders, 2639–2648
antisocial personality disorder,
2646
avoidant personality disorder,
2645, 2646
borderline personality disorder,
2645, 2646, 2647, 2751–2752
dependent personality disorder,
2646
goals of treatment, 2644–2647
histrionic personality disorder,
2646, 2729–2733
indications and contraindications,
2647–2648
narcissistic personality disorder,
2738–2739, 2742
obsessive compulsive personality
disorder, 2777
paranoid personality disorder,
2645, 2646, 2647
schizoid personality disorder,
2645, 2646
schizotypal personality disorder,
2645, 2646
simple phobias, 2019–2022

Psychodrama group therapy for
alcoholism, 1121
Psychodynamic psychotherapy
alcoholism, 1103–1111
adult children of alcoholics, 1110–
1111
indications for, 1105–1106
psychoanalytic theory, 1103–1105
technique, 1106–1108
transference and
countertransference, 1108–1110
treatment setting, 1106
anxiety disorders, 2010–2025
and inhibited female sexual
response, 2290
mood disorders, 1729, 1731–1732,
1944
effectiveness, 1841
obsessive compulsive disorder,
2105–2111
pedophilia, 625
personality disorders, 2635, 2639–
2648, 2650, 2659, 2689
antisocial personality disorder,
2745–2746
avoidant personality disorder,
2760
dependent personality disorder,
2767–2769
goals of treatment, 2644–2647
histrionic personality disorder,
2729–2733
indications and contraindications,
2647–2648
passive-aggressive personality
disorder, 2646, 2786–2787
schizoid personality disorder, 2714
posttraumatic stress disorder, 2080
schizophrenia, 1518, 1519–1529
communicative processes, 1520–
1521
distance maneuvers, 1522
purpose, 1519–1520
sadness and grief, 1523
security operations/background of
safety, 1520, 1521

technique, 1520–1529
therapist-patient relationship,
1524–1525, 1526–1529
uncontrollable behavior, 1522–
1523
sexual disorders, 2256, 2339–2440
See also Brief dynamic
psychotherapy; Individual
psychotherapy; Psychotherapy
Psychodynamic theories
of anxiety, 2010–2012
of impotence, 2319
language and integration of
psychiatric theory and practice,
2009
of rumination, 568–569
Psychoeducational Profile (PEP), 185,
193
Psychogenic amnesia, 821, 822
amobarbital interview, 2188
anosognosia, 2187
associated symptoms, 2186
case vignettes, 2188–2190
differential diagnosis, 2187
DSM-III-R diagnostic criteria, 2186
flight as response, 2187
hospitalization, 2187
hypnosis, 2187–2188
memory functioning, 2186–2187
other amnesia types, 2186
and personality disorders, 2186, 2190
and psychogenic fugue, 2187
stress, 2188
Psychogenic drugs
stroke-related syndromes, 874
Psychogenic fugue
age as factor, 2193
and alcohol abuse, 2194
amytal interview, 2192, 2195–2196
automatic writing, 2195
case studies, 2192–2194
dependency, 2196
and depression, 2191, 2192, 2193,
2194
diagnostic criteria, 2191
DSM-III-R diagnostic criteria, 2191

duration and frequency, 2193
and encephalitis, epilepsy, and head
injury, 2194
ethical issues, 2194–2195
etiology, 2194
hypnosis, 2195
hysteria mechanisms, 2193, 2194
and illicit activity, 2195
medication as factor, 2194
and organic brain disease, 2193–
2194
and other psychiatric disorders, 2191
phenomenology, 2191–2194
and psychogenic amnesia, 2187
psychotherapy-anamnesis, 2195
and schizophrenia, 2193
and senile dementia, 2194
stress, 2193
Psychogenic megacolon. *See* Functional
encopresis
Psychogenic pain disorders. *See*
Somatoform pain disorder
Psychogenic polydypsia and
hyponatremia, 898
Psychogenic psychosis, 1672, 1677
See also Brief reactive psychosis;
Schizoaffective disorder
Psychological factors affecting physical
condition, 2148
Psychological programming therapy in
ritualistic and tyrannical
behavior, 56–57
Psychological rating scales for
pervasive developmental
disorders, 187
Psychomotor epilepsy. *See* Epilepsy,
partial seizures
Psychomotor stimulants
mood disorders, 1729, 1735, 1744
Psychoneurotic depressive reaction,
1743
See also Dysthymia
Psychopathology
alcoholism, 1067–1072
anorexia nervosa patients, 459–460,
507, 513–514

Psychopathology (cont)
  cannabis abuse and dependence,
    1250–1252
  childhood gender identity disorder,
    667
  drug abuse, 1185, 1189–1190
  mentally retarded persons, 4–8
  multiple personality disorder, 2198,
    2204
  opioid abuse, 1313, 1314, 1316
  parasomnias in children, 2420
  rumination, 567–568
  somatoform pain disorder, 2125
Psychopathy. See Antisocial
    personality disorder
Psychopharmacology. See
    Pharmacotherapy
Psychoses of association. See Induced
    psychotic disorder
Psychosexual disorder not elsewhere
    classified. See Atypical
    psychosexual disorder
Psychosexual dysfunctions. See Sexual
    disorders
Psychosis, brief reactive. See Brief
    reactive psychosis
Psychosis, drug-induced
  cannabis abuse and dependence,
    1251–1252
  hallucinogen abuse, 1206
  phencyclidine abuse and
    dependence, 1214
Psychosocial Factor Evaluation in
    somatoform pain disorder
    diagnosis, 2125
Psychosocial stressors, response
  adaptation, 2502
  age as factor, 2500–2501, 2504
  birth cohort as factor, 2501
  categories, 2498, 2499
  experience as factor, 2501
  identification, 2499–2500
  personality as factor, 2501–2502
  severity and specificity, 2503
  sociocultural expectations as factor,
    2501

Psychosocial treatment
  mood disorders, 1729, 1730–1734
  pica, 589
Psychostimulant drugs. See Stimulants
Psychosurgery
  hypochondriasis, cautions, 2146
  mood disorders, 1729, 1741, 1896–
    1897
  obsessive compulsive disorder,
    2104–2105
  obsessive-compulsive personality
    disorder, 2780–2781, 2782
Psychotherapy
  adjustment disorders of adulthood
    and old age, 2509, 2510
  adolescent treatment issues, 789–790
  alcoholism
    adult children of alcoholics, 1110
    differential diagnosis, 1093–1094,
      1104
    indications for individual therapy,
      1097, 1102, 1105–1106
    psychodynamic, 1103–1111
    role of Alcoholics Anonymous
      (AA), 1101–1102, 1107, 1134
    stages of recovery, 1098–1099
    techniques, 1099–1100, 1106–1108
    therapeutic leverage, 1099
    transference and
      countertransference, 1099–1100,
      1104, 1108–1110
  anorexia nervosa, 510–516
  anxiety disorders, 2010–2025, 2027,
    2033, 2056
  anxiety disorders of childhood or
    adolescence, 408–411, 418–421
  attention-deficit hyperactivity
    disorder, 378
  atypical eating disorders, 593
  atypical impulse control disorder,
    2478, 2480
  atypical psychosis, 1705–1706
  autistic disorder, 192, 266–268
  avoidant disorder of childhood, 437–
    439
  brief reactive psychosis, 1681, 1684,
    1685

bulimia nervosa, 525–526, 555–563
cannabis abuse and dependence, 1249, 1257–1258
childhood gender identity disorder, 665–670
conduct disorder, 386
conversion disorders, insight, 2157
crisis intervention, 2557–2558
dementia, 829
elective mutism, 764–767
exhibitionism, 672–673
factitious disorder with physical symptoms, 2163–2164
fetishism, 638–639
functional enuresis, 722
hypochondriasis, 2141–2143
identity disorder, 788–791
immature personality disorders, 775, 776, 778, 779, 781, 782
impotence, 2330
and inhibited female sexual response, 2290
intermittent explosive disorder, 2476
late paraphrenia, 1642
Medicare reimbursement, 981
mentally retarded persons
    anxiety disorders, 18
    caretaker role, 105
    eating disorders, 62
    goals, 109
    group therapy, 110–111
    individual therapy, 108–110
    issues, 108–109
    parent sessions, 106
    socially appropriate behavior, 105
    transference, 110
methadone maintenance programs, 1327
mood disorders, 1729, 1730, 1744–1745, 1756, 1766, 1801
    adjustment disorder with depressed mood, 1743, 1948, 1949
    bipolar disorders, 1929, 1936–1937
    children and adolescents, 1956
    depressive disorders, 1743, 1817, 1818, 1819–1820, 1821, 1839,
        1909, 1911, 1915, 1921, 1943–1945
        effectiveness, 1814–1823
        new technologies, 1814–1823
        versus pharmacotherapy, 1818
obsessive compulsive disorder, 2105–2111
opioid abuse and dependence, 1327
organic aggressive syndrome, 848
organic personality syndrome, 859–860
overanxious disorder of childhood, 428–431
pedophilia, 623–627, 628, 630
persecutory delusional disorders, 1636–1637
personality disorders, 2635, 2637, 2695
    antisocial personality disorder, 2642, 2646, 2665, 2666, 2668, 2674, 2745–2746
    available evidence, 2642
    avoidant personality disorder, 2642, 2645, 2646, 2671, 2674, 2759–2762
    borderline personality disorder, 2642, 2645, 2646, 2647, 2665, 2666, 2668, 2673–2674, 2688, 2689, 2738, 2741, 2750–2754, 2759
    combined with pharmacotherapy, 2683, 2688–2689
    dependent personality disorder, 2642, 2646, 2675, 2766–2769, 2770
    duration and frequency, 2642–2644
    histrionic personality disorder, 2642, 2646, 2671–2672, 2717, 2729–2735
    narcissistic personality disorder, 2639, 2642, 2645, 2665, 2666, 2672–2673, 2737–2741, 2742
    obsessive compulsive personality disorder, 2642, 2646, 2675, 2717, 2771, 2773–2779, 2781

Psychotherapy *(cont)*
  paranoid personality disorder, 2642, 2645, 2646, 2647, 2670–2671, 2707–2710
  passive-aggressive personality disorder, 2642, 2646, 2675, 2786–2788
  schizoid personality disorder, 2642, 2645, 2646, 2665, 2666, 2713–2718
  schizotypal personality disorder, 2642, 2645, 2646, 2671, 2719–2725
  pervasive developmental disorders, 266–268
  and pharmacotherapy, 1733–1734, 1785, 1786–1787, 1791, 1817, 1819–1820, 1821, 1839, 1885, 1886, 1888, 1890, 1943, 1945
    future directions for research, 1823
  posttraumatic stress disorder, 2075–2081
  and residential treatment, 2699
  schizoid disorder of childhood or adolescence, 755–757
  schizophrenia, 1486, 1515–1529, 1660
    evaluation studies, 1516–1518
    potential negative effects, 1518
    psychodynamic, 1518, 1519–1529
  schizophreniform disorder, 1659–1660
  separation anxiety disorder of childhood, 418–421
  sexual disorders, 2244, 2247, 2256–2264, 2334–2343, 2358
  sexual sadomasochism, 653, 655
  somatization disorder, 2168–2169
  somatoform pain disorder, 2126–2128, 2135
  stimulant abuse, 1235, 1240
  substance abuse
    countertransference, 1428
    efficacy studies, 1418–1419
    goal setting, 1423
    "helping relationship" development, 1424–1425
    integration into ongoing programs, 1420
    lifestyles, 1419
    listening, 1425
    methadone treatment as factor, 1423
    patience, 1427
    patient types, 1419–1420, 1429–1430
    pharmacology, 1419
    preliminaries, 1423
    psychiatric disorder prevalence in drug abusers, 1417–1418
    rationale, 1417–1418
    responding, 1426–1427
    services delivery, 1420–1421
    supportive and expressive therapy, 1422–1429
    symptoms, 1425
    termination, 1428–1429
    therapeutic communities, 1420
    therapist qualities, 1421, 1430
    time-limited treatment, 1428–1429
    treatment settings, 1420–1421
    treatment types, 1419–1420
    understanding, 1425–1426, 1427
    urine tests, 1421
  therapist characteristics, 1815
  Tourette's syndrome, 699–701
  transsexualism, 656, 658, 659, 660
  transvestic fetishism, 643–644, 645
  trichotillomania, 2482, 2483
  vaginismus, 2297
  voyeurism, 672–673
  See also Family therapy; Group therapy; Individual psychotherapy; Marital therapy
Psychotherapy of Schizophrenia Project, 1517, 1518
Psychotic depression. *See* Major depression
Psychotic depressive reaction. *See* Brief reactive psychosis
Psychotic disorder not otherwise specified (NOS). *See* Atypical psychosis

Psychotic disorders in drug addicts, hospital treatment, 1371, 1372, 1375–1376

Psychotic symptoms, pharmacotherapy, 2589

Psychotomimetic drugs. *See* Hallucinogen abuse

Psychotropic drugs
  alcoholism, 1076
  dependent personality disorder, 2675
  effects on cardiovascular system, 901–907
  hepatic disease, 937–938, 939
  interaction with other drugs, 921, 927
  lipophilic agents and renal disease, 920–921
  pedophilia, 631
  postpartum psychosis, 1708
  secondary depression, 1906–1907
  with a sensory-impaired patient, 957, 958–959
  sexual effects, 2346–2348
  somatization disorder, 2170
  somatoform pain disorder, 2129–2130
  See also names of specific drugs

PTSD. *See* Posttraumatic stress disorder

Puerperal psychosis. *See* Atypical psychosis; Postpartum psychosis

Pulmonary disease. *See* Lung disease

Punishment
  autistic children, 197, 224–226
  in behavior therapy, 46, 54, 113, 403
  ethical issues, 225
  mentally retarded, 46, 54, 113
  personality disorders, 2650, 2659

Pupil-teacher fit for learning disabled child, 305–307

Pure obsessions in obsessive compulsive disorder, 2096

Purpura and alcoholic liver disease, 933

Pyridoxine
  multi-infarct dementia, 962
  neuropsychiatric effects, 912

Pyritinol
  multi-infarct dementia, 962, 963

Pyromania
  age as factor, 2469
  alexithymia, 2457, 2471
  behavior therapy, 2471
  in children, 2457, 2460, 2461, 2469
  community-based treatment programs, 2472
  and cruelty to animals, 2469
  DSM-III-R diagnostic criteria, 2468
  and enuresis, 2469
  family therapy, 2471
  firefighting skills instruction, 2472
  follow-up studies, 2472–2473
  graphing interview technique, 2472
  and impulse control disorders, 2457, 2460, 2461
  interventions, 2471–2472
  nurturing need, 2470
  prevalence, 2469
  psychodynamic formulations, 2470
  rage, 2470
  recidivism, 2472, 2473
  self-esteem problems, 2471, 2472
  and sexual perversion, 2470
  shame, 2471
  stress, 2470
  tension discharge, 2469, 2470

Quaalude. *See* Methaqualone

Quality of life as issue for mentally retarded persons, 138–139

Quinidine
  effects on cardiovascular system, 901, 906
  hepatic disease, 938
  interaction with other drugs, 891, 913, 915
  neuropsychiatric effects, 909, 910

Radcliffe Infirmary, 2336

Rape trauma syndrome
  anxiety induction, 2536
  behavior therapy, 2538, 2541, 2542–2543
  hypnosis, 2061–2063
  imipramine treatment, 2355
  systematic desensitization, 2535

Rapid orgasm in the female, 2251

Raskin depression scale, 1919

Rational emotive therapy (RET) in stress management, 2542

Rational group therapy for alcoholism, 1122

Rauwolfia alkaloids and secondary depression, 1912, 1913

RDC. See Research Diagnostic Criteria

Reactive attachment disorder of infancy
  diagnosis, 738–740
  DSM-III-R diagnostic criteria, 738
  etiology, 737–738
  history and definition, 734–737
  legal intervention, 744–745
  prevention, 746
  prognosis, 745–746
  and teenage mothers, 2368
  treatment, 740–744

Reactive confusion. See Brief reactive psychosis

Reactive depression. See Mood disorders, depressive disorders

Reactive excitation. See Brief reactive psychosis

Reactive mania. See Mood disorders, bipolar disorders

Reactive paranoid psychosis, 1616–1618

Reactive psychosis, 1672
  See also Schizoaffective disorder

Reactive psychosis unspecified. See Brief reactive psychosis

Reading comprehension
  code-emphasis approach, 335–336
  decoding, 334, 336
  meaning-emphasis approach, 334

  strategic instruction, 337

Reading disorders, developmental
  ability and process training, 332–333
  academic skills training, 333
  and attention-deficit hyperactivity disorder, 365
  and conduct disorder, 298, 365
  diagnosis, 328–329
  modality matching, 333
  prevalence, 298
  remediation, 332–337

Reading skills acquisition, 334–337

Reality-adaptive supportive (RAS) psychotherapy for schizophrenia, 1517–1518

Reality group therapy for alcoholism, 1122

Reasoning errors in anorexia nervosa, 486–488

Reattribution techniques in cognitive therapy, 490

Recidivism
  exhibitionism, 619, 672
  pedophilia, 619, 622–623, 626, 627, 629, 632
  personality disorders, 2695
    antisocial personality disorder, 2747–2748, 2749
  pyromania, 2472, 2473

Reciprocal inhibition and pedophilia, 627

Reconstructive surgery in transsexualism, 656, 657
  See also Gender reassignment, transsexualism

Recovered schizophrenia, 1672
  See also Schizoaffective disorder

Recovery, Incorporated, 2596, 2598, 2600, 2604, 2611

Recreational therapy
  pedophilia, 623
  with residential treatment, 2695

Rectal digging in mental retardation, 43–44

Reduplicative paramnesia
  from brain damage, 835

and stroke, 874

Refeeding-psychotherapy combination in eating disorders, 512

Reflux management in rumination treatment, 576–577

Reframing
adjustment disorder therapy, 2581
somatoform pain disorder therapy, 2125

Regression
personality disorders, 2697–2698
in group therapy, 2667
in psychotherapy, 2643, 2694
in residential treatment, 2699, 2701, 2702–2703

Regressive transference neurosis, 2642–2643

Rehabilitation
self-help and mutual aid groups for adults, 2599
somatoform pain disorder, 2130, 2133–2134

Rehabilitations Act, 271

Reinforcement
aggressive behavior, 22
anorexia nervosa, 467, 476–477
avoidant disorder of childhood, 434
behavior therapy, definition, 113, 116
bulimia nervosa, 532
drug abuse therapy, 1442–1444
mentally retarded persons
differential, in self-injurious behavior therapy, 35
eating disorders, 64–65
rectal digging, feces smearing, and coprophagy, 43–44
stereotyped behavior, abnormal, 47–49
overanxious disorder of childhood, 424
pervasive developmental disorders, 218–221
rumination, 569–570
separation anxiety disorder of childhood, 414

substance abuse, 1282, 1312–1313, 1315, 1431–1432, 1441–1444
trichotillomania, 2484
See also Behavior therapy

Relationship problems and sexual disorders, 2252
See also Marital discord

Relaxation-induced anxiety (RIA), 2064

Relaxation therapy and training
adjustment disorders, 2534–2535
alcoholism, 1076
anxiety, 901
anxiety disorders, 2052–2065
case histories, 2056–2063
cultural perspective and effectiveness of treatment, 2055
depressive disorders, 1855, 1856
elective mutism therapy, 768
epilepsy, 893–894
generalized anxiety disorder, 2034–2035, 2054–2055
major depression, 1819
panic, 2035
patient-therapist relationship, 2055
personality disorders, 2650, 2652, 2653, 2657
phobias, 2055–2056
primary insomnia, 2430–2431
schizoid disorder therapy, 759–760
sexual disorders, 2361–2362
smoking, 1278
somatoform pain disorder, 2131
stress management, 2534–2535
Tourette's syndrome, 701, 702
trichotillomania, 2484
vaginismus, 2297–2298

Releaser pheromones, 2355

Religion as ego disruptive
cultism, 2595
and family, 2594
guilt feelings and self-contempt, 2594, 2595
hazardous religions, 2595
misuse and misapplication, 2594

Religion as ego support
aging, 2592

Religion as ego support *(cont)*
  birth and death, 2591
  care centers, 2592
  change in emphasis, 2594
  child rearing, 2591–2592
  disasters, 2592
  healthy versus unhealthy religious
      groups, 2595
  life meaning, 2593
  life passages, 2591
  logotherapy, 2593
  marriage, 2591
  mobile life styles, 2592
  rationale, 2590–2591
  relatedness aspirations, 2593–2594
  suicide deterrent, 2594
  therapeutic adjunct, 2593–2594
  traditional ways, 2592–2593
Religion as family, 2594
Religious/mystical aspects of
      dissociative disorder not
      otherwise specified, 2223–2224
Remitting schizophrenia, 1672
  See also Schizoaffective disorder
Renal disease
  causes, 918
  decreased binding, 922
  and dementia, 917–919
  dialysis dementia, 917–918, 919, 929
  dialysis disequilibrium syndrome,
      917, 919, 929
  differential diagnosis, 918–919
  hemodialysis, 916, 917, 926, 927, 929
  and impotence, 2319
  and lithium, 1930
  and organic mental syndrome, 915–
      929, 918
  and orthostatic hypotension, 928
  patient evaluation, 919–920
  pharmacotherapy, 920–929
    drug metabolism and excretion,
        923–924
    hydrophilic agents, 924, 929
    lipophilic agents, 921, 929
    volume of distribution, 922–923,
        924

  sexual effects, 2241, 2379
  uremic brain syndrome, 916–917
  uremic delirium, 919
Research Diagnostic Criteria (RDC)
  improved patient specification, 1815
  indications for cognitive-behavioral
      therapy, 1845
  mood disorders, 1733, 1849, 1868,
      1891, 1942
  schizoaffective disorder, 1667, 1668,
      1671
  schizophrenia, 1499, 1500
Research issues
  ethical issues, 1005–1008
  Medicare reimbursement guides,
      982–983
Reserpine
  and dementia of the Alzheimer's
      type, 974
  and electroconvulsive therapy,
      1807
  interaction with other drugs, 913
  mood disorders, 1734
    secondary depression, 854, 1754,
        1912, 1913, 1914
  neuropsychiatric effects, 910, 911
  and neurotransmitters, 1795
  and organic mood syndrome, 854
  tardive dyskinesia, 1513
Residential treatment programs
  alcoholism, 1141–1142, 1150–1151
  autistic disorder, 268–271
  controversies, 2702–2704
  discharge planning and aftercare,
      2695
  and family therapy, 2699
  indications, 2689, 2691–2692, 2698–
      2699
  personality disorders, 2637, 2656,
      2658, 2668, 2689–2704
    antisocial personality disorder,
        2689, 2690, 2747–2749
    borderline personality disorder,
        2690, 2697, 2741, 2755–2758,
        2759
    controversies, 2689, 2702–2704

dependent personality disorder, 2764, 2770

histrionic personality disorder, 2736

long-term treatment, 2689, 2698, 2700–2701

narcissistic personality disorder, 2741–2742

obsessive compulsive personality disorder, 2781

paranoid personality disorder, 2711

schizoid personality disorder, 2718

schizotypal personality disorder, 2726

short-term treatment, 2689, 2698–2700

pervasive developmental disorders, 268–271

schizoid disorder of childhood or adolescence, 761

special milieus, 2694–2695, 2696

staffing considerations, 2692

treatment strategies, 2693–2695

See also Nursing home care; Therapeutic communities for substance abuse

Residential treatment programs for substance abuse. *See* Therapeutic communities for substance abuse

Residual amnesia and stroke, 873

Residual subtype of schizophrenia, 1498

Resistance

personality disorders, 2640

in behavior therapy, 2651

passive-aggressive personality disorder, 2786, 2787

in psychotherapy, 2647, 2656

residential treatment, 2697

in psychoanalysis, 1825, 1830

brief dynamic psychotherapy, 1876, 1879, 1880

in psychotherapy for mentally retarded persons, 110

Respiratory failure

and delirium, 806

and organic mental syndromes, 940–941

See also Lung disease

Respite care services for autistic individuals, 262, 269

Respondent conditioning

anorexia nervosa, 475

anxiety disorders of childhood or adolescence, 403

mental retardation, 112, 114–115

See also Behavior therapy

Response prevention

in anorexia nervosa, 475

in obsessive compulsive disorder, 2098–2099

Response specificity, 664

Restless leg syndrome, 692

and dementia, 828

differentiation from nocturnal myoclonus, 2437

Restoril. *See* Temazepam

Restraint, physical

behavior therapy, guidelines, 117

legal issues, 991–992, 993

pica, 588

self-injurious behavior, 36, 37

Restricted Environment Stimulation Therapy (REST)

cigarette smoking cessation, 1278

Restrictive procedures. *See* Restraint, physical

Retarded ejaculation

age effects, 2280, 2285

and alcohol consumption, 2313–2314

and depression, 2254

distinguished from anejaculatory orgasm, 2243 ˙

distinguished from retrograde ejaculation, 2243, 2314

DSM-III-R definition, 2313

incidence, 2312–2314

medical work-up, 2314–2315

organic causes, 2313–2314

pharmacotherapy, 2357

Retarded ejaculation (cont)
  psychological causes, 2315
  and sexual sadomasochism, 650
  speculative pharmacotherapy, 2357
  and stroke, 876
  tests for physical causes, 2243
  treatment, 2315–2316
Retarded maturation in adolescent
    pedophilia, 620
Retention control training, 722
Retinitis pigmentosa
  and neuroleptic drugs, 1514
Retrograde amnesia, 817
  and stroke, 872–873
  See also Amnestic syndromes
Retrograde ejaculation, 2243, 2314
Reverse diurnal variation
  and depressive disorders, 1753
Review of a Generation of Progress, 1814
Rewards in behavior therapy. See
    Reinforcement
Rheumatic chorea and mania, 1761
RIA. See Relaxation-induced anxiety
Rigid-akinetic syndrome and
    antipsychotic drugs, 1511
Rigidity in families of anorectic
    patients, 495, 497
Rinne's test, 956
Ritodrine
  side effects, 944
Ritualistic behavior
  mentally retarded persons, behavior
    therapy, 55–57
  obsessive compulsive disorder,
    2095–2096, 2099, 2106, 2108,
    2110
Ritvo-Freeman Real Life Rating Scale
    for Autism, 229
Roentgenologic examination for
    organic mood syndrome
    diagnosis, 855
Rogerian group therapy for
    alcoholism, 1121
Role models in therapeutic
    communities, 1387

Role-playing
  avoidant disorder therapy, 434
  personality disorders therapy, 2650,
    2654, 2657, 2668
    in family therapy, 2664
    passive-aggressive personality
      disorder, 2788
  somatoform pain disorder therapy,
    2134
Rorschach test, 1549
Rumination
  in adolescence, 566
  in adulthood, 566
  behavioral theory of origin, 569–570
  behavior therapy, 577–578
  biologic determinants, 571–574
  biopsychosocial stimulus, 578–579
  and bulimia nervosa, 566, 567
  and central nervous system
    disorder, 568
  delayed gastric emptying in, 572
  and depression in infants and
    children, 570
  developmental theories of etiology,
    568–569
  esophageal motor dysfunction as
    cause, 572
  esophageal sphincter pressure as
    cause, 573
  etiology, 578–579
  exploitation by patient, 566
  family psychiatric history, 567
  gastroesophageal reflux in, 571–572
  gastrointestinal neurohormonal
    substrate in, 573
  guilt feelings in mother, 574
  hospital treatment, 574–576
  hypersensitivity to touch and sound,
    575
  incidence, 564
  in infancy and early childhood, 565
  in infants of narcotic-addicted
    mothers, 574
  latency, 566
  maternal anxiety as cause, 579
  maternal depression, 576

maternal psychopathology as cause, 569
medical-surgical treatment, 576–577
mentally retarded persons, 8, 53–55, 568
and mood disorder, 570
mortality, 565
neuropeptide role, 573
opioid treatment, 573–574, 577
overcorrection in behavior therapy, 578
overstimulation-understimulation in infants as cause, 568–569
pharmacotherapy, 574, 576–577
presentation, 565–568
psychodynamic theories of origin, 568–569
psychopathology, 567–568
reflux management in treatment, 576–577
reinforcement, 569–570
and Sandifer's syndrome, 571
satiation in behavior therapy, 578
and self-injurious behavior, 566
self-stimulation, 566, 568
sensory stimulation program, 576
stress and tension in children as cause, 579
symptoms, 564
treatment in adults, 577
treatment in infants and children, 574–575
See also Mental retardation
Rush Presbyterian Medical Center
treatment manual for administration of antidepressants, 1731, 1816

SAD. *See* Seasonal affective disorder
Salbutamol
side effects, 944
Salicylate drugs
hepatic disease, 938
interaction with other drugs, 891

Sandifer's syndrome and rumination, 571
Sandoz Clinical Assessment Geriatric Scale, 972
Sarason's General Anxiety and Test Anxiety Scales, 402
Satiation
behavior therapy, definition, 113
pedophilia, 626, 627
rumination therapy, 55
Schedule for Affective Disorders and Schizophrenia, 1733, 1849
Schedule for Affective Disorders and Schizophrenia, Lifetime, 1189
Schedule of Recent Experience, for handling stress, 2501
Schizoaffective disorder
acute and chronic management, 1675–1676
age factor, 1668
and atypical psychosis, 1698, 1699
cognitive therapy, 1675
and delusional (paranoid) disorders, 1612, 1613, 1618
diagnostic criteria, 1666–1672, 1900
differential diagnosis, 855, 1655, 1666, 1671–1672, 1674, 1676, 1679, 1709
distinguished from mood disorders, 1762–1763
distinguished from schizophrenia, 1495–1497
duration, 1672
family history, 1669–1670, 1674, 1676
family therapy, 1656
gender factor, 1669
incidence, 1668–1669
pharmacotherapy, 1656, 1675, 1676
outcome, 1672–1674
prognosis, 1710
Schizoid disorder of childhood or adolescence
case study, 761–762
classification dropped from DSM-III-R, 733, 750, 762
clinical course, 751–752

Schizoid disorder of childhood or
    adolescence (cont)
  debate on continuing need for
      category, 733–734, 750, 762
  diagnosis, 748–750
  distinguished from other personality
      disorders, 749–750
  distinguished from pervasive
      developmental disorders, 750
  distinguished from schizotypal
      personality disorder, 750
  DSM-III diagnostic criteria, 748–749,
      750
  etiology, 752–753
  history and definition, 747–748
  pharmacotherapy, 760
  prevalence, 751
  prognosis, 751
  relationship with schizophrenia, 747,
      750, 751, 752–753
  treatment, 753–762
Schizoid personality disorder
  behavior therapy, 2717
  definition, 2712
  diagnostic criteria, 2712–2713
  differential diagnosis, 2706
  distinguished from schizophrenia,
      1497
  and induced psychotic disorder, 1690
  pharmacotherapy, 2679, 2680, 2682,
      2718
  psychotherapy, 2642
    effectiveness, 2718
    family therapy, 2665, 2666, 2716
    group therapy, 2671, 2717–2718
    individual psychotherapy, 2713–
      2716
    psychoanalytic psychotherapy,
      2645, 2646
    psychodynamic psychotherapy,
      2714
  relationship to schizophrenic
      disorders, 2712
  residential treatment, 2718
  resistance, 2697
  splitting, 2712, 2714

Schizoid personality in adults
  distinguished from schizoid
      personality disorder, 751–752
Schizophrenia, 1483–1606
  and alcohol abuse, 1094
  associated with violent behavior, 848
  and atypical psychosis, 1698, 1706
  behavior therapy, 1569–1570, 1576–
      1580
  and cannabis abuse and
      dependence, 1250–1252
  case management, 1579–1580
  combined treatment approach, 1515,
      1519, 1543, 1557, 1580–1583
  community-based programs, 1506,
      1569, 1578–1580
  concept, 1489–1493
  and conversion disorders, 2153, 2156
  deinstitutionalization, 1547, 1568,
      1576
  and delusional (paranoid) disorders,
      1609, 1612–1613, 1614–1616,
      1647
  described, 1489–1493, 1548
  diagnosis, 1486, 1493–1501, 1751,
      1752
  diagnostic systems other than DSM,
      1498–1501
  diathesis-stress theory, 1548
  differential diagnosis, 806, 834, 855,
      859, 883, 884, 1493–1497, 1655,
      1656, 1660, 1666, 1671, 1674,
      1676, 1679, 1682, 1689, 1709
  distinguished from dissociative
      disorder not otherwise
      specified, 2225
  distinguished from mood disorders,
      1764
    children and adolescents, 1951
  distinguished from organic mental
      disorders, 1493–1498
  drug abuse-induced, 1372
  DSM-III-R diagnostic criteria, 1493
  early theories of family role, 1544–
      1545
  electroconvulsive therapy, 1805

expressed emotion and
communication deviance, 1493,
1549–1552
family history, 1669–1671
family therapy, 1543–1567, 1575–
1576
group therapy, 1529–1543, 2668
and hepatic disease, 935
heterogeneous nature of, 1489–1493
history of concept and treatment,
1487–1489
hospitalization, 1569, 1576–1578
and hyponatremia, 898
incidence, 1752
and induced psychotic disorder,
1694
in mentally retarded persons, 27–28
and mood disorders
secondary depression, 1762, 1765,
1898, 1901, 1915, 1922
and morbid jealousy, 1642–1643,
1644
negative symptoms, 1492, 1501,
1517–1518, 1548
neuropathology, 874
and opioid abuse, 1314, 1329
and organic aggressive syndrome,
841
and paranoid personality disorder,
2705
and Parkinson's disease, 863–864
personal grooming training, 1572
pharmacotherapy, 1486, 1501–1515
phenomenology, 1690
positive symptoms, 1492, 1501, 1517
and prelingual deafness, 951
prognosis, 1710
and psychogenic fugue, 2193
psychosurgery, 1897
psychotherapy, 1486, 1515–1529,
1660
rehabilitation, 1567–1583
relapse after drug discontinuation,
1661
relapse factors, 1493, 1509, 1545,
1550, 1551, 1555–1556

from renal disease, 916
residential treatment, 2701
and schizoid disorder of childhood
or adolescence, 747, 750, 751,
752–753
and schizotypal personality disorder,
2719
and sexual disorders, 2255
social adjustment, 1510
social skills training, 1570–1571, 1582
and stress management, 2534
subtypes, 1498
type I syndrome, 1498, 1633
type II syndrome, 1498, 1633
vulnerability-stress-protective model,
1568–1569
Schizophrenia, childhood type, 180–
182
reformulation in DSM-III, 179
See also Autistic children; Autistic
disorder
Schizophrenic disorders. *See*
Schizophrenia
Schizophrenics Anonymous, 2604–
2605
Schizophreniform disorder
from antituberculosis drugs, 944, 947
and atypical psychosis, 1698, 1699
delusional (paranoid) disorders,
1613, 1617, 1618
and depressive disorders, 1662
differential diagnosis, 806, 1655,
1660, 1671, 1679
distinguished from schizophrenia,
1497
DSM diagnostic criteria, 1656–1657
duration, 1657
electroconvulsive therapy, 1659
and epilepsy, 881, 882
family therapy, 1656, 1663–1665
group therapy, 1662–1663, 1665
"holding pattern", 1657, 1664, 1665
hospitalization question, 1660–1661
individual therapy, 1662, 1665
and induced psychotic disorder,
1695–1696

Schizophreniform disorder *(cont)*
  and infective endocarditis, 896
  milieu, 1659
  and negative symptoms, 1662
  pharmacotherapy, 1656, 1657, 1658,
    1659–1660, 1661–1662
  prodromal symptoms, 1657
  psychotherapy, 1658, 1659–1660
  "true," 1657, 1664, 1665
Schizophreniform psychosis, 1672
Schizotypal personality disorder
  behavior therapy, 2724–2725
  and brief reactive psychosis, 1678
  concreteness, 2721
  distinguished from schizoid disorder
    of childhood or adolescence, 750
  distinguished from schizophrenia,
    1497
  DSM diagnostic criteria, 2719, 2720
  ego diffusion, 2721–2722
  and hypochondriasis, 2723–2724
  limitation of available research
    material, 2636
  and paranoid psychotic episodes,
    2726
  pharmacotherapy, 2680, 2681, 2682–
    2683, 2725–2726
  psychotherapy, 2642
    duration of treatment, 2724
    goals of treatment, 2724
    group therapy, 2671, 2725
    marital therapy, 2725
    psychoanalytic psychotherapy,
      2645, 2646
  residential treatment, 2726
  and schizophrenia, 2719
Schlerosing cholangitis and liver
    transplantation, 933
Schneider diagnostic system for
    schizophrenia, 1499, 1500
Schneiderian criteria for depressive
    personality, 1757
Schneiderian symptoms
  and bipolar disorder, 1760, 1761
  and schizoaffective disorder, 1671
  and stroke, 874

School-work transition for mentally
    retarded persons, 129–132
Scintillation for organic mood
    syndrome diagnosis, 855
Scopolamine
  forgetfulness effect, 967, 968
  secondary depression, 1906
  with a sensory-impaired patient, 958
Scotomas
  and digitalis toxicity, 908
  and systemic lupus erythematosus,
    952
Seasonal affective disorder (SAD)
  atypical SAD, 1892
  phototherapy, 1801, 1891–1896
    efficacy, 1892–1893
  seasonal energy syndrome, 1892
  subsyndromal SAD, 1892
Seasonal energy syndrome. *See*
    Seasonal affective disorder
Seatbelts in the prevention of brain
    damage, 846
Seborrhea
  and Parkinson's disease, 861
Seclusion and restraint
  legal issues, 991–992, 993
  See also Physical restraint
Secondary amine tricyclic
    antidepressant drugs
  dementia, 827
Secondary depression
  and delirium, 805
  differential diagnosis, 918, 1910
  and digitalis toxicity, 908
  and drug abuse, 1901, 1920–1922
    hallucinogens, 1207
    methadone maintenance, 1357–
      1358
    opioids, 1185, 1329
    phencyclidine, 1217
    stimulants, 1223–1224, 1228–1229
  family history, 1900–1901, 1917
  incidence, 1899
  with medical illness, 1899–1915
    AIDS, 1792, 1912
    cancer, 1901, 1904–1907

cardiovascular disease, 901–905, 1900, 1901, 1902, 1907–1908
chronic pain, 1901–1904
endocrine disorders, 1901, 1902, 1908–1909
epilepsy, 882, 1910
hepatic disease, 933, 935
hypernatremia, 898
hypertension, 1729
hyponatremia, 898
lung disease, 939, 942, 947
malaria, 1902
metabolic disorders, 1901, 1902
neurologic disorders, 1901, 1902, 1909–1912
Parkinson's disease, 861, 862–863, 864, 865
renal disease, 916, 918, 919
sensory impairment, 950, 951
stroke, 876, 1910–1911
subacute cerebellar degeneration, 941
systemic lupus erythematosus, 952, 1902
Tourette's syndrome, 701
pharmacotherapy, 1903–1904, 1905–1915
from prescribed and over-the-counter medication, 1764, 1898, 1901, 1912–1915
antineoplastic drugs, 944
antituberculosis drugs, 947
disopyramide, 910, 1912, 1913
diuretics, 912
guanethidine, 912
long-acting neuroleptic drugs, 1514
methyldopa, 911, 1912, 1913, 1914
procainamide, 910
propranolol, 908, 1912, 1913, 1914
reserpine, 910, 1754, 1912, 1913, 1914
with psychiatric illness
alcoholism, 1067, 1068, 1069, 1070–1071, 1094, 1898, 1901, 1918–1920, 1924

anorexia nervosa, 460, 1901, 1915, 1916–1917
avoidant personality disorder, 2668
borderline personality disorder, 2656, 2681
brief reactive psychosis, 1682
bulimia nervosa, 520–525, 1901, 1916, 1917–1918
dementia, 818, 821, 827–828
dementia of the Alzheimer's type, 976
dependent personality disorder, 2764
drug addiction, 1901, 1920–1922
histrionic personality disorder, 2735, 2736
induced psychotic disorder, 1689
multi-infarct dementia, 964
obsessive compulsive personality disorder, 2780
organic delusional syndrome, 837
organic mood syndrome, 853–854, 855
organic personality syndrome, 857, 858
passive-aggressive personality disorder, 2784, 2785, 2787
personality disorders, 2750
schizoaffective disorder, 1667, 1671
schizophrenia, 1898, 1922, 1924
schizophreniform disorder, 1662
substance abuse, 1920, 1924
tobacco dependence, 1285
transvestic fetishism, 642, 645
psychotherapy, 1906, 1921
Secondary gain in anxiety disorders of childhood, 404, 405
Secondary impotence, 2321–2325
See also Male erectile disorder
Secondary mania, 1914–1915
and hepatic disease, 935
Second generation antidepressant drugs
mood disorders, 1737–1738

Sedative and hypnotic drug abuse
  amnestic disorder, 1300
  anxiety, 1373
  and cannabis, 1244
  delirium, withdrawal, 1300
  dependence, 1301
  drug switching, 1307
  DSM-III-R diagnostic criteria, 1295,
    1299, 1300
  high-dose dependence, 1304–1305
  intoxication, 1294–1295
  low-dose dependence, 1305–1307
  overdose, 1301, 1302
  phenobarbital substitution
    technique, 1296, 1297
  phenobarbital withdrawal
    conversion, 1297
  recovery, 1308
  withdrawal, 1295–1300
Sedative drugs
  and delirium, 806
  and epilepsy, 887
  interaction with other drugs, 915
  organic aggressive syndrome, 850
  sexual effects, 2344
  side effects, 850
  uncomplicated bereavement, 1743
  See also names of specific drugs
Sedative-hypnotic drugs
  adjustment disorders, 2587–2588
  depersonalization disorder, 2221
  epileptic children, adverse effects
    96-97
  mentally retarded persons, 89–90
  See also names of specific drugs
Seizures
  delirium, 805, 806, 811, 814
  digitalis toxicity, 908
  hepatic disease, 935
  hypernatremia, 899
  hyponatremia, 898
  lung carcinoma, 942
  organic delusional syndrome, 836,
    839
  organic hallucinosis, 836, 839

phencyclidine abuse and
    dependence, 1213
  renal disease, 918
  subacute sclerosing panencephalitis,
    952
  See also Epilepsy
Selegiline. See Deprenyl
Self-concept and traumatic events,
    2071–2072, 2082
Self-contempt from unhealthy religious
    groups, 2594, 2595
Self-control in anxiety disorders of
    childhood, 405
Self-Control Scale (SCS), 1845
Self-control therapy for depressive
    disorders, 1858, 1859, 1861
Self-destructive behavior in atypical
    impulse control disorder, 2477
Self-Efficacy Questionnaire for tobacco
    dependence, 1270, 1291–1292
Self-esteem problems
  adjustment disorders, 2550, 2552
  anorexia nervosa, 487–488, 515
  attention-deficit hyperactivity
    disorder, 365, 371
  bulimia nervosa, 520–521, 536, 538
  child's self-image and sexuality, 2376
  conduct disorder, 365, 371
  learning disabled children, 305
  mentally retarded persons, 14, 108,
    109, 110
  obsessive compulsive disorder, 2106,
    2107
  pyromania, 2471, 2472
  sexual disorders, 2258–2259, 2263
  substance abuse, therapeutic
    communities, 1382–1383, 1389,
    1390, 1393
Self-expression techniques
  in treatment for exhibitionism, 672
  in treatment for voyeurism, 672
Self-help and mutual aid groups for
    adults
  adjustment disorder therapy, 2550

aftercare, 2599
altruism as therapy, 2603
belief systems, 2602, 2603
cancer groups, 2605, 2606
characteristics, 2597, 2602
cognitive antidotes, 2603
effectiveness, 2596–2597, 2600–2602
feminism, 2604
helper therapy principle, 2599, 2603
helping mechanisms, 2602–2604
history, 2597
hope as element, 2603–2604
Huxley Institute for research on
    nutrition and mental health,
    2605
identity sharing, 2603
ideologies, 2603
information transmission, 2602, 2604
member participation, 2603
motivation, 2601
mutual aid groups
    Alcoholics Anonymous. *See*
        Alcoholics Anonymous
    Alliance for the Mentally Ill, 2604–
        2605
    Alzheimer's Association, 2605
    Compassionate Friends, 2598,
        2599–2600, 2602
    epilepsy groups, 2598, 2605, 2606
    GROW, 2598, 2604
    Integrity Groups, 2598, 2599, 2600,
        2604
    League for Emotionally Disturbed
        Children, 2601
    Mended Hearts, 2600, 2601, 2602,
        2603
    Muscular Dystrophy Association,
        2601
    NAIM, 2602
    National Gay Alliance, 2604
    New York Association for Help to
        Retarded Children, 2601
    Parents Anonymous, 2598, 2599,
        2600, 2601, 2611
    Recovery, Incorporated, 2596,
        2598, 2600, 2604, 2611

Schizophrenics Anonymous, 2604–
        2605
    Theos, 2600, 2601
networks, 2602, 2603, 2605
nutritional basis of pathology, 2605
pathologic gambling, 2464, 2465,
    2466
prevention, 2605–2606
redefinitions, 2604–2605
rehabilitation, 2599
relations with professionals, 2597–
    2600
research findings, 2600–2602
self-help centers, 2606–2607
stressors and trauma, 2596
substance abuse
    cannabis abuse and dependence,
        1259
    opioid abuse and dependence,
        1327
    phencyclidine abuse, 1217
    stimulant abuse, 1234–1235, 1237
    therapeutic communities for
        substance abuse, 1381, 1386
viewpoints, 2604
See also Family support groups;
    Group therapy; Mutual-help
    services for youth; Self-help
    services for youth
Self-help services for youth
    behavior changes, 2610–2611
    Body Awareness Resource Network
        (BARNY), 2611
    categories, 2610
    characteristics, 2609–2610
    computer services, 2611
    definitions and roles, 2608
    family communication, 2611
    health and nutrition, 2611
    origins, 2607–2608
    political issues, 2609
    sexuality, 2611
    strategies, 2610–2611
    stress management, 2611
    substance abuse, 2611

Self-help services for youth *(cont)*
  See also Mutual-help services for
    youth; Peer-helping services for
    youth
Self-hypnosis
  for anxiety disorders, 2052–2053,
    2055, 2058, 2063–2065
  See also Hypnosis
Self-injurious behavior
  autistic disorder, 224–226
  elimination by electric skin shock, 225
  mentally retarded persons
    behavior therapy, 34–36, 119
    definition, 32
    noncontingent physical restraint,
      36–37
    pharmacotherapy, 36
    prevalence, 32
    symptoms and etiology, 8, 32–33
  rumination, 566
Self-monitoring
  bulimia nervosa, 524, 535, 538, 551
  in substance abuse, 1433
  Tourette's syndrome, 701
Self-stimulation in rumination, 566,
    568
Selvini-Palazzoli model of
    schizophrenia, 1545
Semantic categories, 205, 215
Semi-rigid rod penile prostheses,
    2332–2333
Senescent pedophilia, 619, 621
Senile artiopathic psychosis
  differential diagnosis, 1689
Senile dementia and psychogenic
    fugue, 2194
Senile dementia of the Alzheimer's
    type (SDAT). *See* Dementia of
    the Alzheimer's type
Senility and organic mental
    syndromes, 800
Sensate focus exercises, 2275, 2307–
    2308
Sensation-seeking needs as factor in
    substance abuse, 1202
Sensory deprivation and delirium, 806

Sensory impairment
  bilateral eye patching, 949, 950
  differential diagnosis, 953–954
  etiology, 951–953
  hallucinations, 949, 950, 951
  loss of hearing, 949, 950–951, 953,
    954, 955–956
  loss of smell, 949, 952, 953, 955
  loss of taste, 949, 953, 956
  loss of vision, 949, 950, 952–953,
    953–954, 955
  lung carcinoma, 941
  and organic mental syndromes, 948–
    960
  patient evaluation, 954–956
  and subacute sclerosing
    panencephalitis, 952
  systemic lupus erythematosus, 952
  tinnitus, 949
  treatment
    pharmacotherapy, 957–959, 960
    special aids, 956–957
  types, 949
Sensory stimulation program for
    rumination, 576
Separation anxiety disorder of
    childhood
  behavior therapy, 413–416
  family therapy, 421–423
  loss theory of anxiety, 409
  and panic anxiety, 406
  pharmacotherapy, 416–418, 2685
  psychotherapy, 418–421
  reinforcement, 414
  sibling rivalry, 418, 419, 421
Separation anxiety in anorexia
    nervosa, 499
Sepsis and delirium, 806
Sequenced Inventory of
    Communication Development,
    187, 208
Serophene. *See* Clomiphene
Serotonergic drugs
  premature ejaculation, 2353, 2357
Serotonergic system in autistic
    children, 245–246

Serotonin
  and antidepressant drugs, 1775–1777
  and chronic pain, 1904
  dementia of the Alzheimer's type, 973
  and electroconvulsive therapy, 1812–1813
  and imipramine, 1735
  and mood disorders, 1800
  and multi-infarct dementia, 962
  and reserpine, 1734, 1795
  Tourette's syndrome, 691
Serum glutamic-oxaloacetic transaminase (SGOT)
  and hepatic disease, 934, 936
Serum glutamic-pyruvic transaminase (SGPT)
  and hepatic disease, 934, 936
Sex as factor
  bipolar disorders, 1752, 1758
  depression in Parkinson's disease, 863
  family therapy in substance abuse, 1416
  histrionic personality disorder, 2728
  parasomnias in children, 2423, 2424
  personality disorders
    dependent personality disorder, 2765
  therapeutic communities for substance abuse, 1380
  trichotillomania, 2481
Sex change operation, 658, 659
Sex drive, 2265–2266
  See also Sexual desire; Sexual desire problems
Sex education, 623, 625, 626, 627, 2360, 2367
Sex offenders, pedophiliacs, 617, 618
Sexological examination, 2241, 2303, 2365
Sex ring activities, 620
Sex therapy
  impotence, 2319, 2322–2323, 2326–2327, 2328, 2329
  inhibited female orgasm, 2286–2290

Masters and Johnson approach, 2238, 2319, 2326, 2327, 2337–2339, 2341, 2363
  pedophilia, 627
  personality disorders coupled with sexual dysfunction, 2256–2264
    areas of intervention, 2260–2261
    character traits to be treated, 2257–2259
    classifications, 2260
    couples therapy, 2261–2264
    treatment considerations, 2259–2260
  premature ejaculation, 2305–2308
  retarded ejaculation, 2315–2316
  sensate focus exercises, 2275, 2307–2308
  surrogate sexual partners, 2363–2364
  treatment approaches, 2337–2343
Sexual activity with prepubertal children. *See* Pedophilia
Sexual aids, 2362–2363
Sexual anxiety, 2320–2321, 2361–2362
Sexual arousal
  female, 2279–2280, 2386–2387
  male, 2384–2386
  See also Female sexual arousal disorder; Male erectile disorder
Sexual attitude restructuring (SAR) programs, 2360
Sexual aversion, 2237, 2248, 2252
  See also Hypoactive sexual desire
Sexual behavior in pedophilia, 617
Sexual concerns
  body image, 2249–2250
  distinguished from sexual difficulties, 2248, 2249
  normalcy, 2249
Sexual desire
  components, 2265–2266
  concept, 2264–2265
  contexts, 2267–2269
Sexual desire problems
  case studies, 2271–2279
  cultural impact, 2275
  diagnosis, 2269–2271

Sexual desire problems *(cont)*
  increased desire, 2270, 2276–2278
  lifelong low sexual desire, 2275–2276
  pharmacotherapy, 2356
  and relationship problems, 2272–2274
  and sexual identity, 2274–2275
  tests for physical causes, 2241
  treatment, 2271–2279
  treatment effectiveness, 2278–2279
  See also Hyperactive sexual desire or
    arousal; Hypoactive sexual
    desire
Sexual difficulties, 2248, 2250
Sexual disorder not otherwise
    specified. *See* Atypical
    psychosexual disorder
Sexual disorders, 2235–2415
  and alcohol and drug use, 2240,
    2309, 2313–2314, 2344
  atypical, 2248–2253
  and bipolar disorder, 2254–2255
  and common physical disorders,
    2378–2380
  and congenital abnormalities, 2376
  and depression, 2253–2254, 2336
  DSM-III-R areas of change or
    controversy, 2237, 2248
  DSM-III-R triphasic model, 2238
  educational approaches, 2360
  effects of commonly prescribed
    drugs, 2344–2345
  evaluation, 2238–2247
    differentiating between organic
      and psychogenic, 2239–2244
    interview, 2239–2241
    physical examination, 2241–2244
    psychological assessment, 2244–
      2246
    treatment planning, 2246–2247
  global versus situational, 2240
  hormonal aspects, 2392–2393
  hypnosis, 2362
  Kaplan's three basic components of
    sexual life, 2265
  and marital discord, 2246, 2328,
    2336–2337, 2358

  mental levels of psychosexual
    dysfunctions, 2244–2245
  and personality disorders, 2256–2264
  pharmacotherapy, 2247, 2343–2359
  prevalence, 2334–2336
  and psychiatric disorders, 2253–
    2254, 2336
  psychophysiology research, 2390–
    2392, 2394
  psychotherapy, 2244, 2247, 2256–
    2264, 2334–2344, 2358
  research limitations, 2334–2335
  research overview, 2384–2394
  and schizophrenia, 2255
  sexual aids, 2362–2363
  special populations, 2366–2384
  speculative pharmacotherapy, 2356–
    2358
  stress management, 2538, 2541
  surrogate sexual partners, 2363–2364
  systematic desensitization, 2290,
    2319, 2361–2362
  treatment approaches, 2337–2343
  treatment planning, 2246–2247
  See also Pedophilia; names of specific
    disorders
Sexual domination of children. *See*
    Pedophilia
Sexual dysfunction not otherwise
    specified. *See* Atypical
    psychosexual disorder
Sexual dysfunctions. *See* Sexual
    disorders
Sexual exhibition
  and personality disorders, 671, 2258,
    2262–2263
Sexual fantasies focusing on children,
    617, 624
Sexual identity problems
  and low sexual motivation, 2274–
    2275
  potential effects of sex-affecting
    drugs on offspring, 2359
  See also Gender identity disorders
Sexuality and aging, 2280, 2285, 2370–
    2375

Sexuality and culture, 2285, 2311–2312,
2380–2383
Sexuality and health, 2375–2380
Sexual masochism, 647–655
definition, 647
detection, 648–649
primary, 650–652
secondary, 650, 652–653
tertiary, 650, 654–655
treatment
behavior therapy, 653, 654
pharmacotherapy, 651, 652
psychotherapy, 651, 652, 653, 654,
655
Sexual motivation, 2266, 2267–2269
See also Sexual desire
Sexual orientation
possible effects on offspring of
sexually potentiating drugs,
2359
and sexual motivation, 2267
Sexual pain, 2251
Sexual perversion
and kleptomania, 2467
and pyromania, 2470
Sexual pheromones, 2355
Sexual provocation from patients, 991–
992
Sexual reassignment. *See*
Transsexualism
Sexual response cycle
and aging, 2280, 2372–2373
female, 2279–2280
and menstrual cycle, 2282
phases, 2279
Sexual sadism, 647–655
definition, 647
detection, 648–649
in pedophilia, 617
primary, 650–652
secondary, 650, 652–653
tertiary, 650, 654–655
treatment
behavior therapy, 653, 654
pharmacotherapy, 651, 652

psychotherapy, 651, 652, 653, 654,
655
Sexual sadomasochism
associated with fetishism, 637
associated with transvestic fetishism,
641
Sexual surrogates, 2363–2364
Shame as motivation for seeking
treatment for fetishism, 638, 639
Shaping in behavior therapy for
autistic children, 223
Shared paranoid disorder. *See* Induced
psychotic disorder
Sheltered workshop programs, 272,
1573
Shock and delirium, 806
Shock therapy. *See* Electroconvulsive
therapy
Shoplifting, 2467–2468
Short-term anxiety-provoking
psychotherapy
depressive disorders, 1877
histrionic personality disorder, 2733–
2734
Short-term psychotherapy
borderline personality disorder, 2752
mood disorders, 1732
narcissistic personality disorder,
2740
obsessive compulsive personality
disorder, 2778
paranoid personality disorder, 2710
Shy-Drager syndrome, differential
diagnosis, 861
SIADH. *See* Syndrome of inappropriate
antidiuretic hormone secretion
Sialorrhea and Parkinson's disease, 861
Sibling counseling for autistic disorder,
262–265
Sibling role in treatment
autistic disorder, 265–266
schizoid disorder, 759
See also Family role in treatment
Sickness Impact Profile in somatoform
pain disorder diagnosis, 2125

Signal theory of anxiety, 2011
Simple phobias
  behavior therapy, 2026–2028
  hypnosis, 2055–2056
  psychoanalytic psychotherapy, 2019–2022
  social skills training, 2029
  See also Phobias
Simpson Scale, 244
Situational depression. See Mood disorders, depressive disorders
Situational hypoactive sexual desire, 2270
Skin shock. See Electric aversion therapy
Slavson's Activity Interview Therapy, 110
Sleep apnea
  obstructive syndrome, 2434–2436
  pathophysiology as cause, 2433–2434
  See also Central sleep apnea; Obstructive sleep apnea
Sleep deprivation
  mood disorders, 1729, 1741
    bipolar disorders, 1762, 1932–1933
  and nonresponsive patients, 1801
Sleep disorders
  insomnia, primary, 2424–2433
  narcolepsy, 2439–2440
  nightmares and night terrors, 2420–2422, 2540, 2562
  nocturnal myoclonus, 2437–2438
  parasomnias in children, 2419–2424
  sleep apnea, 2433
  See also Sleep disturbances in late life; Sleep-wake schedule disorders
Sleep disturbances in late life
  clinical assessment, 2445
  etiology, 2444–2445
  geriatric insomnia, 2446
  pharmacotherapy, 2447–2448
  prevalence, 2444
  sleep-wake rhythm reinforcement, 2446, 2449

sundowning, 2445
  treatment guidelines, 2446–2447
Sleep disturbances in organic mental syndromes, 804
Sleep hygiene, 2429–2430
Sleep-wake cycle in primary insomnia, 2426
Sleep-wake schedule disorders
  advanced sleep phase syndrome, 2443–2444
  circadian realignment, 2442, 2443
  circadian system, 2440–2441
  delayed sleep phase syndrome, 2443
  jet lag, 2442–2443
  pharmacotherapy, 2442
  shift work, 2441–2442
  sleep deprivation as occupational hazard, 2441
  social problems, 2442
  therapy, 2442, 2443, 2444
  zeitgebers, 2442, 2443, 2444
Sleepwalking, 2422–2423
Slowness, primary obsessional, 2096
Small-Carrion penile prosthesis, 2332, 2333
Smelling salts to treat fetishism, 639
Smoking
  abstinence violation effect, 1282, 1283
  and alcohol abuse, 1283–1284
  American Lung Association program, 1278, 1279
  aversion therapy, 1277
  behavior therapy, 1276–1278
  and cannabis abuse and dependence, 1284–1285
  carbon monoxide in cigarette smoke, 1262–1263, 1271
  contracts, 1276–1277, 1293
  Daily Smoking Record, 1269, 1288–1289
  group therapy, 1279
  hypnosis, 1277–1278, 1279
  maintenance of nonsmoking, 1279–1283

and multi-infarct dementia, 962

and organic aggressive syndrome, 852

physiologic effects of cigarette smoke, 1262–1264

and psychiatric disorders, 1285–1286

relapse prevention, 1280–1282

relaxation training, 1278

rewards, 1276

Smoking Cessation Group Treatment Protocol, 1274–1275

stress as factor, 1265

and stroke, 869

treatment, 846–847

weight management, 1280

withdrawal, 1280

See also Cannabis abuse and dependence; Nicotine dependence; Tobacco withdrawal and tobacco dependence

Smoking Cessation Group Treatment Protocol, 1274–1275

Smoking Contract form, 1293

Smoking History Interview, 1269, 1287–1288

Social factors and organic mental syndromes, 803

Social interaction therapy for depressive disorders, 1858–1859

Socialization of mentally retarded persons, 114, 134

Social learning group therapy schizophrenia, 1530, 1534, 1535, 1536, 1537, 1538, 1542, 1543

See also Social skills training

Social learning in therapeutic communities for substance abuse, 1381

Social phobias

behavior therapy, 2028–2029

flooding, 2028

hypnosis, 2055–2056

psychoanalytic psychotherapy, 2022–2023

systematic desensitization, 2028

See also Phobias

Social problems of drug abusers, 1185–1186

Social Security

age of entitlement, 995

and Medicare, 980

Social skills deficits

in mentally retarded persons, 8, 20

in substance abuse, 1445

Social skills training

anorexia nervosa, 477

attention-deficit hyperactivity disorder, 378

attention-focusing procedure, 1571–1572

autistic disorder, 197, 198, 267, 268

bulimia nervosa, 522, 536

conduct disorder, 384–385

exhibitionism, 673

mentally retarded persons, 120, 130, 131

mood disorders, 1944

depressive disorders, 1859, 1861, 1862, 1945

pedophilia, 626

personal grooming, 1572

personality disorders, 2650, 2653, 2654, 2668, 2670, 2695

avoidant personality disorder, 2761

dependent personality disorder, 2675

schizophrenia, 1555–1557, 1570–1571, 1582

schizophreniform disorder, 1663

social phobias, 2029

transvestic fetishism, 644

voyeurism, 673

See also Social learning group therapy

Social therapy for conversion disorders, 2159

Sociopathic personality disorder, differential diagnosis, 843

Sociopathy. *See* Antisocial personality disorder

Sodium bicarbonate
  and acidosis, 897
  and alkalosis, 897–898
Sodium lactate
  effects on cardiovascular system, 903
Sodium valproate
  bipolar disorders, 1932
Soft neurologic signs and organic
    personality disorder, 840
Somatic component of anxiety in
    mentally retarded persons, 14–
    15
Somatic disorders and exhibitionism/
    voyeurism, 671
Somatic paranoid disorder, 1645–1646
Somatization disorder
  Briquet's syndrome, differentiation,
    2167
  diagnostic considerations, 1764
  DSM-III-R diagnostic criteria, 2166–
    2167
  electroconvulsive therapy, 2170
  group therapy, 2168
  hysteria, chronic, 2167
  and mood disorders, 1755
  and pain disorder, 2169
  psychotherapy, 2168–2169
  stress as cause, 2168
  therapeutic alliance, 2169
  treatment and prognosis studies,
    2167–2168
Somatoform disorder not otherwise
    specified. *See* Undifferentiated
    somatoform disorder
Somatoform disorders
  body dysmorphic disorder, 2146
  conversion disorders, 2152–2159
  DSM diagnostic criteria, 2119–2120
  factitious disorders, 2159–2166
  hypochondriasis, 2138–2146
  psychotropic drugs, 2170
  somatization disorder, 2166–2171
  somatoform pain disorder, 2120–
    2138
  undifferentiated somatoform
    disorder, 2147–2152

Somatoform pain disorder
  acupuncture, 2132
  adjustment disorders of adulthood
    and old age, differentiation,
    2507
  anxiety, 2529
  behavior alteration, 2134
  biopsychosocial assessment, 2124–
    2125
  categories, 2121
  compensation and disability
    payments, 2136
  diagnosis and etiology, 2120, 2121–
    2123
  evaluation, 2136–2138
  family therapy, 2135
  follow-up studies, 2136–2137
  frequency, 2121
  International Association for the
    Study of Pain, 2122
  management, 2124–2136
  medical/surgical events as initial
    cause, 2123
  multimodal treatment programs,
    2137–2138
  and other disorders
    affective disorder, 2121
    conversion disorder, 2121–2122
    depression, 2121, 2123, 2129
    dysthymic disorder, 2121
  outcome evaluation, 2136–2138
  pain management, 2124
  peer support, 2136
  primary physician role, 2136
  psychological tests, 2125
  psychopathology assessment, 2125
  re-entry planning, 2135
  reframing pain problem, 2125
  rehabilitative approach, 2130, 2133–
    2134
  rewards, environmental, 2135
  and secondary depression, 1901–
    1904
  skills training, 2134
  stress/tension, 2125
  symbolic significance of pain, 2127

symptom control
  assertiveness training, 2134
  biofeedback, 2131
  cognitive therapy, 2130–2131
  drug detoxification, 2128
  electroconvulsive shock therapy,
    2133
  hypnosis, 2131–2132
  innovative techniques, 2133
  managing pain complaints, 2126
  nerve blocks, 2132–2133
  pharmacotherapy, 2129–2130
  psychotherapy, 2126–2128, 2135
  rehabilitation, 2130
  relaxation training, 2131
  sensory stimulation, 2132
  surgical procedures, 2133
  therapeutic alliance, 2124–2128
  transcutaneous nerve stimulation
    (TNS), 2132
  treatment goals, 2125–2128
  See also Pain, chronic, somatoform
Somatostatin-like immunoreactivity in
    dementia of the Alzheimer's
    type, 977, 978
Somerset Court, 273
Somnambulism. *See* Sleepwalking
Soteria project, 1663
Speakeasy International, 2613
Special education. *See* Early childhood
    education; Education; Education
    for All Handicapped Children
    Act
Special treatment centers for sexual
    offenders, 624
  Adult Diagnostic and Treatment
    Center, 625
  Fort Steilacom, Washington, 625
  Massachusetts Treatment Center,
    627
  Western State Hospital, 625
Specific developmental disorders
  academic skills disorders, 298, 328–
    339
  clinical description, 308
  controversial therapies, 326–327

developmental disability, 297, 298
differential diagnosis, 320–321
disorder-development relationship,
  302–303
distractibility, 310
educational evaluation, 321
educational programs, 304–305, 347–
  352
emotional problems, 311–312
environment as factor, 301–307
evaluation and intervention, 319–352
family counseling for education,
  322–324
family problems, 311–312
fluency disorders, 315–316
hyperactivity, 310
incidence, 298
input and integrative disabilities,
  319–320
language and speech disorders, 299,
  300, 313–314, 339–347
language problems, assessment,
  316–317
learning disabilities, 297, 308–312
legal aspects of education, 304, 347–
  352
mathematics disorders, specific, 317–
  318
memory disabilities, 320
motor impairments, effect on
  development, 301–302, 303
neurologic evaluation, 321
output disabilities, 320
overview, 297–301
parent as factor, 303–304, 305–307
phonologic disorders, 314–315
psychological intervention, 325
psychological testing, 321
reading disorders, 298, 332–337
school environment, 322
social problems, 311–312
testing, 329–332
treatment, 321–327
Spectatoring and impotence, 2319,
  2320–2321

Speech and language dysfunctions in
   fragile X syndrome, 40
Speech Foundation of America, 315
Speech therapy for autistic children,
   198
"Speed." *See* Methamphetamine abuse
Spinal cord injury, sexual effects, 2241,
   2376, 2377, 2378
Spironolactone
   renal disease, 925
Split personality, self-characterization
   in transvestic fetishism, 641
Splitting, 2013
   personality disorders, 2669, 2690
      antisocial personality disorder,
         2743
      narcissistic personality disorder,
         2739
      schizoid personality disorder,
         2712, 2714
Spouse abuse reporting, 993
Spouse role in paraphilias
   pedophilia, 621
   sexual sadomasochism, 651, 653, 655
   transvestic fetishism, 643, 644, 645
SST penile deformity, 2332
St. Louis Criteria for schizophrenia,
   1499, 1500, 1501
Standardized tests, limitations for
   autistic children, 208, 209
Stanford Achievement Test, 330
Stanford-Binet Intelligence Scale, 193,
   330
Stanford Diagnostic Arithmetic Test,
   331
State-Trait Anxiety Inventory for
   Children, 402
Status epilepticus
   and phencyclidine abuse, 1213
   as result of ending
      pharmacotherapy, 888
Stereotyped behaviors, abnormal
   mentally retarded persons
      age as factor, 45
      amphetamines, contraindications,
         92

   behavior therapy, 46–49, 119
   definition, 44
   description, 8, 44–49
   environmental factors, 45–46
   etiology, 45
   pharmacotherapy, 49, 73, 76
   prevalence, 45
Steroid contraceptive drugs
   interaction with other drugs, 893
Steroid drugs
   interaction with other drugs, 891
   and secondary depression, 1914
   and secondary mania, 1761, 1928
   side effects, 947
Stilbestrol
   transvestic fetishism, 643
Stimulant abuse
   abstinence, 1227–1228
   behavior therapy, 1233–1234
   and bulimia nervosa, 519
   and cannabis use, 1244
   chronic abuse treatment, 1232–1239
   crashing, 1223–1224, 1228–1229
   craving, conditioned cues, 1231–
      1232, 1238
   cycle disruption, 1233–1237
   delirium and delusions, 1223
   diagnosis, 1239–1240
   dysphoria, 1223–1224, 1228–1229,
      1230–1231
   euphoria, 1220, 1221, 1226
   extinction, 1231–1232, 1238
   history and epidemiology, 1218–1220
   hospitalization, 1236
   intoxication, 1222–1223
   manic-like effects, 1223
   medical complications from chronic
      abuse, 1224–1225
   neurochemical activity, 1220–1222
   outcome studies, 1238–1239
   overdose management, 1224, 1225
   pharmacotherapy for relapse
      prevention, 1236–1237, 1240
   prevalence, 1225
   psychiatric complications from
      chronic abuse, 1225–1232

psychosis induction, 1371
psychotherapy, 1235, 1240
recovery stages, 1238
relapse prevention, 1237–1239
research, 1240–1241
self-help groups, 1234–1235, 1237
symptoms, 1222
withdrawal, 1229–1231
See also Cocaine abuse
Stimulants
atypical impulse control disorder,
2479
autistic disorder, 241
dementia, 829
dopamine agonist effect, 242
hyperactivity, 241, 367, 373–376
and inhibited female orgasm, 2286
mentally retarded persons,
contraindications, 92, 93
minimal brain dysfunction, 2686
mood disorders, 1787, 1799
secondary depression, 1912
personality disorders, 2687
antisocial personality disorder,
2746, 2747
prevalence of use, 91
stroke, 871
Tourette's syndrome, 690, 707–708
See also Stimulant abuse; names of
specific drugs
Stimulus fading. *See* Prompting and
fading
Stimulus specificity, 664
Streptomycin
auditory effects, 958
Stress
adjustment disorders, response,
2500–2502, 2513
biologic response, 2070–2071
conversion disorders, 2153
depersonalization disorder, 2219
dissociative disorder not otherwise
specified, 2226
family relationships, 2566, 2568,
2569, 2570, 2571, 2572–2578
job-related, 2578, 2579, 2580

parasomnias in children, 2421, 2422,
2424
primary insomnia, 2427, 2428
psychogenic amnesia, 2188
psychogenic fugue, 2193
psychological response, 2071–2072
pyromania, 2470
social response systems, 2072–2073
somatization disorder, 2168
traumatic stress response, 2070–2071
See also Stress management
Stress and tension as cause of
substance abuse, 1198, 1201–
1202
Stress inoculation training (SIT), 2543
Stress management
affective-autonomic behavior
therapies, 2534–2537
anxiety induction and relaxation
control, 2535–2536
anxiety management training
(AMT), 2536–2537
behavior therapy, 2532–2548
clinical issues, 2544
cognitive behavior therapies
cognitive restructuring, 2542–2543
rational emotive therapy (RET),
2542
skills training, 2543, 2546
stress acquisition, 2541
stress inoculation training (SIT),
2543
systematic rational restructuring
(SRR), 2542
competency retrieval, 2539
coping, 2532, 2538–2540, 2543, 2547
and depression, 2539, 2542
flashbacks, 2536, 2540
group therapy, 2578–2585
implosion/flooding, 2535, 2536
learned helplessness, 2540–2541
models, 2532, 2533, 2539–2540
overlapping treatment, 2546–2547
parents of autistic children, 257–262
parents of mentally retarded, 106–
107

Stress management (cont)
  personality disorders, 2657
  rational emotive therapy, 2542
  relaxation training, 2534–2535
  and schizophrenia, 2534
  secondary symptom prevention/
    reduction, 2540–2541
  self-help and mutual aid groups,
    2596–2607, 2611
  self-regulation strategies, 2537, 2547
  and sexual dysfunction, 2538, 2541
  stimulus control, 2538
  stressor-variable paradigm, 2533
  stress response system, 2532
  systematic desensitization, 2535
  termination, 2547–2548
  treatment guidelines, 2545–2548
  worry, concept, 2538
  See also Adjustment disorders
Stressors
  adjustment disorders, 2572, 2575
  long-term, 2514, 2515
  psychosocial, 2498–2500
  responses to, 2500–2502, 2513
  self-help and mutual aid groups for
    adults, 2596
Stress-related disorders,
    pharmacotherapy, 2586, 2587,
    2590
Stress response syndromes
  adjustment disorders, 2548–2549,
    2587
  etiology, 2548–2549
Striatonigral degeneration, differential
    diagnosis, 861
Stroke
  age factor, 875
  and amnestic syndromes, 819, 871
  cerebral vasculature, 868
  and delirium, 871
  and delusional syndromes, 874
  and dementia, 822, 827, 871, 872
  differential diagnosis, 868
  DSM-III-R diagnostic criteria, 870–
    871
  and hypertension, 846–847

  incidence, 867
  and mood disorders, 875–876, 1741
    secondary depression, 876, 1910–
      1911
    secondary mania, 1761
  and multi-infarct dementia, 962
  and organic aggressive syndrome,
    842, 848
  and organic delusional syndrome,
    833
  and organic personality syndrome,
    840, 858, 859
  and perceptual abnormalities, 873–
    874
  pharmacotherapy, 867, 871, 874, 875
  psychosexual disorders, 876–877
  treatment, 869–870
Structural-strategic therapy for
    schizophrenia, 1545
Students Against Drunk Driving
    (SADD), 2613
Stupor
  and atypical psychosis, 1699, 1700
  and bipolar disorder, 1760
Stuttering
  description, 315–317
  stress and tensions as factors, 345,
    346
  treatment, 345–346
Subacute cerebellar degeneration and
    lung disease, 941
Subacute sclerosing panencephalitis
    and sensory impairment, 952
Subaffective dysthymia, 1758
  See also Mood disorders, bipolar
    disorders
Subdural hematoma
  in alcoholics, 934
  and brief reactive psychosis, 1680
  and delirium, 811
  and dementia, 821
  differential diagnosis, 1910
  and renal disease, 917, 919
Subjective doubles, 836
Subject Treatment Emergent Symptom
    Scale, 381

Sublimation difficulty, 2457
Substance abuse
  adaptive difficulties, 1200
  addiction as life style, 1193, 1194
  adolescents, characteristics, 1192
  and alcoholism, 1918
  anxiety, 1373
  behavior therapy
    abstinence-oriented multimodal
      treatment, 1436
    behavioral assessment, 1431–1433
    behavioral counseling, 1435–1436
    behavioral model, 1430, 1431, 1432
    behavioral observation, 1433–1434
    behavioral perspective, 1430
    biologic testing, 1434–1435
    cognitive-behavioral strategies,
      1436
    collateral behaviors, 1444–1446
    contingency contracts, 1436, 1440–
      1444
    contingency management, 1431,
      1438–1440, 1446
    coping techniques, 1437
    diagnosis, 1434
    environmental restructuring, 1435
    extinction, 1437–1438
    motivation for treatment, 1435
    reinforcement, 1441–1444
    reinforcing aspect of drugs, 1431–
      1432
    relapse prevention, 1432, 1436–
      1437, 1446
    residential treatment, 1439
    role playing, 1444
    self-report, 1433
    skills training, 1431, 1436–1437
    social competency assessment,
      1444
    social skills deficits, 1445
    stimulus counterconditioning,
      1437–1438
    termination, 1441
    therapist qualifications, 1447
  concepts and theories, 1197
  as coping strategy, 1196
  dependence cycle, 1194
  as dependence disorder, 1192–1193
  developmental stages, 1200–1201
  differential diagnosis, 859
  ego deficits, 1201
  environment as factor, 1197, 1199–
    1200, 1201
  etiology, 1192–1202
  family therapy, 1397–1416
  models, 1194–1195
  motivation for use, 1193, 1196, 1198–
    1199
  mutual-help services for youth, 2613
  parental factors, 1200–1201
  peer pressure, 1200
  personality deficiency, 1197
  pharmacology, 1419
  psychiatric disorder prevalence,
    1417–1418
  psychotherapy, individual, in
    substance abuse, 1417–1430
  relapse, 1202
  self-help services for youth, 2611
  self-rejection, 1201
  sexual effects, 2240, 2344
  stimulants, 1218–1241
  stress and tension reduction, 1198,
    1201–1202
  symptoms versus syndromes, 1193–
    1194
  therapeutic communities, 1379–1396,
    1420
  urine testing, 1434–1435, 1436, 1446,
    1447
  user types, variations, 1193
  See also Alcohol abuse; Drug abuse;
    Therapeutic communities for
    substance abuse; names of
    specific substances and classes
    of substances
Substance-induced chronic psychosis,
  1709
  See also Atypical psychosis; Drug
    abuse
Substance-induced organic mental
  disorders. *See* Alcohol-related

organic mental disorders;
Organic mental disorders;
names of specific mental
disorders
Substance use disorders. *See* Alcohol
abuse; Alcoholism; Drug abuse;
Substance abuse; names of
specific substances
Substance withdrawal. *See* Withdrawal
Succinylcholine
alcohol withdrawal, 1088
and electroconvulsive therapy, 1809
and hyperkalemia, 899
Suicidal ideation in transvestic
fetishism, 645
Suicide tendencies
and adjustment disorders of
adulthood and old age, 2510
alcoholism evaluation factor, 1074
and brief reactive psychosis, 1681,
1682, 1684
epilepsy, 882
and induced psychotic disorder,
1689, 1693
and long-acting neuroleptics, 1514
and mood disorders, 1740, 1742,
1745, 1760, 1764, 1765, 1767,
1907, 1911, 1925
secondary depression, 1682, 1900
and pathologic gambling, 2465
and pedophilia, 631
and personality disorders, 2653,
2676, 2688, 2698, 2726–2727
borderline personality disorder,
2784
histrionic personality disorder,
2736
narcissistic personality disorder,
2741
passive-aggressive personality
disorder, 2784
psychoanalytic psychotherapy, 1833
religion as deterrent, 2594
risk assessment, 2529
and schizoaffective disorder, 1674
and sensory impairment, 950, 951

Sulfafurazone
interaction with other drugs, 891
Sulfinpyrazone
stroke, 869
Sulpiride for mentally retarded
persons, 72
Superego
and personality disorders, 2640,
2644, 2646, 2661, 2674
antisocial personality disorder,
2743
avoidant personality disorder,
2760
Supplemental Security Income and
Medicare, 980
Supported employment concept, 273
Support groups for families
of alcoholics, 1091, 1115–1116, 1120,
1160, 1161, 1399, 1401, 1411
of the mentally ill, 1543, 1548, 1560,
1563
of substance abusers, 1316, 1378,
1399
See also Mutual-help services for
youth; Self-help and mutual aid
groups for adults; names of
specific organizations
Supportive-expressive (SE)
psychotherapy
drug abuse, 1422–1429
mood disorders, 1732
depressive disorders, 1822, 1882–
1883, 1921
Supportive group therapy for
schizophrenia, 1517, 1518, 1534,
1537, 1538
Supportive psychotherapy
borderline personality disorder, 2752
narcissistic personality disorder,
2739
Support networks for alcoholics, 1115,
1133–1134, 1135–1136
See also Alcoholics Anonymous
Support networks for employment of
mentally retarded persons, 137

Surgery
  chronic pain, 2133
  obstructive sleep apnea, 2436
Surrogate sexual partners, 2363–2364
Symbiotic psychoses. *See* Induced
    psychotic disorder
Symmetrel. *See* Amantadine
Sympatholytic drugs
  impotence, 2357
  neuropsychiatric effects, 911–912
Sympathomimetic drugs
  effects on cardiovascular system, 905
  interaction with other drugs, 913,
    914, 959
  and monoamine oxidase inhibitors,
    1785
  and organic aggressive syndrome,
    852
  and organic delusional syndrome,
    833, 834
  orgasmic dysfunctions, 2357
  orthostatic hypotension, 903
Synanon, 2611, 2613
Syndrome of inappropriate antidiuretic
    hormone secretion (SIADH), 898
Synkinesias in Tourette's syndrome,
    692
Syphilis and secondary depression,
    1902
Systematic desensitization
  agoraphobia, 2033
  anorexia nervosa, 475
  in behavior therapy, 2098
  exhibitionism, 673
  in family therapy, 2663
  in group therapy, 2582
  obsessive compulsive disorder, 2098
  pedophilia, 628
  personality disorders, 2649, 2650,
    2654, 2656, 2657
    avoidant personality disorder,
      2761
    obsessive compulsive personality
      disorder, 2780
  rape trauma syndrome, 2535
  sexual disorders, 2290, 2319, 2361

  simple phobias, 2026–2027
  social phobias, 2028
  stress management, 2535
  voyeurism, 673
  See also Behavior therapy
Systematic rational restructuring (SRR)
    for stress management, 2542
Systemic lupus erythematosus
  differential diagnosis, 1701
  and loss of vision, 952
  pharmacotherapy, 952
  and renal disease, 927
  and secondary depression, 854, 1902
  and secondary mania, 1761, 1928

T actual Performance Task, 1071
Tamoxifen
  sexual effects, 2355
Tanner, Goetz and Klawans Protocol,
    693
Tar and Nicotine Content of 28
    Selected Cigarettes, tabulation,
    1292–1293
Tarasoff warning, 1000
Tardive dyskinesia
  American Psychiatric Association
    task force report, 1513
  and antipsychotic drugs, 387, 1511,
    1512–1513, 1704
  and anxiety disorders of childhood
    or adolescence, neuroleptic
    drugs, 408
  assessment, 232
  from carbamazepine, 1674
  in children, 244–245
  distinguished from tic disorders, 692
  experimental treatments, 1513
  and haloperidol, 234, 243
  hypersensitivity of dopaminergic
    neurons, 1512–1513
  and neuroleptic drugs, 70, 80, 408,
    827, 849–850, 875, 1510, 1514,
    1631, 1662, 1763, 1775, 1925

Tardive dyskinesia (cont)
  risk factors, 1513
  and Tourette's syndrome, 706, 709
Tar in cigarette smoke, 1263
The Tavistock Group. See Brief
      dynamic psychotherapy
Taylor and Abrams diagnostic system
      for schizophrenia, 1499, 1500,
      1501
Teacher and Parent Separation Anxiety
      Rating Scales for Preschool
      Children, 402
Teaching methods
  autistic children, 194–197
  mentally retarded, 125–126, 127
  See also Education
Teenagers. See Adolescents
Teenagers Anonymous, 2613
Teenage support groups. See Mutual-
      help services for youth; Peer-
      helping services for youth;
      names of specific organizations
Teen pregnancy, 2368–2369
Tegretol
  secondary depression, 1904
Temazepam
  anxiety and lung disease, 945
  delirium, 809, 810
  dementia, 828
  mental retardation, 90
Temperature dysregulation and
      delirium, 806, 809
Temper outbursts
  in adults, 2473, 2474, 2475, 2476
  in children, pharmacotherapy, 2476
Temporal lobectomy to control
      fetishism, 637
Tennessee Self-Concept Scales, 1382–
      1383
Terbutaline
  side effects, 944
Tertiary amine tricyclic antidepressant
      drugs
  dementia, 827
  See also Tricyclic antidepressant
      drugs

Test anxiety, 402, 2054
Test for Auditory Comprehension of
      Language, 208
Testicular atrophy and hepatic disease,
      933, 935
Testing, psychological
  learning disabilities, 321
  pervasive developmental disorders,
      187
  Wechsler Intelligence Scale for
      Children (WISC), 321, 330
Test of Language Development, 208,
      330
Test of Written Spelling, 331
Testosterone
  impotence, 2354
  sexual effects, 2350–2351
Testosterone level
  pedophilia, 629–630
  transvestic fetishism, 635, 645
Tests for learning disabilities
  cognitive tests, 330
  criterion-referenced tests, 331
  language and learning, 329–330
  language comprehension in autistic
      children, 208–210
  mathematics, 331
  nonstandardized tests, 331–332
  reading, 330–331
  spelling, 331
  standardized tests, 329–331
Tetrabenazine
  Tourette's syndrome, 690
Tetracyclic antidepressant drugs
  dementia, 827
  pharmacokinetics, 1780
    neurotransmitter blockade, 1776
  seizures, 884
Tetrahydroaminoacidine
  dementia of the Alzheimer's type,
      970
Tetrahydrocannabinol (THC). See
      Cannabis abuse and
      dependence
Thematic Apperception Test, 1549

Theophylline
  effects on respiratory system, 943,
      947
  interaction with other drugs, 947
Theos, self-help and mutual aid
      groups for adults, 2600, 2601
Therapeutic alliance
  adjustment disorders, 2549, 2550,
      2552
  atypical impulse control disorder,
      2480
  multiple personality disorder, 2203,
      2211
  obsessive compulsive disorder,
      2107–2108, 2110
  paranoid personality disorder, 2707
  somatization disorder, 2169
  somatoform pain disorder, 2124–
      2128
  in substance abuse, 1424–1425
  transvestic fetishism, 645, 646
Therapeutic communities for
      personality disorders, 2696–2697
Therapeutic communities for substance
      abuse
  admission procedures
    client characteristics, 1385
    criteria for residential treatment,
        1384–1385
    detoxification arrangements, 1384
    exclusion policies, 1384–1385
    interview, 1383–1384
    psychiatric diagnosis, 1383
    psychological profiles of patients,
        1382–1383
    referrals, 1383
    social profiles of patients, 1382,
        1385
  approach
    induction stage of process, 1387–
        1388
    peer group structure, 1385–1386
    peers as role models, 1387, 1389
    primary treatment process, 1388–
        1390
    process stages, 1387–1391

    re-entry stage of process, 1390
    staff as rational authorities, 1386,
        1387
    structure, 1385–1386
    work as education and therapy,
        1386
  cannabis abuse and dependence,
      1256
  concept and attitudes, 1382
  detoxification, limitations, 1384
  effectiveness
    alternatives, 1395–1396
    drop-out and retention rates, 1395
    follow-up studies, 1395
  and mental health, 1396
  and methadone maintenance, 1344
  opioid abuse and dependence
      treatment, 1326–1327, 1330
  patient motivation, 1381, 1385
  perspective, 1380–1382
  process elements
    community enhancement, 1392–
        1393
    contracts, 1394
    counseling, 1392
    discipline, 1393–1394
    encounters, 1391
    management, 1386, 1393–1395
    marathons, 1391–1392
    privileges, 1393
    probes, 1391
    sanctions, 1393–1394
    seminars, 1390, 1392
    surveillance, 1394
    therapeutic-educative element,
        1391–1392
    tutorials, 1392
    urine testing, 1394
  psychotherapy, contraindication,
      1420
  psychotherapy, individual, in
      substance abuse, 1420
  self-esteem problems, 1382–1383,
      1389, 1390, 1393
  self-help, 1381, 1386
  sex as factor, 1380

Therapeutic communities for substance abuse *(cont)*
    social learning, 1381
    traditional type, 1379–1380
    See also Residential treatment programs, alcoholism
Therapeutic environment in phencyclidine abuse, 1217
Thiamine
    alcohol intoxication, 1082
    alcoholism, 1092
    alcohol withdrawal, 1085, 1087
    Wernicke's encephalopathy, 826
Thiamine deficiency
    and amnestic syndromes, 818, 819
    and delirium, 806, 807, 808
    and dementia, 818
    See also Wernicke's encephalopathy
Thiazide
    interaction with other drugs, 913, 914, 927
    and lithium, 1930
    renal disease, 925
Thiazines
    mood disorders, 1736
Thin-layer chromatography for urine testing in drug abuse, 1434
Thioridazine
    bipolar disorders, 1929, 1930
    dementia and amnestic syndromes, 827
    effect on seizures, 839
    effects on cardiovascular system, 906, 907
    and ejaculatory pain, 2316–2317
    interaction with other drugs, 852, 915, 1341
    mentally retarded persons, 73–75
    personality disorders, 2679
    premature ejaculation, 2309, 2357
    and retarded ejaculation, 2243
    schizoid disorder, 760
    schizophrenia in adolescents, 234
    with a sensory-impaired patient, 958
    side effects, 876
Thioridazine-naltrexone interaction, 1341

Thiothixene
    autistic disorder, 242
    bipolar disorders, 1928
    borderline personality disorder, 2681
    dementia and amnestic syndromes, 826
    effect on seizures, 839
    and electroconvulsive therapy, 1805
    interaction with other drugs, 914, 928
    mentally retarded persons, 74
    organic mood syndrome, 856
    in patients with lung disease, 946
    premature ejaculation, 2309
    schizophrenia, 2726
    schizophrenia in adolescents, 234
    schizotypal personality disorder, 2681, 2683, 2726
Thioxanthenes
    effects on cardiovascular system, 906
Thought control and thought reform cultism, 2222, 2223, 2225–2226
Thought-stopping, transvestic fetishism, 644
Thresholds psychosocial rehabilitation center, 1573
Thymoleptic drugs
    mood disorders, 1764, 1766
Thyroid disease and personality disorders, 2687
Thyroid disorders and brief reactive psychosis, 1680
Thyroid hormone
    autistic disorder treatment, 240–241
    mood disorders, 1785
        adjunct treatment in nonresponding patients, 1792, 1794–1795, 1797
        secondary depression, 1912, 1913
Thyrotoxicosis and secondary mania, 1761
Thyrotropin-releasing hormone (TRH) autistic disorder, 240–241
Thyrotropin-releasing hormone (TRH) stimulation test for major depression diagnosis, 1905

Thyroxine (T$_4$)
elevation in autistic children, 240
periodic catatonia, 1709
Tic disorders, 687–714
and brain injury, 691
complex tics, 687, 688
differential diagnosis, 692
differentiation from other
neurological disorders, 687–688
etiology, 691
simple tics, 687, 688
variability of manifestations, 687–688
See also Tourette's syndrome
Tic douloureux
carbamazepine, 1739
Timed Stereotypies Rating Scale, 229
Time-limited dynamic psychotherapy
for depressive disorders, 1877–
1878, 1881–1882
Time-out technique in behavior
therapy, 34, 47, 113, 222, 586
Timolol
and secondary depression, 1913
with a sensory-impaired patient, 959
side effects, 959
Tinofedrine
multi-infarct dementia, 963
Tobacco as euphoriant, 1261
Tobacco withdrawal and tobacco
dependence
abstinence violation avoidance, 1282
and alcohol abuse, 1283–1284
and cannabis abuse, 1284–1285
demographic and social factors, 1266
diagnosis and assessment, 1267–
1271
DSM-III-R diagnostic criteria, 1261–
1262
etiology of smoking, 1264
high-risk situations, 1280–1281
history of addiction, 1288
intervention, 1271
maintenance of nonsmoking, 1279–
1285
motivation for smoking, 1261, 1289–
1291

patient progress, monitoring and
evaluating, 1279–1285
physiologic effects
addiction, assessment, 1267–1269
addiction treatment techniques,
1273, 1275
addictive behavior, 1261
factors in smoking, 1264–1265
morbidity and mortality, 1263–
1264
withdrawal, 1280
psychological effects
addiction, assessment, 1269–1270
factors, 1265–1266
psychiatric disorders, 1285–1286
psychologic effects
dependency treatment techniques,
1276, 1279
quit date, 1279
and secondary depression, 1285
Self-Efficacy Questionnaire, 1270,
1291–1292
smokeless tobacco, drawbacks, 1283
smoking behavior, 1264–1266
smoking patterns, 1288
social assessment, 1270
social support, 1278–1279, 1288
treatment
aversion therapy, 1277
behavior change strategies, 1276
behavior therapy contracts, 1276–
1277, 1293
cognitive-behavioral techniques,
1276–1277
goal setting and commitment in
therapy, 1271–1273
group protocol, 1274–1275
group therapy, 1279
issues, 1266–1267, 1283–1286
options, 1273
recommendations, summary,
1282–1283
relapse prevention, 1280–1282
relaxation training, 1278
Why Do You Smoke? questionnaire,
1269, 1289–1291

See also Nicotine dependence;
    Smoking
Tobramycin
    auditory effects, 958
Toilet training
    encopresis development, 724
    enuresis development, 720
Token economy programs for
        personality disorders, 2651, 2652
Tolmetin
    and secondary mania, 1914
Tonic-clonic seizures. *See* Epilepsy,
    generalized seizures
Tooth grinding. *See* Bruxism
Tourette's syndrome, 687–714
    aggressive behavior, 700
    assessment, 692–695
    and attention-deficit hyperactivity
        disorder, 373, 688–689, 692, 694,
        695, 697, 707–708
    behavior therapy, 701–702
    complex tics, 687, 688
    echolalia in, 687, 688
    effect on educational functioning,
        692, 695, 696–698, 702–703, 709
    effect on family functioning, 692,
        698–699, 700, 701
    effect on occupational functioning,
        695, 698, 702–703, 709
    effect on social functioning, 692, 695,
        700, 701, 710
    environmental factors, 690
    etiology, 689, 690–691, 696
    genetic factors, 689, 690, 696, 710
    mentally retarded persons, 7
    neurotransmitters, 690
    and obsessive compulsive disorder,
        688, 689–690, 692, 693, 694, 700,
        708–709
    pharmacotherapy, 692, 695, 696, 697,
        701, 703–709, 911
    psychotherapy, 699–701
    and secondary depression, 701
    simple tics, 687, 688
    and tardive dyskinesia, 709
    variability of manifestations, 692–694

Tourette's Syndrome and other
        Behavioral Disorders
        Questionnaire, 693, 694
Tourette's Syndrome Global Scale, 693,
        694–695
Tourette's Syndrome Questionnaire,
        693, 694
Tourette's Syndrome Severity Scale,
        693, 694–695
Tourette's Syndrome Symptom List,
        693, 694
Tracheostomy, chronic, for obstructive
        sleep apnea, 2436
Trails B, 1071
Training in Community Living
        program, 1663
Trance-like states in dissociative
        disorder not otherwise
        specified, 2223–2225
Tranquilizers
    alcoholism, 1090, 1096, 1101
    antisocial personality disorder,
        2746
    passive-aggressive personality
        disorder, 2787
    premature ejaculation, 2309, 2357
    schizoid disorder, 760
    sex drive reduction, 2356
    See also names of specific drugs
Transcutaneous nerve stimulation
        (TNS) for pain relief, 2132
Transference
    fetishism, 638, 639
    maternal transference, 2729, 2731
    mood disorders in children and
        adolescents, 1956
    personality disorders, 2667, 2699–
        2700
        avoidant personality disorder,
            2760
        borderline personality disorder,
            2688, 2751, 2755
        dependent personality disorder,
            2767
        narcissistic personality disorder,
            2738, 2741

paranoid personality disorder,
2709
passive-aggressive personality
disorder, 2786, 2787
schizotypal personality disorder,
2722
in psychoanalysis, 1825, 1829, 1830,
1831, 1832
brief dynamic psychotherapy,
1876, 1879, 1881
and sexual motivation, 2268–2269
Transformation theory of anxiety,
2010–2011
Transient global amnesia
differential diagnosis, 884, 885
distinguished from amnestic
syndrome, 821
and stroke, 872
Transient ischemia
and amnestic syndromes, 822
differential diagnosis, 884, 885
and myocardial infarction, 869
side effect of guanethidine, 912
treatment, 870
Transitional employment concept, 1573
Transsexualism, 656–660
and childhood gender identity
disorder, 661–662, 669
differential diagnosis, 859
distinguished from transvestic
fetishism, 640–641
evaluation for treatment, 657–659,
660
gender dysphoria, 657–658
gender reassignment, 656, 658, 659
hormonal treatment, 658, 659
moral/professional issues for
participating physicians, 460,
461
primary, 657, 658–659, 660
psychotherapy, 656, 658, 659, 660
as psychotic transvestic fetishism,
642
secondary, 657, 659–660
Transurethral resection of the prostate
(TURP), sexual effects, 2373

Transvestic fetishism, 633–646
borderline personality organization,
642
characteristics, 636, 641–642
in childhood, 642
childhood trauma, 642
definition, 640
distinguished from transsexualism,
640, 640–642
etiology, 634–636, 644, 646
gender dysphoria, 638, 641–642, 644,
645–646
homosexuality, 640, 641, 642
marginal transvestite, 641
nuclear transvestite, 641
Oedipal complex, 643
parent effect, 643
spouse role, 643, 644, 645, 646
treatment, 636, 642–646
aversion therapy, 646
behavior therapy, 643, 644–645
biological therapy, 643, 644
covert sensitization, 644
pharmacotherapy, 643, 644, 645–
646
psychotherapy, 643–644, 645
unreliability of self-report, 642–643
Transvestism. *See* Transvestic fetishism
Tranylcypromine
borderline personality disorder,
2682, 2684
classification, 1774
dementia, 828
effects on cardiovascular system, 905
hepatic disease, 937
hypochondriasis, 2145
low sex drive, 2356
mood disorders, 1797
bipolar disorders, 1929, 1930
pharmacokinetics, 1780
secondary depression, 1917
Trazodone
classification, 1774
dementia, 827
effects on cardiovascular system,
903, 904

Trazodone *(cont)*
  interaction with other drugs, 913
  mood disorders, 1799
    secondary depression, 1904, 1906,
      1917, 1918
  pharmacokinetics, 1780
    neurotransmitter blockade, 1775,
      1776, 1777
    neurotransmitter receptor
      blockade, 1779
  premature ejaculation, 2353, 2354,
    2357
  priapism as side effect, 2354
  sexual anxiety, 2247
  sexual effects, 2353, 2354
  side effects, 876
  and specific medical diseases, 1782,
    1783, 1784
  in treatment nonresponders, 1798
Treatment Outcome Prospective Study
    for methadone maintenance,
    1343
Trexan. *See* Naltrexone
Triacetyloleandomycin
  interaction with other drugs, 893
Triamterene
  renal disease, 925
Triazolam
  delirium, 809, 810
  dementia, 828
  mental retardation, 90
Triazolobenzodiazepines
  borderline personality disorder, 2682
Triazolopyridine
  dementia, 827
  pharmacokinetics, 1780
    neurotransmitter blockade, 1776
Triazolopyridines
  effects on cardiovascular system, 904
Trichotillomania
  age as factor, 2481, 2486
  alopecia, 2481
  aversion conditioning, 2484, 2485
  behavior therapy, 2482, 2484, 2486
  cognitive therapy, 2484
  competing responses, 2484

  definition, 2481
  family therapy, 2485–2486
  feedback, 2484
  history of treatment, 2482
  hypnosis, 2483, 2485, 2486
  incidence, 2481
  medical origin, 2483
  and obsessive compulsive behavior,
    2483
  and other psychiatric disorders, 2481
  pharmacotherapy, 2482–2483, 2486
  psychotherapy, 2482, 2483
  reinforcement, 2484
  relaxation techniques, 2484
  sex as factor, 2481
  treatment evaluation, 2486
Tricyclic antidepressant drugs
  alcoholism, 1075
  anxiety disorders of childhood or
    adolescence, 406, 408
  attention-deficit hyperactivity
    disorder, 374, 376
  atypical psychosis and depression,
    1704
  bulimia nervosa, 530–531
    with secondary depression, 2685
  classification, 1773–1774
  contraindicated for depression in
    myocardial infarction, 903
  and delirium, 812
  dementia, 827, 828, 829
  dementia of the Alzheimer's type,
    975
  depression
    due to hallucinogen abuse, 1207
    and lung disease, 946
    risk of orthostatic hypotension,
      903
  dosage, 1779–1781
  effectiveness, 1738, 1803
  effects on cardiovascular system,
    901–904, 906
  and electroconvulsive therapy, 1808
  enuresis, cautions, 2423–2424
  extrapyramidal symptoms, 866
  and hypertension, 847

hypomanic response, 1758
and inhibited female orgasm, 2286
insomnia, 2430
insomnia in opioid detoxification,
1318
interaction with other drugs, 851,
866, 890, 891, 892, 912–913, 921,
928
with lithium, 1792, 1793–1794, 1930
and mania, 854
mentally retarded persons, other
disorders, 81–84
with monoamine oxidase inhibitors,
1787, 1796
mood disorders, 1729, 1734, 1736,
1737, 1767
bipolar disorders, 1742, 1760,
1927, 1929, 1934, 1935–1936
depressive disorders, 1742–1743,
1869–1870, 1904, 1906, 1907–
1908, 1918, 1919–1920, 1924,
1943
with neuroleptic drugs, 1794, 1795,
1804
neurotransmitter blockade, 1775–
1779
obsessive compulsive disorder,
2100–2103
obstructive sleep apnea, 2435
ocular effects, 958
organic mood syndrome, 1741
and orthostatic hypotension, 928
panic attacks, 2685
panic disorder in drug addicts, 1376,
1420
Parkinson's disease, 865, 866
personality disorders, 2687, 2688
avoidant personality disorder,
2762
borderline personality disorder,
2682, 2754, 2755
dependent personality disorder,
2770
obsessive compulsive personality
disorder, 2685

paranoid personality disorder,
2710
with secondary depression, 2684
posttraumatic stress disorder, 2074
in pregnancy, 1806
premature ejaculation, 2357
and psychotherapy, 1733, 1863,
1869, 1870
renal disease, 921, 922, 923–924
schizoaffective disorder, 1672, 1673,
1674, 1675
schizophrenia, 1506
seizures, 884
sexual anxiety, 2247
side effects, 902, 1788
sleep disturbances in late life,
2448
somatic symptoms, 2151
somatoform pain disorder, 2129
trichotillomania, 2482
See also Antidepressant drugs; names
of specific drugs
Trifluoperazine
autistic disorder, 230, 242
borderline personality disorder,
2682, 2684
and ejaculatory pain, 2317
interaction with other drugs, 928
late paraphrenia, 1641
mood disorders
bipolar disorders, 1928
secondary depression, 1903
schizoaffective disorder, 1673
stroke, 875
Trifluperidol
autistic disorder, 242
side effects, 242
Trihexyphenidyl
and hypokinetic syndrome, 1512
Triiodothyronine (T$_3$)
autistic disorder, 240
dementia, 828
Trimethadione
epilepsy, 889

Trimethaphan
  hypertension from electroconvulsive
    therapy, 1810
Trimipramine
  classification, 1774
  dementia, 827
  pharmacokinetics, 1780
    neurotransmitter blockade, 1776
  and specific medical diseases, 1782,
    1783, 1784
Trisomy 21 as cause of Down's
    syndrome, 30
Tryptophan
  dementia of the Alzheimer's type,
    975
L-Tryptophan
  insomnia, 2430
  mood disorders, 1800
  obstructive sleep apnea, 2435
TS. See Tourette's syndrome
Tuberculosis
  and dementia, 821
  and organic mental syndromes, 939
  and secondary depression, 1902
Tuberous sclerosis and secondary
    depression, 1902
Tumultuous course through
    adolescence, 784–785
Twelve Step program for substance
    abuse
  in Alcoholics Anonymous, 1152,
    1154–1155
  cannabis abuse and dependence,
    1255, 1256, 1259–1260
  in family therapy, 1400
  sedative and hypnotic drugs, 1299
Twilight states, epilepsy-related, 880,
    881
Tybamate for somatic symptoms, 2152
Tyramine
  effects on cardiovascular system, 905
  interaction with other drugs, 867
Tyrannical behavior in mentally
    retarded persons, 55–57
Tyrosine
  cannabis withdrawal, 1254

mood disorders, 1800
multi-infarct dementia, 962

UCLA Longitudinal Study, 1551
UCLA Neuropsychiatric Institute, 256
UCLA Registry project, 232, 256
Uncomplicated alcohol withdrawal,
    1067, 1084–1086
  See also Alcohol withdrawal
Uncomplicated bereavement
  anniversary reactions, 1755
  treatment, 1743–1744
Undifferentiated somatoform disorder
  antidepressant and antianxiety
    drugs, 2151–2152
  cognitive strategies, 2150
  functional somatic symptoms, 2147
  headaches, psychotherapy, 2150
  irritable bowel syndrome, 2149
  peptic ulcers, 2149
  prevalence, 2147
  psychotherapy, disadvantages, 2151
  somatic complaints, psychotherapy,
    2148–2149, 2151
  veterans, disabled, 2149
Undifferentiated subtype of
    schizophrenia, 1498
University of California, San Francisco
    Center for the Study of
    Neuroses, 2078
University of Michigan, Children's
    Psychiatric Hospital, 1953
University of Oregon, Depression
    Research Unit, 1847, 1855
University of Southern California
    study on efficacy of
    nortriptyline, 1871
University of Tennessee
  Mood Clinic, 1935
  studies on depression, 1755, 1757,
    1759
  study of bipolar offspring, 1763
  study of cyclothymia, 1939

Unpleasant Events Schedule (UES). *See* Behavior therapy, mood disorders

Urea
  lithium excretion, 906

Uremia
  and delirium, 806
  and epilepsy, 885

Urethritis, sexual effects, 2243

Urine tests in drug abuse
  abstinence verification, 1191, 1421
  amphetamines, 1235
  cannabis, 1246–1247, 1253–1254
  cocaine, 1235
  enzyme multiplied immunoassay test (EMIT), 1434
  hospital treatment of addicts, 1361
  therapeutic community, process element, 1394
  thin-layer chromatography, 1434

Urologic disease and antidepressant drugs, 1782

U.S. Army draftee study, adjustment disorders, 2497

U.S. Bureau of the Census
  statistics on the elderly, 980

U.S. Department of Health, Education and Welfare, study on aging, 803

U.S. Department of Health and Human Services
  Medicare, 981
  Steering Committee on the Chronically Mentally Ill, 1663
  Task Force Report on Alzheimer's disease, 802
  Vocational Rehabilitation Division, 272–273

U.S. Navy enlisted personnel study, adjustment disorders, 2513

U.S. Office of Education, 269

U.S. Office of Special Education and Rehabilitation Services, 273

Uvulopalatopharyngoplasty (UPPP) for obstructive sleep apnea, 2436

Vaginismus
  and depression, 2254
  diagnosis, 2296–2297
  DSM-III-R diagnostic criteria, 2291
  etiology, 2294–2296
  pharmacotherapy, 2358
  tests for physical causes, 2244
  treatment, 2297–2299

Valium. *See* Diazepam

Valproate
  epilepsy, 887, 888, 889
  interaction with other drugs, 891, 892

Valproic acid
  bipolar disorders, 1934
  seizure management in mentally retarded persons, 96, 99

The Vanderbilt Group. *See* Brief dynamic psychotherapy

Vascular disease
  and delirium, 806

Vasoactive intestinal polypeptide (VIP)
  sexual effects, 2352–2353

Vasodilators
  dementia, 829
  dementia of the Alzheimer's type, 971–973
  impotence, 2357
  multi-infarct dementia, 962, 963
  renal disease, 928–929

Vasopressin
  dementia of the Alzheimer's type, 976–977

Vasovagal attacks
  differential diagnosis, 884

Verapamil
  bipolar disorders, 909, 1932, 1934
  interaction with other drugs, 909, 915
  neuropsychiatric effects, 909
  side effects, 909

Verbal aversion therapy for alcoholism, 1127–1128

Vertigo and digitalis toxicity, 908

Veterans Administration
  Cooperative Study Group on
    Antihypertensive Agents, 908
  methadone maintenance treatment
    study, 1344
  Penn project on substance abuse
    therapy, 1428
Vicious cycle of bulimia nervosa, 538–
  539
Videotaping in assessment and
    treatment
  multiple personality disorder, 2202,
    2205
  personality disorders, 2654
    passive-aggressive personality
      disorder, 2788
  pharmacotherapy efficacy and safety
    assessment, 229, 232
  reactive attachment disorder of
    infancy, 741
  social skills training, 1571
  supervision of group therapy, 1539
  Tourette's syndrome, 694
Vietnam veterans
  community response and posttrau-
    matic stress disorder, 2072–2073
  See also Posttraumatic stress disorder
Viloxazine
  low sex drive, 2356
  sexual effects, 2353
Vinblastine
  and secondary depression, 1913
Vincamine
  dementia of the Alzheimer's type,
    973
  multi-infarct dementia, 963
Vincristine
  side effects, 944, 948
Vineland Adaptive Behavior Scales,
  187
Vineland Social Maturity Scale, 187
Violence
  alcohol-related
    alcoholic blackout, 1083
    guidelines for managing, 1074,
      1083–1084

    pharmacotherapy, 1084
  and atypical impulse control
    disorder, 2477
  and impulse control disorders not
    elsewhere classified, 2461
  and intermittent explosive disorder,
    2475
  in pedophilia, 619
VIP. See Vasoactive intestinal
    polypeptide
Viral infection
  and depression, 854
  and organic mood syndrome, 853
Viscosity and organic personality
    syndrome, 858
Vistaril. See Hydroxyzine
Visual agnosias and stroke, 868
Vitamin B6
  language effects in autistic children,
    241
Vitamin deficiency
  and depression, 854
  differential diagnosis, 1701
  and hepatic disease, 934, 936
Vitamin therapy
  alcohol withdrawal, 1085, 1087
  autistic disorder, 241
  schizophrenia, 1502
Vocational rehabilitation. See
    Vocational training
Vocational Rehabilitation Act, 1568
Vocational training
  alcoholics, 1093
  autistic disorder, 271–274
  bulimia nervosa, 521
  epileptics, 886
  mentally retarded persons
    competitive employment models,
      132
    legislation, 132
    person-environment fit, 136–
      137
    policy issues, 137–138
    quality of life, 138–139
    services, 135–136
    training, 130–131, 133–135

pervasive developmental disorders,
271–274
schizophrenics, 1573–1575
See also Employment
Vomiting. *See* Bulimia nervosa;
Rumination
Voodoo, factitious disorder, 2165
Voyeurism, 670–673
definition, 671–672
deriving from somatic disorders, 671
incidence, 670–671
in pedophilia, 618–619
physical causes, 673
recidivism, 672
sexual sadomasochism, 653
and sexual sadomasochism, 670
treatment, 672–673
Vulpe Assessment, 187

War Department Technical Bulletin
Nomenclature and Method of
Recording Diagnoses, 2762–2763
Warfarin
and hypertension, 847
interaction with other drugs, 891
stroke, 869
Washing, obsessive compulsive
disorder, 2095
Weber's test, 956
Wechsler Adult Intelligence Scale
(WAIS), 71, 1071, 1092
as mortality predictor, 801
Wechsler Intelligence Scale for
Children (WISC), 71, 187, 321,
330, 697
Weight loss therapy for obstructive
sleep apnea, 2434–2435
Weight management
after cigarette smoking cessation,
1280
in bulimia nervosa, 524

Weight restoration
anorexia nervosa, 456–458, 466–467,
479–480
atypical eating disorders, 592–593
Wellbutrin. *See* Bupropion
Wernicke-Korsakoff syndrome
and brief reactive psychosis, 1680
and dementia, 818
transketalase activity, 1092
Wernicke's encephalopathy, 1092
and delirium, 808
and dementia, 818
and secondary depression, 1902
and stroke, 870
treatment, 826
See also Thiamine deficiency
Western State Hospital, treatment of
sexual offenders, 625
Westhaven-Yale Multidimensional Pain
Inventory (WHYMPI), 2125
Whitiko psychosis, differential
diagnosis, 1685
Why Do You Smoke? questionnaire,
1269, 1289–1291
Wide Range Achievement Test, 331
Wilson's disease
differential diagnosis, 861, 934–935,
1700
and liver transplantation, 933
and organic personality syndrome,
858
and secondary depression, 1902
treatment, 934
See also Hepatic disease
Windigo, 1699
Wisconsin Psychosocial Pain
Inventory, 2125
Wisconsin Scoring Test, 1092
Withdrawal
benzodiazepines, 1298, 1299, 2039,
2042–2044, 2052
cigarette smoking, 1280
cocaine abuse, 1229–1231
delirium due to barbiturate-sedative-
hypnotic drugs, 1300

Withdrawal *(cont)*
   drug abuse, 1190
   hospital procedures in drug abuse,
      1362, 1363, 1364
   methadone, 1311, 1312, 1317, 1319
   methadone maintenance, 1351–1352
   nicotine dependence, 1262, 1280
   opioid abuse, 1311–1312, 1315, 1316–
      1319
   phenobarbital withdrawal
      conversion, 1297
   and schizoaffective disorder, 1667
   sedative-hypnotic drugs, 1295–1300,
      1304, 1305
   stimulant abuse, 1229–1231
   treatment of multiple drug users,
      1088–1089
   See also Alcohol withdrawal; Alcohol
      withdrawal delirium
Withdrawal dyskinesia
   assessment, 232
   in children, 244–245
   and haloperidol, 234, 243
Wittigo, 2165
Work, role in therapeutic community,
   1386
World Health Organization, 1667
World Psychiatric Association, 1499
Worry as concept, 2538

Xanthine
   multi-infarct dementia, 962
X-ray for atypical psychosis diagnosis,
   1701

Yale Center of Alcohol Studies, 1143
Yale Plan, 1143–1144
Yohimbine
   dementia of the Alzheimer's type,
      975
   impotence, 2354, 2357
   low sex drive, 2356
   sexual effects, 2354
   Tourette's syndrome, 691
Young Fighters, 2613
Your Perfect Right, 1856
Youth Anonymous, 2613

Zeitgebers in sleep-wake schedule
   disorders, 2442, 2443, 2444
Zinc deficiency in pica, 588
Zung Self-Rating Depression Scale,
   1849, 2125
   secondary depression, 1920

Name Index

Aaron H, 1912, 1913, 1920
Abarbanel A, 2297
Abassi V, 241
Abbott DH, 2352
Abel GG, 619, 626, 627, 671, 2276, 2277, 2385, 2387, 2392
Abel JG, 922
Abel TM, 2713, 2715
Abeles M, 2193, 2194, 2195
Abeloff MD, 1904
Abels N, 2767
Abelson HI, 1219
Abend S, 2750
Abernethy DR, 1780
Abernethy V, 998
Abikoff H, 374, 377, 378, 379
Abildskov JA, 909, 910
Ablon J, 1115, 1120, 1160, 1161
Abplanalp JM, 2389
Abraham K, 511, 541, 700, 1824, 1827, 2015, 2634, 2640, 2762
Abraham SF, 533
Abram HS, 1900
Abramowicz M, 1912, 1913, 1920
Abrams J, 1418, 1810
Abrams R, 814, 875, 1495, 1498, 1499, 1500, 1501, 1761, 1804, 1809, 1811
Abramson L, 2542
Abramson LY, 1848
Abramson R, 2741
A'Brook MF, 944
Abruzzi W, 2747

Abse DW, 1693
Abshagenu, 938
Abuiso P, 1806
Achenbach TM, 351, 367, 369, 373, 382, 389, 402, 435, 720, 772
Achenback TM, 1951
Ack M, 109
Ackerman N, 2660
Ackerman NW, 2340
Adams EH, 1219
Adams F, 1914
Adams HP, 867, 869
Adams J, 2072
Adams RD, 87, 837, 870, 873, 895, 896, 897, 941, 942
Adams RO, 930, 931
Adamson WC, 72
Adatto C, 790
Addonizio G, 1804
Adinolfi A, 1124
Adinolfi AA, 1122
Adler G, 2013, 2140, 2676, 2690, 2693, 2697, 2703, 2737, 2751
Adler K, 1532
Adler S, 911
Adolfsson R, 974, 975, 976
Adomakoh CC, 2159
Adsett CA, 2583
Aduan RP, 2161
Agid Y, 861, 863
Agijian H, 1579, 1581
Agle D, 2322

Agle DP, 939
Agnoli A, 862
Agras W, 2534
Agras WS, 476, 477, 530, 534
Ahad A, 2104, 2773
Aherwadker SJ, 907
Ahmad S, 1912
Aichhorn A, 2458, 2459
Aiken LR Jr, 338
Akerly M, 260
Akhtar S, 2191
Akil H, 1310
Akins T, 2532, 2534
Akiskal HS, 1751, 1752, 1753, 1754,
    1755, 1756, 1757, 1758, 1759, 1760,
    1762, 1763, 1764, 1765, 1790, 1792,
    1886, 1898, 1925, 1929, 1932, 1933,
    1934, 1935, 1936, 1938, 1939, 1941,
    1942, 1945, 2097, 2636, 2681, 2682,
    2683, 2684, 2725
Al-Anon, 1160, 1161
Al-Issa I, 2337
Aladjem M, 723
Alarcon-Segovia D, 912
Albala AA, 1813
Alban J, 2158
Albert DM, 953
Albert H, 2717, 2724
Albert M, 823
Albert MS, 974
Albert N, 1951
Alberti PW, 957
Alberti RE, 1856
Albin JL, 52, 53, 108
Alcoholics Anonymous, 1152, 1153,
    1157, 1159
Alcoholics Anonymous World Service
    Center, 1152
Alden L, 1130, 2761
Aldridge CR, 974
Alexander BK, 2765, 2766
Alexander CS, 906
Alexander F, 511, 1874, 1875, 2127,
    2459, 2509
Alexander HE, 915
Alexander J, 2763

Alexander JF, 385, 2640, 2665, 2746,
    2767, 2778
Alexander MP, 874
Alexandris A, 73, 92
Alexopoulos GS, 974
Alford JD, 24
Alfrey AC, 918
Algozzine B, 125
Ali CJ, 904
Ali Salih M, 1689
Alibrandi LA, 1154
Allan JD, 585
Allen BA, 1068
Allen C, 673
Allen DW, 672
Allen RD, 2476
Allen RP, 967, 968
Allison J, 2281
Allison M, 1439
Allison T, 894
Allman M, 1117, 1118
Alloy LB, 1848
Allyon T, 2652
Alonso A, 2677
Alper J, 138
Alper S, 138
Alpern GD, 185
Alpert C, 213
Alpert E, 933
Alterman AI, 1073
Altman N, 2140
Altschule MD, 1708
Altshuler KZ, 951
Alzate H, 2281, 2286
Amado H, 2746
Aman MG, 6, 7, 68, 73, 74, 75,
    76, 91, 92, 93, 94, 97, 98, 226,
    401
Amatruda CS, 365
Ambelas A, 1761
Ambrosi B, 2350, 2393
Amdisen A, 924, 926
American Academy of
    Ophthalmology, 326
American Academy of Pediatrics, 326,
    327

American Association of Retired
 Persons, 980
American Medical Association, 1296
American Psychiatric Association, 10,
 15, 17, 28, 41, 109, 179, 180, 182,
 226, 231, 234, 239, 256, 298, 299,
 308, 327, 347, 349, 365, 367, 647,
 689, 717, 718, 723, 733, 738, 747,
 772, 783, 799, 804, 806, 815, 817,
 831, 840, 853, 857, 870, 949, 965,
 999, 1001, 1005, 1063, 1067, 1079,
 1082, 1084, 1112, 1184, 1211, 1227,
 1228, 1246, 1261, 1294, 1349, 1361,
 1417, 1488, 1493, 1499, 1513, 1517,
 1611, 1655, 1666, 1667, 1668, 1677,
 1686, 1687, 1697, 1698, 1726, 1743,
 1751, 1753, 1790, 1815, 1822, 1868,
 1873, 1891, 1900, 1902, 1925, 1940,
 1946, 1951, 2007, 2010, 2034, 2064,
 2066, 2097, 2119, 2121, 2146, 2147,
 2148, 2152, 2160, 2165, 2166, 2168,
 2185, 2186, 2191, 2198, 2219, 2222,
 2237, 2248, 2254, 2257, 2258, 2276,
 2282, 2283, 2291, 2301, 2313, 2335,
 2393, 2419, 2425, 2439, 2457, 2462,
 2469, 2474, 2475, 2477, 2497, 2503,
 2505, 2506, 2511, 2512, 2513, 2529,
 2566, 2567, 2589, 2634, 2636, 2639,
 2642, 2674, 2678, 2679, 2689, 2690,
 2705, 2712, 2713, 2719, 2727, 2737,
 2743, 2749, 2759, 2763, 2771, 2783
 Commission on Psychotherapies,
  1516, 1730
 Psychiatric News, 2464, 2466
 Report of the Task Force on
  Electroconvulsive Therapy of the
  American Psychiatric Association,
  1805, 1806
 Task Force, 1779, 1786, 1789, 1791,
  2043
 Task Force on Tardive Dyskinesia,
  243
American Speech-Language and
 Hearing Association, 313
Amsterdam JD, 1795
Ananth J, 2101

Ananth P, 2103, 2104
Anders TF, 718, 720
Andersen AE, 456, 473, 487, 590, 594
Andersen J, 865, 866, 867, 1678, 1684
Anderson CM, 1405, 1531, 1545, 1551,
 1552, 1559, 1560, 1561, 1563, 1564,
 1575, 2716
Anderson EW, 2165
Anderson HW, 1680, 1681
Anderson K, 1784
Anderson LT, 38, 76, 225, 226, 230,
 231, 233, 234, 237, 243, 248, 977
Anderson PO, 1156
Anderson RJ, 920
Anderson SC, 1111
Anderson V, 2514
Anderton CH, 2064
Andreasen NC, 1493, 1498, 1569, 1633,
 1761, 1898, 2254, 2508, 2513
Andrews G, 316, 345, 2509, 2765
Andrews JDW, 2735
Andrulonis PA, 2656, 2686
Ang L, 696
Angel A, 720
Angevine JB, 868
Anggard E, 1221
Anglin MD, 1330, 1331, 1345, 1350,
 1441
Angrist B, 833, 838, 1548
Angrist BM, 838
Angst J, 1669, 1671, 1672, 1758, 1764,
 1929
Angus WR, 945
Anker AL, 1232, 1233, 1234, 1236,
 1237, 1238
Annesley PT, 2103
Annis HM, 1074, 1124
Annon J, 2338, 2380, 2541
Annon JS, 2323
Ansari JMA, 2322, 2324
Ansbacher HL, 1532
Ansbacher RR, 1532
Ansell JE, 585
Anthony EG, 1691
Anthony EJ, 260, 724, 1949, 1952, 1957,
 2642

Anthony WA, 1533, 1543, 1563, 1568, 1574
Anton AH, 92
Anton PG, 2386
Antonuccio DO, 1858, 1862
Anyan WR, 452, 465
Aono T, 2684
APA. *See* American Psychiatric Association
Appelbaum PS, 984
Appenzeller O, 2317
Appleton WS, 1548, 2254
Aquilera D, 2525
Arajii S, 618
Aram DM, 313, 315
Araoz D, 2362
Arcasoy A, 582, 584
Archibald H, 2514, 2517
Arensberg CM, 1545
Arentewicz G, 2320, 2327, 2339, 2341
Argyle M, 1571, 2668
Arick JR, 199
Arieff AJ, 917, 919, 940
Arieli A, 1116, 1119, 1124
Aries N, 2369
Arieti S, 1732, 1749, 1825, 1826, 1833, 1864, 1873, 1947, 2012, 2020, 2472
Armbruster B, 1666, 1671, 1676
Armor DJ, 1075, 1148
Armstrong H, 2159
Armstrong PM, 54
Arndt IO, 1340
Arnhoff FN, 1547
Arnold LE, 241, 2479
Arnow B, 2032
Aronoff GM, 2127, 2128
Aronoff GR, 1780
Aronow R, 1351
Aronowitz E, 2607
Aronson MD, 1779, 1782
Arras JD, 1008
Arter JA, 333
Asana N, 1698
Asarnow J, 337
Ascher E, 700
Aschoff J, 2440

Aserlind R, 348
Ashem B, 1127
Asher R, 2160
Ashley M, 1074
Ashlock RB, 338
Asnis G, 2103
Asperger H, 180, 747
Astrachan BM, 1499
Atkinson G, 1278
Atkinson RM, 1147
Atwell C, 45
Auchincloss E, 2634
August GJ, 230, 236, 246, 256
Aurell M, 926
Ausman J, 586
Austen FK, 940
Austin L, 2559
Austin NK, 1579
Ausubel DP, 1197
Avery D, 1787, 1803, 1805
Avnstorp C, 2146
Axelrod J, 1775
Ayd FJ, 1808, 1928
Ayd FJ Jr, 810
Ayd FL Jr, 814
Ayllon T, 476, 2649
Azerrad J, 476
Azrin N, 2652
Azrin NH, 48, 49, 54, 224, 701, 702, 1122, 1128, 1129, 1442, 1443, 1446, 1574, 1860

Babigian HM, 1910
Babor TF, 1065, 1067, 1068, 1069, 1183
Babott D, 2319
Bach-y-Rita G, 2475, 2478, 2674, 2686
Bachrach AJ, 476
Bachrach HM, 1876
Bachrach LL, 1538, 2690
Bacon MK, 1094
Badel DW, 1829
Badgley RF, 621, 622, 623, 632, 633
Baekeland F, 1102, 1103

Baer DM, 114, 121, 133
Bagley CR, 833
Bahler JF, 894
Bailey EJ, 127
Bailey MB, 1120, 1157, 1160
Baittle B, 2460
Bak RC, 643
Bakalar JB, 813, 814, 1219
Bakalar JD, 1249
Baker A, 1502
Baker AF, 185
Baker BL, 25
Baker EFW, 1209
Baker KG, 2583
Baker L, 250, 256, 299, 300, 332
Baker PS, 212
Baker SP, 846
Baker TB, 1127
Bakker CB, 1204
Bakker LW, 52
Bakow H, 725
Bakwin H, 718, 719
Balaschak BA, 894
Baldessarini RJ, 827, 1627, 1628, 1629,
    1661, 1787, 1788
Baldwin B, 2524
Bale RN, 1326, 1344, 1395, 1439
Bales RF, 1155
Balint M, 1104, 1874, 1878, 2012, 2024,
    2635, 2710, 2712
Ball JC, 1420
Ball JRB, 637
Ball TS, 54, 59
Ballard J, 348
Balldin J, 974
Ballenger JC, 882, 1700, 1931, 2050
Ballmer U, 1306
Balster RH, 1210
Ban TA, 975, 976, 1502, 2221
Bancroft J, 673, 2266, 2297, 2338, 2350,
    2385, 2388, 2389, 2390
Bancroft V, 646
Bandura A, 21, 22, 114, 115, 1266,
    1270, 1276, 1283, 1570, 2025, 2027,
    2028, 2072, 2340, 2539, 2540, 2550,
    2649, 2652

Banerjee SP, 1230
Bank L, 801
Bank S, 262
Bankier RG, 944
Banks MH, 2122
Bannatyne A, 335
Bant W, 1305
Bant WP, 913, 1913, 1914
Bantle JP, 518, 519
Banzett LK, 1578
Bar-Levav R, 2671
Barabasz AF, 1277, 1278
Barbach L, 2342
Barbeau A, 691
Barber TX, 2157
Barbero G, 738, 742
Barcai A, 473
Barchas JD, 982
Barclay J, 945
Barclay LL, 966
Bardon TH, 574
Barken R, 2209
Barker P, 759
Barker WJ, 2255
Barkley RA, 48, 373, 374, 375, 377, 379
Barlow A, 751
Barlow DH, 627, 673, 2025, 2026, 2029,
    2031, 2032, 2035, 2276, 2385, 2390,
    2534, 2536, 2656
Barlow J, 530
Barltrop D, 51
Barmann BC, 578
Barnes DM, 1914
Barnes GM, 1149
Barnes R, 826
Barnes RJ, 2679
Barness LA, 241
Barnett G, 248
Barnett HJM, 869
Barnett LR, 482, 538
Baroff GS, 34
Baron M, 1490, 1669, 1670
Baron RA, 844
Barr AN, 864, 866
Barraclough B, 882, 883
Barrera M, 1857

Barrera RD, 212, 215
Barret RP, 4, 7
Barrett JE, 1752
Barrett RJ, 1221, 1230
Barrios BA, 401, 405
Barron J, 45, 90
Barrowclough C, 1552
Bartak L, 194, 195, 203, 215, 243
Bartlett J, 1897
Bartolucci G, 2514
Barton ES, 37
Barton W, 2591
Bartus RT, 967, 968, 969, 970, 971
Basalt RC, 1206
Bashir AS, 313
Bassett DL, 2126
Bates E, 340, 341
Bates P, 121, 132
Bateson EM, 584
Bateson G, 1154, 1155, 1544
Batki SL, 1921
Batrinos ML, 2393
Battegay R, 2714
Baudry F, 2640
Bauer A, 2143
Baum GL, 939
Baum WM, 121
Bauman MH, 1402
Baumeister AA, 7, 20, 33, 45, 46, 47, 49, 121
Baumgarten HG, 2385
Bawkin H, 2422
Baxter L, 2681
Baxter LR Jr, 1801
Bayer AJ, 1780
Bayer R, 1003
Bayle ALJ, 1490
Bayley N, 188
Beach FA, 648
Beach R, 2339
Beahrs JO, 2198, 2200, 2202
Beal EW, 2566
Beale EW, 2201
Bean M, 1154
Bear D, 846, 882, 2194, 2210
Beard JH, 1573

Beardsley JV, 865
Beatrice DF, 1580
Beatty LD, 331
Beaumont PJV, 492, 511, 533, 541
Beavers WR, 494, 496
Bebbington PE, 1156
Beck A, 2539
Beck AT, 482, 485, 486, 487, 489, 490, 491, 536, 551, 1186, 1566, 1731, 1815, 1820, 1822, 1825, 1834, 1835, 1836, 1837, 1838, 1839, 1841, 1842, 1844, 1845, 1846, 1847, 1849, 1916, 1951, 2009, 2036, 2072, 2542, 2550, 2761, 2778
Beck JG, 2320, 2391
Beck M, 2590
Becker J, 627, 1846, 1864, 2541
Becker JT, 1071
Becker JV, 578, 626
Becker RE, 1944
Beckey RE, 302
Bednar RL, 1123, 1533
Bedrosian RC, 1566
Beech HR, 2098, 2780
Beecher HK, 996
Beels CC, 1531, 1544, 1547, 1563, 1564
Beerends JJ, 725
Beery ED, 330
Beethoven L Von, 948
Begleiter H, 1072
Behrens MM, 835, 873
Beier DC, 28
Beier E, 2760
Beigel A, 1768
Beiman I, 2054, 2055
Beinart H, 533
Beisler JM, 215, 216
Beitchman JH, 300
Beitman BD, 1733, 1734, 1885
Bell A, 92
Bell AH, 1157
Bell DS, 833, 838, 1223
Bellack A, 2761
Bellack AS, 1445, 1571, 1821, 1846, 1859, 2670
Bellack L, 2669

Bellak L, 1702, 1874
Bellamy GT, 138
Bellamy T, 272, 273
Bellizzi J, 865
Bellman M, 724
Bem DJ, 1155
Bemis KM, 464, 477, 482, 483, 485,
    486, 487, 488, 523, 539, 550, 552,
    554
Bemporad J, 1732, 1749, 1873
Bemporad JR, 1825, 1864, 1952
Benaroya S, 212
Bender LA, 235, 330
Bender ME, 378
Benedek T, 511, 513
Bengston V, 2370
Bengtson VL, 995
Benjamin H, 635, 661
Benjamin JD, 2011
Benkert O, 2349, 2350, 2351, 2392
Bennet WM, 920, 921, 924
Bennett D, 2353
Bennett R, 952
Bennett TM, 780
Benoit M, 372
Benowitz NL, 1273
Benson DF, 818, 819, 835, 858, 862,
    864, 868, 870, 872, 873, 874, 876,
    877, 942, 943, 949, 1911
Benson H, 1856, 2052, 2055, 2064, 2361
Bentler PM, 637, 640, 641
Benton AI, 995
Bentovim M, 386
Bentoviv A, 62
Berenson CK, 1000
Berenson D, 1116, 1401
Beresford HR, 1003
Beresin E, 804, 805, 806, 2691, 2692,
    2693
Berg C, 694
Berg I, 725
Berger C, 137
Berger F, 1075
Berger PA, 247, 691, 813, 814, 976, 977,
    978
Berger R, 2611

Berger SH, 2317
Bergin A, 2532
Bergler E, 2464
Berglund M, 1918
Bergman I, 975
Bergman P, 569, 575
Bergman PJ, 835
Bergsholm P, 1809
Berkowitz DA, 758, 2662, 2665, 2740
Berkowitz R, 1548, 1552, 1553, 1554,
    1562, 1563
Berkson G, 44, 45, 46, 47
Berkson J, 689
Berlin FJ, 1708
Berlin FS, 620, 626, 627, 629, 638, 645,
    2276, 2277, 2356
Berlin I, 54
Berlin RM, 1305
Berman E, 2201, 2735
Berman K, 1119
Bernal ME, 64, 65
Berner P, 1621, 1622, 1761
Bernhardson G, 1251
Bernheim KF, 1548, 1559, 1560, 1564
Bernstein GA, 238, 248
Bernstein IC, 2146
Bernstein SB, 2700
Berquist, 571
Berrington WP, 2193, 2194
Berrios GE, 950
Berry S, 2201
Bertlesen A, 1937
Berwish N, 1795
Berzins J, 1358
Besalel VA, 1574, 1860
Besant A, 2224
Besser CM, 2352
Besser GM, 1370
Best C, 2536
Best JA, 1278
Besyner JK, 1838, 1839, 1840
Bewley TH, 1344
Bexell G, 1003
Bhagavan HN, 2104
Bianchine JR, 865, 866, 867
Biase DV, 1382

Bibb RC, 2170
Bibring E, 1827, 1873
Bibring GL, 1004
Bickel WK, 1325
Bicknell DJ, 244
Bidwell BH, 881, 882, 2122
Biederman J, 473, 1916
Bielski RJ, 1790, 1803
Bigelow G, 1127, 1129
Bigger JT Jr, 828, 902, 903, 913
Biglan A, 1852, 1862, 1885
Bijou S, 112
Biller HB, 2615
Billings AG, 1285, 1885, 1886
Binder JL, 1816, 1875, 1881, 2740, 2768
Binder LM, 876, 903
Binet A, 636
Binswanger L, 511
Biological Therapies in Psychiatry, 1661
Bion W, 2717
Bion WR, 1529
Bird B, 2459
Bird J, 2158
Bird RL, 1813
Birk L, 2339, 2340
Birmaher B, 92
Bishop DS, 1559, 1564, 1565
Bishop ER Jr, 836, 839
Bishop JM, 1490
Bishop N, 2312
Bishop S, 1819, 1842, 1843
Bitar KN, 571
Bixler EO, 945
Bjorksten OJW, 2326
Blachly PH, 1344, 1354
Black A, 2098
Black DW, 1928
Black FW, 870, 933, 934
Blackburn IM, 1819, 1820, 1821, 1822, 1839, 1840, 1842, 1843, 1845
Blacklidge VY, 92
Blackman N, 2469
Blackwell B, 1514, 1904, 2123
Blackwood DHR, 1812
Blagooyen TJ, 1121
Blaine SD, 1359

Blanchard EB, 2034, 2131, 2150
Blanchard M, 1761
Blanchard P, 297
Bland K, 2030
Bland RC, 1758
Bland W, 20
Blane HT, 1094, 1257
Blaney PH, 1834, 1846
Blanken AJ, 1219
Blaschke TF, 928
Blashfield RK, 1067
Blass FP, 977
Blass JP, 966, 971, 1092
Blay L, 2348
Bleiberg E, 665, 667
Blessed G, 823, 972
Bleuler E, 1487, 1490, 1498, 1499, 1692, 1898, 2712
Bleuler EP, 2165
Blinder BJ, 564, 566, 567, 570, 572, 573, 574, 577, 579, 580, 581, 584
Bliss EL, 511, 2197, 2198, 2202, 2205, 2206
Bloch DA, 2460
Bloch HI, 1344
Bloch S, 401
Block A, 2135
Block AJ, 940
Block D, 2514, 2515, 2517
Block J, 249
Block S, 1533
Blockley J, 61
Blomquist HK, 40
Bloom B, 2523, 2525, 2527
Bloom BL, 1865
Bloom JR, 2131
Bloom L, 202, 204, 205, 207, 211, 342
Bloom WA Jr, 1344
Blos P, 783, 789, 790, 2368, 2460
Blott JP, 215
Blouin AG, 530
Blount RL, 665
Blowers AJ, 244
Blue FR, 2221
Blum A, 1283
Blume SB, 1117, 1121, 1257

Blumer D, 819, 858, 876, 877, 882, 2129
Blumer DB, 1762, 1902, 1903, 1904, 1936
Bobo J, 1284
Bock JL, 904
Boddie HG, 1366
Bodenheimer C, 263
Boe RB, 22
Boesky D, 2640, 2641
Bogen J, 2223
Bohince EA, 1154, 1156, 1158
Bohlen JG, 2387
Boisaubin EV, 1004
Bok S, 997
Boland BJ, 1127
Bolen DW, 2464
Boller F, 862
Bolstad OD, 117
Bolter A, 1216
Bolwig TG, 810
Bond GR, 1573
Bond MJ, 2159
Bond R, 908
Bondareff W, 829, 966, 974
Bonica JJ, 1902
Bonime W, 2715, 2716
Bonime WT, 1944
Boning J, 2042
Bonn J, 883
Bonner J, 2319
Bonvillian J, 212
Boor M, 2199
Booth A, 2337
Booth AM, 2384, 2386
Boots, 638
Borck LE, 2607
Borders OT, 1440, 1441
Borga O, 922, 923
Borison RL, 1230
Borkovec T, 2532, 2538
Borkovec TD, 2064, 2428
Borman LD, 2597, 2598, 2599, 2600, 2601, 2602, 2605
Bornet A, 1157
Bornstein B, 2013
Bornstein M, 385

Bornstein R, 940
Borowski T, 1534
Borriello JF, 2674
Boshes GA, 1936, 1937
Boskind-Lodahl M, 526, 527, 543, 549
Boskind-White M, 525, 526, 527, 538
Bosley E, 61
Boston Collaborative Drug Surveillance Program, 943
Boszormenyi-Nagy I, 431, 1566, 2665
Bottomley V, 668
Botvin R, 1253
Boudewyns P, 2536
Boudewyns PA, 1577
Boudin HM, 1233, 1433
Bouldin HM, 1443
Boulos Z, 1895
Bowden CL, 1344, 1345, 1351
Bowen DM, 968, 974, 978
Bowen FP, 865
Bowen M, 1403, 1406, 1544, 2566, 2569, 2571, 2660
Bowers MK, 2201, 2203
Bowers TK, 452
Bowes PF, 1542
Bowlby E, 568, 570
Bowlby J, 409, 734, 1825, 1828, 1864, 1952, 1953, 2011
Bowman KM, 1065
Boyce P, 1892
Boyd D, 2133
Boyd S, 2514, 2517
Boyd T, 2535
Boyd WH, 2464
Boylin ER, 1121
Bracha S, 1808
Braden V, 1673
Bradford JMcDW, 630
Bradley K, 2201, 2202
Bradley SJ, 666, 763, 769
Bradley WG, 870
Bradshore W, 2380
Brady JP, 25, 475, 476, 1532, 1542, 2337, 2654, 2670
Brady JV, 1252
Braestrup C, 1306

Braha R, 2133
Brahen LS, 1333, 1337
Brain WR, 941, 942
Braithwaite RA, 1782
Brambilla F, 247
Branch CHH, 511
Branconnier RJ, 1779
Brandsma JM, 1117, 1122, 1123, 1158, 2202
Brandt KD, 952
Brantley JT, 644
Bratter TE, 1122
Braun BG, 2198, 2199, 2202, 2204, 2205, 2207, 2208
Braunwald E, 895, 896, 910
Brawley E, 47
Brazelton TB, 340, 2011
Breese GR, 33, 38
Bregman S, 105
Breier A, 1531, 1532
Breitner C, 2098
Brem J, 1708
Bremmer WJ, 2388
Brena SF, 1904
Brende JP, 2199, 2204
Brenner BM, 917, 921
Brenner I, 2191
Bresnitz E, 1363
Breuer J, 1824, 2157
Briant RH, 913, 1783
Bricker DD, 127
Bridge TP, 1498
Brief DJ, 533, 538
Brierley H, 643, 644
Brierley JB, 942
Brigance AH, 187
Brindley GS, 2385, 2387
Brink T, 2504, 2507
Brinkley-Birk AW, 2339, 2340
Brinkley JR, 2479, 2680
Brinkman SD, 967
Briquet P, 2167
Briscoe CW, 1865, 1885
Bristol MM, 249, 250, 251, 253, 255, 257, 258, 259, 260
British Medical Journal, 873

Brockbank EM, 564, 565, 566, 567
Brockbank R, 791
Brockington IF, 1496, 1500, 1666, 1668, 1669, 1670, 1671, 1672, 1673, 1707, 1708, 1711
Broden M, 117
Brodsky CM, 2135
Brody DS, 998
Brogden RN, 577
Broman HJ, 769
Brook P, 950
Brook RC, 1382, 1395
Brorson L, 1782
Brotman AW, 1704, 1792, 1800, 2146
Broughton R, 2419
Broughton RF, 719
Brown A, 1276, 1280
Brown AL, 333, 337
Brown AS, 332
Brown B, 1214
Brown BB, 2052
Brown BS, 1324, 1344
Brown D, 1277, 1279
Brown E, 764, 2349
Brown GW, 1550, 1748, 1749, 1765, 1865, 1885
Brown HN, 2141
Brown J, 2537
Brown JB, 763
Brown JL, 192
Brown L, 127, 190
Brown LO, 1559
Brown MA, 1535
Brown NK, 1003
Brown R, 1857, 1858, 1862
Brown RA, 1273
Brown RD, 2662, 2663, 2665
Brown RF, 1158
Brown RP, 1792
Brown RT, 374, 378, 379
Brown S, 1159
Brown WA, 1221
Brown WR, 564, 566, 567
Brown WT, 40, 41
Brown v Board of Education, 984
Browne E, 763, 769

Browne-Mayers AN, 1124
Browne TR, 97
Brownell KD, 672, 673
Bruch H, 458, 463, 464, 467, 468, 482,
    483, 487, 488, 511, 513, 515, 589
Bruhn CM, 583
Bruhn JG, 2583
Bruininks RH, 21, 144
Brulle AR, 25
Brundage V, 1154
Bruner EC, 126, 335
Bruner J, 299, 340
Bruni J, 888, 889
Brunstetter RW, 311
Brunt MY, 1691
Brust JCM, 835, 872, 873, 1366
Brutten E, 316, 346
Bruun RD, 697, 710
Bry B, 1202
Bryan E, 1578
Bryant DM, 126
Buchanan GR, 582
Buchkramer C, 1564
Buchsbaum MS, 1491, 1633
Bucht G, 926
Buckingham WB, 940
Buckley P, 86
Budman SH, 2509
Budzynski T, 2534
Budzynski TH, 112
Buffum J, 2348, 2353
Bugliosi V, 1693
Buhler KE, 1087
Buhrich N, 635, 641, 644
Buhrich NA, 2154
Buie D, 2751
Buie DH, 2013
Buie TH, 2676
Bukberg J, 1900, 1904
Buktenica N, 330
Bulpitt CJ, 2319
Bumpass ER, 2470, 2471, 2472, 2473
Bunney BS, 706
Bunney WE, 1754, 1758
Bunney WE Jr, 1762, 1914, 1935

Burchard JD, 23, 25, 26, 2649, 2652
Burchfield SR, 582
Burckhardt D, 904
Burden R, 2517
Burg L, 2370
Burgess AW, 671, 2527
Burgess CD, 904, 913
Burgoine E, 180
Burk HW, 75
Burling TA, 1283
Burman D, 60
Burns BH, 2145
Burns D, 1566, 2031
Burns DD, 2784, 2786
Burns LE, 2024
Burns NR, 45, 46
Burns WJ, 569, 574
Burrel RH, 2780
Burrows GD, 902, 926, 2390
Burstein A, 2076, 2355, 2685
Bursten B, 2162
Burt Associates, 1344
Burton BT, 810
Burton G, 2336
Burton H, 108
Burton K, 865
Buschke H, 967
Bush MN, 1225
Busse EW, 994, 2141
Butcher B, 218, 224
Butcher J, 2525, 2526
Butcher JN, 2342
Butler G, 2028, 2537
Butler IJ, 690
Butler M, 1200
Butler RN, 900, 989, 1001, 1005, 2509
Butler TC, 892
Butlin AT, 96
Butterfield EC, 45
Butterworth A, 1920
Button EJ, 590
Butz G, 1447
Byck R, 1219, 1369
Byerley B, 809

Byrne JE, 904
Byrne WJ, 571, 572

Cabral RJ, 894
Caccia S, 1780
Caddy G, 1097
Caddy GR, 1126, 1130, 2201
Cade JFJ, 1734, 1738, 1928
Cadogan DA, 1116, 1119, 1124
Cadoret R, 1070
Cadoret RJ, 1314
Cahalan D, 1065
Caine ED, 697, 709, 821
Caldwell T, 2585
Callner DA, 1444
Calne DB, 863
Calne DL, 865
Cameron N, 1523
Cameron R, 2761
Camfield CS, 96, 97
Camic PM, 1266
Campbell L III, 1122
Campbell M, 36, 76, 79, 82, 92, 180,
    182, 184, 185, 226, 228, 229, 230,
    231, 233, 234, 235, 236, 237, 238,
    239, 240, 241, 242, 243, 244, 245,
    246, 247, 248, 375, 377, 387, 1936
Campbell MA, 947
Campbell PH, 58, 63, 64
Campbell S, 2393
Cancro R, 1488, 1493, 1510, 1515, 1517,
    1519
Canino IA, 1936
Cannon DS, 1127
Cantalapiedra MA, 110
Canter A, 2054
Canter SM, 204
Cantril H, 1152
Cantwell DP, 249, 250, 256, 299, 300,
    303, 306, 350, 374, 375, 377, 379,
    492, 1950, 2746, 2747
Cantwell DR, 1763
Caplan G, 1559, 2508, 2514, 2516, 2520,
    2521, 2524, 2525, 2557, 2558

Caplan LR, 871, 873, 874
Caplin H, 474
Caplow T, 1566
Capobianco RJ, 109
Capone T, 1322
Cappleman M, 2370
Capstick N, 1629
Caracci G, 1217
Carasso RL, 1783
Carbone PP, 1912
Carek DJ, 2561, 2565
Carey W, 753
Carlen PL, 1071
Carlisi JA, 1411
Carlisle R, 2104
Carlson CR, 2655, 2769
Carlson G, 1754, 1756, 1763, 1929
Carlson GA, 375, 377, 1761, 1935
Carlson PV, 326
Carlsson A, 974
Carney A, 2393
Carney FL, 2669, 2674, 2748
Carney MWP, 945, 1803
Carpenter CB, 921
Carpenter WT, 1495, 1499, 1502, 1517,
    1518, 1519, 1530, 1531, 1548, 1553,
    1561, 1564, 1662, 1703
Carpenter WT Jr, 1681, 1684
Carr AC, 908
Carr EG, 33, 195, 212, 215, 216, 222,
    225
Carr RE, 955
Carrier JK Jr, 213
Carrington CH, 1838, 1839, 1840
Carrion HM, 2332
Carroll BJ, 1762, 2681
Carroll JFX, 1383, 1396
Carroll JL, 1157
Carron H, 2136
Carrow E, 208
Carryer HM, 452
Carson GA, 1950
Carson R, 2762
Carson RC, 2340
Carstens C, 2471
Carter AB, 2154

Carter C, 82
Carter EF, 1366
Carter JN, 2392, 2393
Carter RB, 2158
Carter WE, 1252
Cartwright RD, 2435
Carver CS, 1848
Casey L, 202, 212
Casey PJ, 736, 737, 740
Casey RL, 2501
Cashdan S, 2761
Casnoff IG, 1366
Casper RC, 485, 487, 511, 512, 513,
    515, 537, 555, 556, 563, 2468
Casriel D, 2599
Cass DJ, 2671
Cassano GB, 1752, 1756, 1758, 1764,
    1886, 1925
Cassel CR, 1002, 1004
Cassem NH, 827, 902, 905, 946, 1779,
    1791, 1792, 1990
Cassidy K, 1580
Cassity JH, 630
Castellani S, 813, 814
Castells S, 38
Castelnuove-Tedesco P, 1875
Castillo-Ferrando JR, 915
Catalan J, 2336
Catalano RF, 1437, 1442
Cataldo MG, 33
Catchlove R, 2133, 2136
Catchlove RFH, 945
Cattell JP, 2218, 2220, 2221
Caul D, 2201, 2202, 2204, 2205, 2207
Cautela JR, 673, 2652
Cavanaugh SV, 1900
Cavdar AO, 582, 584, 586
Cavenar JO, 2507
Cawley JF, 338
Celesia GG, 863, 864, 866
Centers for Disease Control, 1365, 2611
Cerreto MC, 105
Certo N, 126
Chabot DR, 464
Chace PM, 1811
Chadsey-Rusch J, 136, 137

Chait LD, 1247
Chalkley AJ, 637
Chall J, 334, 335
Chamberlain P, 382, 384, 385, 389,
    2657
Chambers HE, 1089
Chambes CD, 1349
Chambless D, 2032
Chambless DL, 2099, 2286
Chan D, 1124
Chancellor AM, 2193
Chanda SK, 1230
Chandler L, 2513
Chandler M, 93
Chandra P, 587
Chaney EF, 1130
Chang J, 2306, 2312
Chaplin E, 2536
Chapman CR, 2130, 2131, 2135, 2137
Chapman RS, 207, 209
Chapple ED, 1545
Charatan FB, 665, 942
Charles GA, 961
Charness ME, 869
Charney DC, 1790
Charney DS, 406, 928, 1237, 1319,
    1322, 1355, 2639
Chase MD, 108
Chase TM, 691
Chasnoff IG, 1225
Chassan JB, 231
Chatoor I, 565, 566, 569, 570, 574, 576,
    577, 578, 579
Chatton MF, 935, 936
Cheadle AJ, 2255
Checkley S, 1892
Chein I, 1197
Chen PS, 936
Chen TS, 936
Cherubin CE, 1304
Chesen ES, 2595
Chess RS, 108
Chess S, 59, 61, 298, 300, 371, 735
Chesser E, 2285
Chessick R, 2635, 2739, 2751
Chester EM, 897

Chethik M, 763, 764
Chevron E, 1816
Chiarello RJ, 1787, 1799
Chick J, 747, 753, 1068
Chien CP, 821
Ch'ien JMN, 1315, 1327
Child CG, 935
Childers RT Jr, 2482
Childress AR, 1315
Childs S, 335
Chisolm JJ, 52
Chmara J, 2146
Cho SC, 718, 720
Chodoff P, 1864, 2514, 2515, 2728,
    2729, 2730, 2731, 2732, 2735
Chopra GS, 1251
Chouinard G, 707, 914, 1629, 1932
Chow B, 46
Christakis G, 1349
Christensen DE, 92
Christian CL, 952
Christian MA, 1341
Christian P, 2147
Christiani TS, 254
Christie JE, 971
Christodoulou GN, 836, 1689
Christoff KA, 1571
Churchill D, 203
Cicero TJ, 1347
Cinciripini P, 2137
Cinciripini PM, 475
Ciompi L, 1530, 1537, 1548, 2154
Ciraulo DA, 1810, 1919
Claghorn JL, 75, 1534
Clancy H, 62, 64, 65
Clare A, 633
Clark AL, 2336
Clark DC, 1900
Clark DM, 2035, 2036
Clark EO, 989
Clark EV, 209
Clark HH, 209
Clark JT, 2354
Clark P, 215
Clarke G, 1862
Clarke RVG, 386

Clarkin J, 639
Clarkin JF, 1885, 2699, 2760
Clarren SK, 1366
Clary WF, 2198
Clausen J, 92
Clayton PJ, 1668, 1669, 1676, 1747,
    1755, 1761, 1762, 1898, 2253
Clayton RR, 1244, 1312
Cleary P, 1264
Cleckley HM, 2199, 2205, 2742
Cleland CC, 22
Clement PF, 542
Clements S, 365
Clerambault G de, 1646
Cleveland SE, 2294
Cloninger C, 1072, 1110
Cloninger CR, 2148, 2747
Clouse RE, 572, 577, 579
Coates S, 667
Cobe GM, 989
Cobliner W, 2367, 2368
Coche E, 1532, 1534
Cochran WG, 231
Cocores JA, 2199
CODAP. See National Institute on
    Drug Abuse
Coddington RD, 2500
Coe FL, 919
Coffee K, 60
Coffey B, 407
Coffey CE, 866, 1809
Coffman DA, 543
Cohen BM, 1658, 1669, 1670, 1704
Cohen D, 965
Cohen DF, 580
Cohen DJ, 180, 233, 237, 241, 242, 245,
    690, 691, 698, 706, 710
Cohen EL, 969
Cohen GD, 801, 802
Cohen HD, 2386
Cohen HG, 100
Cohen IH, 2022
Cohen IL, 231, 243, 244, 248
Cohen K, 2136
Cohen L, 1691
Cohen LS, 1793

Cohen M, 1070, 1157, 1351
Cohen MB, 1732, 1788, 1870
Cohen MM, 835
Cohen MN, 77
Cohen NJ, 375
Cohen S, 1208, 1904, 1944
Cohn MA, 945
Cohn R, 94, 317
Cohnheim J, 1490
Coid J, 1074
Colarusso C, 2371
Colarusso CA, 2645, 2647
Colby KM, 213
Cole CL, 136
Cole DA, 109
Cole J, 1508, 2590
Cole JO, 243, 1682, 1737, 1799, 2047,
    2152, 2680, 2682
Cole M, 826
Cole MJ, 2305
Cole O, 1787
Cole P, 342
Cole SA, 1531, 1533, 1539, 1545, 1548,
    1560, 1561, 1563, 1564, 1565
Coleman M, 182, 245, 246
Coleman RE, 1885
Coleman RM, 2439
Coleman SB, 1199
Colletti G, 266
Collins AH, 2614
Collins DJ, 2769
Collins JJ, 1439
Collins M, 672
Collins RC, 941
Colm NJ, 2611
Colpaert FC, 1221, 1230
Colson DB, 1117
Coltman CA Jr, 583, 585, 586, 587
Comas-Díaz L, 1838, 1839, 1841
Comfort A, 984, 995
Comings BG, 375, 708
Comings DE, 375, 708
Comitas L, 1252
Compton A, 2024, 2264
Comptroller General of the United
    States, 1343, 1345

Condiotte MM, 1266, 1270
Conell LJ, 1305
Confer WN, 2202
Conn HD, 930
Conn JH, 631
Connell PH, 691, 832, 1222, 1226, 1227,
    1229, 1230, 1231, 1232
Conners CK, 95, 373, 374, 378, 379,
    413, 427, 694, 695, 850
Connett G, 1418
Connolly AJ, 331
Connolly FH, 2146
Connors ME, 550, 551, 552
Conrad RD, 768
Conroy JW, 20
Conte HR, 1733, 1787, 1791, 1820,
    1885, 2148
Conti G, 2385
Conture E, 316, 317
Cook GC, 938
Cook P, 962
Coons PM, 2197, 2198, 2199, 2201,
    2202, 2213
Coons WH, 1534
Cooper A, 2024, 2636
Cooper AF, 80, 950, 951, 1642
Cooper AJ, 638, 2256, 2305, 2320, 2322,
    2326, 2337, 2350, 2353, 2355
Cooper B, 882
Cooper DG, 2139, 2144, 2149
Cooper EB, 345
Cooper G, 905
Cooper J, 694
Cooper JE, 2098
Cooper M, 584
Cooper PJ, 537, 540, 564, 565, 566, 567,
    570
Copeland PM, 1917
Copeman CD, 1439
Coppen A, 926, 974, 1794, 1800, 1802,
    2336
Corbett JA, 10, 95, 96, 97
Corder BF, 1124
Cordle CJ, 485, 525, 526, 527, 534, 538,
    543
Cornfield RB, 2074, 2076, 2588, 2685

Corsellis JAN, 854, 942, 972
Coryell W, 1669, 1670, 1672, 2167, 2210
Coryell WH, 1497
Costa E, 239, 406
Costain DW, 1812
Costello CG, 1847
Costello J, 2758
Cotman CW, 868
Cott A, 327
Cotzin M, 110
Couch JR, 1783
Couchells S, 720
Coughlan AK, 870
Coull DC, 1907
Couture M, 633
Covi L, 1307, 1819, 1820, 1839, 1841,
    2145, 2151
Covino N, 2132
Cowdry R, 2637, 2682
Cowdry RW, 1760, 2755
Cox A, 249
Cox DJ, 670, 672
Cox GM, 231
Cox M, 625, 925, 927
Coyle JT, 829
Coyne JC, 1866, 1886
Craddock SG, 1283, 1343, 1344
Craddock VM, 1359
Crafoord C, 2703
Craft M, 1768
Cragan M, 2534, 2537
Craig TJ, 1904
Craighead WE, 1846
Cramer Azima F, 2674
Crammer J, 1909
Crane GE, 944
Cranson A, 838
Crasilneck H, 2132
Cravan R, 768
Crawford J, 60
Creak M, 185
Creedon M, 212
Creer C, 1547, 1575
Cregler LL, 1224
Crenshaw T, 2355
Crenshaw TL, 2353

Crepault C, 633
Crisp AH, 454, 458, 463, 464, 466, 468,
    469, 473, 475, 476, 477, 483, 487,
    492, 493, 508, 543
Cristol AH, 1814
Crittinger JW, 874
Crocker J, 61
Crocker R, 1117, 1118
Croghan LM, 768
Crome P, 904
Croog SH, 1914
Crook T, 965, 967, 969, 971, 972, 973,
    975, 978
Crosby TW, 951
Crosby WH, 583
Cross AJ, 974, 1812
Cross PS, 817
Croughan JL, 643, 1668
Crow TJ, 1491, 1492, 1498, 1633
Crowe MJ, 2322, 2338
Crowe RR, 875
Crowe TA, 342, 343
Crowley FJ, 108
Crowley T, 1333
Crowley TJ, 1232, 1233, 1234, 1236,
    1237, 1239, 1442, 1443
Crowley WF Jr, 2352
Crown S, 631, 2337, 2339
Cruikshank BM, 724
Crumley FE, 2784
Crystal D, 204
Csillag ER, 2385
Cull A, 751
Cullen MR, 1910
Culpan RH, 2780
Culver CG, 634
Culver CM, 999
Culver KW, 2469, 2472
Cumin R, 1307
Cummings JL, 818, 833, 834, 838, 868,
    871, 872, 873, 874, 875, 942, 943
Cunningham CE, 374
Curran J, 2761
Curran JP, 1532, 1533, 1542
Curry FK, 316
Curry JF, 385

Curry SH, 923
Cushman P, 1352, 1353
Cushman P Jr, 1344
Custer RL, 2464, 2465
Cutler B, 2199, 2216
Cutler M, 92
Cutter HS, 1120
Cutting J, 835, 1530, 1548, 1625
Cutting JC, 1708
Cvetkovitch G, 2368
Cytryn L, 1885, 1950, 1951
Czeisler CA, 1895, 2442, 2443

Daan S, 1891, 1895
Dackis CA, 1237, 1366, 1369, 1370, 1372, 1921
Daghestani AN, 1214, 1255
Dagon E, 2373
Dahl EK, 180, 665
Dahl G, 2651, 2655, 2696
Dahmus NE, 338
Dai WS, 2388
Daitzman RJ, 672
Dalby T, 378
Dale PG, 850
Dalen P, 866
D'Alessio GR, 672
Dally P, 2147
Dally PJ, 463, 466, 471, 476, 491, 492, 493, 1753
Dalquist LM, 2481
Dalton P, 2663, 2665
Dam M, 893
Damasio AR, 863, 865, 866, 867
Danford DE, 52, 565, 568, 580, 583, 584, 588
Daniel AE, 24
Daniel WF, 814
Danielczyk W, 863
Daniels AC, 942
D'Ardenne P, 2337, 2339
Darvish HS, 1747
Dashef SS, 784

Dasheiff RM, 38
Davanloo H, 1732, 1874, 1875, 1879, 1880, 1881, 1883, 1884, 2768
Davenport AE, 2341
Davenport CW, 642
Davenport RK, Jr, 45
Davidson CS, 930, 931
Davidson DM, 862
Davidson J, 338, 1787, 1796, 2129
Davidson JM, 2388, 2392
Davidson PW, 238, 248
Davidson V, 1424
Davies P, 966, 968, 969, 970, 971, 977, 978
Davies RK, 1892
Davies TF, 2392
Davies TS, 913
Davis, 574
Davis CM, 582
Davis D, 1069, 1070
Davis DH, 2201
Davis DI, 1159
Davis G, 2266, 2372
Davis H, 955
Davis J, 2683
Davis JM, 1507, 1627, 1661, 1787, 1929, 1942, 2039
Davis JR, 1280
Davis JW, 924, 938, 969
Davis KL, 968, 970, 2567
Davis KR, 110
Davis KV, 73, 76, 92
Davis RR, 105
Davison GC, 115, 116, 1276
Davison K, 833, 1625, 2218, 2219, 2221
Davison LA, 1912
Dawley HH, 1286
Dawling S, 923, 924, 1779, 1780
Dawson ME, 1530, 1548, 1570
Dawson MJ, 54
Day JD, 337
De Alwis C, 1779, 1798
De Angelis GG, 1217
De Dimone D, 2346
De La Horne D, 2482, 2484, 2485
De Leon G, 1380, 1382, 1383, 1395

De Luca RV, 2481, 2484
De Montigny C, 1787, 1793, 1794, 1927
de Silva P, 2028
de Wied D, 976
Deakin JF, 1812
DeBakey M, 585
Dec GW, 1811
DeCarolis V, 1804
DeCencio DV, 939
DeChateau P, 736
Decker J, 2520
Deffenbacher J, 2534, 2536, 2537
deGroat WC, 2384, 2386
Deiker T, 1089
Deitch D, 1382
Dekaban AS, 95, 96
Dela Fuente JR, 2315
Delabar J-M, 1490
Delacato C, 326
DeLeo D, 2347, 2353
DeLeon G, 1326
Delgado RA, 2481, 2482, 2483
D'Elia A, 2468
D'Elia G, 1800, 1810
Delis D, 865
DeLisi LE, 1491, 1700
DeLisio G, 1755
DeLong GR, 1936
Delong R, 372
Delongis A, 259
Dement WC, 2444
DeMeyer MK, 217
Demirel T, 2132, 2133
Demitz S, 108
DeMyer MK, 180, 184, 235, 243, 249,
    259, 261, 263
Denaut M, 945
Denckla MB, 180, 315, 707
Deneau G, 1431
Dengler HG, 1775, 1969
Dengrove E, 2319
Denham MJ, 1005, 1007
Denmark JC, 950, 951
Dennerstein L, 1708, 2390
Denney D, 2534
Denton JA Jr, 2225

Denton LR, 108
Department of Health and Human
    Services Steering Committee on
    the Chronically Mentally Ill, 1663
Depaulo JR Jr, 927
Depner TA, 922
DeRiemer SA, 706
DeRisi WJ, 1447
Dermer SW, 2476
Derogatis LR, 1267, 1900, 1904, 2254,
    2256
DeRubeis RJ, 1821, 1846
Desmedt JE, 955
Desmond DP, 1186, 1236, 1357, 1442
Despotovic A, 1122
Detre T, 1760
Deupree JD, 890, 892
Deutsch H, 1691, 2015, 2367, 2368,
    2714
Deutsch JA, 1088
Deutsch SI, 237, 238
Dever SW, 850
DeVilliers JG, 213
Devin-Sheehan L, 2614
Devins GM, 919
Dewey MA, 259, 273
Dewhurst K, 1686, 1687, 1688
Dhadphale M, 2159
Di Mascio A, 1708
Diamond DB, 2017
Dibb GS, 2765
Dickes RA, 2158
Dicks H, 2660
Dickson L, 565, 569, 576
DiClemente CC, 1271
Die Trill ML, 184, 230, 245
Dies RR, 1123, 1535, 1814, 2668, 2674,
    2676
Dietch D, 1380
DiLorenzo TM, 197
Dilsaver SC, 1786
DiMascio A, 1821, 1863, 1868, 1869
Dinaburg D, 1532, 1539
Dincin J, 1580
DiPonte P, 977
Directory of Self-Help/Mutual Aid Groups,

Chicago Metropolitan Area, 1983-84, 2596
Dishotsky NI, 1209
Distiller LA, 2389
Ditman KS, 1158
Dixon KN, 525, 527
Dixon S, 2527
Djaldetti M, 565
Doane JA, 1545, 1549, 1550, 1551, 1555, 1702, 1703
Dobbs WH, 1344
Docci D, 923
Doctor RM, 1443
Dodds WJ, 571
Dodes L, 1106, 1108
Dodrill C, 95, 96
Dodson ME, 945
Doghranji K, 1910
Doke LA, 49
Dolan MP, 1441
Dole VP, 1313, 1323, 1324, 1342, 1350, 1352
Doleys DM, 2130
Doll E, 187
Doll W, 1547
Dollard J, 843
Dollery CT, 912, 2319
Doman G, 326
Domer FR, 2385
Donaldson SR, 1658
Done AK, 838
Dongier S, 881
Donlon PT, 1534
Donnelly M, 375, 376, 377
Donner L, 1127
Donovan A, 257
Doran AR, 1493
Dores PC, 212, 340
Dorfman LJ, 942
Doris J, 402
Dornbrand L, 1004
Dornbusch SM, 717, 720
Doroff DR, 1117
Dorpat TL, 1900, 2639
Dostal T, 79
Doty RL, 2355

Doueck E, 953, 955
Douglas A, 1707
Douglas JWB, 720
Douglas VI, 91, 367, 374, 378
Dow MG, 1852, 1862
Dow MGT, 2393
Dowrick PW, 664
Drachman DA, 967, 968
Drake RE, 1518
Drane JF, 999
Dranger P, 1120
Draper RJ, 1092
Draughon M, 1070
Dravet C, 893
Drayer C, 2514
Dresser RS, 1004
Dressler DM, 1806
Drossman DA, 2140
Dubey DR, 665
Dubin WR, 1910
Dubois A, 474
Dubourg GD, 1122
Dubovsky SL, 909, 1932
Duchan J, 340, 342
Duckworth GS, 821
Dudley CA, 2351, 2352
Dudley DL, 946
Dudley WHC Jr, 810
Duggan HA, 2615
Dujovne CA, 937
Dulcan MK, 377, 2558
Dulfano MJ, 940, 941
Dullinger SJ, 2220
Duncan CC, 1894
Duncan JA, 2614
Dundee J, 945
Dunn LM, 125, 209, 330
Dunn MJ, 813, 814
Dunn P, 2017
Dunner DL, 1758, 1934, 2253
Dupkin C, 665, 666
Dupont H, 664
DuPont RL, 1344
Durden-Smith J, 2346
Durell J, 1219
Durkheim E, 2594

Durkin H, 2667
Durso P, 977
Duvoisin RC, 813
Duyck F, 76
Dwan C, 2169
Dy AJ, 2481, 2485
Dyche L, 758
Dyck AJ, 1004
Dyken ML, 869
Dykens E, 697
Dymond RF, 108
Dyrud JE, 2339
Dysken MW, 864, 2587

Eade NR, 914
Eadie MJ, 888, 890, 892
Eames P, 848
Earle BV, 1794
Earnhart T, 105
Eastman CI, 1891, 1896
Eastwell HD, 584
Eaton LF, 10, 15, 28
Eaton LM, 942
Eayrs JT, 240
Ebert MH, 937, 1781
Ebrahim SBJ, 875
Eckert ED, 452, 459, 476, 477
Eckert EE, 1916, 1917
Eckhardt M, 1067, 1071, 1158
Eckman T, 2653
Eddy E, 53
Edelbrock CS, 351, 367, 369, 373, 382,
    389, 402, 435
Edelbroek PM, 1783
Edeleman B, 541
Edelman R, 537
Edelson M, 2692, 2758
Edelstein BA, 1570
Edelwich JL, 2579
Edwards CH, 584
Edwards D, 1155, 1157
Edwards G, 1067, 1068, 1148, 1154,
    1184

Edwards IS, 2317
Edwards JG, 904
Edwards JN, 2337
Edwards P, 1116
Eeg-Oloffson O, 720
Egbert LD, 2141
Egel AL, 195, 221
Egeland B, 736
Egeland JA, 1490, 1752
Eglash A, 2613
Ehrhardt AA, 21, 656
Ehrlich P, 1235
Eichelbaum M, 893
Eichelman B, 2476
Eidelberg L, 2715
Eisdorfer C, 965, 2508
Eisenberg J, 2103
Eisenberg L, 184, 378
Eisler RM, 1570, 1571
Eissler KR, 511
Eissler RM, 2469, 2471
Ekblad RL, 92
Ekvall SW, 59, 60
El-Fakahany E, 1775, 1778
El-Ganzouri AR, 1808
Elal-Lawrence G, 1075
Elbert MF, 315
Eleftheriou BE, 21
Elizur E, 719
Elkin I, 1732, 1816, 1817, 1821, 1845,
    1871
Elkin J, 1420
Elkind D, 299
Elkins I, 1732
Elkins RL, 1127
Ellenberg M, 2319
Ellenberger HF, 2199, 2216
Ellenor GL, 70
Ellingboe J, 1333, 1340
Ellingwood EH, 833, 1219, 1221, 1222,
    1223, 1226, 1229, 1230, 1231, 1237
Elliott FA, 839, 842, 844, 845, 849, 851,
    2480, 2686
Elliott GR, 2656
Elliott HW, 945
Ellis A, 482, 489, 1856, 2323, 2542

Ellsworth RB, 2694
Elsenga S, 1801
Emergy G, 2036
Emerson R, 888
Emery L, 241
Emmelkamp PMG, 2028, 2099
Emmons ML, 1856
Emory G, 2550
Empey LT, 386
Emrick C, 1134, 1156, 1158
Emrick CD, 1148, 2611, 2613, 2616
Ende J, 2335
Endicott J, 567, 695, 1670, 1849, 2713
Endicott S, 1189
Endo M, 1708
Ends EJ, 1121, 1124
Engel G, 1901, 1903, 1952, 2126, 2127, 2135
Engel GL, 1684
Engel J Jr, 893
Engelhardt DM, 237, 242, 243, 244, 248
Engelhardt HT, 999
Englemann S, 126, 335, 338
Enoch MD, 1686, 1687, 1688, 1692
Epanchin A, 348
Epstein AW, 637
Epstein H, 49
Epstein LH, 49
Epstein N, 2765, 2784, 2786
Epstein NB, 1547, 1559, 1564, 1565
Erenberg G, 692
Erickson MH, 2202
Erickson ML, 386
Erikson E, 2721, 2729
Erikson EH, 782, 783, 785, 789, 1522, 1524, 2509, 2511, 2521, 2525, 2527, 2590, 2634
Eriksson M, 1367
Erlich HS, 2693
Erman MK, 1810
Eron LD, 22
Erry B, 2317
Ervin FR, 21, 883
Escalona SK, 569, 572, 575
Espelin DE, 838
Esquirol E, 1891

Essen J, 720
Essen-Moller E, 2712
Esser AH, 22
Esser PH, 1116
Estes D, 952
Estroff TW, 1361, 1363, 1371
Eth C, 1007
Eth S, 986, 999, 1001, 1007
Ettenburg A, 1221
Eubanks R, 470
Evans C, 1581
Evans CJ, 944
Evans DR, 672, 673
Evans IM, 196, 2389
Evans LE, 1905, 1910
Evans MD, 1532
Evans PH, 972
Evans RW, 95, 97
Evans SL, 736, 737, 740
Evanson JM, 912
Everaerd W, 2322, 2338
Ewalt P, 2526
Ewing C, 2523, 2525, 2527
Ewing J, 1103
Ewing JA, 1097, 1116, 1135
Extein I, 1370, 1929, 1938
Eysenck H, 2535, 2759
Eysenck HJ, 1490, 2318, 2336, 2339, 2355
Ezriel H, 2340

Fabbri R Jr, 2481, 2485
Faergeman PM, 1613, 1616, 1618, 1677, 1684, 1685
Fagan J, 2200, 2203
Fagerstrom KO, 1265, 1267
Faguet KF, 1689
Faguet RA, 1689
Fahn S, 687, 692, 866
Fahnenkrug J, 2385
Fahs JJ, 89
Faillace LA, 1904
Faiman C, 2355

Fairbairn WD, 1623
Fairbairn WRD, 2634, 2712, 2714
Fairbank JA, 2535
Fairburn CG, 482, 485, 523, 525, 526,
     527, 528, 533, 534, 537, 538, 540,
     541, 542, 550, 551, 552, 554, 558,
     564, 565, 566, 567, 570
Fairweather GW, 1516, 1533, 1534
Falaschi PA, 2350
Falcon S, 2076, 2589
Falconer MA, 884, 893
Falk JR, 452, 453
Falk RH, 910, 943
Falkowski WF, 1706
Fallaci O, 2225
Fallon RH, 1420
Falloon FRH, 2668
Falloon I, 1663
Falloon IR, 1675
Falloon IRH, 1548, 1552, 1554, 1555,
     1560, 1562, 1564, 1565, 1566, 1575,
     1576, 1581
Falret J, 1685, 1686, 1689, 1691, 1694
Faltus FJ, 2682
Fanaroff A, 735
Fann WE, 914
Faquet KF, 1692
Faquet RA, 1692
Farber B, 258
Farber L, 2731
Farberow NL, 1192
Faretra G, 237, 242, 248
Farina A, 1572
Farkas T, 1491
Farmer AE, 1706
Farrell GC, 937
Fash I, 666
Faunce EE, 1549
Faust R, 1312
Fava GA, 1901
Favell JE, 37, 46, 200
Fawcett J, 1919
Fay WH, 198, 203, 207, 215
Feder SL, 1768
Federn S, 1520
Fedio P, 882

Feeny DJ, 1120
Fehrenbach PA, 2655
Feibel JH, 875
Feighner JP, 1499, 1668, 1761, 1798,
     1799
Feil WB, 1886
Feinberg T, 862
Feinglass EJ, 952
Feingold BF, 379
Feingold I, 301
Feinstein A, 2136
Feinstein S, 2517
Feinstein SC, 787, 788
Felice M, 2369
Felner R, 2516
Felthous AR, 1708
Fenichel O, 568, 700, 1873, 2015, 2154,
     2157, 2470, 2478, 2640, 2641, 2759,
     2760
Fenn HH, 1532, 1539
Fennell MJV, 1801, 1843, 1844
Fensterheim, 672
Fenton GW, 839, 883
Fenton WS, 1493, 1499
Ferber R, 2421, 2422, 2423, 2424
Ferenczi S, 569, 1874
Ferguson HB, 367, 369
Fernald G, 335
Fernandez JV, 836
Fernando FP, 1695
Ferreira A, 1692
Ferreri CA, 327
Ferris RM, 2353
Ferris SH, 967, 971, 973, 976
Ferster CB, 217, 1847
Fertel N, 2297
Fezler WD, 2056
Fibeles N, 2766
Fibiger HC, 861, 974
Field P, 1277
Fielding D, 722
Fielding JE, 1262, 1263, 1264, 1283
Fielding LT, 68, 69
Fields HA, 1365
Fieve RR, 1758, 1927
Figley C, 2073

Filicori M, 2352
Finch AJ, 402
Finch BE, 1532, 1534, 1571
Finch SM, 781
Fine S, 2473, 2665
Fineman KR, 2470
Fink M, 807, 1206, 1787, 1803, 1806,
    1810, 1812, 1927
Finkelhor D, 618
Finklestein S, 875
Finley WW, 894
Finnegan LP, 1328, 1349, 1356
Finney R, 2332
Finnie NR, 61
Firestone P, 374, 377
Fisch C, 905
Fisch M, 1001
Fischer RG, 947
Fischer-Williams M, 941
Fischhoff J, 665, 667, 736, 737, 740
Fischman HC, 1221
Fish B, 230, 231, 235, 236, 237, 240,
    242, 306
Fishbain D, 580
Fishel R, 1225
Fisher B, 1124
Fisher C, 2193, 2195, 2385, 2387, 2391
Fisher CM, 837, 868, 872
Fisher GW, 82
Fisher HA, 344
Fisher L, 110
Fisher S, 2281, 2284, 2286, 2294, 2336
Fishman AP, 945
Fishman G, 2080
Fishman HC, 1408, 1409, 1410, 1415
Fishman RA, 912
Fiske DW, 1729
Fitch JH, 632
Fithian MA, 2338
Fitzgerald RG, 950
Fix AJ, 940
Flachs H, 891
Flacks H, 892
Flagg W, 2438
Flament M, 2097
Flament MF, 2101, 2102

Flanagan CH, 570
Flannery RB, 777, 2651, 2656, 2658,
    2766, 2784, 2785, 2786, 2787
Flannery RB Jr, 2657
Fleck S, 1545
Fleiger DL, 1127
Fleischer DR, 564, 565, 571, 572
Fleiss JL, 1500
Flemenbaum A, 838
Fleming J, 2013
Fleminger II, 1502
Fleminger JJ, 821
Flemming J, 2024
Fletcher EC, 939
Flick A, 1532, 1534
Flinn SK, 1559
Flomenhaft K, 2520
Flood JF, 976
Flor-Henry P, 882
Floreen A, 2137
Florenzan R, 1075
Floru L, 2143
Flynn NM, 380
Foa EB, 2099, 2100
Foa ER, 2780
Foenander G, 2065
Fogelson DL, 1497
Foley JM, 930, 931
Foley SH, 1871, 1872
Folk J, 1806
Folkard S, 2441
Folkman S, 1886, 2547
Folkman SK, 2071
Folks DG, 850
Follick MJ, 2125
Folstein MF, 805, 817, 821, 823, 825,
    854, 875, 919
Folstein S, 256, 257
Forbes GB, 465
Ford CS, 648
Ford CV, 2144, 2151, 2162, 2163, 2169
Fordney DS, 2297
Fordyce DJ, 848
Fordyce WE, 2128
Forehand R, 20, 45, 46, 47, 385
Forness SR, 20, 300, 350, 379

Forno FS, 942
Forrest G, 1124
Forsythe A, 97
Forsythe WI, 721
Foster FM, 894
Foster R, 208
Foster WS, 22
Fouts R, 212, 215
Fowler GB, 723
Fowler RC, 1074, 1498
Fowlie HC, 80
Fox MR, 1545
Foxman B, 721, 722
Foxx RM, 22, 43, 48, 52, 224, 578, 586, 1273
Foy DW, 1581
Fraiberg S, 301, 743, 2012, 2024, 2368, 2369, 2560
Frakowiak RSJ, 870
Framo JL, 1405
France K, 2615
France R, 2121
France RD, 1902
Frances A, 639, 749, 1106, 2017, 2636, 2639, 2699, 2733, 2760
Frances AJ, 1888, 1941
Frances R, 1104
Francis JJ, 665
Francis PT, 974
Franco DP, 2654
Frank AF, 1517, 2692
Frank D, 2249, 2318, 2335
Frank E, 2248, 2301, 2336, 2536, 2542
Frank J, 2532
Frank JD, 485, 1864, 2055, 2127
Frank L, 2255
Frank OS, 2339
Frankel F, 45, 218, 225, 385
Frankel FH, 2055
Frankena WK, 1003
Frankl FH, 2205, 2206
Frankl V, 2593
Frankl VE, 2099
Franklin GS, 909
Franklin JL, 1580
Frankowski RF, 846

Franks CM, 2338, 2649
Franks RD, 1932
Franks S, 2389, 2392
Franzen MD, 848, 849
Frary LG, 718
Fras I, 709, 1904, 2162, 2163, 2469
Fraser AR, 2193, 2353
Fraser HF, 1296
Fraser HS, 908
Frederiksen LW, 22, 2655
Fredman B, 998
Freed JS, 909
Freeman BJ, 186, 229, 243, 244, 250
Freeman C, 550, 551, 552
Freeman ED, 718
Freeman F, 315, 316
Freeman RD, 73, 88
Freemon FR, 811
Freese KJ, 1808
Freidman AS, 1819
Freidman E, 108
Freis ED, 1912
French T, 2509
French TM, 1874, 1875, 2640, 2778
Freud A, 2459
Freud S, 510, 512, 635, 638, 643, 1220, 1520, 1610, 1622, 1623, 1747, 1824, 1825, 1827, 2010, 2020, 2071, 2157, 2265, 2269, 2280, 2458, 2459, 2470, 2595, 2598, 2633, 2634, 2639, 2640, 2642, 2644, 2647, 2723, 2729, 2730, 2771
Freund K, 582, 627, 629, 2356
Freund S, 618
Freyschuss U, 902
Friberg TR, 1366
Fried E, 2667
Friedel RO, 876, 903, 1790, 1803, 1805
Frieden BD, 43
Frieden J, 914
Friedin BD, 588
Friedlander S, 1951
Friedman AS, 1886
Friedman DE, 2022, 2369
Friedman HJ, 2703
Friedman M, 2539

Friedman MJ, 902
Friedman S, 2337
Friend MR, 642, 665
Frieze M, 1695
Frisbie LV, 632
Frisch RE, 479
Frischholz E, 2202, 2206
Frischholz EJ, 2065
Fristoe M, 344
Fritz GK, 718, 720
Froberg JE, 2441
Fromm E, 1277, 1279, 2053, 2593, 2595
Fromm-Reichmann F, 2729
Frosch J, 1529, 2477, 2478, 2479, 2480,
　2690, 2724
Frosch WA, 1250, 1625
Frostig M, 335
Fry TJ, 1577
Frye FV, 1122
Frykholm B, 1705
Fryns JP, 30, 41, 42
Fuchs C, 2539
Fuchs CZ, 1857
Fuchs K, 2297, 2298
Fuchs RM, 2734
Fugere R, 2468
Fuld PA, 967
Fuller GB, 1157
Fuller R, 1150
Fuller RK, 1134
Fullerten DT, 1911
Fulwiler R, 212, 215
Fundudis T, 763
Furlow WL, 2333
Furman W, 1571
Fusner JE, 944
Futterman S, 2515

Gabel S, 725
Gabuzda GJ, 930, 931
Gadbois C, 2442
Gaddes W, 313

Gaddini E, 564, 569, 570, 574, 576
Gaddini RD, 564, 569, 570, 574, 576
Gado M, 825
Gadow KD, 91, 93, 94, 326, 374
Gahwiler BH, 977
Gaines GY, 1806, 1807, 1808, 1809
Gainotti G, 875
Galanter M, 1063, 1119, 1122, 1133,
　1136, 1693, 1694
Galef H, 665
Galenson E, 666
Gall CMC, 2193
Gallagher D, 1838, 1839, 1841
Gallagher T, 340
Gallant D, 1213, 1214
Gallant DM, 1078, 1086, 1087, 1089,
　1090, 1091, 1092, 1116, 1119, 1123,
　1124, 1920
Gallanter M, 1255
Gallup G, 2594
Galski TJ, 2481, 2482, 2483, 2485
Gamblers Anonymous, 2464
Gambrill E, 2761
Gammon C, 2464
Gammon GD, 1779, 1784
Gandelman R, 21
Ganser SJM, 2165, 2166
Gaoni B, 2765
GAP. *See* Group for the Advancement
　of Psychiatry
Garbarino J, 2614
Garber HJ, 1702
Garbutt JC, 2681
Gardner D, 2637, 2682
Gardner DL, 2755
Gardner EA, 2353
Gardner GG, 2481, 2484, 2485
Gardner H, 179
Gardner LI, 564, 565, 569, 570
Gardner TA, 311
Gardner WI, 25, 81, 136
Gardos G, 243
Garfield AH, 2337
Garfinkel BD, 376
Garfinkel PE, 456, 457, 462, 463, 464,

465, 466, 467, 476, 482, 484, 490,
492, 493, 510, 511, 537, 539, 1917,
1928
Garmezy N, 365, 367, 369, 382, 385,
2500, 2501
Garner DM, 463, 464, 465, 466, 467,
477, 482, 483, 484, 485, 486, 487,
488, 490, 493, 523, 537, 538, 539,
540, 541, 552, 554, 591
Garraway WM, 867
Gartner A, 2609
Gartrell N, 2383
Garvey MJ, 1927
Gastaut H, 882
Gaston EH, 1285, 1286
Gatchel RJ, 2054, 2064
Gates IA, 330
Gattegno C, 335
Gaultieri CT, 914, 915
Gaupp R, 1610, 1613, 1616, 1634, 1648
Gauthier J, 2468
Gautieri CT, 913
Gavin H, 2160
Gaviria M, 2636
Gawin FH, 838, 1184, 1185, 1220, 1221,
1222, 1226, 1227, 1228, 1229, 1230,
1231, 1232, 1233, 1235, 1236, 1237,
1238, 1239, 1240, 1920
Gawin M, 1922
Gay GR, 838, 1224, 1226, 1363
Gaylord-Ross RJ, 25, 199
Gearing FR, 1344
Gebhard PH, 634, 649, 671, 2285
Gediman HK, 2024
Gedo JE, 563, 2643, 2644
Geer JH, 2283, 2387
Geffen N, 565, 566, 571, 572
Gelder M, 624
Gelder MG, 2026, 2027, 2028, 2029,
2031, 2033
Geleerd EB, 2193, 2194
Gelenberg AJ, 89, 1786, 1797, 1798,
1800, 1928
Gelfan MC, 585
Geller B, 92, 242
Geller E, 236, 246

Geller JL, 491
George K, 945
George RL, 254
Georgotas A, 1781, 1785, 1792
Gerard DL, 1123, 1445
Gerner R, 974
Gerner RH, 875, 1792, 1916
Gerschman J, 2065
Gershon E, 926
Gershon ES, 492, 908, 1758, 1762,
1916, 1937, 2736
Gershon M, 2615
Gershon S, 833, 904, 967, 1738
Gerson S, 827
Gerson SN, 1701
Gersten JC, 2500
Gert B, 634
Gertenrich RL, 59
Geschwind N, 949
Gesell A, 365
Gessner PK, 1088
Getto C, 2122
Ghadirian AM, 2348
Ghoneim M, 945
Ghosh A, 2029
Giambra L, 2372
Giannini AJ, 838, 909, 1237
Giardinia EG, 902
Gibaldi M, 1781
Gibberg FB, 885
Gibbons ISE, 724
Gibbs DA, 38
Gibbs FA, 882
Gibson GE, 969, 971, 973, 1092
Gibson M, 2146
Gifford JL, 135
Gifford S, 2194
Gift TF, 2736
Gilbert GJ, 909
Gilbert HH, 316
Gilbert S, 38
Gilchrist L, 1284
Giles TO, 907
Gill D, 1804
Gill H, 2007
Gill JH, 386

Gillan P, 2033, 2387
Gillberg C, 182, 238, 245, 246, 248
Giller H, 367, 382, 385, 386, 388
Gillespie RD, 2140
Gillies C, 1909
Gillin JC, 809, 813
Gillingham A, 335
Gilman A, 1220
Gilpin DC, 665, 667, 775
Gilson BS, 2125
Gilson SB, 1003
Gingras M, 2130
Ginzburg HM, 1329
Giovacchini P, 2635
Gitlin B, 2035
Gitlin MJ, 909, 1938
Gitlow SE, 1133
Gittelman-Klein R, 378, 379, 406, 407
Gittelman R, 301, 365, 366, 367, 374,
    375, 377, 378, 379, 406
Gittleson NL, 670
Giurgea C, 973
Gjessing LR, 1709
Gjessing R, 240
Glanville K, 460, 491
Glaros AG, 1280
Glaser FB, 1153
Glaser GH, 942
Glass GV, 1729
Glass R, 2151
Glassman AH, 531, 828, 902, 903, 904,
    913, 929, 1275, 1782, 1795, 1800,
    1907
Glatzer HT, 2672, 2675
Glaze DG, 688
Glazzard P, 348
Glenn MD, 1807, 1811
Glennon VJ, 338–339
Glick G, 896
Glick ID, 1553, 1768, 1887, 1888, 2668,
    2734
Glick R, 2523, 2525, 2527
Glicklich LB, 717
Gliedman LH, 1116
Glithero E, 2154
Glover E, 2460, 2743

Glover J, 2321
Glover JH, 2468
Glowinski J, 1775
Goddard H, 27
Goeders NE, 1220
Goetz CG, 863, 864, 865
Goetz L, 216
Goetze U, 79
Goff DC, 1799
Goh K, 50
Goismian R, 2022
Golan N, 2521, 2525, 2528
Gold M, 272
Gold ME, 848
Gold MS, 838, 911, 1222, 1226, 1227,
    1229, 1232, 1237, 1319, 1360, 1361,
    1363, 1364, 1366, 1369, 1370, 1372,
    1375, 1929, 1938
Gold P, 263
Gold PE, 976, 977
Goldberg A, 563, 2644
Goldberg AJ, 2739
Goldberg DC, 2387
Goldberg HL, 1708
Goldberg JB, 94, 95
Goldberg MJ, 1779
Goldberg P, 249, 259, 261
Goldberg RJ, 1905
Goldberg S, 2681, 2683, 2726, 2754
Goldberg SC, 472, 1517
Goldberg SR, 1431
Golden GS, 697, 707, 708
Goldfine PE, 40
Goldfinger, 1252
Goldfrank L, 1363
Goldfried MR, 112, 115, 116, 482, 1276,
    2036, 2534, 2542
Goldfriend MR, 2339
Goldie A, 904
Goldin S, 2166
Goldman A, 2768
Goldman H, 1547
Goldman HH, 802, 979, 980
Goldman L, 2330
Goldman R, 344, 1877
Goldman T, 333

Goldsobel AB, 1784
Goldstein A, 1310, 1338, 1355, 2032, 2099
Goldstein AP, 26
Goldstein E, 1217
Goldstein G, 1066, 1067, 1071
Goldstein M, 38, 245, 493
Goldstein MJ, 1545, 1548, 1549, 1551,
     1553, 1663
Goldstein MS, 1553, 1560, 1581
Goldstein N, 2319
Goldstein NP, 934
Goldstein SC, 933
Goldstein SG, 1065
Goldstein SJ, 758
Goleman D, 2199
Goll K, 769
Golosow, 642
Gomez J, 491, 492, 493, 2147
Gomoll AW, 904
Gonce M, 691
Gonzales LR, 1862, 1943
Gonzalez R, 82
Goodman B, 862
Goodman Gilman A, 891
Goodman L, 110
Goodman LS, 1220
Goodman RE, 2353
Goodnick PJ, 1936
Goodsitt A, 487
Goodstein RK, 867, 876
Goodwin D, 2097
Goodwin DW, 811, 1073, 1431, 2194
Goodwin F, 1761
Goodwin FK, 863, 864, 910, 1754, 1755,
     1758, 1760, 1794, 1928, 1929
Goodwin J, 2197, 2207
Goodwin JS, 1787, 1912
Gordon C, 2691, 2692, 2693
Gordon J, 467, 2030, 2135
Gordon JR, 1237, 1238, 1271, 1276,
     1280, 1282, 1436
Gordon MA, 998
Gordon RA, 1202, 1313, 2748
Gormally J, 537
Gorman JM, 1160, 2104
Gorsuch RL, 1200

Gossett JT, 2692
Gostason R, 16
Gottesman II, 234, 256
Gottfries CG, 974
Gottheil E, 2763
Gottlieb BH, 2603
Gottlieb F, 2609
Gottlieb J, 125
Gottschalk LA, 850, 1884
Gouge AL, 59, 60
Gould E, 2668
Gould RJ, 915
Goyal, 573
Grabowski J, 1335
Grabowski SW, 75
Grad J, 1547
Grady PA, 869
Graff-Radford NR, 871
Graham DM, 585
Graham P, 365
Graham V, 218
Gralnick A, 1686, 1687, 1688, 1689,
     2655, 2694
Granacher RD, 946
Granacher RP Jr, 810
Granatz JE, 1630
Granger R, 1397
Granick S, 800
Grant I, 940
Gray JA, 87
Gray KG, 671
Gray W, 1545
Gray WS, 330
Grayson JB, 2099
Greaves C, 2583
Greaves GB, 2198, 2199
Grebb JA, 1701
Green AI, 2051
Green BL, 1884, 2506
Green J, 1329
Green JB, 94
Green JM, 781
Green MH, 1344
Green R, 2385, 2391
Green RJ, 47, 642, 661, 662, 664, 666,
     668, 669

Green RS, 528, 529, 539, 2700
Green WH, 180, 182, 184
Greenacre P, 409, 636, 637, 643
Greenan J, 1808
Greenbaum GH, 241
Greenbaum H, 1120
Greenberg GD, 939, 940
Greenberg HP, 1685, 1689
Greenberg HR, 2481, 2482
Greenberg R, 1836
Greenberger D, 2422
Greenblatt DJ, 88, 809, 811, 812, 821,
    907, 908, 909, 922, 933, 1373, 1912,
    2043, 2448
Greenblatt M, 1803
Greenblatt RB, 2350
Greene S, 2364
Greene SL, 1784
Greenhill LL, 387
Greenley JR, 1552
Greenson, 649, 665, 667
Greenson R, 1825, 1826
Greenson RR, 2641
Greenspan S, 133, 136
Greenspan SI, 1521, 2479
Greenspan SL, 1822
Greenspoon NK, 326
Greenstein RA, 1332, 1333, 1336, 1338
Greenwald H, 2743
Greenway FL, 529
Greenwood R, 1304
Greer M, 92
Greer S, 1905
Gregory HH, 316
Greist JH, 924, 925, 926, 927, 1729
Grek A, 834
Grey S, 2536
Gribbens, 632
Griest DL, 385
Griest J, 1902
Griest T, 1902
Griffen A, 1382
Griffin A, 997
Griffin JB, 565, 566
Griffin JC, 36
Griffith E, 2375

Griffiths RR, 1431, 1432, 1437
Grimshaw L, 2098
Grinberg L, 2714
Grinc GA, 525, 527, 538, 541, 542
Grinker RF, 2154
Grinspoon L, 813, 814, 1219, 1248,
    1249, 1503, 1516, 1658
Grinstein A, 2470
Gritz ER, 1348
Groat R, 530, 558
Grobman J, 2673
Grof P, 1930
Grose D, 2219, 2221
Gross HA, 473
Gross HH, 474
Gross MD, 94
Gross MM, 1067, 1184, 1919
Gross RT, 717, 720
Grosser BI, 1000
Grossman LS, 1670
Grossman SH, 922
Grote B, 2368
Groth AN, 626
Grotjahn M, 2667, 2672
Grotjohn M, 995
Group for the Advancement of
    Psychiatry, 348, 774, 776, 1559,
    2014, 2223, 2511
Grover D, 1215
Groves JE, 2676
Growdon JH, 974
Gruber AR, 2469
Gruenberg AM, 1497
Gruenewald D, 2202, 2204, 2205, 2206
Gruhle HW, 1614
Gruman G, 2371
Grunberg NE, 1280
Grunebaum H, 1566, 2676, 2734
Gryboski JD, 564, 565, 576, 577
Gualtieri CT, 7, 68, 69, 74, 81, 88, 93,
    95, 243, 244, 245, 1781
Gudjonsson GH, 2194
Gudmundsson G, 882
Guerin PJ, 1403
Guerrant J, 882
Guerrero-Figueroa R, 1088

Guess D, 45, 203
Guey J, 96, 97
Guidano VF, 485, 488
Guidotti A, 87
Guidry JR, 910
Guilleminault C, 2435, 2436, 2437, 2438, 2439
Guinn MM, 838
Guitar B, 346
Gujavarty K, 1805
Gulens V, 668
Gull WW, 455, 456, 458, 463
Gulyassy PF, 922
Gunderson E, 2513
Gunderson J, 2635
Gunderson JG, 1517, 1533, 1543, 1547, 2636, 2639, 2656, 2688, 2692, 2693, 2698, 2725, 2751, 2753, 2756
Gunn J, 839, 883
Gunn RC, 1280
Gunne LM, 1221, 1251, 1344, 1346
Guntrip H, 2712
Gupta C, 63
Gur RE, 1491, 1492
Gurland BJ, 817
Gurman A, 1547
Gurman AS, 1404, 1886, 2273, 2340, 2566, 2663, 2762
Guskin SL, 125
Gustafson JM, 1002
Gustafson JP, 2560, 2672, 2677
Gutelius MF, 52, 582, 583, 585
Gutman RA, 1366
Guttmacher L, 2104
Guttmacher MS, 617
Guttman D, 2372
Guze SB, 1073, 2167, 2170, 2336, 2743
Gwirtsman HE, 519, 1916

Haapanen E, 916, 917
Haas GL, 1885, 1887
Hachinski V, 867, 872
Hachinski VC, 820, 961

Hacker L, 2600
Hackett TP, 950, 1900, 2583
Haddon JW, 846
Hadley E, 630
Hadley SW, 1884
Haefely WE, 407
Haegeman RJ, 76
Hafez H, 1779, 1782
Hafner RJ, 2658
Hage R, 348
Hagerman RJ, 40, 41, 42
Hagerman S, 2537
Haggerty JJ, 2164
Hagin RA, 697, 698
Hagman A, 906
Haier JR, 1495
Hakoloa HP, 850
Hakstian AR, 1819, 1861
Hale AS, 1802
Hale E, 2200
Hale MS, 865
Haley J, 494, 504, 1406, 1409, 1545, 1564, 1566, 2761, 2779
Halgin R, 865
Hall GH, 1285
Hall H, 1778
Hall ME, 59
Hall RC, 2202
Hall RCW, 1700, 1901, 1912, 1913
Hall RV, 378
Hall S, 1351
Hall SM, 1438, 1444, 1445, 1447
Hall TB III, 836
Hallahan DP, 328
Hallam R, 2030
Halleck SL, 646, 2734
Hallen O, 2146
Hallgren B, 718, 1498
Hallgrimsson O, 1344
Hallopeau X, 2481
Hallsten EA, 475
Halmi KA, 449, 452, 453, 456, 457, 465, 469, 472, 473, 476, 537, 564, 590, 1916, 1917
Halmstrom LL, 2527
Halpern WI, 194, 767

Hamann K, 2146
Hambridge KM, 588
Hamburg BA, 2614
Hamburg D, 2072
Hameroff SR, 1783
Hamill PVV, 245
Hamilton J, 46
Hamilton M, 1789, 1891
Hamm JE, 1918
Hammill DD, 208, 330, 331, 333, 335
Hammond JJ, 912
Hand I, 2028, 2030
Handleman JS, 190, 195, 197, 215
Handley R, 1550
Hanlon TE, 1681
Hansen C, 1779, 1784
Hansen E, 2132
Hansen HE, 926
Hansen J, 2132
Hanson B, 1419
Hanson DR, 234, 256
Hanson PG, 1116, 1119
Hanssen T, 1502
Hansten PD, 866, 867, 928, 959, 960
Harbaugh RE, 971
Harbin HT, 1559, 2746
Harcherick DF, 695
Harding CM, 1568
Harding T, 1251
Hardy JC, 62
Hare EH, 1514, 1647
Harford RJ, 1439
Haring N, 138
Harley JP, 95, 96
Harley M, 2020
Harmon TM, 1857
Harms E, 1344
Harper C, 1092
Harper G, 463, 502
Harper M, 2218, 2219, 2221
Harper RA, 1856
Harriman P, 2197
Harris A, 335
Harris GM, 2539
Harris J, 33, 347, 349, 350, 351, 1910
Harris M, 316, 345, 2523, 2595

Harris SL, 195, 215, 253, 266
Harris TO, 1748, 1749, 1765, 1885
Harrison HE, 52
Harrison MJG, 818, 821, 965
Harrison W, 1942
Hart H, 2135
Hart J, 95
Hart K, 2537
Hart P, 2761
Hart V, 63, 65
Hartcollis P, 2255
Hartland J, 2055
Hartman LM, 2337
Hartman V, 631
Hartman WE, 2338
Hartmann E, 2421
Hartmann H, 1527, 2012, 2644
Hartnoll RL, 1325
Hartocollis P, 2691, 2700
Harvey J, 348
Harvey SC, 921
Hasan MK, 78
Haskell D, 2043
Haskett RF, 1909
Haslam J, 1487
Haslam MT, 2336, 2337
Hasler JF, 451, 517
Hass WK, 869
Hassanein RS, 1783
Hassibi M, 371
Hatch JP, 2391
Hatcher R, 1077
Hatfield AB, 1543, 1547, 1548, 1552,
    1559, 1560
Hathaway SR, 1844
Hatsukami D, 1919
Hauri P, 2424, 2426, 2427, 2429
Hauserman N, 491
Havassy B, 1351
Havens LL, 935, 2731
Haward LRC, 2194
Hawkins D, 241
Hawkins JD, 1437, 1442, 1445
Hawkins RC, 539, 541
Hawks RL, 1247
Hawton K, 625

Hay GG, 2165, 2166
Hay WM, 664, 665
Hayden TL, 771
Hayes JR, 902
Hayes M, 108
Hayes RL, 904
Hayes SC, 1844, 2653
Hayman, 1135
Hayman M, 1104
Haynes R, 2138
Hays P, 1707
Hazaleus S, 2537
Head H, 2152
Heath GA, 2469, 2470
Heath RG, 2386
Heather N, 1124
Heaton RK, 940, 2125
Heaton-Ward WA, 6, 82
Hecht F, 39
Hechtman LT, 365, 366, 370, 374
Hecker D, 1487
Hedberg AG, 1122
Hedberg DL, 2684
Hedblom JE, 459
Hedlund B, 1862
Hedrick DL, 187, 208
Heffernan MM, 1891
Heffley J, 60, 63, 65
Heiby EM, 1862
Heide FJ, 2064
Heilbronn M, 1902, 1903, 2129
Heiman J, 950
Heiman JR, 2283, 2322, 2327, 2336,
    2341, 2391
Heimberg RG, 1944
Heimlich EP, 768
Hein HA, 725
Heinrichs DW, 1530, 1531, 1532, 1539,
    1543, 1548, 1553, 1561, 1564
Heinz ER, 454
Heiser JF, 813
Heiser KF, 108
Heistad GT, 74, 76
Helfer RE, 735
Helfgott E, 326
Helgason T, 1752

Hellekson CJ, 1892, 1893
Hellman DS, 2469
Hellstrom I, 451
Helmer SH, 212, 215, 216
Helms PM, 826
Helstone FS, 2763
Helzer JE, 1500, 1761
Hemseley DR, 1530
Hemsley DR, 1548
Hemsley R, 253
Henderson DA, 1372
Henderson DC, 1111
Henderson IWD, 1344
Henderson JQ, 2652
Henderson M, 1807
Henderson R, 348
Henderson S, 1864
Hendin H, 1200
Hendren RL, 1916
Hendricks WJ, 1398
Hendriksen GF, 881
Heninger GR, 1793, 1927
Henker B, 91, 373, 427
Henningfield JE, 1261, 1276
Henry CE, 94
Henry J, 2072
Henry JA, 904
Henson C, 2385, 2387
Henson RA, 941
Herbert M, 385, 735, 736, 1641
Herbert W, 2472
Herbst JJ, 564, 565, 571, 572, 576, 577,
    579
Herceg-Baron RL, 1869
Herman BH, 248, 574
Herman M, 2194, 2195
Herman SP, 665
Hermann HT, 1123
Herridge CF, 944
Herrington RE, 1421, 1429
Herrnstein RJ, 121
Hersch R, 1397
Hersen M, 1570, 1820, 1821, 1822,
    1846, 1859, 2651, 2656, 2658, 2670,
    2761
Hersov L, 371, 386

Herz FM, 1412
Herz MI, 1534, 1535, 1553, 1561, 1564, 1662, 1663
Herzog DB, 542, 1917
Hes JP, 1808
Hess ND, 2201
Hesselbrock MN, 1067, 1068, 1069, 1070, 1072, 1185
Hestbech J, 926
Hester R, 1148
Hester RK, 1068, 1150
Heston LL, 31, 819
Hewitt PM, 202
Hibbert GA, 2035
Hicks RE, 93
Higgenbottam JA, 46
Hilgard ER, 2053
Hilgard JR, 1278, 2064
Hill BK, 21, 86, 89
Hill DEC, 2766, 2767, 2768
Hill JW, 272, 274
Hill LP, 1520
Hill R, 1559, 2521
Hillbom E, 833
Hillbom M, 847
Hillman RE, 316
Himmelhoch J, 952
Himmelhoch JM, 866, 904, 924, 927, 1669, 1670, 1760, 1761, 1927, 1930
Hinton GG, 91
Hippins H, 2104
Hirsch SJ, 1683, 2736
Hirsch SM, 1124
Hirsch SR, 1547
Hirschfeld RMA, 1732, 2764
Hiskey M, 188
Hitchcock J, 2525
Hite S, 2281, 2284
Hixon TJ, 62
Hlusko P, 407
Ho AD, 1919
Hobbs N, 348, 386
Hoberman H, 1858, 1862
Hoberman HM, 1846, 1853
Hoch Z, 2281, 2286
Hockfelt T, 406

Hodgkinson S, 1490
Hodgson NB, 719
Hodgson RJ, 639, 1067, 1068, 1131, 2095, 2099
Hodson BW, 344
Hoefnagel D, 958
Hoehn-Saric R, 406, 911, 2151
Hoenig J, 641
Hoenk PR, 2513
Hoffer A, 327
Hoffer W, 570, 2459
Hoffman AR, 2352
Hoffman D, 2520, 2523, 2525
Hoffman L, 463, 1565, 2779
Hoffman PB, 2748
Hogan DP, 2501
Hogan MJ, 876
Hogarty GE, 1517, 1551, 1555, 1556, 1576, 1581, 1662
Hogben GL, 2074, 2076, 2588, 2685
Hohman L, 2133
Holborn SW, 2481, 2484
Holcer P, 64
Holcomb HH, 865, 866
Holden DF, 1548
Holden MA, 2670
Holden NL, 836
Holder E, 666
Holfstetter A, 1279
Holland CJ, 2471
Holland J, 944, 1904, 1905
Holland JC, 1905, 1906, 1912
Holland S, 1382, 1395
Hollender MH, 671, 1683, 2185, 2221, 2728, 2736
Hollis JH, 72, 76
Hollister L, 1333, 1340, 2586
Hollister LE, 829, 946, 972, 1304, 1338
Hollon SD, 1532, 1819, 1822, 1834, 1846
Holloway HC, 811, 812
Hollowell JG, 564, 565, 569, 570
Holmes MR, 1489
Holmes TH, 1865, 2500
Holmgren S, 462
Holmsen R, 1912

Holmstrom LL, 671
Holroyd I, 1277, 1278, 1279
Holroyd JC, 2131, 2150
Holschneider A, 724
Holser-Buehler P, 61, 62, 63, 65
Holt S, 466
Holvoet JF, 54
Holzbach E, 1087
Holzbauer M, 583
Hong CY, 1366
Hood DD, 1811
Hooley JM, 1550, 1552
Hoon EF, 2282, 2386
Hoon PW, 2282
Hooper JF, 810
Hopkin B, 838
Hopkins A, 2165
Hopkins J, 666
Hoppe K, 2223
Horenstein S, 871
Horevitz RP, 2198
Horne RL, 530, 1810
Horner JA, 2672
Horner RD, 37
Horner RH, 127
Horney K, 489, 2773
Horowitz M, 2019, 2066, 2067, 2068,
    2069, 2070, 2071, 2072, 2073, 2075,
    2078, 2081, 2517, 2728, 2732, 2752,
    2768
Horowitz MJ, 1532, 1542, 1874, 1884,
    2509, 2548, 2549, 2550, 2551, 2554,
    2555, 2556
Horton PC, 2224, 2226
Horwitz L, 1117, 2673
Höschl C, 909
Hoshino AY, 812
Hoskins RG, 240
Hotvedt M, 2371
Hoult J, 1580
House R, 933
Howard G, 875
Howard-Peebles PN, 40
Howarth BG, 1704
Howlin P, 215, 253

Hoy RM, 1124
Hoyumpa AM, 936, 937, 938
Hresko WP, 338
Hsu LKG, 460, 476, 491, 531
Huba G, 1200
Hubbard RI, 1323, 1324
Hubbell FA, 823
Huber AM, 52, 565, 568, 580, 583, 584,
    588
Huch A, 945
Huch R, 945
Hucker SJ, 629
Hudgens A, 2135
Hudson JI, 473, 492, 519, 530, 539, 545,
    1917, 2468
Huesmann LR, 22
Huey CJ, 2285
Hughes CP, 823, 825, 966
Hughes JM, 1161, 2347, 2613
Hughes PL, 530, 1917
Huguenin NH, 25, 125
Hull JG, 1202
Humphrey M, 870
Humphries T, 374
Humphris FH, 1890
Hung DW, 219
Hunt CH, 2256
Hunt GM, 1122, 1128, 1129, 1442,
    1443, 1446
Hunt HF, 2339
Hunt M, 2284
Hunt WA, 1278, 1432
Hunyor SN, 911
Huppert FA, 940
Hurley AD, 7, 10, 18, 78
Huschka M, 724
Huse DM, 509
Hussain MZ, 2104, 2773
Husted JR, 222
Hutchings D, 2150, 2534, 2537
Hutchinson RR, 21
Hutt SJ, 96
Hwineixha SQ, 1561
Hyler SE, 2163
Hymowitz P, 2683

Hypertension Detection and Follow-Up Program Cooperative Group, 847
Hyyppa MT, 2349

IASP. *See* International Association for the Study of Pain
Idestrom CM, 95, 96
Iglehart JK, 979
Ilfeld FW, 1865
Illingworth R, 58, 62
Ilson JM, 38
Imber-Mintz L, 1583
Imerek DE, 1310
Imhoff J, 1257
Imlah NW, 1813
Incagnoli T, 697
Inderbitzen LB, 2559
Ingham JG, 1865
Inglehart JK, 980
Ingram D, 344
Innes IR, 944
Inoue F, 70
Inoue K, 1705
Insel T, 2104
Insel TR, 406, 911, 1800, 2096, 2097, 2100, 2101, 2102, 2103, 2685, 2780
Institute for the Study of Learning Disabilities, 333, 337, 338
Institute of Medicine, 982
Insurance Institute for Highway Safety, 846
Intaglia JC, 1130
Intagliata J, 86, 89, 1579, 1580
International Association for the Study of Pain, 2122
Inwood DG, 1707
Irwin DS, 1581
Irwin J, 345
Irwin M, 904, 1779, 1782
Irwin S, 233
Isaacs B, 823
Isaacs G, 1892, 1893

Isbell H, 1296
Isenberg DH, 2603
Isenstadt L, 2013, 2014
Ishihara A, 2381
Ishikawa S, 940, 941
Ismond DR, 180
Ison MG, 71
Issa FG, 2434, 2436
Isselbacher KJ, 933
Istvan J, 1283
Itard JM, 27, 123
Itil TM, 839, 1206, 1783
Itkonen J, 1225
Ivers R, 2319

Jabbari B, 1779, 1783
Jack R, 917
Jackson AH, 812
Jackson DD, 1545, 2569, 2716
Jackson G, 1184
Jackson GM, 55, 122
Jackson J, 2667
Jacob R, 2534
Jacob T, 1111, 1545, 1549
Jacobi GH, 2332
Jacobides GM, 407
Jacobs D, 1700
Jacobs HE, 1574
Jacobs L, 873
Jacobs PA, 21
Jacobs S, 1563
Jacobsen E, 2534
Jacobsen FM, 1892, 1893
Jacobsen S, 1641
Jacobson E, 1826, 1829, 1833, 1856
Jacobson G, 2527
Jacobson JW, 4, 20
Jacobson N, 1887, 2614
Jacobson NS, 1566
Jaffe I, 1262
Jaffe JH, 1070, 1071, 1310, 1311, 1325, 1329, 1333, 1347, 1351, 1359, 1419, 1919

Jagger J, 688
Jain VK, 2103
Jainchill N, 1383, 1395
Jakab I, 74, 105, 108, 588
Jakobson R, 343, 344
James DH, 69
James IM, 2590
James SP, 1892, 1893
James W, 1745, 2595
Jameton AL, 1002, 1004
Jamieson WG, 2121, 2140
Jamison KR, 1760, 1938
Jampala VC, 875
Jampola VC, 1917
Janet P, 2191
Janicak PG, 1936, 1937
Jannoun L, 2029, 2030, 2035, 2537
Janowsky D, 904, 1779, 1782
Janowsky DS, 914, 1548
Jarrett RB, 1834, 1844
Jarvik LF, 801, 816, 817, 821, 827, 828,
    829, 830, 872, 902, 972, 984, 994,
    1821
Jarvik ME, 1275
Jasinski DR, 1319, 1325, 1334, 1353
Jasper K, 2469
Jaspers K, 1610, 1613, 1616, 1618, 1619,
    1642, 1677, 1680, 1683, 1690, 2728
Jasperse C, 2594
Jastak JE, 331
Jastak SR, 331
Jatlow P, 1224
Javaheri P, 2334
Javid M, 917
Jayaprakash S, 2469
Jayne C, 2280
Jefferson JW, 895, 896, 897, 898, 899,
    903, 908, 910, 914, 916, 917, 919,
    924, 925, 926, 927, 930, 931, 934,
    935, 936, 937, 939, 1708, 1891,
    1912, 1926, 2162, 2165, 2166
Jefferys PM, 1007
Jehu D, 2336
Jellinek EM, 1065, 1066
Jellinek MS, 946
Jellinger K, 862

Jenike MA, 828, 913, 945, 946, 947,
    974, 975, 976, 1704, 1792, 2103,
    2104, 2146
Jenkins JR, 333
Jenkins JS, 977
Jenkins RL, 369
Jenner FA, 925
Jensen I, 882
Jesness CF, 386
Jessor R, 1244, 1246, 1250
Jessup B, 2131, 2150
Jeste DV, 849, 862, 1491
Jew CC, 2674
Joffe JR, 1912, 1913·
Joffee WG, 1828, 1947
Johannessen SI, 893
Johanson AJ, 474
Johanson CE, 1226, 1231, 1431
Johanson E, 1637, 1642, 1643, 1648
Johansson J, 2150
John R, 2065
Johns CA, 967, 968
Johnson AM, 2459, 2660
Johnson CL, 485, 526, 527, 534, 538,
    541, 542
Johnson DAW, 1673, 1922
Johnson DG, 317, 332, 333
Johnson HK, 43, 588
Johnson HR, 967
Johnson J, 670, 2321, 2322
Johnson JA, 2353
Johnson L, 1810
Johnson NE, 52
Johnson NS, 337
Johnson P, 1912
Johnson RN, 21
Johnson SB, 401, 404, 405, 2539
Johnson SM, 117
Johnson V, 1400
Johnson VE, 2238, 2264, 2279, 2280,
    2281, 2285, 2290, 2297, 2298, 2299,
    2301, 2303, 2307, 2310, 2311, 2312,
    2315, 2319, 2321, 2322, 2325, 2326,
    2327, 2337, 2338, 2341, 2363
Johnson WG, 533, 538
Johnston A, 1783

Johnston CE, 1204
Johnston D, 2364
Johnston DW, 2029, 2031
Johnston J, 2535
Johnston LD, 1242
Johnston M, 64
Jolley SG, 571
Jonas AD, 1194
Jonas DF, 1194
Jonas U, 2332, 2333
Jones A, 59
Jones AB, 2165
Jones BM, 1077
Jones CM, 838
Jones E, 510, 2641, 2642, 2773
Jones FA, 736
Jones FD, 2654
Jones FDE, 2471
Jones GH, 1149
Jones HR, 896
Jones I, 962
Jones J, 1549, 2205
Jones KV, 643, 725
Jones MC, 1069
Jones MK, 1077
Jones MS, 213, 2634, 2667, 2674, 2696,
    2747
Jones RB, 2035
Jones RM, 1805, 1807, 1809, 1810
Jones RT, 1254
Jones SD, 2353
Jones SL, 1862
Jones T, 59, 60, 63, 65, 66
Jones W, 337
Jones WL, 1344
Jonker C, 961
Jonsen AR, 984, 993, 995, 1003
Jonsson LE, 1237
Jorgensen P, 1684
Josef NC, 904, 2682, 2747
Joseph H, 1324, 1352
Joseph-Vanderpool JR, 1891, 1896
Josephson AM, 1913
Josselson R, 784
Jourard S, 468
Jouvent R, 911

Joy VC, 1547
Joyce MA, 1130
Judd FK, 1912, 1913
Judson BA, 1338, 1340, 1344
Julian A III, 2674
Jung CG, 2225
Jusko WJ, 1285
Justice V, 2469

Kadden R, 1068
Kaerscher D, 2516
Kafer ER, 945
Kaffman M, 719, 2525
Kagan J, 2765
Kagle A, 2339
Kahlbaum KL, 1487
Kahn MD, 262, 577
Kahn RJ, 2024, 2047, 2129, 2151
Kahn RL, 807, 821, 823, 2187
Kalachnick JE, 70, 91
Kalant H, 1224, 1237
Kalant OJ, 1224, 1237
Kalat JW, 238, 248
Kales A, 828, 2419, 2421, 2422, 2439
Kales JD, 2421
Kalfus GR, 2481
Kalinowsky LB, 2104
Kallman FJ, 1689
Kallman RJ, 1690
Kaloupek DG, 2081
Kaltreider NB, 2509
Kalucy RS, 492, 493
Kammeier ML, 1156
Kampman R, 2197
Kanas N, 1532, 1533, 1534, 1537, 1539,
    1543
Kanba S, 1778
Kandel D, 1200, 1201, 1411
Kandel DB, 1312, 1431
Kandel E, 2071
Kane CA, 821
Kane F, 2368
Kane FJ Jr, 1909, 1912

Kane JJ, 243
Kane JM, 1662
Kane R, 697
Kanfer F, 2537, 2547
Kannel W, 847
Kanner L, 53, 55, 179, 180, 185, 564, 565, 2511
Kanno PH, 2341
Kansas N, 1117
Kanter J, 1564
Kanter JS, 1551, 1552
Kantor D, 494
Kaplan AS, 530, 531
Kaplan B, 894
Kaplan D, 2514, 2527
Kaplan DM, 1546, 1559
Kaplan HB, 1201
Kaplan HM, 2336
Kaplan HS, 2244, 2247, 2253, 2264, 2265, 2275, 2281, 2283, 2284, 2286, 2288, 2289, 2290, 2313, 2320, 2325, 2328, 2335, 2338, 2339, 2341, 2342, 2355, 2372, 2373
Kaplan L, 348
Kaplan RF, 1068, 1071
Karacan I, 2239, 2241, 2385
Karagulla S, 884
Karalese RH, 1912
Karan OC, 133, 136, 137
Karasu TB, 636, 1729, 1730, 1822, 2148
Kardener SH, 2525
Kardiner A, 2532
Karhunen U, 950
Karlavage J, 709
Karlen A, 2360
Karliner W, 875
Karno M, 1550
Karoly P, 405
Karon B, 1658
Karon BP, 1516
Karpel MA, 1000
Karpman B, 630, 631
Karpman G, 2743
Kasanin J, 1613, 1666, 1667, 1670, 1671, 2712, 2713
Kashani J, 1951

Kaske M, 847
Kaskey GB, 1787
Kasper S, 1892
Kass MP, 2342
Kassel V, 2374, 2375
Kastin AJ, 976, 977, 978, 2351
Kates W, 2676
Kathol RG, 1899
Katon W, 829, 2121, 2147
Katona CL, 974
Katona CLE, 1928
Katz AH, 2601
Katz J, 984, 997, 1005
Katz JL, 1916
Katz L, 1151
Katz R, 813
Katzman R, 965
Kauffman JM, 128, 328
Kaufman, 1315
Kaufman AS, 189
Kaufman BS, 984
Kaufman E, 1111, 1112, 1116, 1119, 1120, 1149, 1258, 1327, 1380, 1398, 1399, 1400, 1401, 1402, 1405, 1407, 1411, 1412, 1413, 1414, 1415, 1416
Kaufman I, 2469, 2470
Kaufman KR, 70
Kaufman ME, 45
Kaufman MW, 1912
Kaufman NL, 189
Kaufman PW, 1258
Kaufman W, 2592, 2593, 2595
Kaufmann P, 1398, 1402, 1412
Kaul TJ, 1123
Kavale KA, 379
Kay D, 1813
Kay DK, 1615, 1629, 1640
Kay DWK, 950, 951
Kay SR, 1492, 1709
Kaye N, 348
Kazdin AE, 6, 108, 114, 121, 133, 370, 373, 381, 384, 385, 386, 388, 389, 1847, 1856, 2033
Kazdin TM, 382
Kealey LS, 2764
Keane JR, 955

Keane TM, 2081, 2535
Kedia K, 2386
Keefe JF, 1902
Keegan DL, 82
Keeler MH, 1909, 1919
Keeney BP, 2567
Kegel AH, 2286
Keith AE, 382
Keith CR, 348, 386
Keith L, 582, 586
Keith SJ, 1516, 1530, 1535, 1537, 1543,
    1547, 1663, 1664, 1665, 1675
Kellam SG, 349, 2500, 2704
Kelleher RI, 1431
Keller MB, 1729, 1753, 1756, 1788, 1942
Kelley D, 1348
Kellner R, 826, 2125, 2138, 2139, 2140,
    2143, 2145, 2146, 2147, 2148, 2152,
    2463, 2464, 2471, 2476, 2746
Kelly C, 1116
Kelly D, 2685
Kelly J, 2374
Kelly JA, 1571
Kelly JT, 78
Kelly WF, 1909
Kelwala S, 866
Kemali D, 1669, 1673, 1676
Kemp CH, 735, 746
Kemp KV, 2689, 2697
Kendall KC, 378
Kendall PC, 378
Kendall RE, 633, 634, 1707
Kendell RE, 1500
Kendler KS, 1497, 1498, 1609, 1615,
    1618
Kendler MS, 1492
Kennard D, 1382
Kennedy A, 2193, 2194, 2195, 2196
Kennedy D, 2527
Kennedy J, 936
Kennedy SH, 530
Kennell J, 735
Kennie AT, 823
Kent RN, 112, 385
Kenyon FE, 2139, 2140, 2145, 2146
Kenyon J, 2132

Kepler M, 2595
Keppel JM, 68, 69
Kernberg O, 638, 1104, 1529, 2013
Kernberg OF, 645, 2199, 2635, 2636,
    2642, 2648, 2667, 2690, 2692, 2700,
    2714, 2737, 2738, 2739, 2740, 2741,
    2751
Kerns RD, 2125
Kerr M, 2572
Kessel WIN, 2140, 2147
Kessler E, 2514
Kety SS, 1497, 2719
Keup W, 1249, 1251
Keyes B, 830
Keyman MM, 1146
Keys A, 458, 464
Kezur E, 2199, 2216
Khan H, 1071
Khan M, 2020
Khan MMR, 640, 2714, 2730, 2731
Khantzian E, 1104, 1105, 1106, 1107,
    1418, 1424
Khantzian EJ, 1185, 1201, 1232, 1237,
    1238, 1239, 1240, 1248, 1250, 1285,
    1313, 1374, 1417, 1920
Khantzian NJ, 1232, 1238, 1374
Khatami M, 2130
Kholsa N, 1910
Khuri R, 1765, 1925
Kibel HD, 2673, 2676, 2677
Kidd KK, 316
Kiecolt-Glaser J, 525, 527
Kielholz P, 1754
Kierkegaard S, 1747
Kiernan CC, 213
Kiersch TA, 944
Kiesler D, 2762
Kiev A, 2784
Kiger R, 2635, 2674, 2747
Killilea M, 2611, 2612
Kilman BA, 268
Kilman PR, 2674
Kilmann PR, 637, 639, 2288, 2290
Kiloh LG, 818, 821, 1629
Kilpatrick D, 2536, 2539, 2543
Kim WY, 1779, 1783

Kimball RO, 2749
Kimura S, 1704, 1706, 1710
Kincaid-Smith P, 926
King A, 459, 589
King D, 1933
King LW, 1571
King MD, 1366
Kinsbourne M, 374
Kinsey AC, 649, 2280, 2281, 2284,
    2285, 2301, 2335, 2371, 2372, 2383
Kipper D, 2535
Kirby D, 2366, 2367
Kirigin KA, 386
Kirk S, 330
Kirkby RJ, 1370
Kirkendall UM, 912
Kirkley B, 551
Kirkley BG, 534, 552
Kirkley RG, 550
Kirkpatrick, 94
Kirsch TB, 2712
Kirschenbaum DS, 534, 550, 551, 552
Kiser R, 2132
Kish GB, 1123
Kissen B, 1075
Kissin B, 1089, 1919
Kistler JP, 869, 870
Kitagawa T, 454
Kivi R, 906
Kiviranta P, 1157
Kjeldgaard JM, 1348
Klaber MM, 45
Klaiber EL, 1796
Klajner F, 1438
Klaus M, 735
Klawans HL, 861, 863, 864, 865
Klawans HL Jr, 2318
Kleber H, 1418, 1420, 1430, 1920, 1921,
    1922
Kleber HD, 838, 1184, 1185, 1221,
    1222, 1226, 1230, 1231, 1232, 1233,
    1235, 1236, 1237, 1238, 1239, 1240,
    1319, 1329, 1330, 1334, 1338, 1344,
    1348, 1352
Kleber RK, 1227, 1228, 1229
Klee S, 2540

Kleeman J, 666
Klein D, 1736, 1756, 1942, 1957
Klein DF, 367, 373, 377, 378, 379, 380,
    384, 385, 387, 388, 406, 407, 408,
    476, 1420, 1507, 1516, 1517, 1519,
    1523, 2015, 2022, 2027, 2032, 2033,
    2039, 2048, 2051, 2052, 2247, 2521,
    2587, 2588, 2589, 2680, 2682, 2683,
    2684, 2685, 2703, 2710, 2736, 2741,
    2755, 2763, 2770, 2784
Klein J, 108, 109
Klein KE, 2442
Klein M, 735, 1515, 1623, 2470, 2661
Klein RG, 375
Kleinknecht RA, 933
Kleist K, 1698
Klerman G, 1958
Klerman GL, 862, 875, 924, 1730, 1731,
    1732, 1737, 1755, 1758, 1761, 1764,
    1786, 1816, 1819, 1822, 1863, 1870,
    1871, 1885, 1901, 1914, 1915, 1942,
    1944, 2736
Klerman L, 2369
Kline C, 335
Kline MV, 2199, 2205
Kline NS, 1734, 1796, 1919
Kline P, 2763, 2765
Klinge E, 2386
Klingman A, 2540
Klipper MZ, 2052
Klonoff EA, 2164
Klorman R, 375, 2540
Klosiewicz L, 1932
Klotter J, 1284, 2043
Klotz U, 937
Kluft RP, 2197, 2198, 2199, 2200, 2201,
    2202, 2203, 2204, 2205, 2206, 2207,
    2208, 2209, 2210, 2211, 2213, 2214,
    2215, 2216
Knauth P, 2441
Knesevich JW, 911, 1497, 2104
Knight F, 1248, 1251
Knight PR, 1805, 1809
Knight R, 2750
Knight RF, 1094
Knight RT, 818

Knights RM, 91
Knisherman DP, 2273
Kniskern DP, 1404, 2566, 2663, 2762
Knobil E, 2352
Knoll J, 2354
Knopp FH, 625, 626, 627, 630
Knorr NJ, 474
Knowles R, 1344
Knudsen P, 1251
Kobayashi A, 1780
Kobrin S, 2460
Koch-Henriksen H, 977
Kockott G, 2320, 2391
Kocsis JH, 1756, 1789, 1928, 1942, 1943
Koegel RL, 217, 221, 223, 224, 249, 253
Koenigsberg HW, 1550
Kofoed L, 1149, 1150
Kog E, 494
Kogeorgos J, 1779, 1798
Kohl RN, 2341
Kohlberg L, 662
Kohlenberg RJ, 2201
Kohler PF, 1366
Kohon G, 2729
Kohut H, 556, 784, 1104, 1527, 2012,
    2024, 2459, 2462, 2639, 2642, 2644,
    2648, 2667, 2721, 2737, 2738, 2739,
    2740, 2741, 2751
Kokkinidis L, 1230
Kolata G, 1008, 1909
Kolb LC, 1829, 2071
Kolko DJ, 1570, 2470, 2471
Kolle K, 1614, 1615, 1642
Koller H, 5, 10
Kolmel HW, 950
Kolodny RC, 1366, 2305, 2311, 2319,
    2320
Kologinsky E, 195
Kolvin I, 182, 249, 763
Komrad MS, 867
Konstantareas M, 212
Kopel SA, 643, 644
Koprowski PF, 2700
Kopschitz DH, 1514
Koptagel G, 580, 581
Korff J, 2283, 2387

Kornblith SJ, 1834, 1846, 1859
Korner I, 2523, 2525
Kornfeld DS, 930, 931, 935
Korsgaard S, 882, 1912, 1913
Korvath TB, 933
Kosanin R, 904
Kosberg JI, 993, 1000
Kosky RJ, 668
Koss M, 2525
Kosseff J, 2667, 2671
Kosten TR, 1183, 1184, 1185, 1313,
    1315, 1324, 1325, 1331, 1338, 1433,
    1920, 1921, 1922, 2071
Kotelchuck M, 736
Kothary S, 945
Kotin J, 1760, 2316, 2348
Kovacs M, 1753, 1821, 1822, 1842, 1845
Kovacs R, 1890
Koval G, 1779, 1783
Kovelman JA, 1491
Kovner R, 830
Kozel NJ, 1219
Kozloff MA, 253
Kozlowski LT, 1269
Kraanen J, 2099
Kraepelin E, 1487, 1490, 1498, 1499,
    1567, 1613, 1614, 1616, 1726, 1757,
    1762, 1863, 1956, 2678
Krafft-Ebing R von, 636, 637, 670, 671
Kraft IA, 82
Kraft T, 2337
Kragh-Sorenson P, 923
Kral VA, 821
Kramer BA, 1808
Kramer JC, 1222, 1227, 1229, 1230,
    1786
Kramer MS, 1708
Kramlinger KG, 945
Kramp P, 810
Kranzler G, 1856
Krasner L, 1570
Kraspa LJ, 2148
Kraus JF, 840
Kraus JM, 937
Krauthammer C, 875, 924
Krauthammer L, 1761, 1764, 1914, 1915

Kreek MJ, 1324, 1347, 1348, 1357
Kreek MS, 1351
Kreger C, 75
Kreisler, 569
Kreisman DE, 1547
Kreitman N, 1865, 2145
Kretschmer E, 1610, 1613, 1616, 1617, 1635, 2678, 2712, 2759
Kreuzer E, 374
Kriegman D, 1693
Kringlen E, 2098
Kripke DF, 1891, 1895
Kris AO, 2012, 2021, 2023
Kris E, 570, 574
Krishnan KR, 2481, 2482
Krishnan R, 1779
Kristeller JL, 1278
Kristensen O, 882, 975
Kroessler D, 1804
Kroger W, 2056
Kroger WS, 2052
Kronenberg RS, 945
Kronig MH, 905, 928
Krop HD, 940
Krueger DW, 635
Krug CM, 2464
Krug DA, 186
Krugman S, 1365
Krupnick J, 2752
Krystal H, 1106, 2471
Krystal JH, 1311
Kuczen B, 2516
Kuehnle CJ, 1680, 1681
Kugler J, 697, 698, 972
Kuhl DE, 870, 908
Kuhlman WM, 894
Kuhnert BR, 1263
Kuhnert PM, 1263
Kuhnley EF, 2469, 2470
Kuipers L, 1550, 1551
Kukopulos A, 1754, 1758, 1928, 1929, 1933, 1934, 1935
Kulenkampff C, 2143
Kulig K, 904
Kulik FA, 2317, 2347
Kulka AM, 572, 579

Kulshrestha VK, 890
Kuman R, 736
Kumar K, 2143
Kumar MSA, 1254
Kumar R, 1707
Kunst L, 2286
Kupfer DJ, 1740, 1742, 1754, 1760, 1762, 1786, 2256
Kurash C, 556
Kurland AA, 94, 95
Kurland ML, 908
Kurtis LB, 239
Kurtz E, 1154
Kurtzke JF, 867
Kushner HS, 2593
Kutchins H, 2613
Kutchins S, 2613
Kutt H, 890, 938

La Ferla JJ, 2352
La Greca A, 105
La Vietes RL, 760
L'Abate L, 2650, 2654, 2761
Labi MLC, 876
Labrie F, 2352
LaBruzza AL, 1680, 1700
Lacey JH, 473, 523, 525, 526, 534, 537, 538, 540, 542, 543, 550, 551, 552, 558
Lacey JJ, 2141
Lachiewicz AM, 40
Lachmann FM, 2017
Ladas A, 2286, 2387
Ladee GA, 2145, 2146
Lader M, 1305, 2043
Laerum H, 1678, 1684
LaGrow SJ, 45
Lahey B, 367
Lahey M, 202, 204, 205, 207, 211, 342
Lahmeyer HW, 1212
Laidlaw J, 938
Laidler J, 59, 60
Laing RD, 1544

Lake CR, 902
Lakein A, 1856
Lam RW, 1701
Lamb HR, 2695
Lamb R, 1519
Lambert EH, 942
Lambert MJ, 1884
Lambourn J, 1804
LaMendola W, 70
Lamont JT, 930
LaMont JT, 931, 932, 933
Lampert F, 452
Lampl-De Groot J, 2201
Lance JW, 835, 873
Lancioni GE, 212
Landau RL, 1002
Lande SD, 2469
Lander CM, 892
Landesman SH, 1328
Landis C, 2336
Landman GB, 725
Lando HA, 1277
Landolt WG, 881
Landsdown FS, 944
Lane TW, 2649, 2652
Lang J, 2527
Lang PJ, 406, 475, 564, 568, 577, 2100
Lange R, 1328
Langer TS, 2763
Langeston JW, 1328
Langevin R, 617, 618, 619, 627, 628,
    629, 630
Langfeldt G, 1499, 1613, 1617, 1642
Langley G, 2132
Langness LL, 14, 1685
Langsley D, 2520
Langsley DG, 1546, 1547, 1559
Lansky MR, 2341, 2354
Lantz JE, 2481, 2485
Lanzkowsky P, 582, 585, 588
Lapierre YD, 1784
Laplanche J, 2641
Laprade K, 365
Laqueur HP, 1563
Large RG, 2124
LaRosa JC, 1418

Larsen JK, 882
Larsen SL, 331, 333
Larson R, 542
Larsson LI, 2385
LaRue A, 820, 829, 872, 961
Lasagna L, 1220, 1226
Laschet U, 629
Laségue C, 455, 458, 671, 1685, 1686,
    1689, 1691, 1694
Laska E, 231
Lasky R, 2201
LaSor B, 2525
Laties VG, 91
Latimer P, 2135
LaTorre RA, 2280
Lauer J, 2770
Laulumaa VA, 850
Lauvetz RQ, 723
LaVeck GD, 86
LaVietes R, 2527
LaVigna GW, 213, 270
Lavigne JV, 569, 574
Lavin P, 491
Lawlis GF, 1070, 1533
Laws DR, 47
Lawson D, 2387
Lawson G, 1111
Lawson GW, 1161
Lawton MP, 2509
Lawton-Speert S, 625
Laybourne PC, 763, 767, 768
Layman WA, 1691, 1694
Layton TL, 212, 215, 216
Lazar I, 126
Lazare A, 634, 2736, 2763
Lazarus A, 1687
Lazarus AA, 2158, 2291, 2298, 2337,
    2361
Lazarus JM, 917, 921
Lazarus LW, 2740
Lazarus R, 2547
Lazarus RS, 259, 1886, 2071
Le Vann LJ, 74, 75
Leach B, 1157
Leaf A, 943, 996
Leaff LA, 1876, 2745

Leary T, 2340, 2759
Leavitt H, 2197
Leavitt J, 967, 968
Leavitt SS, 1580
LeBaron S, 2064
LeBellec M, 1305
Leber P, 966
LeBoeuf A, 977
Leboy T, 584
Lebwohl P, 474
Lechtenberg R, 835, 836
Leckman JF, 690, 691, 696, 709, 710
Lee AC, 665
Lee JT, 1810
Lee L, 204, 208
Lee NF, 550, 551, 552
Leeman CP, 2766, 2767, 2768
Lees AW, 1912
Leff J, 1493, 1550, 1552, 1553, 1554,
    1562, 1575, 1576, 1663, 1702
Leff JP, 1496, 1509, 1547, 1666
Leff ML, 1746, 1747
Lefkowitz MM, 850
Lefley HP, 1552
Legalos CN, 2065
Lehman AF, 1559
Lehman EJB, 95, 96
Lehman HE, 1560, 1699
Lehmann H, 1925
Lehmann HE, 1502, 1507, 1510, 1511,
    1688
Lehmann J, 975
Lehmann LS, 2218, 2219, 2220
Lehr W, 494
Lehrich JR, 952
Leib SA, 742
Leiblum S, 2390
Leiblum SR, 2297, 2298, 2335
Leibovich M, 2752
Leibowitz JM, 64
Leibowitz MR, 570
Leicester J, 2478
Leitch M, 572
Leitenberg H, 525, 526, 532, 538, 543,
    552
Leiter RG, 188

Leith NJ, 1221, 1230
Lejins PB, 2748
Leland H, 100, 108
Lemberger L, 838
Lemere F, 1127
Leming PD, 582, 587
Lennard C, 984
Lennard HL, 1344
Lennox WG, 881
Lentz RJ, 1535, 1576, 1577, 1578
Leon G, 2515
Leonard A, 78
Leone N, 2680, 2754
Leonhard K, 1671, 1698, 2141, 2143,
    2169
Lerer B, 1931
Lerner B, 2647
Lerner J, 333
Lesar T, 904, 913
Lesch M, 37
Lesieur HR, 2464
Lesse S, 2145
Lessel S, 835
Lesser IM, 2421, 2471
Lester D, 2470
Lester DM, 939, 940
Lester EP, 2560
Leszcz M, 1533, 2668
Lettick AL, 271
Lettieri D, 1192, 1195, 1196, 1197
Levay AN, 2256, 2339
Levene HI, 1534
Levenson H, 2075, 2076
Levenson J, 2201
Levenson JL, 903, 1805
Leventhal A, 2616
Leventhal BL, 230, 236, 247, 387
Leventhal H, 1264
Levere F, 2313
Levey A, 2538
Levin RJ, 2386
Levine B, 2536
Levine DF, 564, 566, 567, 570, 572, 577
Levine DN, 834
Levine FJ, 1425
Levine HG, 14

Levine J, 1066
Levine MD, 724, 725
Levine PM, 1744, 1904, 1905
Levine S, 2070
Levine SB, 2275, 2276, 2305, 2320,
    2321, 2322, 2325, 2327, 2341
Levinsky NG, 897, 898, 899
Levinson DJ, 2509
Levinson HN, 326
Levinson UR, 1123
Levis D, 2535
Levis DJ, 2099
Levitt H, 45
Levy A, 1305
Levy D, 776, 2518, 2519
Levy G, 1781
Levy H, 2381
Levy J, 2662, 2663, 2665
Levy JS, 2218, 2220, 2221
Levy LH, 2603, 2611
Levy R, 576
Levy RI, 899
Levy RL, 2318
Levy SM, 274
Lewin BD, 2020
Lewin K, 1532
Lewin L, 1220, 1222, 1226
Lewin W, 2104
Lewine RRJ, 1548
Lewinsohn P, 2539
Lewinsohn PM, 1731, 1732, 1846, 1847,
    1848, 1850, 1853, 1855, 1857, 1858,
    1862
Lewis A, 2121
Lewis C, 975
Lewis CE, 2656
Lewis DE, 1074
Lewis DJ, 2081
Lewis DO, 384, 385, 386, 844
Lewis JL, 1762, 1934
Lewis JM, 496
Lewis MH, 45, 49, 410, 720
Lewis MI, 900, 1001
Lewis NDC, 2469, 2470, 2471
Lewith G, 2132

Lewy AJ, 1801, 1891, 1892, 1893, 1894,
    1895, 2442
Ley P, 2142
Lezak MD, 876
Liberman RP, 849, 1503, 1532, 1542,
    1563, 1568, 1569, 1570, 1571, 1575,
    1577, 1578, 1579, 1580, 1581, 1583,
    2653, 2694, 2714, 2717, 2725
Libnoch JA, 582, 584, 586, 587
Libson E, 719
Lichtenstein E, 1266, 1270, 1271, 1276,
    1280
Lidz T, 496, 1520, 1544, 1545, 2660
Lieber LL, 2598, 2599, 2601
Liebergott JW, 313
Lieberman JA, 923
Lieberman M, 1731, 1814, 1834, 1846
Lieberman MA, 1865, 2598, 2600, 2601,
    2602, 2613
Liebman R, 476, 495
Liebowitz M, 911
Liebowitz MR, 88, 1791, 1796, 2354,
    2590, 2680, 2682, 2683, 2684, 2685,
    2736, 2755, 2762
Liebson I, 2158
Liebson IA, 1440
Lief HI, 2247, 2248, 2253, 2360
Liem JH, 1545, 1549
Lifton R, 2072
Like Other People, 2378
Lilienfeld AM, 297
Lilius H, 2319
Lim MH, 668
Lim ML, 875
Lindblad MB, 770
Lindemann E, 468, 2507, 2515, 2520,
    2521, 2527
Linden JD, 1065
Linden RD, 2465
Linden W, 538, 543
Lindsley DB, 94
Lindsley OR, 2649
Lindy J, 2515, 2517
Linehan M, 2653, 2754
Linet LS, 697, 707

Ling W, 1325, 1329, 1335, 1359
Lingjaerde, 1892
Linn L, 950, 2197, 2225
Linn MW, 1579, 1581
Linnoila M, 2447, 2448
Lion JR, 80, 1711, 2470, 2475, 2476, 2506, 2674, 2745
Liotti G, 485, 488
Lipinski JF, 893, 1495, 1499, 1704, 1752, 1762
Lipman L, 2202
Lipman RS, 77, 85, 89, 91, 1839, 1841
Lipowski ZJ, 804, 805, 810, 811, 820, 900, 940, 941, 943, 944
Lipper S, 863
Lippman G, 904
Lipsey JR, 875, 1910, 1911
Lipsky M, 2542
Lipton MA, 240, 241
Lipton SD, 2199, 2216
Liptzin B, 980
Lishman WA, 818, 820, 840, 844, 854, 859, 861, 868, 876, 880, 883, 885, 917, 932, 935, 936, 941, 942, 1091
Liskow B, 812
Liss JL, 2255
Lister J, 58, 62
Liston EH, 805, 806, 807, 820, 871, 872, 961
Litin EM, 805
Litman GK, 1130
Liu WS, 1810
Ljungberg L, 2154
Llewellyn LJ, 2165
Lloyd BL, 909
Lloyd KG, 37
Lloyd L, 763
Lo B, 1004
Lobb H, 92
Lobitz GK, 2244, 2245, 2246
Lobitz WC, 2244, 2245, 2246, 2341, 2361
Locke BJ, 24
Lockyer L, 184
Loeb L, 665
Loeb-Lundberg F, 1307

Loening-Baucke VA, 724
Loew DM, 975
Loewald H, 2645
Loewald HW, 2012
Lofts R, 52
Logeman JA, 344
Logothetis J, 884
Logue M, 974
Lohr JM, 525, 526, 527, 534, 543
Loizou LA, 1366
London P, 1730, 1822, 2008
Lonergan EC, 2585
Loney J, 367, 369
Long CF, 566, 567, 572
Long CG, 485, 525, 526, 527, 534, 538, 543, 565
Long KD, 2144, 2169
Longcope C, 2388
Longstreth WT, 869
Longwell B, 1349
Looker A, 95
Looney J, 2513
Looney JL, 348
LoPiccolo J, 2283, 2322, 2327, 2338, 2341, 2361, 2541
LoPiccolo L, 2283, 2541
Lorand S, 1107
Loranger AW, 862, 865
Lord C, 187, 204, 205, 207, 215, 268
Loriaux DL, 472
Loro A, 482, 537, 538, 542
Lothstein LM, 665
Lott IT, 31
Lotter V, 249, 253
Loucas KP, 2104
Loughman PM, 890
Louria DB, 1364
Lourie D, 2473
Lourie RS, 51, 564, 565, 568, 569, 570, 574, 575, 576, 581, 583, 589
Lovaas OI, 34, 35, 46, 48, 122, 194, 200, 202, 203, 218, 221, 223, 224, 225, 233, 253, 664, 665, 767
Lovell MR, 848, 849
Lovett-Doust JW, 1806
Lovibond SH, 720, 1097, 1126, 1130

Low AA, 2598, 2600
Lowe TL, 375, 707
Lowenthal DT, 2147
Lowery JB, 95
Lowy FH, 2147
Loyd DW, 1700, 1704
Lubar JF, 894
Luborsky L, 1193, 1421, 1422, 1423,
    1424, 1425, 1426, 1428, 1429,
    1430, 1732, 1814, 1815, 1816, 1821,
    1882, 1883, 1884, 2642, 2668,
    2768
Lucas AR, 455, 460, 487, 509, 543
Luchins D, 2422
Luchins DJ, 850, 902, 2479
Ludwig AM, 1075, 2202
Luisada P, 1214
Luisada PV, 2728
Luke JL, 1328
Lukianowicz N, 642, 2255
Lukton R, 2527
Lund N, 342
Lundahl W, 2513
Lundberg PO, 2318, 2392
Lundberg T, 2132
Lundell FW, 73, 92
Lunzer M, 936
Luria A, 342
Lustman PJ, 572, 577, 579, 2746
Luthe W, 2052, 2053
Lutz R, 2137
Lweitenberg H, 467
Lydiard RB, 1791
Lykouras E, 1787
Lynch DM, 80
Lyon R, 20
Lyons H, 2728

Maany I, 1341
Maas J, 2674
Maas JW, 1775, 1777
Maberg D, 1146
Mabry JH, 2142

Macalpine C, 583, 584
MacCallam WAG, 836
MacCulloch MJ, 629
MacDonald JD, 202, 215
Macdonald JE, 2166
Macdonald WB, 1808
MacGinitie W, 330
Machin D, 2132
MacHovec FJ, 2195
MacIntosh BA, 2560
Mack JE, 1104, 1154
Mackenzie TB, 905, 906, 1912, 1913
MacKinnon GL, 1305
MacKinnon R, 2759, 2760
MacKinnon RA, 845, 846, 997
Mackworth NH, 91
Maclay WS, 1811
MacLean G, 2560
MacLeod CM, 96
MacMillan DL, 125
MacMillian JF, 1551
MacNamara J, 209
MacPhillamy DJ, 1850
Madakasira S, 836
Madanes C, 1404, 1545, 1564
Madden R, 330
Maddox JF, 1344, 1345, 1348, 1442
Maddrey WC, 936
Maddux JF, 1186, 1236
Madison LS, 40, 42
Madsbad S, 938
Madsen CH, 378
Magers BD, 1838, 1840
Magliozzi JR, 1675
Magni G, 2347
Magnus RV, 2353
Maguire GP, 1900
Magulesparen M, 2393
Mahaffey KR, 52
Maher BA, 1202
Mahler M, 1105, 1524, 1953
Mahler MS, 409, 556, 700, 2012, 2644,
    2645
Mahoney DT, 719
Mahoney K, 532, 533, 537, 538

Mahoney M, 2539
Mahoney MJ, 482, 485, 488, 532, 533, 537, 538, 1154, 2340
Maier HW, 1222, 1231, 1232
Maisto CR, 45
Maj M, 1495, 1666
Malan D, 1422
Malan DH, 1874, 1878, 1879, 1880, 1883, 1884, 2343, 2640, 2668, 2669, 2677, 2710, 2734, 2740, 2768, 2778
Maletsky BM, 1284, 2043
Maletta GJ, 818
Maletzky BM, 672, 673, 850, 1083, 1127
Malimquist C, 1950
Malinow KL, 2675, 2767, 2784, 2785, 2787
Malitz S, 638, 1809
Mallams JH, 1159
Malliara-Loulakaki S, 836
Mallinger AE, 777
Mallinger AG, 1780
Mallinson WP, 2165
Malloy TR, 2330, 2332, 2334
Mally MA, 2169
Mallya G, 1752, 1754, 1755, 1758, 1759, 1929, 1935, 1939
Malm U, 1532, 1535, 1539, 1663
Malone M, 868
Maltbie AA, 1806
Maltsberger JT, 2676
Maltz P, 775
Malyon AK, 2128
Mamelak M, 2440
Mandel M, 1909
Mandel MR, 814, 829, 1662
Mandel W, 1075
Mandler JM, 337
Mangotich M, 1701
Mann DMA, 974
Mann ET, 1128
Mann HB, 2479
Mann J, 1732, 1874, 1877, 1878, 1880, 2734, 2752, 2778
Mann JJ, 867, 905
Mann SC, 1804
Mannino FV, 2481, 2482, 2483, 2609

Manuzza S, 375
Marantz SA, 666
Marc M, 2468
March CM, 2350
Marcotte DB, 1249
Marcus E, 2700
Marcus LC, 585
Marcus LM, 185, 253, 259, 262
Margolis J, 935
Margolis R, 2354
Margraf J, 2035
Marholin D, 73
Marholin D II, 568
Mark M, 1224
Mark VH, 21, 883
Markland C, 2386
Markowitz J, 1911, 1912
Marks I, 2029, 2146, 2535
Marks IM, 636, 639, 2022, 2027, 2028, 2030, 2031, 2032, 2034, 2081, 2099, 2101, 2143, 2322, 2338, 2341, 2761, 2762, 2780
Marks J, 2040
Marks JW, 587
Marks P, 451
Marlatt G, 467, 2135
Marlatt GA, 1237, 1238, 1255, 1271, 1276, 1280, 1282, 1436, 2030
Marlow N, 2657
Marlowe J, 1580
Marlowe RA, 142
Marmer SS, 2201
Marmor J, 485, 649, 2340, 2558, 2560, 2561, 2640
Marmor JMD, 647, 648, 672
Marohn RC, 386, 2459, 2460, 2461
Marquis JF, 947
Marsden CD, 818, 821, 865, 965
Marshall, 2076
Marshall A, 105
Marshall DS, 2285
Marshall JR, 895, 896, 897, 898, 899, 910, 916, 917, 919, 930, 931, 934, 935, 936, 937, 939, 2589
Marshall R, 2074
Marshall W, 2653

Marshall WL, 627, 1839, 1840
Martin A, 136
Martin C, 2372
Martin CE, 2265
Martin ED, 43, 52, 586
Martin G, 222
Martin HP, 62
Martin I, 2538
Martin JB, 943
Martin JC, 976
Martin JE, 133
Martin MF, 2198
Martin MJ, 1904, 1908, 1910
Martin PL, 22
Martin RJ, 939
Martin RL, 1765
Martin WR, 1310, 1312, 1313, 1322,
    1325, 1333, 1334, 1347, 1353
Martinez JL Jr, 977
Martyn MM, 345
Maruyama M, 1545
Marx JL, 1365
Marzillier JS, 2654, 2656, 2761
Mash E, 378
Masland RL, 147
Maslansky R, 1344
Maslow AH, 2593
Masm AS, 946
Masnik R, 1533
Mason E, 2514
Mason JW, 2498
Mason RW, 924
Mason WA, 45, 46
Massel HK, 1572, 1578
Masserman JH, 511
Massey SG, 917, 919
Massie HN, 1547
Massie MJ, 1905, 1906
Massimo JL, 386
Masters JC, 533
Masters WH, 2238, 2264, 2275, 2279,
    2280, 2281, 2285, 2290, 2297, 2298,
    2299, 2301, 2303, 2304, 2307, 2310,
    2311, 2312, 2315, 2319, 2321, 2322,
    2325, 2326, 2327, 2337, 2338, 2341,
    2363

Masterson J, 468, 2513, 2635, 2701,
    2738, 2739, 2751, 2757, 2758
Mastri AR, 819
Matarazzo JD, 1283
Mates TE, 263
Mather MD, 2099
Mathew RJ, 1285, 2199
Mathews A, 2360, 2393
Mathews AM, 2026, 2027, 2028, 2029,
    2030, 2032, 2033, 2099, 2339, 2341
Mathews SM, 1675
Mathis JL, 672, 673
Matson JL, 4, 7, 52, 105, 108, 138, 197,
    385
Mattes JA, 375, 379, 1787, 2476, 2479,
    2480, 2686
Matthews, 2749
Matthews CG, 95, 96
Matthews SM, 1530, 1535, 1537, 1543,
    1547, 1663, 1664
Mattson MR, 1766
Mattson RH, 888, 894
Matussek P, 1886
Maudal G, 2526
Maurer R, 367
Maurice WL, 1806, 2336
Mavissakalian M, 408, 475, 2032, 2033,
    2101
Mavromatis M, 2470
Maxmen JS, 1532, 1533, 1539
Maxwell JD, 937
May E, 1342
May J, 2514
May PRA, 1502, 1503, 1515, 1516,
    1518, 1534, 1535, 1574, 1659, 1922
May W, 946
Mayeda T, 144
Mayer-Gross W, 1614, 2146
Mayer SE, 967
Mayeux R, 860, 861, 862, 863, 865, 866
Mayo JP, 2164
Mayou R, 2140, 2147
Mazer H, 2701
Mazure CM, 1794, 1795, 1927
McAdoo WG, 249
McAllister TW, 821, 1807

McAndrew JB, 244
McArney ER, 452
McArthur JW, 479
McAuley R, 385
McAuliffe WE, 1202, 1313, 1315, 1327, 1437, 1442
McCabe OL, 1443
McCann BM, 28
McCarthy BW, 2338
McCarthy D, 189
McCarthy JJ, 1440, 1441
McCaul ME, 1324, 1439
McClain CJ, 935
McClellan AT, 1918
McClelland DC, 1095
McClelland H, 1666
McClelland HA, 863, 865, 866, 950, 951, 1628
McConaghy N, 641, 644
McConahey OL, 72
McConnell J, 2385
McConnell TR, 92
McConville B, 1954
McCord J, 1094
McCord W, 1094
McCormick RA, 2465
McCoy PL, 2583
McCoy S, 348
McCracken J, 904
McCrady BS, 1116, 1406
McCrum ED, 910
McCubbin H, 259, 2609, 2613, 2614
McCulloch DJ, 2336
McCullough CM, 330
McCullough LB, 999
McCurdy L, 1786, 2045
McDermott JF, 402
McDonald AC, 1839, 1840
McDonald LK, 1345
McDonald RJ, 972
McDowell FH, 861, 865, 869
McDowell JJ, 225
McElfresh O, 1120
McEvoy JP, 807, 808
McFall RM, 136, 1571
McFarlane AH, 590

McFarlane WR, 757, 1503, 1544, 1560, 1563, 1564
McGaugh JL, 976
McGee CS, 2614
McGee GG, 195, 268
McGeehan M, 1235
McGehee FT Jr, 582
McGill D, 1413
McGinnis CA, 1124
McGlashan GH, 2693
McGlashan T, 2758
McGlashan TH, 1501, 1516, 1518, 1531, 1548, 1675, 1702, 1705, 1706, 2644, 2645, 2690, 2691, 2692, 2695, 2701
McGlothlin W, 1443
McGlothlin WH, 858, 1184, 1185, 1330, 1345, 1349, 1350, 1441
McGoldrick M, 1412, 1413
McGovern GP, 942
McGovern L, 2336
McGovern PG, 1277
McGrath JC, 2386
McGrath P, 2471
McGrath PJ, 1797
McGraw RB, 2196
McGregor AM, 2393
McGuiness TP, 2055
McHale A, 720
McHale SM, 198, 199, 263
McHugh PR, 821, 919
McIntyre PM, 777
McKay AC, 945
McKeith IG, 974
McKellar A, 2219
McKenna GJ, 1248
McKhann G, 818, 965
McKinlay AP, 1065
McKinlay WW, 840
McKinley JC, 1844
McKinney WT, 1754
McKnew DH, 1950, 1951
McKnight DL, 1862
McKrensky M, 59
McLean JD, 2347
McLean JE, 202
McLean JM, 213

McLean LP, 213
McLean P, 1850, 1851, 1852, 1854, 1855, 1858, 1859
McLean PD, 1819, 1861, 1862, 1886
McLellan AT, 1071, 1183, 1185, 1187, 1232, 1315, 1324, 1326, 1327, 1329, 1331, 1344, 1358, 1418, 1420, 1433, 1444, 1445
McLemore C, 2761
McLeod C, 2028
McLeod WR, 1344
McMahon CD, 959
McMahon D, 670
McMahon PP, 2200, 2203
McMahon RJ, 385
McNamara E, 2681
McNamara ME, 835
McNamara PJ, 922
McNeil GN, 909
McNichol RW, 812
McNicholas LF, 1322
McNiel JN, 1689
McPherson FM, 2031
McReynolds LV, 315
McSweeney AJ, 639, 909, 912, 940, 943, 944, 947
Mead S, 664, 669
Meador A, 665
Meaes R, 2221
Meares R, 2219
Mecca RS, 1811
Mecklenburg M, 2369
Medical Research Council Clinical Psychiatry Committee, 1803
Medina JL, 871
Meecham MM, 344
Meehl PE, 2712, 2715
Meeks DE, 1116
Meeks JE, 789, 790, 2457, 2471
Meerman R, 502
Meichenbaum D, 378, 482, 1856, 2035, 2543, 2652, 2761
Meichenbaum DH, 112, 114
Meichenbaum N, 337
Meijer A, 769
Meineche CF, 2276, 2277

Meinecke CF, 629, 638, 645, 2356
Meisel A, 993
Meiselas KD, 234, 243
Meissner SJ, 750
Meissner WW, 1623, 1624, 2340, 2707
Melamed B, 2532, 2540
Melamed BG, 401, 404, 405, 564, 568, 577
Melisaratos N, 1075
Mellgren A, 2309
Mellinger GD, 2040
Mellman LA, 2104
Mello NK, 1069, 1070, 1156, 1284, 1325, 1437
Mellsop G, 2639
Melman A, 2385
Melmon KL, 928
Melson SJ, 2169
Melville C, 1663
Melzack R, 2131, 2132
Mendell D, 666
Mendels J, 1754, 1786, 2133
Mendelson G, 2136
Mendelson J, 1108
Mendelson JH, 1069, 1070, 1156, 1325, 1333
Mendelson WB, 2437
Mendelwicz J, 1669
Mendez MF, 839, 875
Mendlewicz J, 1761
Mengel CE, 585
Menking M, 569
Menninger K, 24, 2475
Menolascino FJ, 7, 10, 14, 15, 28, 54, 74, 75, 148, 568, 569
Menyuk P, 209
Mercer JR, 124
Mercer SO, 1001
Merrill DC, 2334
Merrill JP, 917
Merrill MA, 193, 330
Merry J, 1096, 1919
Merskey DM, 2651, 2655, 2696
Merskey H, 2121, 2122, 2123, 2124, 2126, 2129, 2136, 2140, 2154, 2157, 2165

Mishler EG, 1549
Misiaszek J, 1701
Miskimins RW, 1534
Mitchell DM, 2150
Mitchell HS, 60
Mitchell JE, 452, 453, 485, 517, 518,
    519, 520, 521, 523, 526, 527, 530,
    534, 538, 541, 543, 558, 581, 582,
    905, 906
Mitchell JR, 912, 928, 1777, 1783
Mitchell KR, 2150
Mitchell W, 637
Mithaug DE, 132, 138
Mitikainen N, 517, 520
Mitler MM, 2437
Mitsuda H, 1698
Miura S, 2481, 2482, 2483
Mizes JS, 525, 526, 527, 534, 543
Mizuno T, 38
Modell AH, 2648, 2693, 2739
Modell JG, 1682, 1704
Modlin RK, 907
Moe GK, 909, 910
Moffic HS, 1900
Mohler H, 1306
Mohr FW, 671
Mohr JW, 618, 620, 630
Mohr PD, 2159
Mohs RC, 966, 967, 970
Moldofsky H, 466, 469, 474, 707
Mollica RF, 995
Molloy JS, 63
Molnar D, 724
Money J, 635, 636, 644, 656, 662
Mong TH, 2442
Monk TH, 2441
Monks R, 2129
Monopolis S, 2475
Monroe RR, 1698, 1701, 1705, 2475,
    2476, 2478, 2773
Monroe SM, 1791, 1862
Montgomery J, 2675, 2769
Montgomery SA, 2101
Monti PM, 1534
Mooney HB, 1629, 1642, 1644
Mooney RP, 78

Moore CA, 2239
Moore DC, 1917
Moore DP, 809
Moore J, 2318
Moore JW, 72
Moore MT, 1806
Moore NC, 950
Moore R, 1108
Moorhead A, 341
Moorhead D, 341
Moos RH, 1111, 1285, 1885, 1886
Mooty J, 52
Mora G, 769
Moran EA, 882
Mordasini R, 453
Morel BA, 1487
Morey LC, 1067
Morgan AH, 1278
Morgan HG, 459, 492, 493, 882
Morgan MY, 936
Morgan SB, 191
Mori A, 138
Morokoff PJ, 2391
Morris JB, 1815
Morris JV, 92
Morris NE, 1838, 1839, 1840
Morris S, 58, 61, 63, 64
Morrison D, 470
Morrison G, 921, 922, 2471
Morrison RL, 1445
Morrison TL, 108
Morse RM, 805
Mortimer JA, 817, 862
Moser M, 913
Mosher L, 1535, 1537, 1560
Mosher LR, 1516, 1533, 1547, 1663,
    2725
Mosk MD, 1571
Moskovitz C, 833
Moskowitz JA, 2465
Mosnaim AD, 1800
Mosovich A, 2386
Moss GR, 2746
Moss H, 2765
Moss JW, 132, 137, 586, 587
Moss RL, 2351, 2352

Mostofsky DJ, 894
Mostyn J, 568, 570
Mouchka S, 143, 144
Mountjoy CQ, 974
Mowat RR, 1643
Mowrer OH, 2598, 2599
Mueller PS, 1892
Mueser KT, 1572
Muhaly R, 838
Mukherjee S, 1779, 1783, 1809
Mulhern T, 47
Mulick JA, 21, 25, 52, 54
Mullaley W, 837
Muller JC, 1898
Mulvery CH, 2766
Mulvey CH, 2767, 2768
Muma J, 340
Munby M, 2029, 2031
Munday L, 108
Munford AM, 1535
Munford PR, 2158
Munich RL, 1492
Muniz CE, 1919
Munjack D, 2341
Munjack DJ, 2256, 2305, 2313, 2316
Munoz RA, 1707
Muñoz RF, 1838, 1840
Munro, 1898
Munro A, 839, 1689, 2146
Munroe RH, 635
Munroe RL, 635
Murdoch RP, 1127
Murphy CV, 2319
Murphy DL, 1785, 2101, 2685, 2780
Murphy GE, 1801, 1820, 1839, 1841
Murphy GH, 212
Murphy HA, 378, 385, 388
Murphy HBM, 1148
Murphy ME, 379
Murray ME, 578
Musisi SM, 1917
Musselwhite CR, 203
Musto DF, 1342
Myerhoff B, 995
Myers J, 1104
Myers JK, 1918, 1942

Myerson AT, 2188, 2193, 2194, 2195
Mykelbust HR, 317, 332, 333
Mykleburst HR, 951
Myrick RD, 664

Nadel I, 914
Nadelson C, 2367, 2368
Nadelson T, 2162
Nagera H, 2514, 2777
Nagler S, 636, 638
Nakada T, 818
Nally M, 2537
Napoli-Farris L, 2350
Nardini JE, 94
Naruse H, 242
Nash JD, 1276
Nasrallah HA, 1631
Nathan PE, 1069, 1070
Nathan SG, 2342
Nathanson MH, 1220
Nation JE, 313, 315
National Cancer Institute, 1272
National Center for Health Statistics, 718, 720
National Commission for the Protection of Human Subjects of Biomedical and Behavioral Research, 1896, 1897, 1986, 2133
National Commission on Marihuana and Drug Abuse, 1219
National Council on Alcoholism, 1112
National Institute of Mental Health, 1579
National Institute on Aging (Task Force), 823, 996
National Institute on Drug Abuse, 1210, 1212, 1309, 1344, 1398
CODAP, 1383
National Household Survey, 1225
National Institutes of Health Consensus Development Conference, 379
National Research Council, 1322

National Research Council on Clinical
　　Evaluation of Narcotic
　　Antagonists, 1355
National Safety Council, 846
Naughton JM, 213
Nausieda PA, 864
Naylor GJ, 78
Nee LE, 705
Needleman HL, 473
Neff KE, 810, 814
Negrete JC, 1066
Neil JF, 585, 1760, 1927
Nelson A, 1776, 1778, 1779, 1783
Nelson JC, 902, 1790, 1794, 1795, 1927
Nelson K, 212, 2370
Nelson RO, 1844
Nelson WE, 53
Nemec PB, 1533, 1543, 1563
Nemeroff CB, 1910
Nemiah JC, 563, 760, 2024, 2151, 2190,
　　2198, 2223, 2226, 2471, 2773
Nemiroff FA, 2645
Nemiroff R, 2371
Nemiroff RA, 2647
Neppe VM, 2476
Nesbitt J, 2169
Neshkes RE, 827, 902, 946
Nettelbladt P, 2318, 2355
Neubauer P, 2590
Neuberger OW, 1127
Neubuerger OW, 1438
Neuchterlein KH, 1530
Neuman M, 2256
Neumann C, 1108
Neville J, 2193, 2194, 2195, 2196
Nevins MA, 1366
New York County Health Services
　　Review Organization, 1769, 1772
Newberger E, 736
Newcomb RD, 958
Newcomer PL, 208, 330
Newcomer RB, 108
Newell FW, 952
Newman B, 904
Newman G, 2372
Newman HF, 2299, 2385

Newman LE, 641, 668
Newman RG, 1343, 1344
Newton R, 904
Ney PG, 215
Ng LKY, 2124, 2136
Nicholi AM, 789, 2340
Nichols C, 2372
Nickel JC, 2270
Nickerson M, 944
NIDA. *See* National Institute on Drug
　　Abuse
Nielsen AC, 1900
Nielsen H, 977
Nieman GW, 372, 1936
Nies A, 1779, 2685
Nies AS, 928
NIH. *See* National Institutes of Health
Nikolovski OT, 836
Nininger JE, 2347
Ninio A, 299
Nitzkin JL, 2159
Nocturnal Oxygen Therapy Trial
　　Group, 940
Noel NE, 1406
Nolan BT, 1913
Nolen WA, 95
Nolke AC, 943
Norberg A, 1003
Nordquist VM, 47
Norell H, 944
Norgaard JP, 719
Norman A, 769
Norman DK, 542
Norris JL, 1152, 1154, 1157, 1159
Norton GR, 2336
Norton JP, 1551
Norton SG, 2167
Noshpitz JD, 779, 2692
Notman M, 2367, 2368
Nott PM, 821
Novaco RW, 1856, 2655
Novick D, 938
Nowinski J, 2541
Nowlin NS, 492
Noy P, 2319
Noyes JH, 2312

Noyes R, 88, 2050
Noyes R Jr, 2145, 2152, 2221
Nuebuerger OW, 1097
Nuechterlein KH, 1548, 1570, 2131, 2150
Nuffield EJ, 105, 108
Nuland W, 1277, 1278
Nuller YL, 2221
Nunes JS, 2099
Nunn RG, 224, 702
Nurco D, 1396
Nurco DN, 1330
Nurcombe B, 2469
Nyhan WL, 37, 38
Nyswander ME, 1313, 1323, 1342, 1350

Oakley WF, 927
Ober RR, 1366
O'Brien CP, 1310, 1333, 1334, 1338, 1354, 1438, 1532, 1534, 1537, 1538, 1543
O'Brien F, 44
O'Brien GE, 1326
O'Brien JE, 1087
O'Brien KM, 2319
O'Brien LS, 890
Ochitill H, 2122, 2154, 2165, 2166
Ochs E, 340
Ochs HR, 922, 1285
Ochsner, 585
Ockene JK, 1265, 1266, 1278
O'Connor JF, 2337
O'Connor S, 746
O'Connor TW, 2347, 2348
Oddy M, 847
Odell WH, 943
Odgen T, 1528
Odom SI, 2615
O'Donnell DJ, 384, 387
O'Donnell JA, 1244
O'Donnell JM, 2143
O'Donnell T, 2590
O'Farrell TJ, 1120, 1285, 1286

Offenkrantz W, 1824, 1825, 2643, 2733, 2768
Offer D, 784, 2460
Offer JB, 784
Offit AK, 2254, 2259
Ogborne AC, 1153, 1157
Ogg HL, 58
Ogle PA, 254, 255, 256, 263
O'Gorman P, 2613
Ogren SO, 1778
Ogston WD, 2169
Oguchi T, 2481, 2482, 2483
Okada T, 1306
Okasha A, 2130
Okazaki H, 941
Okuma T, 1931
Olarte SW, 1533
Oldham JM, 843, 1539
O'Leary KD, 117, 378, 379, 385, 2025, 2028, 2032, 2036, 2663
O'Leary MR, 1067, 1153
O'Leary R, 1065
O'Leary SG, 665
Oliver AP, 839
Oliver JF, 2196
Oliveras JC, 977
Ollendick DG, 15, 19
Ollendick TH, 15, 19, 665, 2652
Oller-Daurella L, 888
Oller DK, 215
Olley JG, 198
Olmstead E, 2426, 2427
Olsen RW, 1307
Olsen S, 926
Olson DH, 494
Olson E, 1361
Olynyk F, 583, 584
Onal E, 2434
O'Neal P, 2154
O'Neill PJ, 215
Opjoerdsmoen S, 1618
Opjordsmoen S, 1615, 1617, 1626
Oppel WC, 718
Oppenheimer E, 1328, 1331
Ordman AM, 534, 550, 551, 552
O'Regan JB, 2104

Orensteen AC, 1154, 1156, 1158
Orford J, 1068, 1075
Oritz A, 904
Orko R, 950
Orleans CS, 537, 542
Orleans CT, 482, 538
Ormont L, 2677
Orne EC, 2059, 2060
Orne MT, 2009, 2053, 2054, 2055, 2197, 2199, 2205, 2207, 2208
Ornstein A, 2468
Orrego H, 1077
Orsulak PJ, 1780
Orth MH, 2660
Orton S, 297
Ortony A, 336
Osborn CA, 2387
Osherson A, 2201
Osmond H, 327
Ost L, 2029, 2150
Oster RA, 2615
Osterman PO, 2318
Osterweis M, 2586
Ostow M, 2225
O'Sullivan M, 2525
Otis GD, 1565
Ottens AJ, 2481, 2484
Otter H, 1285
Ottesen B, 2352, 2353
Otteson JP, 1532, 1534
Ottosson JO, 1810, 1812
Ounsted C, 97, 744, 881
Overall JE, 1920
Oversey L, 638, 642, 644, 657
Ovesey L, 2253
Owen RT, 1305, 2043
Owens WA, 800
Oziel LJ, 2305, 2313, 2316

Pacific Crest Outward Bound School, 2749
Paden EP, 344
Padfield PL, 910

Padilla-Borjes E, 670
Page CW, 1121, 1124
Page TJ, 50, 51
Pagle S, 20
Paglietti E, 2350
Painter J, 2135
Palfrey JS, 348
Palij M, 182, 185, 228, 229, 244
Palmer S, 59, 60, 61, 62, 63, 64, 65
Palmer TB, 386
Palmon N, 2540
Palmore E, 803
Paluck RJ, 22
Paluzny M, 255
Pancoast DL, 2614
Pancsofar E, 132
Pandey GH, 1812
Pandit SK, 945
Panepinto W, 1119
Pangborn RM, 583
Panksepp J, 234, 238, 248, 574
Pantuck EJ, 1285
Pao P-N, 1519
Paolino TJ, 1116
Papajohn JC, 2658
Papp P, 1410
Parad H, 2520, 2521
Parad HJ, 1559
Parad L, 2520
Parfitt DN, 2193
Parikh MD, 2218
Parikh RM, 1911
Paris JJ, 1004
Parish RA, 947
Park CC, 273
Park S, 2076
Parker G, 1892
Parker R, 263
Parker WA, 1305
Parkes JD, 936, 2421, 2422, 2424
Parks SL, 185
Parloff MB, 1123, 1535, 1730, 1732, 1814, 1815, 1822, 2668, 2674
Parnas J, 882, 1497
Parras A, 1532
Parsons B, 2665

Parsons BV, 385, 2746
Parsons OA, 1092
Parsons RD, 777
Partington MW, 246
Pasamanick B, 94
Patel MM, 946
Pato MT, 2102
Patrick GM, 1159
Patterson CR, 382
Patterson GR, 22, 23, 25, 384, 385, 389, 774
Patterson JH, 338
Patterson JW, 938
Patterson P, 2159
Patterson RD, 800
Patterson V, 2525
Pattison EM, 1075, 1084, 1103, 1112, 1116, 1117, 1119, 1120, 1123, 1132, 1413, 1414, 1533
Patton D, 1820
Patton MQ, 1156
Paul GL, 1535, 1576, 1577, 1578, 2725
Paul L, 2525
Paul SM, 1804
Paulak A, 630
Pauleikhoff B, 1698
Pauling L, 241
Pauls DL, 690, 691, 696
Paulsen GW, 2318
Paulson GW, 244
Pavlov EP, 54
Pawl RP, 2132
Paykel E, 908, 911, 912
Paykel ES, 1767, 1768, 1792, 1865, 1870, 1885, 1900, 1942
PDR. See Physician's Desk Reference
Peachy R, 1304
Peacock EP, 1534
Pearce I, 863
Pearce JK, 1413
Pearce JMS, 863
Pearlin L, 2072
Pearlin LI, 1865
Pechacek TF, 1277
Peck BB, 780
Peck CA, 195

Peck S, 2593, 2595
Peckham C, 720
Pecknold JC, 2050
Pederson J, 1555, 1576
Pederson LL, 1272
Pekala RJ, 1532, 1539, 1542
Pelham WE, 373, 374, 378, 379, 385, 388
Pellegrini AJ, 1700
Pellegrini DS, 378, 379, 385
Pellerin D, 2468
Pelletier LL Jr, 896
Pendagast EF, 1403
Pendergrass VE, 47
Pendery ML, 1097
Pendry ML, 1075
Penick E, 1065, 1066, 1069, 1104
Penn JR, 1912
Penton KW, 914
Pepper B, 1538
Perkins KA, 1921
Perkins ME, 1344
Perl M, 991, 996
Perlas AP, 1904
Perley MJ, 2167, 2170
Perrault R, 2336
Perret JT, 1158
Perris C, 1699, 1706, 1708, 1709, 1711, 1758
Perry A, 1813
Perry EK, 968, 978
Perry J, 2281
Perry JC, 777, 1700, 2651, 2656, 2658, 2690, 2745, 2754, 2764, 2765, 2766, 2784, 2785, 2786, 2787
Perry MA, 105
Perry MC, 584
Perry PJ, 1674
Perry R, 234, 237, 244
Perry SW, 1911, 1912
Persky H, 2350, 2389, 2390
Person E, 644, 2743, 2745
Person ES, 638, 642, 657, 667
Personage M, 888
Pertschuk MJ, 457, 458
Perucca E, 892

Pervin LA, 2335
Peselow ED, 1927, 1934
Petchkovsky L, 1370
Peterfreund E, 1825
Peters KG, 367
Petersdorf RG, 869, 896
Petersen-Kelley A, 1161
Peterson AL, 701, 702
Peterson C, 969, 971, 973
Peterson GA, 105
Peterson GL, 22
Peterson R, 945
Peterson RA, 720
Peterson RC, 1285
Petrie WM, 826, 908, 975, 976, 1231, 1237
Petti TA, 239, 407, 408, 427, 2682
Pettinati HM, 1809
Petty F, 1899
Petursson H, 1709, 2043
Pevnick JS, 1305
Peyser HS, 1133
Pfafflin F, 2256
Pfeffer CR, 2473
Pfeiffer E, 2266, 2372
Pfenning M, 1775, 1776, 1777
Pfohl B, 1493, 2639
Pfohl D, 1340
Phelps G, 2313
Philips I, 10, 15
Phillips I, 1951, 1952
Phillips S, 2369
Physician's Desk Reference, 232
Piafsky KM, 922, 923
Piaget J, 340, 341, 464
Pichot P, 1620, 1621
Pickar D, 248
Pickens RW, 1919
Pierloot R, 460, 461, 471, 492
Pierson PS, 1356
Pietrotesa JJ, 254
Pigache RM, 976
Pilkington TL, 82
Pilkonis P, 2761
Pilkonis PA, 2668, 2759
Pillay M, 477

Pilowsky I, 1767, 2126, 2127, 2128, 2129, 2139, 2140, 2145
Pincus JH, 886, 982
Pincus LH, 942
Pinderhughes C, 2381
Pine F, 752, 1691, 2367, 2368
Pinel P, 1487
Pines M, 2673
Pinessi L, 974
Pinsky JJ, 2122, 2128, 2136
Piorkowsky GK, 1128
Pious WL, 1521
Piper WE, 2640
Piran N, 1917
Pitman J, 335
Pittendrigh CS, 1895
Pitts F, 903, 2095, 2097
Pitts FN, 1810
Pitts FN Jr, 1215
Pizzo PA, 944
Placidi GF, 1931, 1932
Platman SR, 1548, 1800
Platt JE, 387
Platt JJ, 1444, 1445, 2784, 2785, 2786, 2788
Pleasure H, 944
Pleuvry BJ, 945
Plotkin DA, 828, 829
Plum F, 871, 940, 943, 965, 1809
Plumb MM, 1904, 1905
Plummer S, 222
Pochedly C, 944
Poe RO, 1701
Pohorecky LA, 1202
Pokorny A, 1063, 1912
Pokorny AD, 1123, 1124
Polakow RL, 1443
Polatajko HJ, 327
Poleck DG, 846
Polich JM, 1067, 1075, 1157
Polinsky RJ, 697
Polivy J, 538
Polizos P, 243, 244
Pollack MH, 1788, 1790, 1792, 1797
Pollack RH, 2387
Pollitt E, 736, 740
Pollock G, 2508, 2517

Pollock GH, 2642, 2645, 2646, 2647
Pollock W, 2635
Polotsek I, 105
Pomeranz J, 1908
Pomerleau CS, 532, 1265
Pomerleau OF, 532, 1130, 1265
Pompeius R, 719
Pond DA, 881, 882, 2122
Pond SM, 1919
Pontalis J, 2641
Pool D, 234
Pope, 577
Pope HG, 520, 521, 525, 530, 567,
    1495, 1496, 1497, 1499, 1752, 1762,
    1917, 1918, 2166, 2636, 2685
Pope HG Jr, 893, 2468
Popham RE, 1075
Porrino L, 367, 374
Port FK, 927
Porter K, 2677, 2734
Porter R, 950, 2525, 2528
Portin R, 862, 864
Portnoy RA, 946
Portnoy S, 1812
Porto R, 2353
Posner JB, 871, 940, 943
Post F, 951, 1641, 1666, 1764, 1927, 2104
Post RM, 833, 876, 882, 1232, 1370,
    1739, 1931
Postma JU, 833, 924
Pototsky C, 723
Pottash ALC, 1361, 1364
Pottenger M, 1918, 1919
Potter HW, 14
Potter WZ, 924
Poussaint A, 2381
Poussaint AF, 719
Powell B, 1073
Powell G, 637
Powell JR, 947
Powell SF, 913, 914, 915
Powell TH, 254, 255, 256, 263
Power SF, 1781
Powers HP, 470
Powers MD, 190, 197
Powers PS, 470

Powles WE, 1532
Poznanski E, 311
Poznanski EO, 1763, 1951, 1953, 1954
Prader A, 50
Prange AJ, 1794
Prange AJ Jr, 1794, 1795
Prange AL Jr, 240
Prasad A, 2104
Prasad AS, 585
Pray BJ, 914
Premack AJ, 213
Premack D, 63, 64, 213, 219
Prentkey R, 627
President's Commission for the Study
    of Ethical Problems in Medicine
    and Biomedical and Behavioral
    Research, 1003
President's Commission on Mental
    Health, 2596, 2605, 2609
Preskorn SH, 408, 836, 1375
Presley AS, 2763
Presthus J, 1912
Price DL, 31, 968
Price J, 2201
Price LH, 1793, 1794, 1795, 1797, 2102
Price RA, 375, 690
Price SL, 1779, 1783, 1811, 1812
Price TR, 875
Prien RF, 1508, 1673, 1786, 1929
Priest PN, 1344
Prigatano GP, 940
Prima A, 2150
Prince V, 637, 640, 641
Printz A, 783
Pritchard PB, 836
Prizant B, 204, 215, 216
Prochaska JO, 1271
Proctor JT, 2154
Protass LM, 873
Prout MF, 2784, 2785, 2786, 2788
Pruett KD, 665
Prugh DG, 724
Pruitt AA, 896
Prusoff B, 1185
Prusoff BA, 1820, 1870, 1922
Prutting C, 340

Prutting CA, 207
Pruyser PW, 1493
Psychiatric Annals, 2572
Psychopharmacology Bulletin, 240, 244
Pucci E, 2352
Pudney H, 1629
Pueschel SM, 581
Pugh CR, 908
Pugh DD, 1787
Puig-Antich J, 383, 387, 408, 1763,
    1951, 1957, 1958
Puletti F, 865
Pulver SE, 1691
Pumpian-Mindlin E, 2515
Purcell JJ, 1920, 1922
Purtell JJ, 2281, 2336
Purvis SA, 1534
Pustrom E, 764
Putman P, 1700
Putnam FW, 2197, 2198, 2199, 2200,
    2203, 2213
Puzantian VR, 1763
Puzynski S, 1932
Pyle RL, 492, 537, 545

Quail M, 1912
Quay HC, 115, 369, 386
Quill K, 209
Quill TE, 2169
Quinn D, 834
Quinsey VL, 628, 632
Quitkin F, 1628, 1704
Quitkin FM, 570, 1788, 1789, 1795,
    1929, 2685, 2703
Quy RJ, 894

Rabach J, 2275
Rabin AS, 1862
Rabins PV, 805, 863, 864, 962, 1002
Rabkin JG, 905, 1797, 1907, 1908, 2022

Rabkin R, 1559
Raboch J, 2255
Racamier PC, 1761
Rachelefsky GS, 1781
Rachman S, 112, 114, 639, 2026, 2028,
    2033, 2541, 2780
Rachman SJ, 2095, 2096, 2099
Rada RR, 1070
Rada RT, 826
Radcinowicz L, 632
Radinsky AM, 36
Radloff LS, 1849
Rado S, 1827, 2255, 2264, 2712, 2722,
    2731, 2759, 2771
Rafal RD, 862, 865
Ragen FA, 1701
Ragheb M, 927
Rahe R, 2583
Rahe RH, 2500
Rahim S, 2655
Rainer D, 2641
Rainer JD, 950, 1761
Rajput AH, 862
Rako S, 2701
Ralph DD, 914
Ramani V, 1701
Ramer JC, 462
Ramey CT, 126
Ramirez AL, 1779, 1783
Rampling D, 915
Ramsey P, 998
Ramsey TA, 925, 927
Rangell L, 700, 2024
Rank O, 1874
Rankin GO, 928
Rankin JJ, 1131
Ranson FG, 958
Rao AV, 1754, 1806
Rao S, 945
Rapaport D, 1522
Raphael B, 2143
Rapoport JL, 91, 180, 366, 367, 368,
    369, 372, 373, 374, 375, 376, 377,
    380, 381, 382, 387, 389, 402, 407,
    723, 726, 2423
Rapoport L, 2521, 2523, 2525, 2526

Rappolt TR, 838
Raskin D, 1809
Raskin M, 2034, 2054
Raskin NH, 912
Raskin NN, 1355
Raskind M, 829, 903, 1641, 1783, 1908
Raskind MA, 974
Rasmussen SA, 2097, 2103
Rast J, 54, 55, 565, 568, 578
Rastegar A, 1630
Ratey JJ, 88, 2686
Ratey JS, 851
Rathod NH, 1124
Ratusnik CM, 213
Ratusnik DL, 213
Ratzan RM, 1005, 1006, 1008
Rau JH, 528, 529, 539
Rauch PK, 913
Rauckman EJ, 1225
Rausch JL, 904, 1779, 1782
Rawson M, 335
Rawson R, 1236, 1239
Rawson RA, 1240
Ray I, 944
Razani J, 1354
Rea WS, 1369
Read AE, 935
Read SL, 819, 872
Reagan TJ, 941
Realmuto GM, 234
Rearden FE, 1004
Rebec GV, 838
Reches A, 866
Records MA, 316
Reder LM, 337
Redick RW, 802
Reding M, 977
Reding MJ, 975
Redl F, 2460
Redlich F, 995
Redmond A, 721
Redmond DE, 405, 406, 407, 408, 474
Redmond DE Jr, 1311, 2071
Reed CF, 764
Reed J, 2199, 2216
Rees I, 1806, 1807, 1808, 1809

Regan M, 1912
Regestein QR, 2426
Reginaldi D, 1928
Rehm L, 2539
Rehm LP, 1834, 1846, 1857, 1859, 1861, 1862
Rehm OP, 1857, 1859
Reich J, 1902, 2121
Reich P, 2161, 2162, 2163, 2426
Reich W, 773, 2634, 2640, 2648, 2784, 2785, 2786, 2787
Reich WT, 1007
Reichard S, 2729
Reichert WH, 977
Reichler RJ, 185, 193, 197, 233, 251, 253, 254
Reichman F, 1952
Reid AH, 5, 6, 7, 10, 28, 78
Reid DH, 200
Reid DK, 338
Reid JL, 928
Reid WH, 2674, 2743, 2747, 2749
Reidenberg MM, 2147
Reifler BV, 821, 827
Reilly TM, 839
Reimann F, 580, 581
Reimann IW, 927
Reiner MA, 909
Reinhardt L, 2137
Reinking RH, 2150
Reisberg B, 823, 926, 965, 966, 970, 972, 973, 977, 990
Reisner H, 1087, 1091
Reiss AL, 41
Reiss D, 1544
Reiss M, 240
Reiss S, 10, 11, 24, 109
Reith M, 1221
Rekers GA, 664, 665, 669
Relman A, 1243
Remick R, 1911
Remick RA, 908, 1806
Remmel M, 2520, 2523, 2525
Remvig J, 950, 951
Renick R, 1237
Renik O, 2020

Renik P, 2219
Renshaw DC, 876, 2301, 2309, 2310, 2328
Renton KW, 947
Renuart, 568
Renzaglia A, 138
Repp AC, 25, 45, 48
Resnick E, 1237
Resnick EB, 833
Resnick M, 810
Resnick RB, 833, 1322, 1334, 1418
Resnick RG, 1319
Retterstol N, 1610, 1613, 1615, 1617, 1618, 1647, 1648, 1678
Reuler JB, 818, 826
Reveley A, 836
Revell AD, 1285
Reyes FJ, 2355
Reynolds BS, 2319, 2337
Reynolds CF, 2448, 2449
Reynolds EH, 96
Reynolds GS, 121
Reynolds I, 1580
Reynolds JR, 2153
Reynolds RD, 585, 588
Reyntjens AM, 2679
Rhead C, 2017
Rhoads FA, 39
Rhoads JM, 670, 673
Rhodes JM, 2022
Rice KM, 2034
Rich CL, 529
Richardson D, 2132, 2133
Richardson F, 2539
Richardson JS, 248
Richardson JW, 1780, 1810
Richardson SA, 16
Richelson E, 904, 1775, 1776, 1777, 1778, 1779, 1780, 1781, 1783, 1784, 2130
Richens A, 892
Richet G, 920
Richman A, 1184
Richmond J, 53
Richmond JB, 564, 566, 569, 570, 574, 576, 723

Richter CP, 582
Richter NC, 405
Richter RW, 1366
Rick GR, 2746
Rickels K, 407, 1373, 1798, 2043, 2055, 2152, 2587
Rickels WH, 2047
Rickets K, 2588
Rickles NK, 671
Ricuarte GA, 1230
Riddle MA, 691, 696, 706
Riding J, 839, 2146
Rie H, 1950, 1951, 1955
Riederer P, 862
Rieger W, 475, 476
Rierdan J, 2516
Ries H, 2201
Ries RK, 1784, 1805
Riess D, 494, 496
Riessman F, 2609
Rifkin A, 1514, 1928, 2479, 2684
Rigter H, 976
Riguet CB, 109
Riko K, 957
Riley DM, 1707
Riley J, 22
Rimland B, 185, 186, 241, 243, 379
Rimm DC, 533
Rimmer J, 1065
Rinck C, 86, 89
Rincover A, 219, 220, 222, 224
Ringelheim D, 105
Rinsley D, 2635, 2692, 2701, 2738, 2739, 2757
Rioch MJ, 2667
Riordan MM, 64
Riotte K, 909
Rioux B, 1694
Risch SC, 905, 906, 907, 913
Riskin J, 1549
Risley TR, 46, 202
Ritvo E, 2469
Ritvo ER, 228, 230, 232, 235, 236, 245, 246, 250, 256
Rivinus TM, 88
Ro-Trock G, 1547

Robb RM, 952
Robbins DM, 384
Robbins E, 2469
Robbins FP, 2642, 2643, 2644, 2645
Robbins L, 2469
Robboy MS, 453
Roberts A, 2137
Roberts AH, 810
Roberts B, 737
Roberts E, 964
Roberts J, 2146
Roberts JR, 1224
Roberts P, 240
Roberts R, 1810, 2146
Roberts W, 2541
Robertson EE, 884
Robin AA, 1735
Robins C, 2036
Robins E, 2154
Robins LE, 818
Robins LN, 365, 368, 401, 773, 1069,
    1312, 1331, 1942, 2007, 2097, 2743
Robinson BA, 724
Robinson C, 2380
Robinson D, 1152, 1154, 1157, 1159
Robinson DS, 905, 1785, 1786, 2736
Robinson GE, 1707, 1708
Robinson GM, 1088, 1089
Robinson HM, 104, 330
Robinson N, 104
Robinson RG, 848, 854, 875, 1780,
    1796, 1911
Robson KM, 736
Rochley GJ, 1689
Rockely GJ, 1690
Rockley GJ, 1688
Rockwell WJ, 2558
Rodin EA, 881, 886, 887
Rodin GM, 1900
Rodin L, 1280
Rodnick EH, 1545, 1548, 1549
Rodriguez-Perez JF, 2714
Roffe MW, 2256
Rogers CR, 108, 1516, 1658
Rogers ES, 105
Rogers RC, 39, 40

Rogers RM, 940
Rogers-Warren A, 136
Roiphe H, 666
Rollings JP, 7, 33, 49, 121
Rolls BR, 582
Rolstein S, 249
Roman PM, 1146, 1153
Romano J, 2121, 2129
Romney DM, 945
Ron MA, 821, 965
Rondot P, 863, 865
Rooney JF, 1160
Roos BE, 974
Roose SP, 902, 1781, 1782, 1783, 1785,
    1795, 1907, 2254
Rooth G, 671, 673
Roouse BA, 1097
Rose JC, 510
Rose RM, 1752
Rosen A, 1159
Rosen AJ, 1577
Rosen AM, 810, 814, 1215
Rosen BK, 1693
Rosen EJ, 1412
Rosen GM, 1856
Rosen J, 467, 525, 526, 532, 538, 543,
    552
Rosen LW, 2653
Rosen M, 702
Rosen RC, 643, 644, 2385
Rosen WG, 820, 961
Rosen ZA, 2712, 2713
Rosenbaum AH, 2315
Rosenbaum JF, 1788, 1790, 1792, 1797,
    1800, 2682
Rosenbaum M, 1845, 2199, 2216, 2540
Rosenberg JB, 770
Rosenberg L, 1264
Rosenberg M, 298, 300, 558
Rosenberg S, 2148
Rosenberg SA, 944
Rosenblatt R, 2129
Rosenfeld H, 1526, 2713
Rosenheim E, 2256, 2765
Rosenthal A, 2517
Rosenthal AJ, 2558

Rosenthal D, 1690
Rosenthal MS, 1395
Rosenthal NE, 1496, 1668, 1740, 1891,
    1892, 1893, 1894
Rosenthal T, 2027
Rosett H, 1071
Rosner F, 587
Ross AO, 122
Ross DM, 373, 378
Ross DR, 1784
Ross ED, 835, 875, 951
Ross H, 821
Ross MW, 1693
Ross RT, 21, 54
Ross SA, 373, 378
Ross SM, 1444
Rossor MN, 977, 978
Rotegard LL, 144
Roth BE, 2670, 2676
Roth BF, 2725
Roth D, 1764, 1820, 1859
Roth LH, 984, 993, 998
Roth LS, 984, 985
Roth M, 865, 950, 951, 1615, 1629,
    1640, 1666, 2104, 2218, 2219, 2221
Roth T, 945
Rothman DJ, 1006
Rothman R, 110
Rothroth D, 2370
Rothstein A, 778
Rotondo D, 580
Rotunno M, 1412
Roughan PA, 2286
Roukema RW, 241
Rounsaville BJ, 1069, 1070, 1071, 1183,
    1184, 1185, 1186, 1187, 1189, 1191,
    1232, 1238, 1257, 1313, 1314, 1327,
    1329, 1330, 1331, 1369, 1417, 1418,
    1420, 1422, 1430, 1791, 1816, 1868,
    1869, 1871, 1885, 1920, 1921, 1942
Rovner BW, 1002
Rowan AJ, 873
Rowbotham M, 1237
Rowe B, 746
Rowe JW, 925
Rowen R, 2481, 2485

Rowland DI, 2391
Roy A, 2336
Roy-Bryne P, 538
Roy-Byrne PP, 850
Royers FL, 2469, 2471
Rubin A, 2319
Rubin HB, 2385
Rubin SE, 1070
Rubin V, 1252
Ruchs CZ, 1859
Ruckebusch Y, 574
Rudel RG, 326
Rudy DR, 1157
Ruhback G, 2592
Rumans LW, 2161, 2162
Rumbaugh CL, 1225
Rumelhart DE, 336
Rund DA, 1148
Rundles RW, 2319
Rusak B, 1895
Rusch FR, 52, 132, 134, 136, 137, 138
Rush A, 2130
Rush AJ, 550, 551, 552, 961, 1675,
    1731, 1732, 1816, 1818, 1821, 1822,
    1834, 1836, 1838, 1839, 1840, 1841,
    1842, 1843, 1846, 1847, 2734
Russakoff LM, 1539
Russell AT, 20
Russell GFM, 451, 456, 459, 487, 492,
    508, 517, 537, 538, 540, 543, 544,
    548
Russell LM, 265
Russell PL, 2021, 2024
Russell R, 2534
Russo AM, 2464
Rutan JS, 2669, 2677
Rutenfranz J, 2441
Ruth DD, 810
Rutherford G, 45
Rutrick D, 2127, 2128
Ruttenberg AJ, 1328
Ruttenberg BA, 186
Rutter GR, 382
Rutter M, 1550, 1864, 2498
Rutter ML, 4, 20, 115, 180, 182, 184,
    194, 195, 197, 198, 203, 215, 243,

249, 253, 256, 257, 268, 298, 299,
347, 365, 366, 367, 369, 371, 379,
382, 384, 385, 386, 388, 724, 735
Rutter MLL, 718, 720
Rybash JM, 1000

S

Sabelli HC, 1800
Sabine EJ, 530
Sachar EJ, 240
Sachs DA, 47
Sachs RG, 2201
Sachs V, 2521
Sack WH, 665
Sackeim HA, 814, 1809, 1813
Sackin HD, 665
Sacks O, 109
Sacks OW, 863
Sacks S, 587
Sadeh M, 862
Sadock VA, 2223, 2225
Sadoff RL, 2769
Saenger G, 1123, 1445
Safer D, 375
Safer DJ, 967, 968
Safford P, 348
Safran J, 2761
Sager CJ, 2246, 2336, 2340, 2341
Sagherian AA, 1920, 1921, 1922
Sahakian BJ, 967
Sahley TL, 234, 248
Saigh PA, 2081
Sainsbury P, 1547
Sajwaj T, 54, 122, 568, 578
Sakheim DK, 2320
Salber EJ, 1264
Saleh JW, 474
Salkind MR, 476, 1900
Sallee FR, 427
Sallustro F, 45
Salter RH, 2140
Saltman V, 2213
Salvatierra O, 2319
Salvia J, 328, 333

Salzman C, 827, 828, 866, 946, 1786,
2043, 2045, 2051, 2076
Salzman L, 2022, 2095, 2773
Sambrailo F, 550, 551, 552
Samenow SE, 2748
Samenow SM, 1070
Sanchez-Craig, 1130
Sanders DJ, 977
Sanderson BA, 581
Sandler H, 2369, 2370
Sandler J, 773, 1520, 1828, 1947, 2508
Sandler M, 867
Sandman CA, 45, 90, 238, 248, 976
Sandmeier M, 1416
Sandok BA, 870, 895, 896
Sandor P, 707
Sandoz M, 923, 1919
Sands DE, 2158
Sands PM, 1116, 1119
Sands R, 2527
Sanford AR, 187
Santos AB Jr, 1786
Sapira JD, 1304, 2140
Sarason SB, 402
Sargant W, 471, 2104, 2154, 2157, 2193
Sargeant J, 367
Sargent W, 1753
Sarlin MB, 951
Sarner CA, 2481, 2482
Sarrel L, 2295, 2297
Sarrel P, 2295, 2297
Sarrel PM, 2292
Sarwer-Foner GJ, 2764
Sataloff J, 956
Sato M, 833
Satterfield JH, 370, 378, 379, 381, 2746,
2747
Saul LJ, 2766, 2767
Saunders JC, 82
Savitz S, 2132
Sawa M, 1698
Sbriglio R, 1243, 1252, 2195, 2196
Scallet A, 2158, 2167
Scavone JM, 2347, 2348
Schachter S, 1265, 2141
Schaefer C, 1886

Schaefer LC, 2336
Schafer R, 2641, 2644
Schaffer C, 2367, 2368
Schaffer CB, 1927
Schain RJ, 96, 97
Schalock RL, 133, 135, 136
Schapiro S, 240
Scharf MB, 945
Scharfetter C, 1690
Scharff DE, 2268, 2339, 2698
Scharschmidt BF, 932, 933, 934
Schatzberg AF, 1800, 2682
Schauf CL, 892
Schaumburg H, 241
Schecter G, 1958
Scheerenberger RC, 123
Scheibel AB, 1491
Scheidlinger S, 2670
Scheie HG, 953
Scheier MF, 1848
Scheinberg IH, 934
Scheinberg P, 917
Schellen AM, 2355
Schenecke OW, 2149
Schenk L, 2194, 2210
Schenker S, 936, 937, 938
Scher M, 1779
Schiavi RC, 21, 2321, 2328, 2391, 2392
Schieffelin B, 340
Schiff HB, 850
Schiffer RB, 1910
Schilder P, 2193, 2194, 2195
Schleifer M, 375
Schlessinger N, 2642, 2643, 2644, 2645
Schmid H, 2470
Schmidt D, 87
Schmidt G, 2320, 2327, 2339, 2341
Schmidt GL, 830
Schmidt HS, 2435, 2440
Schmidt K, 379
Schmidt M, 1862
Schmidt P, 58, 63
Schmidt SS, 2317
Schmidt W, 1075
Schmitt B, 721, 722
Schmitt GW, 2319

Schneck M, 900
Schneider JA, 534
Schneider K, 1490, 1499, 1500, 1614, 1619, 2678, 2712, 2759
Schneider LS, 828
Schneider NG, 1275
Schneider RJ, 1313
Schneiderman LJ, 1008
Schnoll SH, 1210, 1211, 1219, 1255
Schnurmann A, 2020
Schoettle UC, 454
Schoffling K, 2319
Schooler C, 1534, 2072
Schooler NR, 1543, 1564, 1665
Schöph J, 1305
Schopler E, 180, 183, 185, 186, 193, 194, 196, 197, 199, 215, 216, 229, 233, 250, 251, 253, 254, 255, 257, 258, 259, 260, 262, 268
Schottenfeld RS, 1910
Schou M, 924, 926, 927, 1738, 1927, 1929, 1931, 1938
Schowalter JE, 465
Schreiber FR, 2205
Schreibman L, 217, 223, 266
Schreiner-Engel P, 2282, 2387, 2389, 2390
Schrier RW, 920
Schroeder JS, 408
Schroeder SR, 7, 21, 25, 32, 35, 44, 45, 74, 75, 114
Schubert DSP, 2447, 2448
Schuckit M, 1066, 1067, 1070
Schuckit MA, 1072, 1073, 1074, 1075, 1076, 1083, 1185, 1431, 1918
Schuffel W, 2149
Schuler AL, 198, 203, 207, 215
Schultz NM, 665, 668
Schultz RS, 2198, 2199, 2203
Schultz S, 2517
Schulz CG, 2703
Schulz P, 1780
Schulz PJ, 950
Schulz SC, 1518
Schuman LM, 817
Schur M, 2014, 2020

Schuster CR, 1232, 1431
Schutz RP, 137
Schwab JJ, 1900
Schwarcz G, 2317
Schwartz B, 1784
Schwartz CJ, 1207
Schwartz DP, 1520, 1521, 1525, 1527
Schwartz JT, 1825
Schwartz L, 1779, 1783
Schwartz MF, 2275, 2347
Schwartz RC, 109, 110, 544, 548
Schwartz RG, 313
Schwartz RH, 1247
Schwartz RM, 1202
Schwartz S, 1395, 2525, 2526, 2527
Schwartz SR, 1252
Schwartzman G, 2672
Schweitzer MD, 1344
Schweitzer PK, 2435
Schwoeri F, 2662, 2663
Schwoeri L, 2662, 2663
Scopetta MA, 1398
Scott BS, 30, 31
Scott DF, 894
Scott DW, 753
Scott FB, 2333
Scott JP, 21
Scott M, 838
Scott NR, 1344
Scott P, 1957
Scott PD, 2165
Scott R, 1580
Seager CR, 1813
Searles H, 1521, 1529
Searles HF, 2716, 2751
Sears HTN, 912
Sebolt N, 2525
Sederer LI, 1518
Seeman P, 1491
Segal M, 1514, 2354
Segal MM, 637, 644
Segarra JM, 871
Séglas J, 1609
Segraves RT, 2251, 2318, 2319, 2320,
    2321, 2322, 2324, 2330, 2336, 2338,
    2339, 2340, 2341, 2342, 2348, 2353

Seguin E, 27, 123
Seibert JM, 215
Seidel WF, 2442
Seiden L, 1232
Seifert AR, 894
Seigel RK, 1226
Seilhamer RA, 1111
Selan BH, 108
Seligman M, 2293, 2535, 2542
Sellers EM, 922
Sells SB, 1323, 1343, 1350, 1351, 1382,
    1395
Selvini MP, 1545
Selvini-Palazzoli M, 463, 488, 494, 495,
    504, 513, 1545
Selye H, 2070
Selzer J, 2354
Selzer ML, 1186
Semel EM, 330
Senatore V, 105, 108
Senay EC, 1074, 1319, 1344, 1349,
    1353, 1355, 1357
Seppecher MF, 2336
Serban G, 2681, 2725, 2754
Serber M, 672
Serby M, 863
Serok S, 1542
Serrano A, 351
Settlage CF, 409, 2020
Settlage P, 917
Seymour RB, 1301
Shader R, 821, 907, 908, 2309
Shader RI, 80, 88, 809, 811, 812, 933,
    937, 944, 1373, 1781, 1912, 2043,
    2747
Shafer J, 1204
Shafer MS, 134
Shaffer D, 369, 371, 695, 717, 718, 719,
    720
Shahar A, 2670
Shaikh SP, 2159
Shakir SA, 1939
Shakkebaek NE, 2388, 2392
Shamsie SJ, 1430, 2652
Shand DG, 938
Shane H, 203

Shane M, 665
Shanfield S, 2135
Shanok S, 2469
Shapiro AK, 375, 695, 707, 708, 709,
    710, 911
Shapiro D, 780
Shapiro E, 375, 695, 707, 708, 709
Shapiro EI, 2317
Shapiro ER, 2661, 2662, 2663, 2664,
    2665, 2666, 2740, 2753
Shapiro J, 332
Shapiro LJ, 110
Shapiro RL, 2661, 2662, 2664, 2666,
    2728
Shapiro RW, 1942
Shapiro S, 1063, 2220, 2514, 2517
Shapiro T, 306, 427
Sharfstein SS, 981, 1822
Sharma M, 318
Sharp SL, 2226
Sharpe DH, 583, 584
Shaw BF, 1816, 1838, 1839, 1840, 1845
Shaw D, 1847
Shaw JA, 1920
Shaw P, 2761
Shaw PL, 1439
Shea T, 1732
Shea V, 191, 257
Sheagran TG, 564, 565, 568, 574, 575
Shear HB, 2748
Sheard MH, 79, 387, 850, 1759, 2476,
    2686, 2747
Sheehan DV, 88, 406, 408, 1373, 2015,
    2050, 2145, 2151, 2247, 2685
Sheehan J, 316, 345
Sheffet A, 1344
Sheffield BF, 2139, 2147
Sheidlinger S, 2734
Shelly CH, 1066, 1067, 1071
Shelokov A, 1372
Shelp EE, 991, 996
Shelton J, 2537
Shelton RL, 62
Shen WW, 2076
Sheppard C, 1358
Sheppard G, 1491

Sherlock S, 935, 936
Sherman EN, 453
Sherman JA, 114
Sherrington R, 1634
Shershow JC, 946
Sherwin AC, 240
Sherwin BB, 2350, 2390
Sherwin I, 874
Sherzer AL, 38
Shew P, 106
Shick JFE, 1354
Shiffman S, 1280, 1281, 1437
Shiffman SM, 1278
Shimoda Y, 454
Shipley R, 2536
Shoemaker D, 316, 346
Shoenfeld Y, 2143
Shontz FC, 1193, 1200
Shopper M, 2012
Shor RE, 2052, 2059, 2060
Shore J, 2070
Shore JH, 1149, 1150, 1151
Shore MF, 386, 2609, 2615
Short AB, 253
Shorvon HJ, 2154, 2157, 2218, 2219,
    2220, 2221
Shou M, 925
Shoultz B, 133, 136
Showalter CV, 813, 814
Shraberg D, 2218, 2219, 2220
Shugart G, 1397
Shukla D, 1366
Shulka S, 1912
Shull HJ, 937
Shulman K, 1764, 1927
Shuping JR, 873
Shurman RA, 995
Siantz J, 348
Siassi I, 387
Sideroff SI, 1333
Sieg S, 2754
Siegel H, 1702
Siegel IM, 955
Siegel RK, 1219, 1222, 1227, 1229,
    1232, 1234, 1236, 1239, 1367
Siegel S, 2681, 2725

Siegler M, 1004
Siever LJ, 2567
Sifneos P, 760, 1422, 1732, 1874, 1875,
    1876, 1877, 1878, 1879, 1880, 1883,
    1884, 2521
Sifneos PE, 2151, 2471, 2509, 2733,
    2734, 2752, 2778
Sigelman CK, 24
Silber A, 1104, 1109
Silber SJ, 2317
Silberfarb PM, 833
Silberman EK, 2199
Silva DA, 86, 89
Silver AA, 700
Silver D, 2676
Silver FC, 1397
Silver JM, 839, 840, 842, 843, 844, 847,
    849, 851
Silver LB, 298, 310, 311, 319, 322, 326,
    327
Silverberg R, 1196
Silverfarb PM, 1905
Silverman A, 588
Silverman M, 348
Sim M, 2165
Simensen RJ, 39, 40
Simeon J, 242, 326
Simeonsson RJ, 198
Simmel E, 2470, 2471
Simmonds J, 1951
Simmons JE, 371
Simmons JQ, 45, 96, 218, 225, 235, 385
Simon FB, 1565
Simon R, 757
Simons AD, 1822, 1842, 1843, 1845
Simpson DD, 1230, 1324, 1328, 1331,
    1343, 1344, 1350, 1351, 1382, 1395
Simpson G, 1796
Simpson GM, 244, 867, 1518, 1534,
    1535, 1631, 2316, 2348
Simpson LL, 914
Sims A, 1688
Sindrup EH, 882
Singer B, 1428
Singer I, 2281, 2387
Singer J, 2281

Singer JE, 2141
Singer JM, 975
Singer M, 1549
Singer MT, 1693, 1694
Singh J, 1907
Singh NN, 6, 7, 33, 37, 52, 54, 73, 74,
    76, 91, 569, 577, 578, 580, 583, 584,
    585, 588
Singhi S, 580, 581
Sipich J, 2534
Siris SG, 1923, 1924, 1928
Sirois F, 1693, 2159
Siskind M, 1904
Sisson RW, 1159
Sitaram N, 970
Sitzman J, 946
Siva Sankar DV, 1209
Sjodin I, 2149
Sjogren T, 1498
Sjoqvist F, 1779
Sjostrand NO, 2386
Skausig OB, 1912, 1913
Skekais B, 1002
Skigen J, 1002
Skinner BF, 113, 121, 1847, 2649
Skinner HA, 1065, 1067, 1068
Skinner L, 2541
Skolnick P, 1307
Skott A, 2146
Skwerer RG, 1895
Skynner ACR, 2663, 2665
Slade PD, 483, 488, 539
Slag MF, 2319
Slater E, 836, 882, 2104, 2154, 2193,
    2335, 2336
Slavson SR, 1532, 1539, 2734
Sleator EK, 91, 374, 377
Sloane RB, 1819, 1871, 1884, 2034,
    2650, 2659
Sloman L, 763, 769
Slovenko R, 983, 993
Sluckin W, 735, 736
Small E, 2381
Small GW, 819, 820, 821, 829, 961,
    1920, 1922
Small IF, 2783, 2784, 2786

Small JC, 814
Small JG, 1503, 1805, 1809, 1928
Small L, 1874
Small MP, 2332, 2333
Smart RG, 1066, 1074, 1146
Smialek JE, 1351
Smith AD, 2344
Smith AJ, 913
Smith CH, 955
Smith CK, 718
Smith CM, 1149
Smith D, 1216
Smith DE, 108, 838, 1207, 1222, 1229, 1295, 1296, 1299, 1302, 1304, 1307
Smith DV, 330
Smith DW, 1366
Smith EH, 82, 109
Smith GR, 2119
Smith JB, 1865, 1885
Smith JE, 1220
Smith JM, 243
Smith JS, 818, 2104
Smith JW, 1251, 2313
Smith L, 2368, 2521
Smith M, 1420
Smith ML, 1729
Smith RC, 970, 974, 2338, 2340
Smith RR, 2654
Smith SR, 671
Smith TW, 907
Smith WL, 95, 97
Smulevitch AB, 1676
Snow SS, 1912
Snowdon CT, 52, 581
Snyder-McLean LK, 202
Snyder S, 2481, 2482
Snyder SH, 832
Soave R, 908
Sobel B, 1383, 1396
Sobell LC, 1075, 1097, 1130
Sobell MB, 1075, 1097, 1130
Soblen RA, 82
Socarides CW, 630, 631, 643
Soininen H, 974
Sokoloff L, 240
Sol P, 577

Soldatos C, 839, 1783
Soledad G, 1208
Sollod RN, 2339
Solnick JV, 47, 222
Solnit AJ, 311
Soloff PH, 2680, 2681, 2682, 2683, 2726, 2754, 2755
Soloman L, 1693
Solomon A, 470
Solomon EB, 2671
Solomon G, 2073
Solomon GE, 878, 885, 887, 888, 889, 890, 893
Solomon GF, 2747
Solomon JR, 1002
Solomon K, 946
Solomon RS, 2198, 2213
Solomon V, 2198
Solyom L, 476, 533
Sommers RK, 316
Soni SD, 1688, 1689, 1690
Sonino N, 1901
Sontag S, 2370, 2371
Sordillo P, 893
Sorgi PJ, 851
Sorosky AD, 2482, 2483
Sorrell M, 52
Soskis DA, 2053
Souetre E, 1801
Sours JA, 556
Sovner R, 7, 10, 18, 31, 78
Sowles RC, 386
Spalt L, 2255
Spangler P, 105
Spanos NP, 2197, 2199, 2205
Spar JE, 829, 864, 904, 974, 1779, 1782
Spark G, 431, 1566
Spark RF, 2392
Sparrow S, 187
Spector R, 1779
Speech Foundation of America, 315, 345
Speers RW, 764
Spellman MS, 2142
Spence DP, 2642
Spence E, 263

Spence N, 2130, 2131
Spence ND, 1767
Spence SH, 2654
Spencer DA, 92
Spencer JH, 1766
Spencer SS, 893
Sperber MA, 643
Sperling, 665, 672, 673
Sperling M, 1950, 2020
Spiegel D, 2131, 2199, 2202, 2206
Spiegel H, 1277
Spiegel JP, 2154
Spiegel R, 972
Spiegler MD, 1579, 1581
Spielberger CD, 402
Spielman AJ, 2444, 2449
Spiker DG, 1787, 1795, 1804, 1907
Spinweber CL, 2422
Spitz HI, 1533, 1535, 1543
Spitz R, 409, 734, 1952, 2011
Spitzer RL, 403, 412, 567, 1183, 1499,
    1667, 1668, 1761, 1815, 1845, 1849,
    1891, 1942, 2020, 2022, 2217
Spivack G, 23, 1444
Spodak MK, 629, 630
Spohn HE, 1534
Spotnitz H, 2673, 2717, 2725
Spotts J, 23
Spotts JV, 1193, 1200
Spradley JB, 1688
Spradlin JE, 62
Sprafkin, 115
Sprague RL, 68, 70, 73, 75, 77, 91, 233,
    374, 378, 379, 380
Spring B, 1575
Springer CJ, 875
Springer NS, 57
Spyraki C, 1221
Squire LR, 1811
Squires RF, 1306
Sreebny LM, 60
Sroka H, 864, 865
Sroufe L, 91
St. Louis KW, 203
St. Omer VV, 72
Staats AW, 115

Staats CK, 115
Stackhouse TU, 780
Staehelin JE, 1610
Stafford-Clark D, 2104
Stafford RL, 476
Stagno S, 585
Stahl SM, 691, 1784
Stainback S, 63
Stainback W, 25, 134
Stambler M, 585
Stampfl T, 2535
Stampfl TG, 2081, 2099
Stancer HC, 906
Standahl J, 46
Standards of Practice: Minimal
    Monitoring, 1808
Stangler RS, 783
Stanley B, 986
Stanton AH, 1518, 1659
Stanton MD, 1199, 1398, 1402, 1403,
    1404, 1418, 1421
Staples FR, 2650
Starfield B, 719
Stark MH, 311
Stark P, 905
Starr R, 738
Stasiek C, 1914
Stason WB, 982
Staub H, 2459
Staunton HP, 2318
Stavrakaki C, 108, 109
Stawar TL, 2471
Steen SM, 945
Stefanis C, 1252
Steffenhagen RA, 1201
Steffy, 628
Stefl ME, 688, 702, 703
Steg G, 866
Stege P, 517
Steif B, 1811
Stein A, 2677
Stein GS, 473
Stein L, 406, 407
Stein LI, 1535, 1580, 1663
Stein ZA, 720
Steinbach E, 2371

Steinberg A, 2469
Steinberg S, 707
Steiner C, 1156
Steiner J, 1532, 1539
Steinert J, 908
Steinglass P, 1076, 1111, 1112, 1116,
    1135, 1415, 2664
Steinhart MJ, 805
Steinhausen HC, 460, 491
Steinman DL, 2282
Steinmetz JL, 1857, 1858, 1862
Stekel W, 2470, 2471
Steketee G, 476, 2780
Steketee GS, 2100
Stënback A, 916, 917
Stengel E, 2193, 2194
Stenhausen H, 374
Stephens JH, 1500, 1501
Stephens S, 2598, 2599
Sterling-Smith R, 1196
Sterman MB, 894
Stern C, 335, 338
Stern D, 299, 340, 2011
Stern GM, 867
Stern L, 735
Stern LO, 2337
Stern MJ, 903, 1900, 1907
Stern R, 2029
Stern RS, 2102
Stern SL, 1786
Stern TA, 813, 2103, 2104
Stern Y, 862, 863
Sternberg DE, 1700, 1701
Sternberg M, 2104
Sternlicht M, 105, 109
Steuer J, 1002
Steuer JL, 1839, 1841
Stevens JR, 874
Stevens MJ, 2481, 2484
Stevenson J, 299
Stewart B, 2536, 2542
Stewart DE, 1707, 1708
Stewart JC, 2336
Stewart JW, 1789, 2685
Stewart M, 365, 367
Stewart MA, 1900, 2469, 2472

Stewart S, 1405
Sticher M, 2481, 2483
Sticher MB, 2482, 2483
Stickler M, 2525
Stillman B, 335
Stimbert VE, 61, 64
Stimmel B, 906, 1184, 1324, 1329, 1352
Stimson GV, 1328, 1331
Stitzer ML, 1184, 1438, 1441
Stock PG, 1212
Stocker B, 317, 345
Stockley I, 893
Stockley IH, 913
Stockwell L, 718
Stokes TF, 121, 133, 665
Stoller RJ, 634, 635, 638, 640, 641, 642,
    643, 644, 648, 649, 661, 662, 666,
    667, 669, 672
Stolorow RD, 2017
Stolorow RS, 2220
Stone AA, 984
Stone AR, 2148
Stone GC, 2763
Stone L, 2470
Stone M, 2758
Stone MH, 1249, 1251, 1939, 2162,
    2163, 2164, 2641, 2682, 2713, 2715,
    2754
Stone WN, 2669, 2672, 2673, 2677
Stores G, 95, 883
Storey R, 2763, 2765
Stotski BA, 2447
Stoyva J, 2534
Stoyva JM, 112
Strachan AM, 1551, 1552
Strachan JG, 2473
Strain PS, 198, 776, 2615
Straker M, 2504, 2507, 2508, 2509
Strandjord RE, 893
Strassberg DS, 1539
Strategy Council on Drug Abuse, 1219
Strauss JS, 1498, 1499, 1531, 1532,
    1666, 1684
Stravynski A, 2668, 2670, 2674, 2676
Strayhorn JM, 92
Strean H, 2677

Stricker G, 2784, 2786, 2787
Stringer AY, 2682, 2747
Strober M, 492, 493, 511, 1754, 1756, 1916, 1929
Strodteck FL, 1551
Strom-Olsen JS, 2104
Strömgren E, 1610, 1613, 1616, 1617, 1677, 1683
Stromgren LS, 1808
Strominger AZ, 313
Strub RL, 870, 933, 934
Strupp HH, 1732, 1816, 1875, 1881, 1883, 1884, 2768
Stuart RB, 1406
Stubblebine J, 2520
Stunkard A, 456, 457
Sturge C, 365
Sturgeon D, 1550
Sturgis E, 2136, 2137
Sturup GK, 2635, 2742, 2748
Stutsman R, 188
Sudderth EW, 1344
Suedfeld P, 1278
Sugarman A, 556
Sugarman M, 746
Suh CS, 1883
Suinn R, 2532, 2534, 2536, 2537, 2539, 2543, 2544, 2547
Sullivan CE, 2434, 2436
Sullivan HS, 1515, 1520, 1532, 1864, 1944, 2634, 2731, 2773
Sullivan TJ, 1784
Sulser FJ, 1775
Summers WK, 970, 1812
Summerskill WHJ, 935
Summit R, 2207, 2210
Sumner D, 952, 955
Sunderland P, 2680
Sung KT, 2370
Sunshine RF, 2254
Surawicz FG, 833
Susman V, 1804
Susser MW, 720
Sussman N, 2163
Sussman S, 1572
Sutcliffe JP, 2205

Sutherland GR, 39, 42
Sutker PB, 1077, 1416
Sutter P, 20
Svedlund J, 2149
Svejda M, 736
Swaminathan S, 1779, 1783
Swanson D, 2137
Swanson DW, 1902, 2707
Swanson J, 374
Swanson PD, 869
Swartz MF, 2392
Swedberg K, 906
Sweet RD, 863, 865
Sweillam A, 839
Swerdlow M, 2130
Swiff WJ, 1915
Swinner P, 1123
Swischuk LE, 572
Sydenham T, 1491
Symthies JR, 1711
Szasz TS, 1490
Szetala B, 848
Szmukler GI, 493, 494, 508
Szurek SA, 2459, 2660
Szymanski LS, 108, 109, 111, 306, 307
Szyszko J, 24

Tahlka V, 1094
Taitz LS, 725, 726
Talalla A, 918
Talbott JA, 1249, 1539, 2523
Talkington LW, 22
Tallafero A, 2386
Tallmann JF, 87
Tamarkin L, 1891
Tamburello A, 2336
Tamerin J, 1108
Tamminga CA, 1703
Tan E, 2381, 2780
Tan SY, 2130, 2131
Tannahill R, 2371
Tanner CM, 694, 861, 863

Tarasoff v Regents of the University of California, 993
Tardiff K, 839, 993
Targum SD, 1497, 1676, 1795, 1888
Tarjan C, 227
Tarler-Benlolo L, 2150
Tarrier N, 1550, 1552
Tarter R, 1065
Tarter RE, 933
Tarver A, 1237, 1240
Task force reports. *See* specific organizations
Tasto DL, 619, 623, 624
Tate BG, 34
Taube CA, 802
Taylor B, 2369
Taylor D, 977
Taylor DC, 882, 884
Taylor DJ, 54
Taylor DL, 1230
Taylor DP, 408
Taylor EA, 365, 366, 367, 373
Taylor FG, 1782, 1839, 1840
Taylor FK, 2219
Taylor MA, 810, 1495, 1498, 1499, 1500, 1501, 1761, 1804, 1811
Taylor P, 1502
Taylor PJ, 839
Taylor WS, 2198
Tchertkoff V, 2385
Teague JW, 1249
Teasdale J, 112
Teasdale JD, 1801, 1839, 1841, 1843, 1844
Tec L, 474
Telch MJ, 2032, 2033, 2034
Tellegan A, 1278
TenHoor WJ, 1580
Tennant C, 2500
Tennant F, 1237, 1333, 1336
Tennant FS, 1217, 1240, 1254, 1325
Tennent FS, 1920, 1922
Tennent JJ, 1921
Tenuta K, 52
Teoh JI, 2159

Teri L, 1858, 1862
Terkelsen K, 1539, 1548
Terman J, 1892, 1893, 1894
Terman LM, 193, 330, 2281, 2285, 2286, 2335
Terr L, 2514, 2515, 2516, 2517, 2519
Terr LC, 2421
Terry RD, 965, 966
Tesar GE, 2103
Test MA, 1535, 1580, 1663
Teuber HL, 835
Thacher B, 665
Thain J, 1266, 1270
Thal LJ, 970
Thalassinos PA, 569
Thaler FH, 2095
Tharp RG, 1565
Thase ME, 31
Theander S, 491, 492
Thelen MH, 2655
Thienhaus OJ, 1910
Thigpen CH, 2199, 2205
Thomas A, 735
Thomas CW, 586
Thomas KB, 2148
Thomas MA, 2653
Thomasma DC, 997
Thompson A, 192
Thompson DJ, 1003
Thompson GN, 2074, 2076
Thompson IM, 723
Thompson LW, 1838, 1839, 1841, 1862
Thompson MK, 908
Thompson P, 2369
Thompson RJ, 59, 61, 62, 64, 96
Thomsen IV, 844
Thomsen K, 927
Thoren P, 2101, 2102, 2103, 2685, 2780
Thorne FC, 108
Thornton JE, 1784
Thornton WE, 813, 814
Thornton WF, 914
Thorpe GL, 2024
Thorpe JJ, 1158
Thurston JH, 5, 451, 888

Thyer BA, 401
Tiebout HM, 1094, 1096, 1152, 2598, 2599
Tilkian AG, 906
Tinker DE, 462
Tinklenberg JR, 976, 977, 978
Tippin J, 2104
Tischler PV, 1701
Titievsky J, 1921
Tizard B, 46
Tobin A, 1824, 1825, 2643, 2733, 2768
Todd J, 1686, 1687, 1688
Todd TC, 1398, 1402, 1404, 1418, 1421
Todres R, 2609
Toenniessen LM, 827
Tolksdorf M, 31
Tollefson G, 833, 913, 915, 1912, 2103
Tolpin M, 2014, 2015
Tolpin PH, 2468
Tolwinski T, 1534
Tomkins S, 1265, 1269
Tomlinson BE, 819, 820, 872
Tomosovic M, 1066
Tomsovic M, 1121, 1123, 1124
Toolan J, 1950
Toone B, 882
Toone BK, 839
Topliss D, 908
Torch EM, 2218, 2219, 2220
Torgersen S, 2769
Torgesen JK, 333
Torrey EF, 1539
Torvik A, 868
Toseland RW, 2600
Tourkow P, 2664
Tourney G, 1502
Towbin KE, 708, 709
Townsend RE, 2052, 2054
Traskman L, 2102
Travers RD, 96
Treece C, 1185, 1417, 1920
Trethowan WH, 1686, 1687, 1688, 1692
Trice HM, 1153
Trieschmann R, 2375
Trifiletti R, 2131, 2135

Trimble MR, 87, 95, 96, 97, 836, 874, 882, 1779, 1783, 2155
Trites RL, 365
Troen P, 2388
Tronick E, 340
Tross S, 1912
Troup CW, 719
Truax CB, 386
Trueblood E, 2595
Trueman DJ, 2218, 2219
Trupin EW, 92
Trussel T, 2369
Tsai CS, 1919
Tsai LY, 215, 216
Tse DT, 1366
Tseng WS, 1688
Tsitouras PD, 2388
Tsoi WF, 2165
Tsuang M, 1813
Tsuang MT, 1497, 1498, 1500, 1609, 1618, 1668, 1670, 1672, 1674, 1700, 1704, 2097
Tu JB, 71, 86, 89
Tuason VB, 1344
Tucker G, 886
Tucker GJ, 2692
Tuddenham R, 2514, 2517
Tuma AH, 1659
Tunks ER, 850, 2476
Tupin J, 1680, 1683
Tupin JP, 850, 2686, 2747
Turk D, 1856, 2131, 2543
Turkat ID, 2655, 2769
Turkewitz H, 2663
Turnbull AP, 103, 123, 259
Turnbull HR, 103, 123
Turnbull JM, 2141
Turner DA, 231
Turner G, 41, 42
Turner J, 2121, 2128, 2129, 2130, 2131, 2135, 2137
Turner JC, 1580
Turner RW, 1838, 1862
Turner S, 2535
Turner SN, 2102

Turner TH, 833
Turnquist K, 2686
Turton LJ, 61, 62
Tuthill JF, 2324
Tyce FA, 2747
Tyhurst J, 2516, 2517
Tyler R, 917
Tyrer B, 1305
Tyrer P, 2043, 2121, 2122, 2124, 2152, 2763
Tyrer SP, 1786, 1928

Ucer E, 75
Uddenberg N, 2318, 2335
Uhde TW, 876
Uhlenhuth EH, 2151
Ulett GA, 1810
Ullmann LP, 1570
Ulman RB, 1693
Ulrich C, 2256
Ultee CA, 405
Unis A, 2682
U'Prichard D, 928
Urbain ES, 378, 379, 385
Urey JR, 1571
U.S. Department of Health, Education, and Welfare, 1262
U.S. Department of Health and Human Services, 802, 803, 981, 1262, 1263, 1265, 1266, 1271
U.S. Fire Administration/National Fire Academy, 2472
U.S. Public Health Service, 2445
U.S. Senate, 803
Usdin E, 406, 407
Usdin GL, 2347
Usher ML, 1116
Usubiaga JE, 1810
Utena H, 1230, 1231, 1232
Utley BL, 58, 64
Utting HG, 945

Vacek J, 2146
Vaillant G, 1069, 1103, 2514
Vaillant GE, 1153, 1161, 2141, 2645, 2690, 2745, 2764, 2765, 2766, 2784
Vaisanen K, 72, 75
Vaisrub S, 918
Valko RJ, 2168, 2169
Van Buskirk EM, 959
van den Berg PJ, 2763
Van den Hoed J, 2439
van den Hoofdakker RH, 1801
Van der Kolk B, 2532
Van der Kolk BA, 2075
Van der Rijt CCD, 936
Van Dyke C, 1220, 1221
Van Hemert JC, 76
Van Kammen DP, 1923
Van Krevelan DA, 748
van Leeuwen AMH, 810
Van Loon JH, 2442
Van Putten T, 1581, 1922, 2158
Van Riper C, 315, 345, 346
Van Spanning HW, 1783
Van Tilburg W, 833, 924
Van Woerkom AE, 1792
van Woert MH, 691
Van Wulfften PP, 2381
Van Zweiten PA, 928
Van Zwieten PA, 1783
Vandenberg JG, 2355
VandenBos G, 1658
VandenBos GR, 1516
Vandereycken W, 461, 471, 472, 492, 502
Vandersall JA, 2469, 2470
Vanggaard T, 2723
Vannicelli M, 1118
Vardy MM, 1709
Varenhorst B, 2615
Varenhorst BB, 2614
Varley CK, 18, 92, 374, 375
Varley WH, 379, 385
Varnaka TM, 1763
Varni JW, 664, 665
Varsamis J, 2255

Varyura-Tobias JA, 2104
Vastayana, 2304
Vasudevan S, 2137
Vattano AJ, 2598
Vaughan M, 2780
Vaughn B, 736
Vaughn C, 1550, 1552
Vaughn CE, 1509, 1551
Vaughn M, 2098
Vauhkonen K, 1643
Veatch RM, 1002
Veith RC, 902, 903, 1782
Venables PH, 1530, 1548
Verbeeck RK, 924, 938
Verebey K, 238, 247, 1247, 1361, 1366
Verhulst J, 2336
Veronen L, 2539, 2543
Verwoerdt A, 2507, 2509
Vessell ES, 913
Vestal RE, 915
Vestegaard P, 1927
Vestergaard P, 925, 927
Veterans Administration Cooperative
    Study Group on Antihypertensive
    Agents, 908
Viamontes JA, 1075
Victor BS, 1704
Victor G, 2205
Victor M, 87, 837, 870, 873, 895, 896,
    897, 942
Victor RG, 2464
Viederman M, 2527
Vigersky RA, 472
Villareal SU, 943
Vilmar T, 1251
Virchow R, 1490
Vischi T, 1063
Vislie H, 881
Viukari M, 2447
Vlok LA, 1547
Voegtlin WI, 1127
Voeller MN, 496
Vogel GW, 1796, 1933
Vogelsberg RT, 132, 133
Vogl G, 1708
Vogler RE, 1126, 1130

Vohra J, 902
Volavka J, 2101, 2103
Volkmar FR, 180
Voller MN, 494
Volpe BT, 908
von Bertallanffy L, 1545
Von Brauchtisch K, 946
Von Hagen KO, 2133
Voshart K, 1900
Voss HL, 1244, 1312
Voth HM, 2660
Vreeland RG, 2470
Vulpe SG, 187
Vygotsky L, 340

Waber D, 473
Wachtel A, 625
Wachtel P, 2651, 2658
Wachtel PL, 2009, 2218, 2220, 2221,
    2340
Wack J, 1280
Waddel WJ, 892
Wadden TA, 2064
Wadsworth MDJ, 2147
Waelder R, 2634
Wagner G, 2384, 2385, 2386, 2391
Wahler RG, 47
Wahlin A, 926
Wai F, 144
Wainwright RB, 327
Waizer J, 242
Walaas SI, 976
Wald A, 724
Wald D, 1709
Waldinger R, 2750, 2751
Waldron VD, 1348
Walford RL, 31
Walinder J, 1800
Walker BB, 976
Walker C, 2541
Walker CF, 94
Walker E, 1670
Walker HM, 125

Walker J, 2133, 2442
Walker K, 1151
Walker RG, 926
Walker S, 934
Wall P, 2132
Wallace CJ, 1530, 1531, 1532, 1534, 1548, 1566, 1571, 1581
Wallach GP, 313
Wallach M, 914
Waller JV, 511
Waller MB, 2470
Wallerstein R, 2642, 2752
Wallin L, 926
Wallin P, 2337
Walls RT, 138
Walsh BT, 530, 539, 558, 1916, 1917, 2685
Walsh H, 344
Walsh RN, 2219, 2221
Walsh T, 2129
Walsh TC, 1783, 1904
Walter CJ, 2158
Walters A, 86, 2127
Walton D, 2099, 2779
Walton HJ, 2763
Walton NY, 1088
Waltzer H, 1688, 1690
Wanamaker WM, 863, 864
Wander TJ, 1776, 1778, 1783
Wanderer ZW, 109
Wang RIH, 1354
Wangh M, 2020
Wanzer SH, 982, 993, 1003
Wapner I, 96
Ward NG, 1942
Wardell DW, 72
Wardle J, 533
Warfield C, 2132
Waring EM, 1820
Warner SL, 2766, 2767
Warren SA, 45, 46
Warren SF, 136
Waryas CL, 342, 343
Wasek P, 2513
Washton AM, 1237, 1238, 1239, 1255,

1319, 1322, 1333, 1335, 1336, 1360, 1366, 1436
Waskow IE, 1815
Wasser WG, 943
Wasserman R, 102
Wassman ER, 705
Watkins HH, 2202
Watkins JG, 2202
Watkins JT, 1838, 1839, 1841
Watkins P, 1208
Watson BU, 300
Watson CP, 2129
Watson LR, 187, 198, 204, 205, 215, 216
Watson MS, 40
Watson R, 1230
Watt DC, 1707
Watt JAG, 1497
Watters GV, 952
Watters RG, 212
Watts CAH, 1764
Watts RD, 1920
Watzlawick P, 1565
Waxenberg SE, 2389
Waxer PH, 1532, 1539
Waxler NE, 1549
Waxman HM, 1002
Way EL, 1310, 1311
Weakland J, 1565
Weaver G, 1911
Weaver GM, 2199, 2216
Weaver LA, 1809
Weber FL, 936
Weber JJ, 2154, 2157
Webster C, 212
Webster P, 2440
Webster RL, 346
Webster TG, 109
Wechsler D, 187, 189, 330, 801
Weeks G, 2761
Weeks M, 25
Weg R, 2371, 2374
Wegmann HM, 2442
Wehl CK, 1838
Wehman P, 121, 132, 133, 272, 274

Wehr TA, 1758, 1892, 1893, 1929, 1934
Weihofen H, 617
Wein AJ, 2330, 2331
Weinberg WA, 1951
Weinberger DL, 1491
Weinberger DR, 1701
Weinberger G, 2525
Weiner BJ, 109
Weiner EA, 109
Weiner H, 453, 519
Weiner MF, 2585
Weiner N, 814, 967
Weiner RD, 875, 1807, 1809, 1811, 1812
Weiner WJ, 946
Weingartner H, 374, 977, 1807
Weinrott M, 385
Weinstein EA, 2187
Weinstein H, 1210
Weinstein MC, 982
Weinstein MR, 1931
Weisbard AJ, 1004
Weisberg P, 48, 125
Weisberg PS, 1532, 1542
Weischer ML, 79
Weise CC, 1781
Weisinger RS, 581
Weisman AD, 950
Weiss B, 91
Weiss E, 2017
Weiss G, 365, 366, 370, 374, 2479
Weiss HD, 944
Weiss J, 909
Weiss RD, 574, 1185, 1225, 1239, 1240
Weiss SM, 1185
Weissman M, 1104
Weissman MM, 1185, 1814, 1815, 1816,
    1817, 1819, 1820, 1822, 1834, 1863,
    1865, 1868, 1869, 1870, 1871, 1885,
    1886, 1887, 1898, 1915, 1918, 1922,
    1942
Weissman R, 2754
Weitzman, 642
Weitzman ED, 2443, 2444
Weizman R, 238, 247
Weksler ME, 966
Welch CA, 1810

Weller E, 1763
Weller EB, 408
Wells CE, 805, 807, 808, 821, 832, 836,
    965, 1764, 1859
Wells DA, 1805
Wells KC, 373, 374, 378
Welner A, 1666, 1667, 1668, 1669, 1676
Welsh RS, 2471
Wender P, 365
Wender PH, 2479, 2686, 2747
Wennerblom B, 1782
Wepman JM, 335
Wergeland H, 763
Wermuth BM, 529
Werne J, 477
Werner DB, 326
Wernicke JF, 905
Werry JS, 68, 70, 73, 75, 94, 226, 233,
    376, 401
Wertheim E, 494
Wesner C, 702
Wesson DR, 1207, 1296, 1299, 1307,
    1335
West DJ, 623, 624, 627
West ED, 1753
West JW, 1079, 1081, 1082
West LJ, 858, 1693, 1694
Westermeyer J, 1358
Westfield DR, 1124
Westlake RJ, 1630
Westman JC, 772, 780
Wetherby AM, 207
Wetli CV, 1366
Wever R, 2441
Wever RA, 1895
Whalen CK, 91, 373, 374, 427
Wharton RN, 1790
Wheat P, 2601
Wheby MS, 585
Whipple B, 2281
Whisnant JP, 867
White AJ, 74, 76
White D, 2392
White DBS, 2136
White DM, 134, 137
White JC, 54

White K, 867, 1796
White NJ, 835
White P, 968
White PT, 1806
White RG, 2150
White WB, 909
White WC, 525, 526, 527, 538, 543, 549
Whitehad P, 2594
Whitehead A, 1834
Whitehead IC, 1382, 1395
Whitehead M, 2297
Whitehill WB, 1343
Whitehouse A, 590
Whitehouse PJ, 968
Whitfield CL, 1082, 1084
Whitling C, 20
Whitlock FA, 853, 1904, 2154, 2165
Whitman R, 2763, 2764, 2765, 2783,
    2784, 2785, 2786
Whitman RM, 2673
Whitman S, 2605
Whitten CF, 736, 740
Whybrow P, 1420, 1794
Whyler AR, 894
Wickramasekera I, 672, 673
Wicks RJ, 777
Wide L, 2392
Widem P, 980
Widlocher DJ, 1755
Wiedemann H, 31
Wiederholt JL, 317
Wiegerink R, 251
Wieland WF, 1349
Wiemann G, 63
Wiener JM, 2469, 2470
Wiig EH, 330
Wikler A, 812, 1135, 1236, 1315, 1334,
    1437
Wikler L, 1692
Wilbur CB, 2199, 2201, 2204, 2205,
    2211, 2212, 2213, 2214
Wilbur R, 2317, 2347
Wilcox B, 192
Wilcox DRG, 1514
Wilder BJ, 888, 889
Wilford WO, 1134

Wilkeson A, 2382, 2383
Wilkie F, 2508
Wilkinson DA, 1071
Wilkinson GR, 1363
Wilkinson JCM, 2143
Wilkinson M, 941
Wilkinson W, 2133
Will D, 501
Will OA, 1525
Willems EP, 136
Willets R, 1580
Willett EA, 1418
Willette RE, 248
Willi J, 2661
Williams DT, 408, 851
Williams GF, 746
Williams JBW, 1183, 1668
Williams JG, 810
Williams N, 10, 15
Williams TA, 1900
Williams W, 668, 2251
Williamson PD, 880
Willison JR, 940
Willner HS, 1007
Wilsher CR, 326
Wilsnack JC, 1095
Wilson G, 2387, 2759, 2761
Wilson GT, 542, 550, 551, 552, 2025,
    2026, 2028, 2032, 2033, 2036, 2072,
    2338
Wilson JW, 339
Wilson LC, 1920
Wilson PH, 1820, 1838, 1839, 1841
Wilson RP, 959
Wilson S, 1382
Wilson W, 2281
Wilson WC, 94
Wilson WH, 1542
Wimmer A, 1610, 1613, 1616, 1618,
    1619
Winblad B, 906, 974
Wincze J, 2541
Wincze JP, 2387, 2391
Wineman D, 2460
Winer J, 2508, 2517
Winer JA, 2644

Winer LR, 1398
Wing J, 1547, 1575
Wing JK, 61, 1499, 1530, 1531, 1548
Wing L, 63, 180, 255, 748
Wingate ME, 345
Winget CM, 2442
Winitz H, 61, 343
Winnicott DW, 738, 1523, 1524, 2012, 2013, 2024, 2460, 2644, 2648, 2739
Winograd CH, 829, 830
Winokur A, 492
Winokur G, 1065, 1066, 1070, 1666, 1756, 1758, 1761, 1762, 1787, 1803, 1805, 1898, 1902, 1903, 1916, 1934, 2255, 2281, 2336
Winslade WJ, 990, 1807
Winstead DK, 1780
Winters SJ, 2388
Winters WD, 914
Winton AS, 52, 569, 577, 578, 585, 588
Wirz-Justice A, 1892
Wise RA, 1220, 1221
Wise RJS, 870
Wise TN, 641, 642, 644, 645, 916
Wiseberg S, 1735, 2014
Wishner GJ, 316
Wishnie HA, 903, 2694, 2703
Witheridge TF, 1580
Witkin HA, 21
Wittchen H, 2028, 2030
Witton K, 1908
Wolberg L, 1874
Wolchik SA, 550, 551, 552
Wold PN, 1917
Wolf M, 34, 54
Wolf MM, 202, 218, 578
Wolf P, 847
Wolf PA, 869
Wolf SM, 97
Wolfe B, 2025
Wolfe E, 2639
Wolfensberger W, 123, 270, 993
Wolff HH, 2671
Wolff K, 1124
Wolff S, 385, 747, 751, 753
Wolfson I, 110

Wolin S, 1110, 1112
Wolkin A, 1491
Wolkon G, 2527
Wolkowitz OM, 51
Wolman BB, 1539
Wolpe J, 112, 2026, 2060, 2337, 2361, 2541, 2598, 2649, 2652, 2779
Wolraich M, 101
Wong BY, 333, 337
Wong J, 2673
Wong MR, 666
Wong N, 2741, 2754
Wong SE, 25, 849, 1569, 1572, 1578, 1583
Wood D, 1124
Wood DR, 2479, 2685, 2747
Wood R, 848
Woodcock RW, 335
Wooden WS, 2472
Woodforde JM, 2123
Woodruff J, 585
Woodruff R, 2095, 2097, 2197
Woodruff RA, 1070, 1078, 1079, 2169
Woods JH, 1310, 2040
Woods SC, 581
Woods SM, 2253, 2254, 2255
Woods SW, 1787, 1799
Woodside M, 2335, 2336
Woodward R, 2035
Woody CP, 1326
Woody GE, 1185, 1193, 1257, 1295, 1313, 1327, 1329, 1349, 1357, 1358, 1417, 1418, 1422, 1429, 1920, 1921
Wooley OW, 483, 485, 540, 541
Wooley S, 2122, 2128, 2134, 2144
Wooley SC, 483, 485, 541
Woolfolk E, 342
Woolliscroft JO, 1005
Woolston, 568
Woolverton WH, 1210
Woosley RL, 928
Worcester A, 997
Working Party, 1002
World Health Organization, 1261, 1499, 1611, 1612, 1667, 1668
World Psychiatric Association, 1499

Worrall EP, 79, 850
Wrate RM, 668
Wright B, 143
Wright J, 2337, 2338, 2341
Wright L, 569
Wright MW, 54
Wright RK, 1366
Wu FCW, 2266, 2388
Wunderlich RA, 1398
Wurmser L, 1232, 1235, 1313, 1417, 1424
Wurtman RJ, 965, 969
Wyant GM, 1808
Wyatt RJ, 849, 1544
Wynne L, 2514, 2517
Wynne LC, 1542, 1544, 1545, 1548, 1549, 1559, 2660

Yager J, 492, 493, 545, 1777
Yagi B, 1230, 1231
Yago KB, 1214
Yahr MD, 861, 865, 942
Yaksh TL, 1311
Yalom ID, 1118, 1120, 1124, 1156, 1533, 1539, 2168, 2583, 2602, 2613, 2667, 2669, 2670, 2671, 2674, 2676, 2677
Yamaguchi F, 961, 972
Yamaguchi K, 1431
Yamamoto M, 961, 962
Yarnell H, 2469, 2470, 2471, 2472
Yaskin JC, 1898
Yassa R, 2164
Yates AJ, 550, 551, 552, 1266, 1270
Yealland LR, 2158
Yerby MS, 883
Yerevanian BI, 1891, 1894, 1895, 2683
Yesavage JA, 829, 830, 962, 972, 973, 1247
Yochelson S, 2748
Yockelson S, 1070
Yokel RA, 1220
Yorke C, 2014
Youdim MBH, 583, 584, 588

Young D, 2760
Young JG, 234, 236, 237, 238, 239, 242
Young JPR, 1796
Young LD, 856, 946, 1919
Young RC, 865, 866
Young TJ, 1161
Younger SJ, 993
Youngerman J, 1936
Younoszai MK, 724
Ysseldyke E, 328, 333
Ysseldyke JE, 125
Yudofsky SC, 839, 840, 842, 843, 844, 845, 846, 847, 849, 851, 865, 866, 1911, 2476, 2480, 2686
Yugari Y, 28

Zacharko RM, 1230
Zaleski WA, 248
Zangwell BC, 1325
Zaphiriou M, 665
Zarcone VP, 2440
Zarkowsky H, 52
Zaudig M, 1708
Zavitzianos G, 637, 638
Zavodnick S, 904
Zeiss A, 2539, 2547
Zeiss AM, 1821, 1848, 1861, 1862
Zellweger H, 51
Zemet RM, 1542
Zeneroli MI, 936
Zetin M, 1792, 1914
Zettel JJ, 348
Zettle RD, 1844
Zetzel E, 2014
Zetzel ER, 2641, 2728
Ziegenfuss J, 1380
Ziegler-Driscoll G, 1397, 1398
Ziegler VE, 902
Ziff DC, 1283
Zigler E, 1066
Zilberg N, 2019
Zimberg S, 1094, 1095, 1117, 1133
Zimmerman GN, 316